THE SOCIAL ORGANIZATION

OF THE GILYAK

D1558383

Lev Iakovlevich Shternberg

Edited with a Foreword and Afterword

by

Bruce Grant
Swarthmore College

ANTHROPOLOGICAL PAPERS OF
THE AMERICAN MUSEUM OF NATURAL HISTORY
NUMBER 82, 336 PAGES, 32 FIGURES, 2 MAPS, 3 TABLES
ISSUED APRIL 5, 1999

ABSTRACT

In 1905, the eminent dean of American anthropology, Franz Boas, commissioned a monograph on the lives of Sakhalin Island peoples from the young Russian exile ethnographer Lev Shternberg. Shternberg's *Social Organization of the Gilyak* was Boas' final requisition for the annals of the Jesup North Pacific Expedition, exploring the origins of Amerindian peoples along both the Russian and American north Pacific rims.

Shternberg's manuscript made it to English translation under Boas' supervision, but political upheaval in tsarist Russia soon overtook events. For decades, this Russian ethnographic masterwork, published twice in Soviet Russia in the 1930s, was lost to English readerships, given political developments in the USSR and the climate of the Cold War. This first English edition includes a fresh analysis of Shternberg's classic work by anthropologist Bruce Grant. For the compelling Afterword, Grant returned to Sakhalin Island in 1995, one hundred years after Shternberg's first field studies, where modern-day Gilyak (Nivkh) offered their own reflections on being among the foremost subjects of Russian ethnographic literature.

Social Organization of the Gilyak is at once a careful reading of indigenous life in far eastern Siberia, as well as an important building block in the ongoing reevaluation of Russian studies of kinship, religion, and nationality policy.

COVER ILLUSTRATION

The Gilyak, organized. Lev Shternberg sits at the far right of a line of Gilyak informants, 1890s.

TITLE PAGE ILLUSTRATION

Birch bark stencil adapted from Berthold Laufer, *Decorative Art of the Amur Tribes*. Jesup North Pacific Expedition, Vol. IV (New York: Memoir of the American Museum of Natural History, 1902).

Copyright © American Museum of Natural History 1999
ISSN 0065-9452
ISBN 0-295-97799-X

Anthropological Paper no. 82 is distributed by the University of Washington Press
P.O. Box 50096
Seattle, WA 98145

CONTENTS

THE SOCIAL ORGANIZATION OF THE GILYAK

Glossary of Terms

affinity	Relationship by marriage
agnates	Blood relatives counting common descent through male links only
akhmalk	[Gilyak] Father-in-law
ang'rei	[Gilyak] Marriageable wife
bride-price or bride-wealth	Compensation to parents for a daughter given in marriage
clan	Group tracing descent to a putative, sometimes mythical, founding ancestor
classificatory terms	Kinship terms that do not distinguish between lineal and collateral relatives
cognates	Relatives of common descent
collateral kin	Relatives of common descent through different lines
consanguinity	Relationship by blood
cross-cousins	Children of opposite-sex siblings
endogamy	A rule prescribing marriage within a residential, kin, status or other group to which a person belongs
exogamy	A rule prescribing marriage outside a residential, kin, status, or other group to which a person belongs
Gilyak	Term of Tungus origin designating 5000 indigenous people on northern Sakhalin Island and the Amur River delta. Since the 1920s, they have been known by their self-naming, Nivkh.
imgi	[Gilyak] Son-in-law
iukola	[Russian] Dried salmon
khlai nivukh	[Gilyak] "The best man" and good orator
kinz	[Gilyak] Spirit
kolkhoz	[From the Russian *kollektivnoe khoziaistvo*] Term introduced in the USSR, normally designating a collective agricultural or fishing enterprise
levirate	The right or obligation of a man to the wives of his living or deceased brothers
lineage	A consanguineal kin group following unilineal descent; includes only kin who can trace their link through one gender to a known founding ancestor
mos'	[Gilyak] Aspic made from seal fat, fish skin, and berries

Nivkh   The predominant self-naming for Gilyaks; adopted for official purposes in the USSR from the late 1920s onwards. The Nivkh-language plural is *Nivkhgu*. The Russian-language plural is *Nivkhi*.

parallel-cousins   Children of same-sex siblings

sagund   [Gilyak] Valuables

sazhen   [From the Russian *sazhen'*] A prerevolutionary Russian measure of length, equal to 7 feet. Five hundred sazhens make a verst. *See* verst.

sororate   The right or obligation of a man to the sister or close female relative of his living or deceased wife

tkhusind   [Gilyak] Penalty, fine, or ransom

tuvng   [Gilyak] Brothers and sisters, real and classificatory

pandf   [Gilyak] Ancestral point of origin of the clan

pu   [Gilyak] Marriageable husband

verst   [From the Russian *versta*] A prerevolutionary Russian measure of length, equal to 3500 feet or 0.6629 miles. *See* sazhen.

yurta   [Russian] Originally referred to a tent made of animal skins, found across Central Asia and Siberia; by the late 17th century it came to include any non-Russian dwelling, including those of the Gilyak semi-subterranean (winter) and raised wooden (summer) types

GLOSSARY OF ETHNONYMS

Earlier American Museum of Natural History (AMNH) and Soviet versions of the Shternberg manuscript used a number of 19th and 20th century Russian and European nomenclatures for the peoples they described. This edition uses Shternberg's terms from the undated AMNH Russian typescript of *Social Organization*, while indicating current Library of Congress terms in brackets on first usage. The use of Library of Congress terms is for the sake of referencing, though the Library's terms are not always consonant with autonyms, or even consistent with the Library of Congress' own system of transliteration from Russian into English (hence, Gilyak rather than Giliak; Gilyak rather than Nivkh).

Autonyms are taken from Wixman (1988). Variations include popular British Library spellings, alternative Library of Congress spellings, and older imperial Russian forms.

Lib. Congress	Autonym	Current Russian Style	Variations
Altai	Altai, Oirot, et al.	Altai	Oirot
Buriat	Buriat	Buriat	Buryat
Chukchi	Lyg Oravetlian et al.	Chukchi	Chukchee
Chuvan	Shelga	Chuvan	Yukaghir et al.
Chuvash	Chavash	Chuvash	Chuvash
Dolgan	Dulgaan	Dolgan	—
Enets	Enets	Enets	Samoyed
Even	Even et al.	Even	Lamut
Evenk	Evenk et al.	Evenk	Tungus et al.
Gilyak	Nivkh	Nivkh	Giliak
Itelmen	Itel'men	Itel'men	Kamchadal
Kamchadal	Kamchadal	Itel'men	Itelmen
Karagasi	Karagass, Tofalar	Karagass	Karagass, Tofalar
Ket	Ostyg, Ket	Ket	Enesei Ostiak
Khakass	Khass	Khakass	Yenesei Tatar
Koriak	Chavchiav et al.	Koriak	Koryak
Kyrgyz	Kyrgyz et al.	Kyrgyz	Kirghiz, Kyrghyz
Mansi	Mansi	Mansi	Vogul
Mari	Mari	Cheremis	Cheremiss
Nanai	Nani et al.	Nanai	Gold, Gol'd, Ulchi
Negidal	El'kan et al.	Negidal	Negda, Amgun
Nenets	Nenets et al.	Nenets	Samoyed et al.
Nganasan	Nia	Nganasan	Tavgi Samoyed
Oroch	Nani	Oroch	Orok, Orochon
Orochon	Orochon	Orochon	Orok, Oroch
Orok	Ul'ta	Orok, Ul'ta	Uilta, Oroch
Ostiak	Khant, Hant	Khant	Ostyak

Lib. Congress	Autonym	Current Russian Style	Variations
Sami	Saami, Lopar	Saami	Lapp
Tofalar	Tubalar	Tofalar	Tofa, Karagasi
Selkup	Sel'kup	Sel'kup	Ostiak Samoyed
Udekhe	Udee	Udegei	Udeghe
Udmurt	Udmurt	Udmurt	Votiak, Votyak
Uighur	Uigur et al.	Uigur	Taranchi et al.
Ulchi	Ulchi	Ul'chi	Nanai
Yakut	Sakha	Sakha, Yakut	Iakut
Yukaghir	Odul	Iukagir	Yukagir

LIST OF ABBREVIATIONS

AAN (RF PF) Arkhiv Akademii Nauk Russkoi Federatsii, Peterburgskii Filial [St. Petersburg Branch of the Archive of the Academy of Sciences of the Russian Federation]

AMNH American Museum of Natural History, New York

APS American Philosophical Society, Philadelphia

E.D. Eastern dialect of the Gilyak language

ESBE *Entsiklopedicheskii Slovar' Brokgausa i Efrona* [*Brockhaus and Efron Encyclopaedic Dictionary*]. Russian Edition. St. Petersburg: Brokgaus–Efron, 1890–1904

GARF Gosudarstvennyi Arkhiv Russkoi Federatsii [State Archive of the Russian Federation, formerly TsGAOR, Tsentral'nyi Gosudarstvennyi Arkhiv Oktiabr'skoi Revoliutsii (Central State Archive of the October Revolution)], Moscow

GASO Gosudarstvennyi Arkhiv Sakhalinskoi Oblasti [Sakhalin Regional State Archive], Iuzhno-Sakhalinsk

IRKISVA Isvestiia Russkogo Komiteta dlia izucheniia Srednei i Vostochnoi Azii v istoricheskom, arkheologicheskom, lingvisticheskom i etnograficheskom otnosheniiakh [Bulletin of the Russian Committee for the Study of Central and East Asia—History, Archeology, Linguistics and Ethnography], St. Petersburg

KIPS Komitet po Izucheniiu Plemennogo Sostava SSSR [Committee for the Study of the Tribal Composition of the USSR]

MAE Muzei Antropologii i Etnografii im. Petra Velikogo [Peter the Great Museum of Anthropology and Ethnography; also known as the Kunstkamera], St. Petersburg

MKIVSA Mezhdunarodnyi komitet po izucheniiu Vostochnoi i Srednei Azii [International Committee for the Study of the East and Central Asia]

NESBE *Novyi Entsiklopedicheskii Slovar' Brokgausa i Efrona* [*New Brockhaus and Efron Encyclopaedic Dictionary*]. Russian Edition. St. Petersburg: Brokgaus—Efron, 1911–1916

SOKM Sakhalinskii Oblastnoi Kraevedcheskii Muzei [Sakhalin Regional Studies Museum], Iuzhno-Sakhalinsk

TsGADV Tsentral'nyi Gosudarstvennyi Arkhiv Dal'nego Vostoka [Central State Archive of the Far East], Vladivostok (formerly in Tomsk)

W.D. Western dialect of the Gilyak language

NOTE ON TRANSLITERATION

The transliteration of Russian words into English follows the Library of Congress system, with the apostrophe indicating the Russian soft sign. Hence, the often-Anglicized versions of Leo Sternberg, Waldemar Bogoras, and Waldemar Jochelson appear here as Lev Shternberg, Vladimir Bogoraz, and Vladimir Iokhel'son, unless their names appeared in the title of an article or excerpted archival correspondence. Exceptions are made for commonly accepted English usages such as yurta (rather than *iurta*) or sazhen (rather than *sazhen'*).

The Gilyak language did not have a script when Shternberg first traveled to Sakhalin in the 1890s. For his early Gilyak monograph (Shternberg, 1904f–h), he developed his own system of transliteration, with extensive diacritics for rendering the language in Russian and English. He modified this system slightly for the American Museum of Natural History (AMNH) Russian typescript of this book, inserting handwritten Gilyak words in the Latin alphabet. In 1931, Shternberg's Gilyak studies protégé Erukhim Kreinovich developed an official Gilyak script for Soviet administration based on the Latin alphabet. Kreinovich shifted to the Cyrillic alphabet in 1936, and the Gilyak (Nivkh) writer Vladimir Sangi proposed a new system in 1981. For the 1933 Soviet editions of the manuscript (Shternberg, 1933a, 1933b), the results were often confusing, as when they used both Cyrillic and Latin letters in the same Gilyak words (such as "чих-чиgynd," a ritual offering of food, or "чauf," the place where the offerings are made, from Shternberg, 1933a: 337). Further variations arise between the two texts when each spells the same Gilyak terms differently.

This edition makes use of Shternberg's handwritten insertions in the AMNH Russian typescript, amending them only when Gilyak (Nivkh) readers of both the language's two main dialects reviewed the typescript on Sakhalin Island in 1995 and urged revisions. Footnotes throughout the text indicate prominent examples, such as *imgi* rather than *ymgi*, *tuvng* rather than *tuvn*, and *ang'rei* rather than *angej* or *angey*. The transliteration of Gilyak words follows the Library of Congress Russian to English system, hence *jox* is rendered as *iokh*.

SHTERNBERG TIME LINE[1]

1861 (May 4)	Born in Zhitomir, now Ukraine.
1866–1870	Receives early education in Jewish Letters, the Bible, and the Talmud.
1874–1881	Studies at the Zhitomir Classical Gymnasium.
1881	Enters Petersburg University, majoring in physics and mathematics.
1882 (November 8)	Arrested and exiled from Petersburg for student activism.
1883–1886	Enters Novorossiisk University in Odessa, majoring in law. Actively participates in *Narodnaia Volia* [The People's Will]; becomes editor of the bulletin, *Vestnik Narodnoi Voli*.
1885	Participates in the organization and meetings of the Ekaterinoslav Congress of *Narodnaia Volia* delegates.
1886 (April 27)	Arrested and incarcerated in the Odessa Central Prison.
1886–1889	Spends 3 years confined in the Odessa Prison before being exiled to Sakhalin by sea (March 19, 1889).
1889 (May 19)	Arrives on Sakhalin, settles in the town of Aleksandrovsk.
1890	Imperial officials, concerned with Shternberg's record for agitating for prisoners' rights, look to sequester him from Anton Chekhov during the writer's study of the island. Shternberg is relocated from Aleksandrovsk 100 km north to the more remote coastal settlement of Viakhta. He begins his studies of Gilyaks.
1891 (winter)	Travels for the first time to Gilyak communities in northwest Sakhalin.
1891 (summer)	Travels down the river Tym' to the shores of the Sea of Okhotsk to study east coast Gilyaks and Oroks.
1892–1893	Travels to southwestern Sakhalin to study Gilyaks, Oroks, and Ainu.
1892	Shternberg's initial findings on Gilyak social organization are reported to the Anthropological Section of the Society of Friends of Natural Science by N. I. Ianchuk and are recorded in the October 14 issue of *Russkie Vedomosti* [*The Russian Gazette*]. Friedrich Engels reprints Shternberg's report, with commentary on its favorable significance for understanding primitive communism in *Die Neue Zeit* (vol. 11, no. 12, Band 2, 373–375).

---

[1] *Source:* Modified from [Anonymous], "Lev Iakovlevich Shternberg, Vazhneishie biograficheskie daty," *Ocherki po istorii znanii VII* (1930), 7–19.

1893	Publishes his first ethnographic work on Gilyaks, "Sakhalinskie Giliaki" [Sakhalin Gilyaks] in *Etnograficheskoe Obozrenie* [*The Ethnographic Review*, Moscow] 17(2): 1–46.
1894	Makes second summer trip to northwest coast Gilyaks, up to Cape Mariia; begins to study the Gilyak language.
1893–1894	Organizes and heads a regional studies [*kraevedcheskii*] museum in the town of Aleksandrovsk.
1895	Temporarily relocates to the Amur region to study continental Gilyaks.
1895–1896	Makes three expeditions to Gilyaks, Oroks, and Ul'chi along the Amur.
1897 (May 7)	Officials remand the final 17 months of his 10-year sentence. Shternberg leaves Sakhalin with permission to return to Zhitomir.
1897–1899	Lives in Zhitomir under police surveillance. Takes part in the preparations of the journal *Dal'nii Vostok* [*Far East*]. Partially edits his Gilyak linguistic material. Meets his future wife, Sarra Arkadievna Ratner, director of the Women's Academy in Zhitomir.
1899	Receives permission to return to St. Petersburg through the intervention of Academician Vasilii V. Radlov.
1900	Becomes editor of the ethnographic sections of the prestigious *Entsiklopedicheskii Slovar' Brokgaus i Efrona* [*Encyclopaedic Dictionary of Brockhaus and Efron*, Russian Edition].
1901	Begins work at the Kunstkamera [later the Museum of Anthropology and Ethnography (MAE)], St. Petersburg, as a volunteer.
1902	Reenters Petersburg University; joins the staff of the MAE as a Junior Ethnographer. Additionally, writes the charter for the Mezhdunarodnyi komitet po izucheniiu Vostochnoi i Srednei Azii (MKIVSA) [International Committee for the Study of the East and Central Asia], Russian Section, and becomes a member of the Russian Writer's Union.
1902–1917	Acts as Secretary of the Russian Section of MKIVSA; edits their newsletter, IRKISVA.
1903	Travels to Berlin and Leipzig to visit ethnographic museums.
1903–1917	Participates actively in both open and underground Russian Jewish movements.
1904	Becomes Senior Ethnographer at the MAE. Travels to Berlin and Stockholm to cultivate museum exchanges.
1904–1914	Lectures on ethnography at the MAE.

1905	Travels to New York; meets with Franz Boas to negotiate publication of *The Social Organization of the Gilyak* in the Jesup North Pacific Expedition series; meets with American Jewish activists.
1906	Travels to the International Congress of Americanists in Quebec City as a delegate from the Russian Imperial Academy of Sciences.
1907 (January 17)	Presides over first congress of the Evreiskaia Narodnaia Gruppa [Jewish People's Group] in St. Petersburg; serves as one of group's chief strategists and ideologists.
1908	Elected to the organizing committee of the Evreiskoe Istoricheskoe Obshchestvo [Jewish Historical Society], St. Petersburg.
1908 (June)	Attends International Congress of Americanists in Vienna.
1908 (September)	Travels to Prague to purchase ethnographic collections.
1910	Returns to Sakhalin and the Amur for the first time since his exile there; it is his last visit.
1911	Travels to Stockholm to purchase ethnographic collections.
1912	Elected to the Organizational Committee of the International Congress of Americanists. Becomes Assistant to the Director of the MAE.
1913	Travels to Stockholm for ethnographic collections; elected to the Berliner *Gesellschaft für Anthropologie, Ethnographie und Urgeschichte.*
1915	Travels to the World War I Russian battle front as a delegate for the Committee to Aid Jewish Refugees.
1917	Serves as Chair of Commission on the composition of an ethnographic map of Russia for the Russian Geographic Society; teaches ethnology in the Eastern Studies Department of Petrograd [St. Petersburg] University.[2]
1918	Becomes Professor of Languages and Material Culture at Petrograd University; organizes the Department of Ethnography within the Geographic Institute; later becomes Professor and Chair of this department. Also works as Chair of the Komitet po Izucheniiu Plemennogo Sostava SSSR (KIPS) [Committee for the Study of the Tribal Composition of the USSR].

[2] [***Editor's note:*** The city of St. Petersburg [*Sankt-Peterburg*], founded by Peter the Great in 1703, was renamed Petrograd by Nikolai II upon Russia's entry into World War I in 1914 to downplay Germanic overtones. Soviet officials renamed the city Leningrad following the death of Lenin in January of 1924. The Russian Republic returned to the original name of St. Petersburg in 1992.]

1921   Becomes Professor in the Department of Primitive Art, Institute of Art History, Petrograd.

1924   Appointed Chair of the Jewish History and Ethnography Society and chief editor of its journal, *Evreiskaia Starina* [*Jewish Antiquity*]. Appointed to the prestigious rank of "member-correspondent" [*chlen-korrespondent*] of the Soviet Academy of Sciences]; attends the International Congress of Americanists in Stockholm. Meets with Boas in the Hague.

1925   Becomes a founding member of the Komitet sodeistviia narodnostiam severnykh okrain pri Prezidiume VTsIK [Committee for the Assistance to Peoples of the Northern Borderlands; commonly known as the Komitet Severa or Committee of the North].

1926   Becomes a founding co-editor of journal *Etnografiia* [*Ethnography*, 1926–1930; later *Sovetskaia Etnografiia* (*Soviet Ethnography*), 1931–1991; and *Etnograficheskoe Obozrenie,* 1992–]. Travels to Tokyo to attend the Third Pacific Rim Congress; visits Hokkaido to study Ainu.

1927 (June 1)   Becomes editor of the KIPS journal, *Chelovek* [*Man*].

1927 (August 14) Dies at his dacha in Dudergof, outside of Leningrad.

1933   Under the supervision of Shternberg's widow, a special commission releases the posthumous publication of the first two major Shternberg collections: *Giliaki, orochi, gol'dy, negidal'tsy, ainy* [*Gilyaks, Orochs, Gol'ds, Negidals and Ainu*] (Khabarovsk: Dal'nevostochnoe Knizhnoe Izdatel'stvo), and *Sem'ia i rod u narodov Severo-Vostochnoi Azii* [Family and Clan Among Peoples of Northeast Asia] (Leningrad: Institut Narodov Severa).

1936   Publication of the third major posthumous Shternberg volume, *Pervyobytnaia religiia v svete etnografii* [*Primitive Religion in Light of Ethnography*] (Leningrad: Institut Narodov Severa).

TABLES

MAPS

ILLUSTRATIONS

Notes on Contributors

Though many people have worked on the *Social Organization* text since Boas commissioned it from Shternberg in 1905 (appendix A), some of the key editors and translators are noted here.

IULIA PAVLOVNA AVERKIEVA [PETROVA-AVERKIEVA] (1907–1980) was born in the small coastal village of Poduzheme in Karelia. She entered Leningrad State University in 1925 to work under Bogoraz, studying to become a specialist on peoples of the American northwest coast. Under a short-lived US-USSR exchange of anthropologists, she went to New York in October of 1929 to study with Boas, later accompanying him to British Columbia in October of 1930 for 6 months of fieldwork among the Kwakiutl. Archival sources (appendix A) show that she assisted Boas in the editing of Shternberg's *Social Organization* text during her stay, and translated at least one chapter into English (Chapter 14). She returned to Leningrad in May of 1931. After a brief marriage to Petr Averkiev, who disappeared in the 1930s and may have perished in Stalinist camps, she married Apollon Petrov, a Sinologist and diplomat. They had three children, and went on to reside in China from 1942 to 1947. Shortly after Averkieva returned to Moscow, she was arrested for purported crimes against the state. Authorities exiled her for 7 years, first to Mordova, and then to Siberia. Petrov died in 1949 during her internment. She returned to Moscow in 1954, and joined the staff of the Institute of Ethnography. During her 26 years there, she rose to considerable prominence, chairing the Sector of American Studies, editing the flagship journal, *Sovetskaia Etnografiia* [*Soviet Ethnography*], and maintaining, as few Soviet ethnographers could, an active network of international colleagues.

FRANZ BOAS (1858–1942), the German-born dean of American anthropology, received his doctorate in geography from the University of Kiel in 1881. After a year-long stay in the Arctic from 1883 to 1884, he shifted to anthropology, soon after beginning his first field studies among Bella Coola Indians in British Columbia. Boas founded the first department of anthropology in the United States, at Clark University in 1888, and later moved to Columbia University, where he taught from 1899 to 1936. He worked as a curator at the American Museum of Natural History in New York from 1895 to 1905, during which time he organized the Jesup North Pacific Expedition. Although he left the Museum in 1905, he maintained close ties. Boas trained a generation of influential American anthropologists; in 1926 alone, former Boas students chaired every single department of anthropology in the country. He published over 600 articles and many books, including *The Kwakiutl of Vancouver Island* (1909), *The Mind of Primitive Man* (1911), and *Anthropology and Modern Life* (1928). He died during a luncheon at the Faculty Club at Columbia University in 1942.

ALEXANDER GOLDENWEISER (1880–1940) was born in Kiev. Having begun his undergraduate degree at Harvard, Goldenweiser received his A.B., M.A., and Ph.D. (1910) degrees from Columbia. Prior to translating portions of Shternberg's *Social Organization* text, he published his first book, *Totemism: An Analytical Study* (1910), and went on to publish nine others, most concerned with native American life. Goldenweiser taught at a number of institutions, including Columbia, the New School for Social Research, Reed College, and the Universities of Washington, Oregon, and Wisconsin.

BRUCE GRANT has worked on ethnographic and historical aspects of Nivkh (Gilyak) life since his first fieldwork on Sakhalin Island in 1990. His book on state intervention in Nivkh lives since the 1890s, *In the Soviet House of Culture: A Century of Perestroikas* (Princeton, N.J.: Princeton University Press, 1995), was a winner of the 1996 Book Prize awarded by the American Ethnological Association. He teaches anthropology at Swarthmore College.

ZOIA IVANOVNA IUGAIN (1929–1996) was born in the town of Muzma on the Amur River in the Russian Far East. She came to Sakhalin Island after World War II and worked for many years in the Red Dawn Collective Fishery in Rybnoe, on Sakhalin's northwest coast. In the summer of 1995, she read through the manuscript with Grant and Lok, making linguistic and ethnographic commentaries.

ALEKSANDRA VLADIMIROVNA KHURIUN works as a correspondent for the Nivkh monthly newspaper, *Nivkh Dif.* She lives in Nekrasovka on Sakhalin Island. In the summer of 1995, she read through the manuscript with Grant, making linguistic and ethnographic commentaries.

IAN PETROVICH KOSHKIN [AL'KOR] was a student of Shternberg and Vladimir Bogoraz in Leningrad in the 1920s. In the 1930s, amidst new ideological demands on scholarship under Stalinism, he wrote ambiguous prefaces for and edited the works of Shternberg and Bogoraz, using the pseudonym Al'kor. He became director of the Institute of Northern Peoples in Leningrad before being arrested in the late 1930s and disappearing.

ERUKHIM [IURII] ABRAMOVICH KREINOVICH (1904–1984) was 17 years old in 1924 when his friend Ian Koshkin took him to one of Shternberg's lectures in Petrograd. He enrolled that year as a graduate student, becoming Shternberg's Gilyak studies protégé. He worked as Native Affairs director on Sakhalin Island in Aleksandrovsk from 1926 to 1928, making extensive field trips to central Sakhalin Gilyak communities. Returning to Leningrad, he assisted in the editing of the Shternberg archive between 1929 and 1935. In 1931, he published the first Gilyak (Nivkh) literacy primer, *Cuz Dif.* Kreinovich's far eastern experience made him the object of suspicion in the Stalin years: He was arrested in 1937 on grounds of conspiring with "a Trotsky-Zinovievite terrorist spy organization in cohorts with the Japanese." He served a 10-year sentence in Magadan, only to be sentenced again, for the same crime, to a further 10 years upon his release in 1947. When he attempted suicide at the outset of his second term, he was allowed to work as a medical assistant for prisoners in a village outside of Krasnoiarsk until 1955. The government exonerated him later that year. After returning to Leningrad, he joined the staff of the Institute of Linguistics.

He defended his first doctoral (*kandidatskaia*) dissertation in 1959 on the Yukaghir language and his second doctoral (*doktorskaia*) dissertation in 1972 on the Ket language. Among his many publications, his 1973 book *Nivkhgu* remains a centerpiece of Gilyak (Nivkh) scholarship. Showing courage in an often anti-Semitic Soviet Union, he published by choice under the name Erukhim, rather than Iurii, which he used more commonly.

GALINA DEM'IANOVNA LOK is the director of the north Sakhalin Nogliki branch of the Sakhalin Regional Museum [SOKM]. She has worked extensively among Nivkh communities on North Sakhalin and the Amur. She read the manuscript with Grant and Iugain on Sakhalin in 1995, making linguistic and ethnographic commentaries.

SARRA ARKADIEVNA RATNER-SHTERNBERG (1870–1942) met her husband Lev when she came to Zhitomir, Ukraine from St. Petersburg in 1897 to head the Zhitomir Academy for Women. Little is known about her early biography or whether she continued to teach when they moved to St. Petersburg in 1899. After the death of Lev Shternberg in 1927, she was active in overseeing his archive and worked as Chair of the Sector of American Studies at the Museum of Anthropology and Ethnography in Leningrad. She died during the German siege of Leningrad in 1942.

ACKNOWLEDGMENTS

Like many Western anthropologists of Siberia, I first came to Shternberg's *Social Organization of the Gilyak* through an unpublished English typescript archived at the American Museum of Natural History. Lev Shternberg was one of the founding deans of the Russian ethnographic school, and the recondite English translation of this cardinal study of Gilyak social relations has long remained an inviting draw for anyone engaged by the history of Russian anthropology. The story of the manuscript's odyssey through the halls of anthropology on both sides of the Atlantic at times has rivaled the importance of the manuscript itself. First commissioned by Franz Boas in 1905—and later passing through the hands of Alexander Goldenweiser, Vladimir Iokhel'son, Erukhim Kreinovich, Roman Jakobson, Claude Lévi-Strauss, and Rodney Needham, among many others—it was an inviting project to assume when I completed my own ethnographic fieldwork among the Gilyaks (Nivkhi, by modern nomenclature), 100 years after Shternberg's imprisonment on Sakhalin Island.

Surely, *The Social Organization of the Gilyak*, in Russian or in English, is one of Shternberg's most difficult texts. Here the reader finds a densely composed tract on the arcana of primitive marriage and a foundational text in the development of prescriptive alliance theory for the anthropological study of kinship. But to be fair to Shternberg, this current edition is also a group effort in the most literal sense. At least three translators, if not more, took part in the production of the Museum's original English typescript, annotated by hand in different places by Shternberg, Boas, and, following Shternberg's death in 1927, at least three Soviet editors (appendix A). To that end, we can think only loosely of Shternberg's work as a "manuscript." The book is a historical artefact, Shternberg's fullest work in English translation, presented here to readers in a renewed and vigorous climate of international exchange in Russian anthropology. As editor, I had recourse to four Russian versions that approximate the current text—a Russian typescript archived with the Museum in New York, Shternberg's serialized 1904 monograph of Gilyak life (Shternberg, 1904f–h), and two Soviet editions of the work, published in 1933. It was at times small comfort when, faced with puzzling English renditions of Gilyak kinship terms, I discovered that the four Russian editions often differed more so among themselves than across the greater Russian–English language divide. Rather than seeing this as a handicap, I have used editorial notes to privilege the divergences in order to generate a maximal context for the book's argument. What I hope to bring to the text, particularly in the Foreword, is an intellectual setting for the lived experience of Shternberg's project; in the Afterword, Gilyak (Nivkh) readers bring an essential perspective on what Shternberg's work means to them today.

Field and archival research for this English edition of Shternberg's *Social Organization* text was conducted over the course of four trips to Russia: to the Archives of the Russian Academy of Sciences in St. Petersburg in March 1994, July 1995, July 1996, and March 1997; to Moscow during June and July 1996 and January through May 1997; and to Sakhalin Island in May through July 1995. I am grateful for financial support from the National Endowment for the Humanities, which generously facilitated the 1995 summer research, and to the Faculty Research Program at

Swarthmore College. Swarthmore's Office of Word Processing got the project off the ground when they agreed to take Shternberg's well-worn, faded typescript and transfer it to the computer age.

A number of colleagues in Russia extended considerable help for this study of a famous ethnographic ancestor. I owe particular debts to Michael Allen, the late Zakharii Efimovich Cherniakov, Galina Ivanovna Dudarets, Nelson Hancock, Aidyn Jebrailov, Aleksandr Krotov, Sergei Murav'ev, Nikolai Pesochinskii, the late Aleksandr Pika, Tat'iana Pika, Sergei Pshenitsyn, Galina Aleksandrovna Razumikova, Natal'ia Sadomskaia, Anna Vasil'evna Smoliak, Ol'ga Stakhova, Masha Staniukovich, Ol'ga Vainshtein, and Nikolai Vakhtin. Many of the archival documents in the Archives of the Academy of Sciences in St. Petersburg would not have been available to me without the kind interventions of Ol'ga Ulanova. The unusually generous staff of the Sakhalin Regional Museum in Iuzhno-Sakhalinsk directed me to many of the sources on Shternberg used here and have provided ongoing logistical support since my first visit there in 1990. I am particularly grateful to the Museum's Director, Vladislav Mikhailovich Latyshev, as well as Tania Roon, Igor' Samarin, Ol'ga Shubina, Sasha Solov'ev, and Marina Ishchenko. The Institute for Advanced Research in the Humanities at the Russian State University for the Humanities in Moscow extended their considerable resources for the final stages of writing and editing during my stay there in the winter of 1997.

On North Sakhalin, Nivkh friends and colleagues took more trouble than usual to entertain their Canadian visitor; many read the manuscript in its entirety in order to share their comments 100 years after Shternberg first arrived on the island to write about their relatives. I am especially grateful to Zoia Ivanovna Agniun, Galina Fedorovona Ialina, Sasha Iugain, the late Zoia Ivanovna Iugain, Rima Petrovna Khailova, Ivan Khein, Vera Khein, Aleksandra Khuriun, Murman Kimov, Lidiia Dem'ianovna Kimova, Nadezhda Aleksandrovna Laigun, Zoia Ivanovna Liutova, Galina Dem'ianovna Lok, Elizaveta Ermolaevna Merkulova, Antonina Iakovlevna Nachetkina, Ol'ga Ngavan, Pavel Nasin, Raisa Taigun, Kirill Taigun, and Natal'ia Dem'ianovna Vorbon.

Outside Russia, friends and colleagues, who might have learned long ago to plead other obligations when I have shown up on their doorsteps with works-in-progress, read through drafts of this volume in many different incarnations. I thank David Anderson, Eileen Consey, Aleksei Elfimov, Claire Feldman-Riordan, Lisa Hajjar, Laura Helper, Jamer Hunt, Karen Knop, Igor Krupnik, Brigitte Lane, Dana Lemelin, Nancy McGlamery, Anne Meneley, Rachel Moore, Patricia Polansky, Nancy Ries, Evelina Shmukler, Nikolai Ssorin-Chaikov, John Stephan, and Robin Wagner-Pacifici. Marjorie Mandelstam Balzer, Lydia Black, and Sergei Kan gave sharp, incisive readings of my own commentaries, as well as the English translations, for the presses of the American Museum of Natural History and the University of Washington. Lawrence Krader and Rodney Needham, each indirectly connected to the manuscript in their earlier careers and for whom my queries might have constituted a spectral return, were generous in consultations. At the American Museum of Natural History, Petica Barry expertly oversaw the illustrations and mapwork, while Brenda Jones shepherded production. Laurel Kendall, the Museum's Curator of Asian Ethnography, brought her keen eye and patience to this book in ways that far exceeded her initial responsibility for overseeing its publication 90 years after Boas preceded her.

More than one friend on Sakhalin Island warned me about "the Shternberg curse" when I first took up this project, and even the briefest perusal of appendix A, chronicling the manuscript's sometimes tortuous, sometimes comic route to completion since it was first commissioned in 1905 lends some support to this shadowy thought. In 1994 I managed to level both my car and a passing deer in a collision on the very day I learned about funding for the summer Sakhalin trip; in 1995 I deftly short-circuited two computer keyboards in as many weeks while transcribing the Sakhalin interviews; and in 1996 my very first troublesome encounter with poison ivy gave way to a month of monstrous disposition beginning the very day I was returning to Shternberg after the school year's hiatus. Thinking, then, that the American Museum of Natural History might not be the only august body to have wanted this long-lingering project to reach completion, my genuine hope is that this book is one Shternberg himself might have recognized and liked.

Bruce Grant, Swarthmore, 1998

FOREWORD

BY *Bruce Grant*

IN 1889, LEV SHTERNBERG, a Russian law student who had been exiled to Sakhalin Island for his participation in an anti-tsarist terrorist organization, met a Gilyak man on the street in the small Sakhalin town of Aleksandrovsk. "I saw a disheveled Gilyak shaman," he entered in his fieldnotes, "with matted gray hair and a strange cordial smile. Small boys surrounded him, shouting 'Look at the old shaman, he'll tell your fortune!'"[1] Shternberg didn't know how to respond, but he remembered the shaman's expression as he walked by. So began one of Russia's most famous ethnographic encounters. From that first meeting, Shternberg went on to produce a corpus of writing on Gilyak life that easily compares to Franz Boas' "five-foot shelf" on the Kwakiutl and Bronislaw Malinowski's epics from the Trobriands. Like his foreign colleagues, he has enjoyed the reputation as a famous ancestor for the generations of anthropologists he trained and influenced. Yet, looking back on Shternberg's work today, what perhaps stands out is not even just what he wrote, but how his work has come to mean so many different things to so many. Shternberg's *Social Organization of the Gilyak*, his most extensive work in English translation, began as a spirited defense of the idea of group marriage first put forth by the American ethnologist Lewis Henry Morgan. To Shternberg's students and colleagues in late imperial and early Soviet Russia, it became a model ethnography for a nascent field. For Soviet social engineers in an age of rising Stalinism, it became a chronicle of everything that needed to be eradicated from Gilyak life. And for Gilyaks themselves, Shternberg's *Social Organization* articulated with strange prescience a politics of primitive communism that influenced how others viewed them for decades.

Who was Lev Shternberg? Born in a small town in Ukraine in 1861, he began his career in the radical Russian movement, Narodnaia Volia [The People's Will], advocating violence in the service of the Russian socialist cause. When banished for his activism to Sakhalin Island on Russia's Pacific coast in 1889, he turned exile to advantage in 8 years of ethnographic research. Together with colleagues Vladimir Bogoraz and Vladimir Iokhel'son, he became a popularizer of the long-standing but little-known Russian tradition of protracted, polyglot field studies. He was a scholar

---

[1] Shternberg, *Giliaki, orochi, gol'dy, negidal'tsy, ainy* (Khabarovsk: Dal'nevostochnoe knizhnoe gosurdarstvennoe izdatels'tvo, 1933), xiii.

of kinship, religion, and psychology. A passionate and charismatic teacher, he trained the Soviet Union's first generation of ethnographers. An energetic institution builder, he oversaw the transformation of St. Petersburg's Museum of Anthropology and Ethnography (the Kunstkamera) into one of the world's leading ethnographic collections. So, at the turn of the century, when American anthropologist Franz Boas was looking to build the publications of the Jesup North Pacific Expedition (1897–1902), it was not surprising that the St. Petersburg museum recommended Shternberg as one of their most promising ethnographers.

The Jesup Expedition, organized in early 1897, was named after its leading patron, the American banker Morris Jesup. One of the late, great expeditions of American anthropology, and surely one of the most ambitious, it was the first to investigate the origins of Amerindian peoples by drawing on ethnographic data from both the Russian and American North Pacific Rim.[2] Though the primary expeditions had already been funded, Boas was looking for an ethnographer to write on Sakhalin and the Amur when Shternberg came to the American Museum of Natural History in New York in 1905. He and Boas struck a deal. Shternberg was to write a book based on his 1890s fieldwork among Sakhalin and Amur Gilyaks, a little-known group of just under 5000 people. It was an agreement that outlasted the first target publication date of 1907, and an agreement that outlasted both men. Delayed at first by the slow pace of writing and revision, *The Social Organization of the Gilyak* navigated its way through Shternberg's active work in Russian Jewish rights, World War I, the October Revolution, the Russian Civil War, Shternberg's death in 1927, funding strains at the American Museum of Natural History in the 1930s, Boas' death in 1942, and finally a Cold War that did little to permit the international scholarship that had given the Jesup Expedition its original verve. Nine decades, eight editors, and eleven translators later, Shternberg's English language text comes to light in this volume.[3]

Shternberg's *Social Organization*, then as now, began as a central contribution to North Asian ethnography, but in its theory and argument it came to represent much more than that. When Shternberg was first sent to Sakhalin in 1889, he had gained a cursory education in kinship theory and evolutionism from a fellow prison inmate in Odessa who had read him aloud Friedrich Engels' book *The Origin of the Family, Private Property and the State*. The book was a detailed commentary on American scholar Lewis Henry Morgan's work on kinship systems and the rise of civilization, and its influence over Shternberg lasted throughout his career. When Shternberg began his studies of the local Gilyak population on Sakhalin in 1891, he wrote excitedly to his friend Moisei Krol', "I've found a kinship terminology and clan system just like that of the Iroquois and the famous Punalua family of the Sandwich Islands, in a word, remains of the marriage form Morgan based his theory on . . . . At first I was scared to believe it . . . but as I went from yurta to yurta and from family to family making my census, I asked everyone

---

[2]   Stanley Freed et al., "Capitalist Philanthropy and Russian Revolutionaries: The Jesup North Pacific Expedition (1897–1902)," *American Anthropologist* 90 (1988), 7–24.

[3]   For a full listing of participants in the editing of the manuscript since 1905, see the archival correspondence in appendix A.

how various kin members are called and who has rights to whom. Then I became convinced."[4]

From his fieldnotes, it is clear that Shternberg was excited by his discovery, one that eventually led him on a theoretical excursion through the rise of restricted cross-cousin marriage.[5] Scholars from Morgan to Rivers to Engels and Freud had postulated an evolutionary paradigm of human social organization, beginning with incest, leading to a generalized "cousin marriage" or "sister-exchange," and later to the kind of more complex systems such as the form of matrilateral cross-cousin marriage Shternberg describes in this volume (see especially Chapter 8). With Morgan's theories of group marriage coming under attack, first from the Scottish juror J. S. McLennan in the 1890s and later more subtly from Boas himself, Shternberg saw the *Social Organization* manuscript as a detailed defense of Morgan's arguments. As Shternberg writes in Chapter 9 of this volume, "What Morgan based on speculation, we find fully realized among the Gilyak." He offered an emblematic illustration of the role of the mother's brother in the generalized exchange of women, and an early milestone in the development of prescriptive alliance theory.

For these reasons, the publication of Shternberg's manuscript is all to the good. But what actually did Shternberg discover? To be sure, in Shternberg's time, Gilyaks used formal terms of address that were complex enough to confuse even themselves, and that required a lifetime for mastery. But did this constitute, in the very confident way we find in *Social Organization*, such a juridical edifice? As David Schneider once wrote, whether we are reading Evans-Pritchard or Lévi-Strauss, Meyer Fortes or Edmund Leach, the tremendous constructedness of the kinship idiom rarely comes into play.

> Fortes says quite clearly that for the Tallensi the ideology of kinship is so dominant that all other modes of relationship are assimilated to that ideology. Leach affirms that kinship is not a thing in itself but rather a way of thinking about the rights and usages with respect to land for the villages of Pul Eliya. They were there. They saw it. They talked to the natives. But just what did Fortes and Leach and Evans-Pritchard actually see and hear?[6]

Schneider's work, along with other critiques of kinship that followed Rodney Needham's cardinal 1971 collected volume, has not diminished kinship's role within anthropological thought so much as return us to the roots of kinship studies as a metaphor for anthropology itself.[7] Reading Shternberg today, a hundred years after

---

[4] Shternberg, *Giliaki*, xii.

[5] AAN RF PF [Archive of the Academy of Sciences of the Russian Federation, Petersburg branch, *hereafter* AAN] f. 282, o. 1, d. 120/1–14.

[6] David Schneider, *A Critique of the Study of Kinship* (Ann Arbor: Univ. of Michigan Press, 1984), 3.

[7] Rodney Needham, ed., *Rethinking Kinship and Marriage* (London: Tavistock, 1971). Some recent critiques of the anthropological study of kinship include Jane Collier and Sylvia Yanagisako, eds. *Gender and Kinship: Essays toward a Unified Analysis* (Stanford: Stanford Univ. Press, 1987); James Faubion, "Kinship Is Dead. Long Live Kinship," *Comparative Studies in Society and History* 38 (1996), 67–91; Jack Goody, *The Oriental, the Ancient and the Primitive: Systems of Marriage and the Family in the Pre-Industrial Societies of Asia* (New York: Cambridge Univ. Press, 1990); and Schneider, *A Critique*.

his fieldwork, we have cause to reflect on his answers to some of Schneider's questions, for whether the anthropological reader has ever heard of Gilyaks or not, Gilyak kinship will be both strange and familiar. On the one hand, after a dizzying round of explanation in Chapter 8, Shternberg concedes that "for the European," the language of Gilyak kinship "naturally produces a sense of total confusion."[8] But it is also a language that became emblematic of anthropology's efforts across the 20th century to systematize our knowledge of other worlds. In the post-Soviet age, we can also reflect on Shternberg's work along with Gilyak readers (Nivkhi, by modern nomenclature) and ask how they look back on their own century of being represented both inside and outside anthropology's purview.[9]

This English-language volume of Shternberg's work takes a long-ago translated English typescript from the archives of the Department of Anthropology of the American Museum of Natural History, editing it for consistency with a handful of other Russian editions and making many new additions. These new portions include glossaries, a Shternberg time line, maps, expository footnotes, an Afterword incorporating 1995 retrospective interviews with Gilyak (Nivkh) women on Sakhalin, archival notes, an interview with one of Shternberg's former students, and a bibliography. Readers looking for a full account of the manuscript's odyssey through editing, near releases, and transformations since 1905 may wish to start with the story as it unfolds in the archival notes in Appendix A. In the meantime, I begin with Shternberg himself.

THE ROUTE TO SAKHALIN

Lev (Khaim) Iakovlevich Shternberg was born on May 4, 1861, in the Ukrainian town of Zhitomir. His childhood friend Moisei Krol' remembers their Jewish neighborhood as crowded, with rundown, one-story wooden homes, and his young companion Lev as energetic but intensely shy with strangers.[10] Their early life, as recounted by Krol', was filled with books, camaraderie, and a powerful mix of Judaism and mysticism. Zhitomir itself was isolated for that time, located some 30 miles from the nearest railroad and without a dominant industry. By the time of Krol' and Shternberg's adolescence, however, Krol' paints a quiet, provincial life grown increasingly turbulent with the disappearances and arrests of older friends who had left Zhitomir to take part in revolutionary activities.

In the 1870s and early 1880s, much of Russian politics oscillated between the autocratic, often repressive rule of the immense state bureaucracy and expectations for political reform brought on by the emancipation of the serfs in 1861. The events of 1861 captured the imagination of many of Russia's urban intellectual classes, beginning a tradition of populist intervention in the lives of the empire's underclasses

---

[8] Shternberg, *Sem'ia i rod u narodov Severo-Vostochnoi Azii.* Edited with a preface by Ian P. Koshkin (Al'kor) (Leningrad: Institut Narodov Severa, 1933), 108.

[9] In the early 1930s, Soviet state planners shifted from "Gilyak," a Tungus (Evenk) term, to "Nivkh," the self-naming for the just under 5000 fishermen, hunters, and traders living on the banks of Sakhalin and the Amur River. Although "Nivkh" came into full use by World War II, the use of Gilyak in this edition defers to Shternberg's original usage.

[10] Moisei A. Krol', "Vospominaniia o L. Ia. Shternberge," *Katorga i Ssylka* 8–9 [57–58] (1929).

FIG. 1. Lev Shternberg in exile, photographed on Sakhalin by prison authorities upon his arrival in 1889. Courtesy of the Sakhalin State Archive.

that would eventually greatly influence Shternberg. Before and after the emancipation, the Russian writers Aleksandr Herzen and Nikolai Chernyshevskii sent thousands of urban intelligentsia, "critically thinking people," peregrinating across the Russian countryside to appreciate, and more importantly educate, Russia's "soulful" peasantry. The belief was that these encounters between city and country [*khozhdeniia v narod*] would strengthen and advance Russia's famous tradition of communal organization, the peasant *mir*.[11] By the 1870s, Russia's urban intellectual classes took to the countryside in unprecedented numbers, with over 200 groups from European Russia's 51 administrative regions [*guberniia*] taking part in this rural invasion in 1874 alone. However, the urban activists were divided over both goal and method, and by the end of the 1870s, two distinct factions had formed. One favored working through small-scale, incremental gestures advanced by propagandists living in local villages, while another militated for higher profile political acts against the state in

---

[11] Nikolai Troitskii, "Druz'ia naroda ili besy?" *Rodina* 2 (1996), 69.

the cities.[12] Shternberg and Krol' inherited both of these traditions when they joined the movement's second faction, Narodnaia Volia [The People's Will], upon entering St. Petersburg University in 1881, months after the group had made an attempt on the life of Tsar Aleksandr II.

Historians have looked back upon Narodnaia Volia through many lenses. Early Bolshevik revolutionaries embraced their use of violence in the defense of the working class, whereas imperial Russian liberals saw them as noble but quixotic men of dangerous means.[13] Notably, however, as Christoph Gassenschmidt has argued, the group also served as a channel for Jewish political activism; up to 25 percent of Narodnaia Volia membership in some regions was of Jewish origin, and five out of the seven leaders of the movement were prominent Jewish activists.[14] Although the government tracked the group's membership at 500, mostly in Ukraine and along the Volga, its real numbers were likely 10–20 times that, with police records counting over 8000 arrests of the group's members between 1881 and 1883 alone.[15]

Along with a young Vladimir (Natan) Bogoraz, Shternberg and Krol' became members of Narodnaia Volia's "Central Student Circle" in 1881. Yet, by 1882, the movement was already in decline under government siege. By the end of their first year in St. Petersburg, police sent Shternberg and Krol' back to Ukraine for having participated in student demonstrations. Shternberg enrolled in law at Novorossiisk University in Odessa a year later, continuing to rise within the movement's ranks and becoming editor of its journal, *Vestnik Narodnoi Voli.*[16]

---

[12] Ibid., 69. Both sides in the 1870s successor movement to Herzen, Zemlia i Volia [Land and Will] had their detractors: Local village policemen had little trouble identifying and arresting the outside agitators because "they were the only village residents who would neither drink nor take bribes"; their urban counterparts had different trouble maintaining secrecy because of the more sensational resistance acts they advocated. Troitskii explains that when the two groups broke off in 1879, forming Chernyi Peredel [Black Partition] and Narodnaia Volia [The People's Will], the first took *zemlia* while the second took *volia.*

[13] Ibid, 67. One of the most detailed accounts of the participation of Shternberg, Krol' and Bogoraz in Narodnaia Volia is found in Erich E. Haberer, *Jews and Revolution in Nineteenth-Century Russia* (Cambridge: Cambridge Univ. Press, 1995), ch. 11. See also V. A. Malinin, *Filosofiia revoliutsionnogo narodnichestva* (Moscow: Nauka, 1972); V. A. Tvardovskaia, "People's Will," *Great Soviet Encyclopaedia* 17 (New York: MacMillan, 1983), 617–618; Christoph Gassenschmidt, *Jewish Liberal Politics in Tsarist Russia, 1900–1914: The Modernization of Russian Jewry* (New York: New York Univ. Press, 1995); Daniel Brower, *Training the Nihilists* (Ithaca, N Y: Cornell, 1975); Abbott Gleason, *Young Russia: The Genesis of Russian Radicalism in the 1860s* (New York: Viking, 1980); and Franco Venturi, *Roots of Revolution: A History of the Populist and Socialist Movements in Nineteenth Century Russia* (New York: Knopf, 1960). Hilda Hoogenboom takes a particularly productive look at the question of genre in Vera Figner's Narodnaia Volia memoirs. See Hoogenboom, "Vera Figner and Revolutionary Autobiographies: The Influence of Gender on Genre," in Rosalind Marsh, ed., *Women in Russia and Ukraine* (Cambridge: Cambridge Univ. Press, 1996), 78–92.

[14] Gassenschmidt, *Jewish Liberal Politics,* 5.

[15] Troitskii, "Druz'ia naroda," 70.

[16] Chuner Mikhailovich Taksami, "Issledovatel', drug i uchitel' nivkhov," in Ivan A. Senchenko, ed., *Issledovateli Sakhalina i Kuril* (Iuzhno-Sakahlinsk: Sakhalinskoe Knizhnoe Izdatel'stvo, 1961), 108. For an example of Shternberg's most provocative political writing at this time, see his "Politicheskii terror v Rossii 1884," in Boris Sapir, ed., *Lavrov—Years of Emigration,* Vol. 2 (Dordrecht, Holland: D. Reidel, 1974), 572–594.

For Shternberg the risks in such work were evident. Between 1879 and 1883, amidst thousands of arrests, the government held over 70 trials to indict Narodnaia Volia members, sending some 2000 people to prison. Authorities arrested Shternberg himself in April of 1886 after police exposed an elderly female street vendor he had recruited for the distribution of literature.[17] Shternberg spent 3 years in the Odessa Central Prison before the court sentenced him to 10 years of exile on Sakhalin Island.

Shternberg's prison diaries from the years 1887 and 1888, 14 notebooks now preserved in the Archive of the Russian Academy of Sciences in St. Petersburg, are documents that astonish for the range of acquired languages and literatures occupying Shternberg while in confinement.[18] Long passages in Russian, Yiddish, English, and French, interspersed with Italian vocabulary lists, fill the pages stamped by prison censors. Many of Shternberg's entries are excerpts from Shakespeare, Milton, Mill, Machiavelli, and, perhaps all too aptly for his imminent sentencing, *Robinson Crusoe*.[19] By the tone of the entries, the prison years were a painful, introspective period that recalled his childhood in Zhitomir as formative for his later intellectual life. Shternberg wrote,

> My education was an imperfect one, though my family gave me more than I could ever absorb. From the ages of five to twelve, I studied the Hebrew language and religion. These years were decisive. I was deprived of all joys of youth, and the lasting impressions of these years are moral ones. Conversations on morality and learning were among the only I had. Sad and hollow . . . . Instead of novels, I studied philosophy and history, creating a chasm between myself and my school friends. I condemned them, and in turn was mocked by them. Even those that liked me took issue with my company, for I was strange to all . . . . That position imbued me with an inexpressible bitterness.[20]

---

[17] Krol', "Vospominaniia," 229.

[18] AAN f. 282, o. 1, d. 120/1–14.

[19] Although Shternberg excerpted the first and best known of Daniel Defoe's Crusoe voyages, *The Wonderful Life and Surprising Adventures of the Renowned Hero Robinson Crusoe* (Philadelphia: Cist, 1789), Defoe sent Crusoe through the Tatar Strait and up the Amur River en route to China in his second volume, *The Farther Adventures of Robinson Crusoe* (1925 (1790)).

[20] AAN f. 282, o. 1, d. 120/12, l. 1–3ob. Although Shternberg wrote this entry, as some others, in his own English, possibly to seek privacy from prison censors, I have modified the original text to avoid grammatical confusion. The original extract reads:

> My education was very imperfect, though from my kindred I received more than was possible to acquire. From five, close to age of twelve years, I studied the Hebrew tongue and theology. These years have decided all my future. I was bereaved of all joys of youth, and the single impressions of these years were moral beliefs. Therefore, ideas of morality and learning grew to me as real things. All conversations of that time had one topic. Sad and hollow. Sad and fitting. When my fellows threw the ball and found delight in fantastical tales, my mind required a more hard enjoyment, the rigors of contemplating. Instead of novels, I studied philosophy and history. This had thrown an impassable abyss between me and my school fellows. I condemned them, and was in turn mocked by them. And even they that esteemed me, they could not find a delight in my society, for I was strange to all . . . . That position imbued me with an inexpressible bitterness.

More important than reading *Robinson Crusoe*, however, was Shternberg's first encounter Friedrich Engels' book, *The Origin of the Family, Private Property, and the State*. Much folklore surrounds what became, at least for later Soviet biographers, a decisive event in Shternberg's life. Shternberg's student Erukhim Kreinovich wrote that Shternberg had to learn German in prison in order to read Engels himself, while others suggest that Shternberg had someone read the German edition aloud to him in Russian translation.[21] Our only hint from Shternberg's archive comes after Shternberg arrived on Sakhalin, when he wrote of "relaxing in the evenings with the *Ursprung*."[22] That the *Ursprung* in question might have been Engels' *Ursprung der Familie, des Privateigentums und des Staats* is an inviting but unnecessary leap; Shternberg's formal ethnographic work, soon to begin, made it clear that he had Engels and Morgan on his mind.

* * * * *

The Sakhalin of Shternberg's day bore the marks of a somewhat recent territorial acquisition by Russia. Both Russia and Japan had been making claims to the island since the 1850s, when Russian governmental presence on Sakhalin became a reality. The Treaty of St. Petersburg in 1875 formally put Sakhalin into Russian hands. Its turbulent waters and rocky shores made the island's economy suffer by contrast with the booming Primor'e region on the mainland. Instead, with so many folkloric visions of Siberia predicated on distance, Sakhalin took on the reputation as one of the most distant outposts of all. At some 6500 km and eight time zones from the Russian capital, Sakhalin remained farther from Petersburg than Newfoundland. Despite its most northerly tip being on the same latitude as Hamburg or Dublin, Muscovites from a hundred years ago through to the close of the Soviet period could receive northern hardship pay for taking jobs there. Despite being only 50 km north of Japan, it is thought of more often not as the Far East but "the Uttermost East," or more commonly, "the end of the world."[23] After his restless journey to the island in 1890, Anton Chekhov began a tradition of prosaic exaggeration about the island's isolation, declaring "This is where Asia ends," at "the end of the world," despite the fact that the booming city of Vladivostok lay only a few hundred miles to the southwest.[24] Following Chekhov, it was a matter of course that when the Polish geographer Ferdinand Ossendowski visited Sakhalin in 1905 he dubbed it "The Banished Island" and, in turn, "The Inaccessible Shore."[25]

Given these impediments to more rapid colonization, the island's indigenous Gilyaks initially fared somewhat better than, for example, their counterparts in northwestern Siberia such as the Nenets or the Ostiak (Khanty), whom Russians had been

---

[21] Ian Petrovich Koshkin (Al'kor), "Predislovie," *Sem'a*, iv; Taksami, "Vospominaniia," 110.

[22] AAN f. 282, o. 1, d. 190, l. 59.

[23] Charles H. Hawes, *In the Uttermost East* (London: Harper, 1904), 269.

[24] Anton Chekhov, *Ostrov Sakhalin: Polnoe sobranie sochinenii i pisem*, vols. 14–15 (Moscow: Nauka, 1978), 45. The English edition has been published in two separate editions under the titles, *The Island: A Journey to Sakhalin*, translated by Luba and Michael Terpak (New York: Washington Square Press, 1967); and *A Journey to Sakhalin*, translated by Brian Reeve (Cambridge: Ian Faulkner, 1993). See also, Cathy Popkin, "Chekhov as Ethnographer: Epistemological Crisis on Sakhalin Island," *Slavic Review* 51, no. 1 (1992), 36–51.

[25] Ferdinand Ossendowski, *Man and Mystery in Asia* (New York: Dutton, 1924), 223.

actively colonizing since the 15th century. However, these literal and metaphoric distances turned against the local island populations in the latter half of the century when the tsarist administration saw in Sakhalin the perfect outpost for its growing exiled population. Officials began considering the penal colony idea in 1870, and by 1881 had established the island prison system. The tsar accorded Sakhalin its own governor, and from 1884 onward over 1000 exiles were shipped to Sakhalin each year. "By 1888 Sakhalin had become," in the words of George Kennan, "the largest and most important penal establishment in Siberia."[26] Indeed, although exiles were banished all across Siberia during the tsarist and Soviet periods, often to places even farther than Sakhalin, such as Chukotka or Kamchatka, the island's choppy seas and perceived isolation made it one of the most dreaded of exile destinations. Any man with a sentence of more than 2 years and 8 months could be sent to Sakhalin, as could any woman under the age of 40 with a sentence of 2 years or more. Exiled political agitators of any stripe were sent automatically.[27] The writer James McConkey notes that by the end of the 19th century Sakhalin had, through the eyes of its Russian prisoners, become synonymous with hopelessness, bestial callousness, moral depravity, obliteration of the self, despair, and miasma.[28]

In March of 1889, Shternberg sailed from Odessa to Sakhalin on the ship *Peterburg*. Although Shternberg later posted a comforting letter to his parents about the voyage, Ossendowski's account of the passage he made on the same boat 16 years later offers us a stark description.

> Russian ships used to sail from Odessa to the western shore of Sakhalin two or three times a year, ships that wore a strange appearance. No passengers were visible on the decks, only a dark flag with some letters on it flew at the masthead. If anyone could have boarded this mysterious ship near Colombo or Shanghai, he would have been struck by the sound of clanking chains and by the continuous buzz below decks that would have reminded him of some enormous bee-hive—only these bees were not free insects . . . . This sea journey of these chained men and women shut up in iron cages recalled the most terrible scenes of *Dante's Inferno*. Storms at sea, heat under the tropics, cold in the North Pacific, dirt surpassing anything the most vivid imagination could picture, persecution of these helpless victims—all this took toll of their ranks by hundreds, a result considered desirable from the Government standpoint, as it diminished costs and saved trouble.[29]

Upon his arrival in 1889, Shternberg's status was that of a political rather than criminal exile, which permitted him to reside in special housing in the small administrative town of Aleksandrovsk, though he joined other prisoners at hard labor during the days. However, by March of 1890, penal officials cited Shternberg's harmful ideological influence over other local exiles and relocated him to the remote

---

26 Kennan *in* John Stephan, *Sakhalin—A History* (Oxford: Clarendon Press, 1971), 68.
27 Hawes, *In the Uttermost East*, 337.
28 James McConkey, *To a Distant Island* (New York: Dutton, 1986), 154. For another of many examples, see also A. A. Panov, *Sakhalin kak koloniia* (St. Petersburg: I. D. Sykin, 1905), 1.
29 Ossendowski, *Man and Mystery*, 223–224.

MAP 1. Sakhalin Island, 1905. Over the course of the 20th century, Gilyaks have numbered from 4000 to 5000 people living on North Sakhalin Island and the banks of the Amur River (shown in shaded areas). At the turn of the century, over 100 small Gilyak villages lined the shores and rivers of North Sakhalin where Shternberg did much of his Gilyak research. The largest of these settlements are shown here. Russian and Japanese regional centers are in bold. Following the Russo-Japanese War of 1905, the Treaty of Portsmouth divided Russia's North Sakhalin from Japan's Karafuto at the 50th Parallel. *Source:* GASO f. 511, o. 2, d. 150, 152.

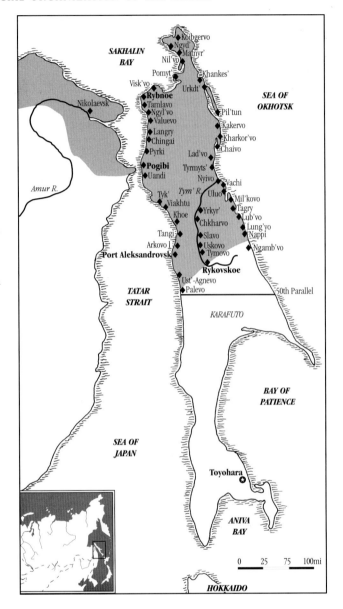

community of Viakhtu some 100 km north of Aleksandrovsk on the Tatar Strait.[30] That the playwright Anton Chekhov was known to be en route to Sakhalin at the same time, and that authorities were likely fearful of having Shternberg brief Chekhov on the finer points of the tsarist penal system, was an additional factor often later noted in Soviet writings.[31]

Viakhtu consisted of five houses for exiles who had finished their prison terms, and was a way station for Gilyaks traveling between the northwest coast and Aleksandrovsk. In his field diaries Shternberg described the small house where he lived under surveillance by imperial police officers as

---

30   The town is now called Viakhta.
31   Nina Ivanovna Gagen-Torn, *L. Ia. Shternberg* (Moscow: Nauka, 1975), 28–30.

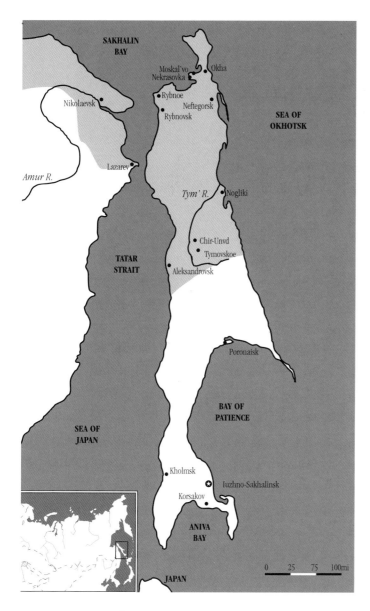

MAP 2. Sakhalin Island, 1995. The USSR reclaimed the southern half of Sakhalin at the close of World War II, further accelerating voluntary migration and involuntary displacement, now from north to south. Gilyak (Nivkh) villages, already diminished by Sovietizing relocation programs of the 1920s and the collectivization of the 1930s, were dealt a final blow when a massive resettlement program in the 1960s reduced the entire number of both Russian and Gilyak settlements across the island from 1000 to 329. The Gilyak (Nivkh) population, still stable from a century ago, is now concentrated in the towns of Okha, Nekrasovka, Rybnoe, Nogliki, Chir-Unvd, and Poronaisk. Shaded areas show traditional Nivkh territory.

a lonely abandoned grave in the empty taiga along the banks of the Tatar Strait . . . . The gloomy sky hung low over the snowy savanna, bordered by a thick fog, and beyond it, it seemed, was the end of the world, a kingdom of endless ice and gloom . . . . In the house [we were five—myself,] three former convicts turned officers and a military supervisor. Vigilantly they kept watch through a tiny window looking out onto the shore, thinking they might find a passerby or runaway convict . . . . The hope for them as for everyone was to win the curious three ruble prize for each fugitive captured.[32]

---

[32] Taksami, "Issledovatel'," 109–110.

FIG. 2. The house where Shternberg resided in Viakhta, Sakhalin Island, starting in 1891. *Source:* AAN f. 282, o. 2, d. 162, l. 117.

"It was here," Shternberg wrote, "that I was ethnographically baptized." In his "Russian Palestine," "A grim land!" where the sea was "eternally stormy," and where the true inhabitants were "bears, powerful winds, punishing hellish blizzards and destructive hurricanes," Shternberg began his investigations of local Gilyak life.[33] Shternberg's Narodnaia Volia comrade-in-exile, Vladimir Bogoraz, himself sent to the Kolyma Peninsula, later coyly described Shternberg's decision to study Gilyak as "owing to the leisure time we all enjoyed then," underscoring the unlikely boost that banishment gave anthropology in Siberia as well as the Trobriand Islands.[34] However, it was more likely the practical interests of the Sakhalin administration, who saw in Shternberg's restlessness someone both to organize a census of the island's Gilyak population and appoint a network of native officials who would report to Aleksandrovsk authorities.[35] In February of 1891, the prison administration allowed Shternberg to undertake what would be the first of dozens of excursions to Gilyak communities across North Sakhalin.[36] It was a new kind of rural

---

[33] Cf. the Preface in this volume.

[34] Bogoraz correspondence cited from the Gosudarstvennyi Arkhiv Rossiiskoi Federatsii [State Archive of the Russian Federation, Moscow; *hereafter* GARF] f. 3977, o. 1, d. 279, l. 110. For a particularly good reading of Bogoraz's early fieldwork in Chukotka, see Igor Krupnik, "The Bogoras Enigma," *in* Vaclav Hubinger, ed., *Anthropological Concepts in the Postmodern Era* (London: Routledge, 1996), 35–52.

[35] Shternberg, *Giliaki,* 112; "Dnevnik puteshestviia L. Ia. Shternberga" (1891), AAN f. 282, o. 1, d. 190, l. 48.

[36] Cf. the Preface in this volume; Shternberg, *Giliaki,* 22–23.

invasion [*khozhdenie v narod*] for Shternberg, but one for which he was ironically well suited, given the very Narodnaia Volia background for which he had been imprisoned.

* * * * *

For Gilyaks, Shternberg arrived at a time when outside influences were widely restructuring their access to natural resources. Hunters and fishermen by tradition, the Gilyak population had never exceeded 5000, divided approximately between the Amur delta and North Sakhalin. Nevertheless, because of the river and coastal locations of their villages they had long been integrated into expansive trade networks with neighboring indigenous groups and the Amur mainland Manchurians. By the 1860s, they were clearly under new pressure to define their rights to resource use as Russian and Japanese fishing fleets began sparring over the prime waters. The arrival of fishing industrialists also introduced the additional draw of paid seasonal labor: Many Gilyaks were lured into taking disadvantageous salary advances and fell into considerable debt.[37]

Although by the late 19th century some Gilyaks had begun to build Russian-style houses, the majority still lived a seminomadic life between summer and winter homes in order to exploit seasonal fishing and hunting grounds. The traditional Gilyak summer dwelling was a large one-room wooden cabin perched on posts 4–5 feet above the ground, whereas winter dwellings were partly underground to ensure warmth.[38] On Sakhalin, both shores of the northern portion of the island as well as the banks of the central Tym' and Poronai rivers were lined with Gilyak villages approximately every 5 km. Anywhere from one or two to 10 families constituted a village, with the maximum number of residents usually around 50. Almost every family kept a dog team for winter transport and shared narrow wooden log boats for navigating the hazardous coastal waters.

Fishing dominated the Gilyak economy in almost all respects. Summer was the busiest period, given the magnitude of the fish runs and the volume of salmon to be dried into *iukola* which would be the main food supply for the rest of the year. Winter, by contrast, they set aside for periodic hunting and almost constant socializing—as Shternberg wrote, *"dolce far niente,"* sweet doing nothing.[39] The Gilyak diet consisted of fresh or dried salmon, a variety of wild berries prepared plainly or in custards, and a range of products adopted from Japanese and Manchu traders, such as low-grade brick tea, millet, potatoes, sugar, alcohol, and tobacco. Traditional Gilyak clothing, in the form of tunics and pants for men and long tunic-style dresses for women, was made from a variety of textiles, including complexly crafted salmon-skin jackets. As with the clothing of other indigenous peoples of the Amur area, Gilyak designs borrowed heavily from local Chinese practices. Few if any Gilyaks were known to be literate, though many had practical knowledge of Chinese, Japanese, Russian, and

---

[37] Anna Vasil'evna Smoliak, *Etnicheskie protsessy u narodov Nizhnego Amura i Sakhalina* (Moscow: Nauka, 1975), 161–182; and "Zametki po etnografii nivkhov Amurskogo Limana," *Trudy Instituta Etnografii* 56 (1960), 96–98.
[38] In *Social Organization,* Shternberg refers to both as yurtas.
[39] Shternberg, *Giliaki,* 27.

FIG. 3. Shternberg drinking tea with Gilyaks, 1890s. *Source:* AAN f. 282, o. 2, d. 162, l. 119.

other languages for trading purposes. Although Shternberg expressed surprise at the number of Gilyaks who knew Russian, he worked largely in Gilyak, a language noted for its grammatical complexity. For example, it includes 26 ways of counting from 1 to 10 based on the spiritual and material qualities of the objects being counted. Linguists consider it to be so distinct as to have no known affiliation with another language.[40]

Despite the fact that Gilyaks, as both Shternberg and later anthropologists observed, came the closest of any of the Far Eastern peoples in the 19th century to adopting Russian ways, late 19th century Russian Orthodox missionaries recorded few efforts to win Gilyak converts. Through to the early 20th century, reports suggest a Gilyak world view that remained animistic, recognizing four spirit masters presiding in turn over the Sky, the Hills, the Water, and Fire. Gilyaks recognized each of these figures through feeding rituals, such as a ritual feeding of the sea with tobacco and *mos'* (an aspic made from seal fat, fish skin, and berries) before commencing a sea expedition. By the same token, Gilyaks had a complex symbolic relationship with the animal world: Bears in particular were regarded as ritual kin and would often be kept in pens inside or alongside family homes for several years as visiting

---

[40] For analyses of the Gilyak (Nivkh) language, see the works of Robert Austerlitz, Bernard Comrie, Erukhim Abramovich (Iurii) Kreinovich, Galina Aleksandrovna Otaina, and Vladimir Z. Panfilov in the bibliography.

guests, culminating in a bear festival that marked the high point of the winter social season.

By virtue of language, clothing, systems of counting, and sheer physical appearance, there was much to set Gilyaks apart from the gradually expanding Russian community around them. Between bear sacrifice, shamanic healing rituals, and Gilyak forest feedings, there was much fodder for the nascent practice of ethnography, which my description only begins to touch upon here, and which has been so excellently treated elsewhere.[41] However, what makes the literature on Gilyak life so striking—Shternberg's *Social Organization* being no exception—is the shifting tides of what counted as useful or important knowledge from one political era to another. This was perhaps most evident in the Soviet period, when Shternberg's posthumous editors published his careful work on the clan system "to ensure the liquidation of patriarchal clans."[42] But with the regnant intellectual trends at the time of Shternberg's field research, it was Gilyak kinship structure and its implications for burgeoning socialist theories of egalitarian primitive society that rose to the fore.

GILYAKS AND GROUP MARRIAGE

By the time Shternberg arrived on Sakhalin in 1889, the American scholar Lewis Henry Morgan had set in motion a series of debates on the nature of classificatory kinship in his pathbreaking books *League of the Iroquois* (1851), *Systems of Consanguinity and Affinity* (1871), and *Ancient Society* (1877). It was the last of these books, *Ancient Society*, that the Russian jurist Maksim Kovalevskii lent to Karl Marx, who made extensive notes on the book between before his death in 1883.[43] One year later, Engels published his and Marx's response to Morgan in the influential *Origin of the Family, Private Property and the State* (1884). While Shternberg states frequently in *Social Organization* that his goal was to test Morgan's hypotheses, it is nonetheless in the context of both Engels and late 19th century theories of group marriage that many of Shternberg's observations on Gilyak life can be understood.

Lewis Henry Morgan's first book, *League of the Iroquois*, grew out of his early commitment to the rights of local Iroquois populations in his native New York state. In this 1858 publication, he paid early attention to what he found to be a uniquely

---

[41] Prior to Shternberg, the German ethnographer Leopold von Schrenck conducted a lengthy survey of Gilyak (Nivkh) life for the Imperial Academy of Sciences in 1859. The Polish scholar Bronislaw Pilsudskii (older brother of the Polish leader Iuzef) was a coeval in exile with Shternberg on Sakhalin. At the outset of the Soviet period one of Shternberg's graduate students, Erukhim Kreinovich, began what would become decades of research on Gilyak life; in the 1960s and 70s and 80s, there have been considerable contributions by Anna Smoliak, the Gilyak (Nivkh) ethnographer Chuner Taksami, and the collective of the Sakhalin Regional Museum. In the English language, Lydia Black put the 19th and 20th century Russian materials to excellent use in her monographs on Nivkh social organization and symbol systems. Bruce Grant has written on the Soviet and post-Soviet periods. See their works in the bibliography.

[42] Shternberg, *Giliaki*, xxxvi.

[43] Lawrence Krader, *The Ethnological Notebooks of Karl Marx* (Assen, The Netherlands: Van Gorcum, 1974), 6; Lester Richard Hiatt, *Arguments about Aborigines* (Cambridge: Cambridge Univ. Press, 1996), 59.

integrative kinship terminology that Iroquois used to reach across clan affiliations. Morgan described Iroquois kin terms as "classificatory," because entire groups of relatives, both lineal and collateral, could be classified as group "brothers" or group "sisters," depending on the angle of relationship. Shortly after the book's publication, however, Morgan found similar patterns among the Ojibwa of Lake Superior and excitedly began sending out questionnaires in preparation for a wide-scale comparison of kinship terminologies.[44]

In 1871, Morgan's ambitious *Systems of Consanguinity and Affinity* analyzed kinship systems set forth by the 139 respondents who had answered his call for data. The seeds of what soon came to be termed "group marriage" came in Morgan's reflections upon "pínalúan" (or punaluan) sexual customs offered to him by Lorin Andrews, a judge of the Supreme Court of Hawaii. Andrews had written, "The relationship of *pínalúa* is rather amphibious. It arose from the fact that two or more brothers, with their wives, or two or more sisters with their husbands, were inclined to possess each other in common; but the modern use of the word is that of *dear friend*, an intimate companion."[45] Andrews offered Morgan a conjectural solution to the "mystery of Hawaiian kinship" that Shternberg would later see by analogy among Gilyaks—how it was that all males and females of a man's parents' generation could be "fathers" and "mothers," how so many members of his own generation could be "brothers" and "sisters," and so on. Morgan's conclusion that these terms were survivals of an earlier age of promiscuity was a milestone in thinking on evolution. Here was a stage of marital development

> Older in point of time than polygamy and polyandria, and yet involving the essential features of both. The several brothers, who thus cohabited with each other's wives, lived in polygynia; and the several sisters, who thus cohabited with each other's husbands, lived in polyandria. It also presupposes *communal families*, with communism in living, which, there are abundant reasons for supposing, were very general in the primitive ages of mankind; and one of the stages through which human society passed before reaching the family in its proper sense, founded upon marriage between single pairs.[46]

In print, Morgan was cautious with his evolutionism. His stages in the development of the family were "landmarks of experience" known to varying degrees among different peoples of the world.[47] Yet many readers saw simpler, unilineal development upon finding his cardinal list of 15 stages of family life in *Systems*, beginning with "Promiscuous Intercourse" and continuing through "The Intermarriage or Cohabitation of Brothers and Sisters" to "The Civilized Family" and, finally, "The

[44] Hiatt, *Arguments*, 36–38.
[45] Lewis Henry Morgan, *Systems of Consanguinity and Affinity of the Human Family* (Washington: Smithsonian Institution, 1871), 453n, original emphasis. For Morgan's fuller account of the Hawaiian case, see *Systems*, 451–458; and Morgan, *Ancient Society*, 427–428. For a concise discussion of the Punaluan category as an example of Morgan's nonsymbolic logic, see Marshall Sahlins, *Culture and Practical Reason* (Chicago: Univ. of Chicago Press, 1976), 58–59.
[46] Morgan, *Systems*, 457, original emphasis.
[47] Ibid., 479.

Fig. 4. A young Gilyak couple, 1890s. Photo by Lev Shternberg. *Source: AAN f. 282, o. 2, d. 162.*

Overthrow of the Classificatory System of Relationship, and the Substitution of the Descriptive."[48] In doing so, Morgan joined the conjecture put forth by Bachofen, Maine, Lubbock, and McLennan that the earliest forms of human society were found in a promiscuous horde.[49]

In his next book, *Ancient Society*, group marriage emerged more clearly as a explanation for kin terms that tied certain societies to these developmental stages. After meeting with Darwin, Morgan had begun to think of family structures as evidence for different stages in human social evolution.[50] He assigned group marriage to the period of savagery; a loose pairing arrangement between husband and wife to the period of barbarism; and the monogamy hegemonic today to mankind's later rise of civilization.

In his 1884 response to Morgan, Engels streamlined Morgan's analyses into a more trenchant indictment of the rise of bourgeois patriarchy. While Morgan concentrated primarily on the first two stages of savagery and barbarism, Engels focused on the civilizing process and how family relations intersected with the rise of private property concepts. Whereas in savagery and barbarism descent was often matrilineal, Engels argued that civilization, by contrast, promoted patrilineal descent through monogamy. When descent was traced through the female line, Engels reasoned, paternity, or more specifically, precise rules of material inheritance, could not be firmly held. "Once it had passed into the private possession of families and there rapidly begun to augment, this wealth dealt a severe blow to the society founded on pairing marriage and the matriarchal gens," Engels wrote. "Monogamous marriage comes on

---

48 Ibid., 480.

49 Krader, *The Ethnological Notebooks*, 63.

50 Darwin's role in the work of Morgan and later Engels was nonetheless a passive one. Reeling from the social arguments being drawn from his work, Darwin reacted in horror when Marx proposed dedicating *Das Kapital* to him. See Maurice Bloch, *Marxism and Anthropology* (London: Oxford Univ. Press, 1983), 5; and Alexander Vucinich, *Darwin in Russian Thought* (Berkeley: Univ. of California Press, 1988).

the scene as the subjugation of the one sex by the other."[51] While modern states presented themselves as products of natural social evolution—"the image and reality of reason," as Hegel said—Engels countered that states were products of society that bound up specific interests in the accumulation of private wealth by a few, and that families governed under a patriarchal system of monogamy served that end.[52] Nonetheless, in order to demonstrate that the bourgeois state was a temporary formation, Marx and Engels were in need of other formations since gone by. For this they prized Morgan's catalog of primitive life.

Many scholars have observed that although there was little to explain how patrilineal descent accounts for property more accurately than matrilineal descent, the details counted less than the framework. "What mattered to Marx and Engels," Maurice Bloch wrote, "was not so much the specific history which had produced these concepts, but the fact that they had a history at all, that the concepts depended on the type of society and economy in which they occurred."[53] Indeed, the most salient part of Engels' book might have been the title, where the rise of family, private property, and the state could all be tied to *one* origin, monogamy.

* * * * *

Where did Gilyaks fit into all of this? Like many indigenous peoples across Siberia in the late 19th century, clan affiliation structured a great deal of Gilyak political, economic, social, and religious life. There were roughly two dozen active clans among Sakhalin Gilyaks during Shternberg's 8 years there. While only one clan or lineage ideally prevailed in a given village, in practice mixed settlements had made the system more complex by the late 1800s. Shternberg's descriptions of the Gilyak kinship system were famously labyrinthine: Gilyaks were exogamous in that they married only outside their lineage in a complex system of reciprocities that bound together, in Gilyak terms, the wife-givers and the wife-takers.[54] But what made Gilyaks unique, Shternberg claimed, was a triangulated system of marital exchange, based on a tri-clan phratry or alliance group (from the Gilyak, *pandf*) that underwrote a complex web of mutual social and economic obligations.[55] Following Morgan's terminology, Shternberg charted Gilyak kin relations under the heading of "group marriage,"

---

[51] Frederick Engels, *The Origin of the Family, Private Property and the State: In Light of the Researches of Lewis H. Morgan* (New York: International Publishers, 1972), 119, 128.

[52] Ibid., 144.

[53] Bloch, *Marxism*, 94.

[54] Shternberg's cardinal writings on Gilyak kinship are in this volume, as well as in *Giliaki*, 30–45, 81–246, and *Sem'ia*, passim. Smoliak, *Etnicheskie protsessy*, 76–88, 150–167 and 222, is an excellent Russian review. The clearest analyses in English are in Lydia Black, "Dogs, Bears and Killer Whales: An Analysis of the Nivkh Symbolic System," Ph.D. diss., Univ. Massachusetts, Amherst, 1973, ch. 4; Lydia Black, "Relative Status of Wife Givers and Wife Takers in Gilyak Society" *American Anthropologist* 74, no. 5 (1972), 1244–1248; and Claude Lévi-Strauss, *The Elementary Structures of Kinship* (Boston: Beacon Press, 1969), ch. 14. For an example of the variety of ways people put a similar social form into practice, see R. H. Barnes' excellent study, *Kédang: A Study in the Collective Thought of an Eastern Indonesian People* (Oxford: Clarendon, 1974), chs. 14–17.

[55] In his 1904 essay, "Giliaki," Shternberg stressed the tri-clan model, although in this book he stresses that minimally four clans, and ideally five, were required for the successful local functioning of any given marrying network. See Chapters 7 and 16 of this volume.

because he found the Gilyak kin system to be remarkably similar to the Punaluan system in Hawaii that Morgan had documented. According to the classificatory nature of Gilyak kin terminology, any married man or woman had several potential "husbands" or "wives" from his or her marrying generation. As a result, "all men of a given lineage had rights of sexual access to women of their own generation in the wife-giving lineage," and by the same token, women had the same access to men of their own generation in the wife-taking lineage.[56] In practice, the system was a loose kind of monogamy: Many Gilyak men and women initiated discreet but permissible affairs, particularly with visiting guests, and under more formal circumstances of levirate, widowed women often married their husband's younger brother. Nonetheless, public displays of affection were uncommon and most Gilyaks considered it indiscreet to discuss extramarital activities in public.[57] The crucial element here is the reference to group marriage, for, according to Morgan's taxonomy, any group still practicing group marriage could only fall under the category of savagery.

When Engels came upon Shternberg's first field report from Sakhalin in the Moscow newspaper *Russkie Vedomosti* in 1892, he seized upon the case as an example of group marriage still extant and had it translated into German for reprinting within days.[58] Shternberg's account was important for Engels not only because it suggested the existence of group marriage in general but because the perceived backwardness of Gilyak life resonated so well with his and Marx's evolutionary framework. What made the Gilyak case relevant was that, in Engels' view, "It demonstrates the similarity, even their identity in their main characteristics, of the social institutions of primitive peoples at approximately the same stage of development."[59] What was good for Morgan, by association, was good for Marx and Engels' evolutionist theory of class struggle. Hence, that Gilyaks were proven to be a primitive people with backward customs became, in its own way, a building block in the edifice of Russian socialism.

* * * * *

While Engels popularized Shternberg's work for Russian and, perhaps more importantly, later Soviet readers, Shternberg swayed little from the basic Morganian position developed in *Systems of Consanguinity and Affinity*. After the Sandwich Islands, the main evidence for Morgan's theory of group marriage came from anthropology's El Dorado of complex kinship systems, Australia. In 1880, Australian researchers Lorimer Fison and A. W. Howitt released their monograph, *Kamilaroi and Kurnai* announcing "the most extensive system of communal marriage the world has ever known."[60] Despite the book's dedication to and approving preface from Morgan,

---

[56] Lydia Black, "Dogs, Bears and Killer Whales," 34. Black's reference to "lineages" resonates with Lévi-Strauss' observation that Shternberg's preference for "clan" might have been better captured by the more specific idea of lineage. Lévi-Strauss, *Elementary Structures,* 301.

[57] Chapter 6 of this volume; Shternberg, *Giliaki,* 169. Kreinovich makes similar observations in "Perezhitki rodovoi sobstvennosti i gruppovogo braka u giliakov," *Trudy Instituta Antropologii, Arkheologii i Etnografii* 4 (1936), 711–754.

[58] *Russkie Vedomosti,* October 14, 1892. Reprinted in German in *Die Neue Zeit* XI (12) (1892), Band 2, 373–375; and in English in Engels, *Origin,* 238–241.

[59] Engels, *Origin,* 239.

[60] Morgan *in* Lorimer Fison and A. W. Howitt, *Kamilaroi and Kurnai* (Melbourne: George Robertson, 1880), 10.

the material on group marriage more closely resembled simple polygyny than proponents of Morgan's theory might have liked. Nine years later, Baldwin Spencer and Frank Gillen published a detailed account of group marriage practice among the Dieri in their book, *The Native Tribes of Central Australia* (1899). W. H. R. Rivers' 1907 essay on the Toda marked a further and final landmark.[61] In *Social Organization*, Shternberg approvingly relies on each of these.

Meanwhile, however, criticisms of Morgan's framework had been mounting in wider anthropological circles. Although his own book, *Primitive Marriage* (1865), met mixed reviews, the Scottish juror J. S. McLennan leveled some of the strongest attacks on Morgan's work in an 1876 response to *Systems*. Beginning at the premise that group marriage was only a postulate to explain a puzzle of kinship terms, McLennan asked why such terms could not be mere salutations with ambiguous meanings. Later, Northcote Thomas furthered this in a 1906 essay by giving the example of the French word *femme,* meaning both woman and wife. Why would someone call an entire class of women "mother," Thomas asked, when it was clearly apparent who one's birth mother actually was? Thomas' alternative was to take the prime examples of group marriage data, such as the fraternal polyandry Fison and Howitt found among Kamilaroi and Kurnai, and explain them as contemporary institutions rather than survivals.[62]

By 1913, Malinowski and Radcliffe-Brown amended Thomas' intervention within the framework of functionalism by reasoning that much of the problem lay with the idea of "marriage" itself, a much broader category of functions and relations than had been considered in earlier debates. Morgan tended to interpret marriage strictly as a right of sexual access, rather than a larger edifice of securities and obligations such as the legalities of reproduction, child raising, and economic support. So, too, with levirate Morgan tended to see the right of a brother to his brother's wife or widow as a choice rather than an obligation that created a social security for clan solidarity. In the context of Morgan and Malinowski, Shternberg fell somewhere in the middle. He vigorously defended Morgan, but recognized (in a handful of lines from Chapter 10) that "To participate in group marriage is the duty of all cousins."[63]

---

[61] W. H. R. Rivers, "On the Origin of the Classificatory System of Relationships," *in* W. H. R. Rivers et al., eds., *Anthropological Essays presented to Edward Burnett Tylor* (Oxford, Clarendon, 1907), 309–324. While Rivers argued in his monograph *The Todas* (London: MacMillan, 1906) that the coexistence of polyandry and polygyny would be a more accurate expression of sexual ties than "group marriage," he continued to refer to group marriage in his work. Rivers, *The Todas,* 518–519, 531. For a further discussion of Fison and Howitt, Spencer, Gillen, and Rivers, see Hiatt, *Arguments,* 43–49. See also R. H. Barnes' excellent study of group marriage in his "Editor's Introduction" to Josef Kohler, *On the Prehistory of Marriage: Totemism, Group Marriage and Mother Right.* Translated from the German by R. H. Barnes and Ruth Barnes (Chicago: Univ. of Chicago Press, 1975), 1–70.

[62] Hiatt, *Arguments,* 40–41, 46–47.

[63] The functionalist approach is deeply implied in Engels' reworkings of Morgan, when Engels used the institution of marriage to fashion an early sophisticated critique of gender roles and obligations. For more on Engels' contribution to Marxist feminism, see Eleanor Burke Leacock's introduction to Engels, "Origin," and Gayle Rubin, "The Traffic in Women: Notes on the 'Political Economy' of Sex," *in* R. Rieter, ed., *Towards an Anthropology of Women* (New York: Monthly Review, 1975), 157–210.

New functionalist critiques notwithstanding, the most subtle figure working against Shternberg's argument for Gilyak group marriage was perhaps Boas himself, who chiseled away at the Morganian evolutionary stages in his 1911 book, *The Mind of Primitive Man.* While conceding the similarities found across early human societies, Boas pointedly wrote, "The theory of parallel development [advanced by Morgan], if it is to have any significance, would require that among all branches of mankind the steps of invention should have followed, at least approximately, in the same order, and that no important gaps should be found. The facts, so far as known at the present time, are entirely contrary to this view."[64] Unexpected similarities in material and social systems, Boas argued, had obscured the differences, which followed from a multitude of causes and consequences.

In the years after Shternberg's death in 1927, further critiques diminished much of the group marriage debate, at least in the way Morgan had framed it. In his 1941 *Structure and Function in Primitive Society,* Radcliffe-Brown described group marriage's place in evolutionary kinship theory as "one of the most fantastic in a subject that is full of fantastic hypotheses."[65] While Radcliffe-Brown's own research in Australia conceded that classificatory kinship terms demanded certain levels of behavior appropriate to the imputed relation, fictive or real, he argued that there were clear distinctions, in every Australian society considered by Morgan, that asserted the primacy of the nuclear family. George Peter Murdock, in his canonic 1949 kinship guide, *Social Structure,* followed Boas in arguing that there was no direct relationship between kinship nomenclature and societal complexity.[66] Lévi-Strauss, who published his essay on Gilyaks in *Elementary Structures of Kinship* the same year, remarked only that Shternberg was ultimately more observer than theoretician, subject to "rash historical interpretations."[67]

Whatever their fate in kinship debates abroad, for Gilyaks the die was cast. Their role as the quintessential savages of Engels' favor made them famous in Russian and Soviet ethnographic literature. Their personification of primitive communism, postulated by Morgan and elaborated by Engels, became axiomatic. What was lost in the process was that the report that found its way into *Russkie Vedomosti* was one of Shternberg's first, outlining a clan system he would later come to recognize as far less fixed than he first had perceived it. Given the swell of non-Gilyaks into the area, the increasing dislocations through travel and trade, and the demographic havoc wrought by disease, he realized that much of what he had been presented was an ideal system. This realization later found confirmation in the work of Soviet ethnographers such as Anna Smoliak, who pointed out that intermarriage with Gol'd (Nanai), Tungus (Evenk), and Manchurian Chinese prefigured the character of many Gilyak (Nivkh) settlements in a way that made close adherence to the marriage rules described by Shternberg difficult. Anthropologist Chuner Taksami, himself a Nivkh, noted that

[64] Franz Boas, *The Mind of Primitive Man* (New York: MacMillan, 1927 (1911)), 182. See also Gladys A. Reichards' "Social Life," *in* Boas, ed., *General Anthropology* (New York: D. C. Heath, 1938), 409–486.
[65] Alfred R. Radcliffe-Brown, *Structure and Function in Primitive Society* (London: Cohen and West, 1952 (1941)), 59, also *in* Hiatt, *Arguments,* 54.
[66] George Peter Murdock, *Social Structure* (New York: MacMillan, 1949), 187.
[67] Lévi-Strauss, *Elementary Structures,* 292, 301.

actual examples of Shternberg's labyrinthine systems were few.[68] That the clan system may not have functioned as methodically as suggested, that group marriage was not as licentious as it sounded, that Shternberg himself was not wholly loyal to the Marxian strain of materialism for which Engels had conscripted him (Shternberg once called Marxism "a hackneyed reworking of the Hegelian triad")[69]—or that Gilyaks at the turn of the century were far from an isolated tribe waiting to be discovered—were points that soon came to be lost in a handful of popular and scholarly accounts that entrenched Gilyaks in an edifice of evolutionary theory.

For Gilyaks of a century ago, there was considerable consequence in Shternberg's chance reading of Engels on the eve of his Sakhalin exile. The irony is that for someone who set out to produce a sympathetic portrait of Gilyak life, one of the results of his path through evolutionism was to emphasize the more sensational aspects of primitive life held in popular thought. Many Russian ethnographers besides Shternberg followed the terminology of the day by making similar claims to group marriage in Siberia in the later 1800s. However, as anthropologist Peter Schweitzer has shown, few if any of the cases actually corresponded to Morgan's criteria. What so many scholars and travelers claimed to document as group marriage more closely approximated extensive extramarital liaisons, and, in some cases, prostitution. The application of Morganian categories was itself awkward in Siberia because, as in Chukotka, for example, there were cases of virtually neighboring ethnic groups, effectively at the same "stage" of social development, with widely divergent kinship systems.[70] One wonders how Gilyak life might have been perceived differently had their most famous ethnographer not foregrounded their social structure so prominently.

THE SAGA OF THE SOCIAL ORGANIZATION TEXT

The odyssey of the *Social Organization* text, which marked the foundation of Shternberg's understanding of Gilyak marriage rules, is itself a small epic in the changing fortunes of Russian and American scholarship over the 20th century.[71] In 1898, when Boas was first looking for fieldworkers who might be recruited for the Russian side of the Jesup project, the German ethnographer Berthold Laufer, accompanied by archaeologist Gerald Fowke, had already begun an expedition to Sakhalin and the Amur, arriving on Sakhalin that spring, only 1 year after Shternberg had been released. When Boas consulted Vasilii Radlov, then head of the prestigious Museum of Anthropology and Ethnography in St. Petersburg, about Russian fieldworkers, Radlov was quick to recommend two former exiles who had emerged as excellent ethnographers:

[68] Smoliak, *Etnicheskie protsessy*; Taksami, *Osnovnye problemy*, 86, 110.
[69] Shternberg, *Giliaki*, xxi.
[70] Peter Schweitzer, "Spouse-Exchange in North-Eastern Siberia: On Kinship and Sexual Relations and their Transformations," *Vienna Contributions to Ethnology and Anthropology* 5 (1989), 17–38. Maurice Bloch expands on general misconceptions held by Morgan in *Marxism and Anthropology*, passim.
[71] Anthropologist Sergei Kan has treated the history of the manuscript in the greatest depth in his insightful forthcoming article, "The Mystery of the Missing Monograph or Why Boas Did Not Include Shternberg's 'The Social Organization of the Gilyak' in the Jesup Expedition Publications" [unpublished manuscript].

Shternberg's Narodnaia Volia colleague Bogoraz, who had been exiled to Kolyma and who had worked with Chukchi; and Vladimir Iokhel'son, another revolutionary sent to northeastern Siberia, where he worked among Koriaks and Yukaghirs. At that time, Radlov himself was only 1 year shy of meeting Lev Shternberg.[72]

From the time he left Sakhalin in May of 1897 to his trip to New York in the summer of 1905, Shternberg's career as an ethnographer and curator had met with its own partial successes. Originally returning to Zhitomir, where he lived under police surveillance as part of his early release from Sakhalin, Shternberg soon received permission to move to St. Petersburg in 1899 through the intervention of Radlov. In 1900, the Russian publishers of the prestigious *Entsiklopedicheskii Slovar' Brokgausa i Efrona* [*Encyclopaedic Dictionary of Brockhaus and Efron*] hired him as a contributing editor, eventually leading to the publication of more than 40 essay-length entries.[73] His early rise within the Museum of Anthropology and Ethnography was equally prodigious, from his start as a volunteer in 1901 to his appointment as a senior ethnographer and lecturer in 1904.

The original agreement by Shternberg and Boas in 1905 was for Shternberg to produce a general text called *The Gilyak and Their Neighbors.* Judging by the impatience Boas began expressing within only a year or two of this first meeting, it is likely that Shternberg's original pledge was to get the book out quickly, given the writing he had already done since leaving Sakhalin 8 years earlier.[74] Indeed, Shternberg had already published preliminary portions of the *Social Organization* text in the leading Russian journal *Etnograficheskoe Obozrenie* [*Ethnographic Review*].[75] But 1905 and the events that followed made for what Shternberg later described as "a difficult year."[76] "Bloody Sunday," the massacre of hundreds of demonstrators by imperial troops on Palace Square in St. Petersburg on January 9, 1905, had already transpired by the time Shternberg went to New York. Later, in October of that year, rioting in the city of Odessa, where Shternberg had many friends and had spent 3 years in internment, led to pogroms claiming the lives of 400 Jews and 100 non-Jews; a further 300, mostly Jewish, were injured, and over 1600 Jewish homes were damaged.[77]

Boas, whose academic career also often melded with political activism, was sympathetic, writing to Shternberg in January of 1906 to express his concern for "the terrible affairs that are happening under your very eyes day after day."[78] By August of the same year, however, Boas needed progress reports from both Bogoraz and

---

[72] For cardinal accounts of Russian contributions to the Jesup Expedition, see Freed et al, "Capitalist Philanthropy," and Nikolai B. Vakhtin, "Franz Boas and the Shaping of the Jesup North Pacific Expedition, 1895–1900: A Russian Perspective" [unpublished manuscript].

[73] Shternberg's contribution to the Brockhaus encyclopedia is discussed most extensively in Vladimir Germanovich Bogoraz, "L. Ia. Shternberg kak etnograf," *in* S. Ol'denburg, ed., *Pamiati L. Ia. Shternberga* (Leningrad: Akademiia Nauk, 1928), 4–30.

[74] Kan, "The Mystery," *passim.* See also appendix A of this volume.

[75] Shternberg, "Giliaki," *Etnograficheskoe Obozrenie* 28, no. 60 (1904), 1–42; no. 61, 19–55; and no. 63, 66–119.

[76] Letter from Shternberg to Boas, 11 August 1906, in the Boas Collection of the American Philosophical Society [*hereafter* APS].

[77] Robert Weinberg, *Blood on the Steps: The Revolution of 1905 in Odessa* (Bloomington: Indiana Univ. Press, 1993), ch. 7.

[78] AAN f. 282, o. 2, d. 2, l. 29.

Shternberg for funding purposes and was urging them to "tear themselves away" from Russia's political maelstrom.[79] However, between the intensity of their political work and the demands of their careers, Bogoraz and Shternberg were clearly working at different paces. Bogoraz spent 2 months in prison in late 1905 along with five members of the Central Bureau of the Farmers' Union (and he would go on to spend a particularly grueling 9 months in solitary confinement in 1911 following further work with the same group). In 1906, Shternberg published his foundational essay on Russian Jewish rights, "Tragedy of the Six-Million People."[80]

Shternberg's professional and political obligations were clearly enormous. In 1907 he presided over the first of three congresses of the *Evreiskaia Narodnaia Gruppa* [The Jewish People's League] in St. Petersburg, emerging as one of its chief ideologists. Later, in 1908, he was elected to the Organizing Committee of the Jewish Historical Society and became director of the Jewish Museum in St. Petersburg. At least one historian has named him among the eight major Jewish liberal figures in Russia at that time.[81] In 1908 he became ill from cholera, but still managed to deliver to Boas the first few chapters of the *Social Organization* text. Two years later, he made his second and final trip to the Russian Far East, using some of the new data he collected to modify the manuscript, although his time on Sakhalin was less than 2 weeks before moving on to the Amur. It was not until 1912 that Boas received the better (but not entire) part of the work reprinted here.

At this stage, Boas arranged for one of his students, Alexander Goldenweiser, of Ukrainian origin, to translate at least one chapter of the Shternberg text for preliminary printing. Goldenweiser had already translated parts of Bogoraz' and Iokhel'son's Jesup works, and he fulfilled Boas' request quickly. Boas requested that Shternberg present a full table of Gilyak kinship terms (Table 1) and refine his transcription system, which often combined both Cyrillic and Latin letters in the same Gilyak words.[82]

If life before World War I had made it difficult for Shternberg to complete this work, then the decade that followed made that goal nearly impossible. In September of 1916 at the height of World War I, Boas wrote Shternberg conceding, "At present it is hardly possible to write about anything serious."[83] Shternberg made an effort, sending a few more short chapters in February of 1917, and charitably Boas let up on the tempo of his reminders.[84] In the difficult early years of the Soviet 1920s, Boas proposed all manner of sustenance to Shternberg, from one offer of $300 in May of 1922 for "some subject on the Amur River tribes" to a pledge of emergency food aid later in July.[85] The turmoil of World War I, the October Revolution, and an equally trenchant Civil War did much to paralyze the workings of academic life. Shternberg spread himself thinly, organizing commissions for the Russian Geographic Society and Committee for Study of Tribal Composition of the USSR [KIPS], traveling to the war front

[79] Ibid., l. 19.
[80] Bogoraz discusses Shternberg's 1906 essay at length in Bogoraz, "L. Ia. Shternberg kak chelovek i uchenyi," *Etnografiia* 2 (1927), 271.
[81] Gassenschmidt, *Jewish Liberal Politics*, 53–57, 74.
[82] See the 1912 archival correspondence in appendix A of this volume.
[83] AAN f. 282, o. 2, d. 29, l. 62.
[84] Letter of 28 February 1917 from Shternberg to Boas, APS.
[85] AAN f. 282, o. 2, d. 29, ll. 64, 66, 70.

FIG. 5. Lev Shternberg, Franz Boas, and Vladimir Bogoraz in an undated photograph, possibly taken at their meeting in the Hague, 1924. Courtesy of Zakharii E. Cherniakov.

on behalf of the Committee to Aid Jewish Refugees, and teaching in a number of institutes and universities around the city rechristened as Petrograd. Where his academic writing was concerned, Shternberg's list of publications in many ways speaks for itself: Between 1914 and 1924 the normally prolific writer produced only three brief essays.

By 1923, the New Economic Policy of the young Soviet government had partially eased the tremendous economic pressures that followed the close of the Civil War (in European Russia). In 1924 the two correspondents, Boas and Shternberg, met one last time in the Hague. Shternberg pledged further installments on Gilyak material culture, religion, and folklore to Boas, all subjects on which he had published previously. But in their final exchange 2 years later in November 1926, Shternberg expressed remorse that he had been unable to keep his promise over so many years.[86] Shternberg died of heart failure 10 months later, in August of 1927, at his dacha outside the city rechristened as Leningrad. He was 66.

Upon Shternberg's death, Bogoraz reflected that "Every Moses dies at the gates of the promised land."[87] But given the frustration he was expressing to Boas over political events in Leningrad, he may have been speaking ironically.[88] Shternberg's demise

---

[86] Letter of 13 November 1926 from Shternberg to Boas, APS.

[87] Bogoraz, "L. Ia. Shternberg kak chelovek," 279.

[88] See, for example, the letter of May 17, 1928, from Bogoraz to Boas, APS.

FIG. 6. Shternberg, Bogoraz, and their graduate students posed for this photograph in Leningrad in 1926. *Top row from left to right:* I. A. Dyshchenko, Saul M. Abramzon, Zakharii E. Cherniakov, Stepan A. Makar'ev; *middle row:* Ian P. Koshkin, Vladimir G. Bogoraz, Erukhim A. Kreinovich, Lev Ia. Shternberg, Pavel Iu. Moll; *bottom row:* Sergei N. Stebnitskii, N. G. Shprintsin, Elena V. Talonova. Courtesy of Galina Aleksandrovna Razumnikova.

spared him much of what Bogoraz' later years did not—the new institutionalized repression of a Soviet Russia entering the "Cultural Revolution" (1928–1931) and the rise of Stalinism. In 1929, the state began enforcing entrance quotas for scholars (and scholarship) of working class origin, markedly changing the tenor of acceptable Marxist and non-Marxist discourse at the Museum, the University, and the Institute of Northern Peoples.[89] Bogoraz, who contemplated emigrating to the United States before his own death in 1936, soon referred to the ethnographic section of Leningrad University as "our incessantly seething cauldron."[90]

Judging from his correspondence, Boas was greatly cheered some months after Shternberg's death when Shternberg's widow, Sarra Arkadievna Ratner-Shternberg (1870–1942), the former Zhitomir schoolteacher and Amerindian specialist, wrote to him about the *Social Organization* text in her possession. Their exchanges over the next 6 years breathed new life into the project. On the Soviet side, Ratner-Shternberg organized an editorial collective to oversee the posthumous publication of her husband's works. The Russian language archival copies of the *Social Organization* typescript show that at least four Soviet scholars made editorial changes after Shternberg's death—Ratner-Shternberg and three of Shternberg's graduate students, Koshkin, Kreinovich, and Isaak Natanovich Vinnikov. For the Gilyak language portions of the *Social Organization* work, she marshaled the assistance of Kreinovich and E. A. Karger, both of whom had studied the Gilyak language under Shternberg, as well as eight

---

[89] Cf. Yuri Slezkine, "The Fall of Soviet Ethnography, 1928–38," *Current Anthropology* 32, no. 4.

[90] Letter of March 9, 1933, from Bogoraz to Boas, APS.

Gilyak students from Sakhalin and the Amur region studying in Leningrad in 1928. Finally, Bogoraz' graduate student Iulia Averkieva, who worked with Boas in the United States between 1929 and 1931, translated Chapter 14 of this edition under Ratner-Shternberg's supervision when she returned to Leningrad in 1931. On the American side, Boas himself took to editing and condensing sections of the text, as he had earlier done with Bogoraz' and Iokhel'son's contributions to the Jesup series. Further sections of the Russian manuscript were translated into English in New York at this time, and Ratner-Shternberg took part in the editing of the English copy.[91] Despite this new round of activity, it was now Boas who was in the awkward position of stalling. By 1933, funds for the Jesup series had long been spent, and the stock market crash of 1929 had taken a heavy toll on the patrons of the American Museum of Natural History. Ratner-Shternberg had greater success in Soviet Russia: In 1933, she oversaw the publication of the *Social Organization* text in Russian, twice, by publishing houses in Khabarovsk and Leningrad.[92] For the English edition, the final exchange of typescripts between Boas and Ratner-Shternberg that same year brought the pre-World War II publication efforts to a close.

The result of so much editing and translating leaves us today with at least four very different versions of the Shternberg text: an undated English typescript in the American Museum of Natural History [AMNH], an undated AMNH Russian typescript, and two 1933 Soviet editions—*Giliaki, Gol'dy, Negidal'tsy, Ainy* [*Gilyaks, Golds, Negidals, Ainu*] and *Sem'ia i rod u narodov severo-vostochnoi Azii* [*Family and Clan among the Peoples of Northeast Asia*].[93] In some parts of the AMNH Russian typescript, the distinctive handwriting of Shternberg, Ratner-Shternberg, Kreinovich, and Vinnikov made it possible to identify their specific additions that surfaced in the later English text. However, beyond that, discrepancies among all four cardinal versions defy easy explanation. Shternberg's two 1933 Soviet editions of *Social Organization* are, in places, as different from each other as they are from their AMNH Russian counterpart, despite the fact that both Soviet versions are listed as having been edited by the same person, Ian P. Koshkin. The AMNH English typescript, contrary to the expectation that it might be less ideologized than conventional Soviet ethnography of the period, sometimes appears more "Soviet" than the Soviet editions, containing extra lines on the deleterious force of religion, for example, not found in any of the Russian language texts.[94]

---

[91] See correspondence between 1927 and 1933 in appendix A.

[92] Shternberg, *Giliaki*, and Shternberg, *Sem'ia*.

[93] Two further copies of the Russian typescript are in AAN f. 282, o. 1, d. 2, "Sem'ia i Rod: Sotsial'naia zhizn' giliakov" (n.d.); and f. 282, o. 1, d. 41, "Obshchestvennoe i bytovoe ustroistvo u giliakov" (n.d.). Since their fragility made working with them in the Russian Academy of Sciences archive difficult, I have not made detailed comparisons with them in the manner of the four other texts. I have also compared sections of this volume to Shternberg, "Giliaki," noting relevant correspondences in chapter footnotes.

[94] It is also unclear whether American and European scholars later consulted by the AMNH about the editing of the manuscript may have modified the English typescript in any way. For example, in 1952, the late Russian emigré anthropologist Demitri Shimkin reported working on the linguistic portions of the text together with Siberianist Lawrence Krader, but conceded in 1954 that "little more than basic spade work was accomplished." See the correspondence from 1950 to 1969 in appendix A.

The Koshkin prefaces to the two 1933 editions of the manuscript are themselves studies in the politics of the early Soviet 1930s. While presenting Shternberg as "the best Russian ethnographer of his time," Koshkin also made it clear that that time was now past. What Koshkin described as Shternberg's "subjectivist" and "populist" education in the works of Kant and Spencer, as with the Russian philosophers Lavrov and Mikhailov, presented a special problem for his Soviet successors. Not only did Shternberg spend little time pondering the materialist causes of Gilyak class struggle, he praised the security and protection that more affluent Gilyaks extended to the less fortunate. "Inequality," he wrote of his time on Sakhalin, ". . . does not manifest itself here. A wealthy man owes everything to his personal abilities and virtues. His accumulations can neither exploit nor degrade another person."[95] Class struggle indeed. In another remark on private property among Gilyak fishermen, Shternberg observed that "Communal possession generally leads to continuous strife."[96] Here Koshkin countered that Shternberg's grasp of primitive communism was "completely incorrect," proposing that Shternberg misinterpreted signs of Gilyak life already corrupted by capitalist influence as earlier, more innocent forms.[97] While Koshkin emphasized how Shternberg's theoretical understandings of kinship helped combat "social-fascist falsifiers of the history of primitive society," he relegated Shternberg's world view, in a scorching admonishment, to "the bourgeois ideas of an English tradesman."[98]

Koshkin was in a particularly awkward position, because the fortunes of Morgan had risen so sharply in the Soviet 1920s. Indeed, many early Soviet planners looked to the new socialist state, in Morgan's words, as "a revival, in a higher form, of the liberty, equality, fraternity of the ancient gentes."[99] Not surprisingly, then, many looked upon Siberian indigenous communities as "already socialist." G. Lebedev wrote in 1920 that Siberian peoples were "the truest proletarians," natural allies of the working masses (and socialist intellectuals), and deserving of special state assistance.[100] In the Sovietized understanding of Morgan, Gilyaks emerged even more clearly than before as living chronotypes, examples of a simpler past who would undertake a "stride across a thousand years," emerging from primitive society directly into socialism, bypassing slaveholding, feudalism, and capitalism along the way.

How Koshkin actually felt about his former mentor or the Soviet ideology then sweeping through the academy is the kind of unanswerable question inherent in daily life under Stalinism. But his position may have been little different from Erukhim Kreinovich's, whose loyalty to Shternberg, according to Kreinovich's relatives, did little to outweigh an unwavering faith in the Soviet system.[101] Their fel-

---

[95] From Chapter 15 of this volume.

[96] From Chapter 7 of this volume.

[97] Shternberg, Sem'ia, xiv–xv.

[98] Shternberg, Sem'ia, xiii; Shternberg, Giliaki, xviii.

[99] Lewis Henry Morgan, Ancient Society (Cleveland: World Publishing, 1963), 562. Nikolai Ssorin-Chaikov discusses the politics of primitive communism advanced by Soviet planners in Siberia in his excellent dissertation, "Stateless Society, State Collective, and the State of Nature in Sub-Arctic Siberia: Evenki Hunters and Herders in the 20th Century," Ph.D. diss., Stanford Univ.

[100] G. Lebedev, "Vymiraiushchie brat'ia," Zhizn' Natsional'nostei 19 (1920), 76.

[101] From an interview with Kreinovich's second wife, Galina Razumikova, in Voronezh, USSR, November 1990.

low graduate student Zakharii Cherniakov observes in this volume, for example, that Koshkin was truly dedicated to Shternberg (appendix B). And indeed, while Koskhin condemned Shternberg's misinterpretations of primitive communism, he also marshaled Shternberg's examples in great detail, possibly incurring risk in the process. This speculation adds ambiguity to one of Koshkin's closing recommendations, "Not for one minute should we let [Shternberg's] idealist stance out of our view."[102]

With events in St. Petersburg taking new turns after Shternberg's death, life for Sakhalin Gilyaks was no less turbulent. While Soviet power came relatively late to North Sakhalin and the Amur in 1925, following the long civil war which had drifted eastward, state planners lost little time in dramatically transforming the social and political landscape.[103] Throughout Siberia and the Soviet Far East, the newly established Committee for the Assistance to Peoples of the Northern Borderlands [*Komitet sodeistviia narodnostiam severnykh okrain pri Prezidiume VTsIK*, commonly known as the *Komitet Severa* or "Committee of the North"] established "Culture Bases" in the furthest and most remote areas to propagate new Soviet political institutions through local idioms. In and around Gilyak settlements, the government began organizing fishing and hunting collectives, electric stations, machine shops, hospitals, veterinary units, boarding schools, adult literacy programs, native councils, and women's groups in a storm of activity that many people who lived through the period look back on today as a frenzy of building.[104] What was particularly striking about this early period of Sovietization was the emphasis on existing Gilyak political and social forms as channels for the new administration to work through. Indeed, one of the first decisions of government overseers was to phase out the word Gilyak, a term of Tungus origin, in favor of the self-designation Nivkh. People used both names in tandem for the next two decades.

Education and language policy were only two areas where the emphasis on native autonomy and self-government took hold. Here the key relevance for small groups such as Gilyaks was the extensive work by linguist-ethnographers, such as Shternberg's student Erukhim Kreinovich, to render education available in as many languages as possible. In order to invite the masses into history, Lenin once wrote, the invitation had to be written in a language the masses could understand. From its inception in 1924, with Shternberg's participation, to its closure by Stalin in 1935, the state-run Committee of the North organized writing systems for 13 Siberian indigenous languages, including Gilyak. In the spirit of freedom and variety,

---

[102] Shternberg, *Giliaki*, xxxv.
[103] Between 1925 and 1945, what Russians now refer to as South Sakhalin below the 50th parallel was the Japanese territory of Karafuto.
[104] For more on the new social order on Sakhalin in the 1920s, see Bruce Grant, *In the Soviet House of Culture: A Century of Perestroikas* (Princeton, NJ: Princeton Univ. Press, 1995), ch. 4. While the work of the Committee of the North (1924–1935) began to be widely implemented only after Shternberg's death in 1927, Zakharii Cherniakov, Shternberg's student and later Bogoraz's personal secretary, recalled that the Committee took up a great deal of Shternberg's time (appendix B of this volume). This runs counter to the general sense that Shternberg's participation was a pro forma endorsement of the more active role played by Smidovich and Bogoraz. Cf. GARF f. 3977; and Yuri Slezkine, *Arctic Mirrors: Russia and the Small Peoples of the North* (Ithaca, NY: Cornell Univ. Press, 1994), 152n.

most of the new scripts were in the Latin alphabet, which linguists argued was more appropriate for Siberian phonetics.[105] In addition to Kreinovich's efforts on Sakhalin from 1926 to 1928, a small handful of promising Gilyak students traveled to Leningrad to receive educations at the Institute of Northern Peoples.

The unexpected conflict behind such rapid "Soviet cultural construction" (as it was known in the campaigns of the day) is that at the very time Sakhalin sped to realize the social policies of the Soviet 1920s, Stalin's rise to power in 1929 and the radical curtailment of certain ethnic rights were working in a very opposite direction. As early as 1931, the government began discouraging Gilyak women from wearing traditional cotton tunics and Gilyak men from keeping their hair in braids. Shamans, whom Shternberg had admired as religious leaders and bards, were being forced underground, and native councils were dissolved. The speed of this turnaround is difficult to overemphasize because, in many cases, the very Gilyaks whom the government had trained as new native cadres were the first people to come under suspicion for antigovernment activities only a few years later. When I asked Shternberg's former student Zakharii Cherniakov, who worked as an ethnographer of the Soviet Saami in the 1930s, about the turnaround in Soviet nationalities policy at this time, he replied, "Of course we felt it. [The change] was evident at every step of our work. I mean, we all started out our work learning native languages, writing literacy primers, promoting native intellectuals. And suddenly, we are told that we are supposed to discourage native language use, to attract people instead to the Russian language. Basically, to Russify them."[106]

In 1932, the newly formed Committee of the New Alphabet, working in tandem with the Committee of the North, released the first Nivkh language primer, *Cuz Dif*, for children and adults alike. Committee members particularly praised the book's Latinized script as more internationalist and "less Russificatory" than previous tsarist work with small nationalities. Politically, however, they were caught in the clash of policy.

By only 1936, dissenters argued that "Peoples of the North [were] hungry for the Russian language, for party literature in Russian, [and] for the central newspapers," while others saw conspiracy in an ideological affinity between Latinized indigenous scripts and the same Latinized alphabet in the service of capitalist enemies.[107] Regardless of whether Siberian peoples hungered for the Russian language, it was evident that the linguistic isolation brought on by being in the Latinized minority had little place in the increasingly centralized state.

Under pressure now to switch to Cyrillic, the Committee of the New Alphabet, fittingly named, introduced its second new alphabet in only 5 years. Sakhalin officials pronounced the Latinized Gilyak textbooks "deficit items" and withdrew them from circulation. Amidst the purges of liberal experimentation that characterized the early Leninist period, Stalinist revisionism of the 1930s outlawed the study of the Gilyak language in schools and punished its use in the mechanized fishing col-

[105] Letter from Kreinovich to Ratner-Shternberg, AAN f. 282, o. 5, d. 27.
[106] From the interview in appendix B.
[107] Tsentral'nyi Gosudarstvennyi Arkhiv Dal'nego Vostoka [Central State Archive of the Far East], Vladivostok (formerly in Tomsk) f. R353, o. 1, d. 88 (1936), l. 16.

FIG. 7. Shternberg at work in his study in St. Petersburg. A portrait of Karl Marx hangs on the wall between the books at right. Photo by Sarra Arkadievna Shternberg. *Source:* AAN f. 282, o. 2, d. 162, l. 1.

lectives where most of the Gilyaks worked. It became only one of many casualties of the Stalinist period's "war against the past."

Back in St. Petersburg, events moved apace. On March 27, 1935, when Ratner-Shternberg convened the editorial board organized for the posthumous publication of her husband's work, they were listed as a group of eight. But in a handwritten note she penned on the back of the same memorandum in August 1936, 17 months later, she reported

> V. G. Bogoraz to be excluded by reason of his death; Busygin, Karger and Koshkin, by their political motives; and Vinnikov, one of Shternberg's closest and most loyal students, by his refusal to participate in the editorial collective for personal reasons.

It was little wonder that Vinnikov might have run for the hills. Koshkin soon disappeared upon arrest, while Kreinovich, already fallen from Ratner-Shternberg's graces when she suspected some pages missing from a document he edited, would go on to 18 years of hard labor beginning only several months later.[108] When Ratner-Shternberg

---

[108] Cf. Slezkine, "The Fall of Soviet Ethnography"; and Kreinovich, "Istoriia moego otnosheniia k arkhivu L. Ia. Shternberga." Kreinovich Archive, SOKM. For more on how Stalinism affected Soviet ethnographers, see A. M. Reshetov, "Repressirovannaia etnografiia: liudi i sud'by," *Kunstkamera* no. 4, 185–221; and nos. 5–6, 342–369.]

died in 1942, the same year as Boas, Soviet participation in the English edition came to a close.

Since World War II, the unpublished English version of *Social Organization* has remained a select source for a series of researchers in the United States. Following Lévi-Strauss, who described the manuscript as "a work of exceptional value and insight," those who were consulted as potential editors, or who worked with the text, included Robert Lowie, Alfred Kroeber, Clyde Kluckhohn, Roman Jakobson, Rodney Needham, and a host of Siberian scholars.[109] Its publication here brings to a close its 90 years of print exile.

★ ★ ★ ★ ★

Why, ultimately, did classificatory kinship systems and the perceived customs of Gilyak group marriage so intrigue Shternberg? No doubt Shternberg's evident pride in building on the works of mentors such as Marx, Morgan, and Engels give us the better part of this answer. For Shternberg the evolutionist, Gilyak group marriage provided a living illustration of where mankind had been at the very time when Russia was debating where to go.

However, we would be remiss not to also remember that kinship as an idiom had also helped keep private lives public since the second half of the 19th century. At once a high modernist charting of order and rationality, kinship charted blood ties that were "everywhere an object of excitement and fear at the same time."[110] Blood, which could be inherited (dynastically), shed (militarily), and corrupted (by association) was a ready symbol of power relations that were of increasing importance to 19th century and 20th colonial administrations. A kinship idiom that worked at the interstices of "bodies and populations," "organized around the management of life rather than the menace of death," Michel Foucault wrote, provided governments with new channels of insight into non-European worlds.[111] With respect to Russia and the former Soviet Union's relations toward Siberian indigenous peoples, this was very much the case.

Shternberg's Gilyak work hinged on a European evolutionist paradigm that we could trace, of course, further back than Morgan. "To be" was "to become," Hegel argued 50 years before Morgan, signaling a tradition of European Enlightenment consciousness so deeply rooted in change as a motor force of being that we could little contend to have broken away from it today.[112] But with Shternberg's work, as anywhere, knowledge was in the eye of the beholder. While Russian readers of *Social Organization* in the 1920s might have focused on its ethnographic contributions to a general evolutionist argument, by the 1930s Koshkin gave that evolution a distinctly Soviet twist, presenting Shternberg's work as an important tool in the proletarian struggle against native backwardness.

---

[109] Lévi-Strauss, *Elementary Structures*, 292. Cf. also Kan, "The Mystery," esp. 33–37, and appendix A of this volume.

[110] Michel Foucault, *The History of Sexuality, Vol. I, An Introduction* (New York: Vintage, 1990), 148.

[111] Ibid.

[112] G. W. F. Hegel, *Theses on the Philosophy of History* (Indianapolis: Hackett, 1988 (1840)).

For the modern reader, Shternberg's algebraic kinship formulae, which at their apex resemble permutations and combinations reminiscent of the high speed digital computing that Lévi-Strauss pledged would revolutionize myth analysis, evoke at times high modernism more than marriage.[113] Indeed, the functioning of Gilyak marriage rules *as a system* is perhaps what stands out most today, as it may have for Shternberg himself, who later in life conceded the simplicity of his original castings of Gilyak group marriage by writing, "I took them all for pure-blooded aristocrats."[114] Some modern Gilyak (Nivkh) readers of *Social Organization* in 1995 have taken this admission one step further. As an accountant from a North Sakhalin shipping port who had grown up in a Gilyak village in the taiga, Elizaveta Merkulova said,

> I've read those stories about how a man would offer his wife to a visitor for the night, but I can't believe any of it. When I was young, my Russian friends would even ask me about it. Everyone thinks it's what we used to do. But I can't believe it, because I remember how jealously all my mother's and father's families treated the women. They were unbelievably protective and jealous. Among [Gilyaks] at least, I mean, I just don't see it. Think of all the instances of men killing their wives out of jealousy. It used to happen more frequently when I was young but it happens today. So to imagine that a man would just offer his wife to another under those circumstances, it seems impossible. It was all a big Russian fantasy.[115]

Yet, if the idea of group marriage has not held up well, Merkulova only smiled when I told her that parts of Shternberg's text left me feeling that I, too, following his observation in Chapter 6, had fallen prey to "the almost hypnotic effect" of Gilyak kinship terms.[116]

> You find it difficult? I don't find it difficult, but that's probably because I grew up with it. I think a lot gets lost in the translation since there are some words that just don't really have translations. Even if you take the simplest words like *imk* and *itk*: Everyone thinks that this means "mother" and "father," and that's true. But neither of those words really give you a sense of what it's like when everyone is connected to each other through formal relations. There's no context to place these words when you have to start saying "the son of my sister of my father . . ."! Whereas we would just say *pu* . . . and you say it knowing that everyone is connected to everyone else in some important way.[117]

Merkulova's response was a laurel branch to the uninitiated, but she also reminds us why kinship became such a regnant and often dazzling way of accessing other people's worlds, promising at once an objective force of reason and a hopeful

---

[113] Claude Lévi-Strauss, "The Structural Study of Myth," in his *Structural Anthropology* (New York: Basic Books, 1963), 206–231.

[114] Shternberg *in* Smoliak, *Etnicheskie protsessy*, 86.

[115] See the interview with Merkulova in the Afterword.

[116] In this context, Chapters 1, 7, 9, and 10 deserve special mention for their complexity.

[117] Ibid.

insight into subjective lives. Shternberg's own evolution of thought on Gilyak kinship reminds us that the elegance of kinship constructions can sometimes be misguiding. As Greg Urban has noted, "Kinship terms seem to us to be closely related to one another—pieces of a jigsaw puzzle—because we, in fact, treat them that way in our discourse practices."[118] Hence, when Lévi-Strauss wrote, "A human group need only proclaim the law of the marriage of the mother's brother's daughter for a vast cycle of reciprocity between all generations and lineages to be organized, as harmonious and ineluctable as any physical or biological law," harmony may have also been in the eye of the beholder.[119] Gilyak marriage rules were evidently not only difficult for Gilyaks themselves to follow, Gilyaks may never have followed them as religiously as Shternberg avowed.

In the decades of Sovietization that followed Shternberg's first drafts of *Social Organization*, the kinds of local knowledge and social circumstances that made Gilyak marriage rules possible have long since been transformed. As the Nivkh ethnographer Galina Dem'ianovna Lok blurted out when we both sat sequestered in the confines of a North Sakhalin oil town in 1995, reading the entire text aloud to each other for review, "You would have to have a head bigger than an entire House of Soviets to understand this!" And yet for all the passage of practice, to some Nivkhi even the most complicated of marriage rules have not lost, in Shternberg's words from Chapter 4, their "mnemonic-adjudicating force." To historians of anthropology, Shternberg's work invites us to reflect on one people's experience of being represented through a language of kinship that became the discipline's flagship idiom in the 20th century. To Gilyaks a century after Shternberg first came and went, he offers a portrait of lives once lived, and the terms of address that still reconstitute that world.

---

[118] Greg Urban, *Metaphysical Community* (Austin: Univ. Texas Press, 1996), 104.
[119] Lévi-Strauss *in* Georges Bataille, *The Accursed Share*, Vol. 2 (New York: Zone, 1993), 47.

THE SOCIAL ORGANIZATION

OF THE GILYAK

Lev Iakovlevich Shternberg

PREFACE

[1–10; 1–10; —; —][1]

I SPENT ABOUT 7 YEARS, interrupted by few intervals, doing fieldwork among the primitive peoples of Sakhalin and of the Amur region, particularly the Sakhalin Gilyak.[2]

I became interested in this study when late one winter I found myself involuntarily on the solitary shore of the Tatar Strait, about 100 kilometers from Aleksandrovsk, near the small settlement of Viakhtu.[3] Here, not far from a Russian settlement consisting of five houses of exiles who had finished their terms of servitude,

---

1. [*Editor's note:* Page sequences at the beginning of each chapter refer to approximate page numbers for the same or similar material in four separate Shternberg publications: the undated AMNH Russian typescript; the undated AMNH English typescript; Shternberg, *Giliaki*; and Shternberg, *Sem'ia*. For example, the numbers below the Preface heading show that this preface is found in the AMNH typescripts only.

   Although the translators of this and most chapters in the book are not precisely known, clues lead to some process of elimination. An undated explanatory note entitled "To Shternberg's Manuscript," filed in the Boas Collection in the Department of Anthropology of the AMNH observed that this preface, as well as the introduction and chapters 13–23 (in this edition, chapters 11–16), had not yet been translated into English. The note, signed, "W.J.," likely indicated Boas' frequent correspondent Vladimir I. Iokhel'son (a.k.a. Waldemar Jochelson, 1855–1937). Presuming that Boas asked Iokhel'son to make a review of the manuscript's status after it had been with the Museum for a time, one can venture that Alexander Goldenweiser, who through his correspondence was in contact with Boas regarding the Shternberg manuscript only on receipt of Shternberg's first installments in 1912, was not the translator of these sections. Iokhel'son's review of the manuscript most likely took place after his emigration to the United States in the early 1920s and before Bogoraz' graduate student Julia Averkieva arrived in New York and began work on the translation of chapter 14. See appendix A for more correspondence on the manuscript at this time.]

2. [*Editor's note:* "Primitive" can be derived from either the Russian *primitivnyi* or the more ambiguous *pervobytnyi* (which can also mean "early"); here Shternberg used the former.]

3. [*Editor's note:* Earlier versions of the text spell this variously as Viachty, Viaxty, and Viakhta. The northwestern Sakhalin coastal town is now known as Viakhta, but I have retained its original designation from the 1890s for the logic and consistency of Shternberg's narrative. For this and other place names on Sakhalin listed in this preface, see Konstantin Makarovich Braslavets, *Istoriia v nazvaniiakh na karte sakhalinskoi oblasti* (Iuzhno-Sakhalinsk: Dal'nevostochnoe Knizhnoe Izdatel'stvo, 1983); and Sviatozar Demidovich Galtsev-Bizuk, *Toponomicheskii slovar'* (Iuzhno-Sakhalinsk: Sakhalinskoe Knizhnoe Izdatel'stvo, 1992).

were several Gilyak yurtas.[4] These Gilyak had entirely preserved their old ways and morals in spite of their contact with Russian neighbors. It was here that I was ethnographically baptized.

The surrounding taiga, rich with reindeer moss, attracted the reindeer-herding Tungus [Evenki] and Orok [Ul'ta],[5] whose camps lay scattered around the settlement, not many versts[6] away. During the summer these herders descended from the mountains to the summer camps of the Gilyak on the seashore and scattered their picturesque conical tents nearby. Here on the broad pasture at the mouth of the Viakhtu River, the representatives of such different tribes as the deer-breeding Tungus and the dog-breeding Gilyak organized annual rendezvous. This close proximity of three tribes differing in language, customs, and beliefs gave me an opportunity for making a comparative ethnographic study. It was a particularly favorable location because our settlement stood on the main route along which sped Russians from Nikolaevsk, Gilyak on dog-harnessed sledges, and Tungus and Orok on the backs of deer or in their primitive sledges.

Settlers traded with the natives in flour, brick-tea, alcohol, and other prisoners' chattels [skarb][7] for sable furs and reindeer meat. The settlement on the solitary shore of the Tatar Strait consisted of a post office and a sentry house established for overtaking fugitives and vagrants. There I lived as a political exile in pleasant company with the guards—a soldier and three watchmen, former convicts. It was the central gathering place for transient natives. Occasionally they spent several days with us, and in exchange for tea and bread they let me into some of the secrets of their primitive life. Among these representatives of three different tribes, the Gilyak, being the least known, interested me particularly. I knew that the scientific expeditions of von Schrenck and later observers had collected a considerable amount of material on the ethnography of this tribe. But since my predecessors were naturalists I thought that they would have paid less attention to the social and spiritual life of the people than to the external ethno-anthropological peculiarities. This proved to be the case, although the works of von Schrenck, and particularly those of Grube published in

---

4   [*Editor's note:* Yurta (from the Russian, *iurta*) originally designated a tent made of animal skins, found across central Asia and Siberia. By the late 17th century, the term came to denote any non-Russian type of dwelling.]

5   [*Editor's note:* Modern self-namings for Tungus and Oroks are given here in brackets. Throughout the text I defer to Shternberg's usages in the AMNH Russian typescript, while acknowledging their later Library of Congress referents both in the text and in the prefatory glossary of ethnonyms. Ian Koshkin discussed 1930s variations within the particularly extensive category of Tungus in Shternberg, *Giliaki*, xxxii*n* (a footnote on page xxxiii). For more on the politics of self-identification among Orok/Oroch/Ul'ta, see Heonik Kwon, "Maps and Actions: Nomadic and Sedentary Space in a Siberian Reindeer Farm," Ph.D. diss., Univ. Cambridge, 1993.]

6   [*Editor's note:* The verst (from the Russian, *versta*) was a prerevolutionary Russian measure of distance equal to 3500 feet or 0.6629 miles. Five hundred "sazhens" (from the Russian, *sazhen'*), each equal to 7 feet, made up a verst.]

7   [*Editor's note:* All italicized terms in editorial square brackets are Russian translations from the AMNH Russian typescript; italicized terms in authorial parentheses are Shternberg's Gilyak translations from the same edition.]

1891, were not accessible to me in the wilderness.[8] I read them only after my return to St. Petersburg in 1900.[9]

Despite my complete ignorance of the language, I was struck from the very beginning by the terminology used by the Gilyak when addressing relatives of various categories. Children addressed by the common name of *imk*, mother, not only their own mother but also all her sisters, and wives of the father's brothers. Similarly, with some variations, they addressed their father and all his brothers as *tuvng*.[10] Brothers' children addressed one another by the word *tuvng* (in German, *Geschwister*).[11] Brothers' wives called each other sisters. In a word, I had before me the terminology which is known to exist among primitive tribes in other parts of the world, and which characterized a peculiar form of family organization that Morgan identified as classificatory.

As the scope of my observations was small, I decided to verify my generalizations by further investigations and a census of the Gilyak. By means of the census I could examine the terminology of relationship and the family relations with greater certainty. For that, a competent interpreter was necessary, one able to understand my questions and the answers of the natives, as well as to be sufficiently liked by the natives to overcome their natural hostility and distrust against a census. Such an interpreter was found in the person of Obon, a Gilyak from the Tonki settlement.[12] The wealthiest man of his tribe, enjoying great fame for this wealth and skill, and famous for his intelligence and arts of oratory, he enjoyed great popularity among his tribesmen. (He learned a great deal from long association with Dr. Suprunenko. It was with Obon's help that Suprunenko obtained his rich natural, historical, and ethnographic collections.)[13] Although Obon's knowledge of Russian was very poor, he fully compensated for it by great zeal and an active intelligence.

---

[8] [*Editor's note:* Shternberg refers to Vladimir Grube, *Linguistische Ergebniss I. Giljakisches Worterverzeichniss nebst Gramm. Bemerkungen. Anhang zum III Bande;* and Leopold von Schrenck, *Reisen und Forschungen in Amur-Lande in den Jahren 1854–1856, 3 vols.* (St. Petersburg: Eggers, 1860–1900).]

[9] [*Editor's note:* For a brief English-language survey of 19th century literature about Sakhalin Island, see Bruce Grant, *In the Soviet House of Culture: A Century of Perestroikas* (Princeton, NJ: Princeton Univ. Press, 1995), ch. 3.]

[10] [*Editor's note:* While Russian versions of this text use *tuvn*, Shternberg's transliteration guide in the AMNH archives and Gilyak (Nivkh) readers on Sakhalin in 1995 indicate that the last "n" is more properly represented by the English diphthong "ng."]

[11] [*Editor's note:* This reference to the German, as well as others later in this edition, are taken from the AMNH English typescript only. Lydia Black has pointed out that the problem in comparing *tuvng* to *Geschwister* is that *tuvng* designates not only children of one father but also children of one's father's brothers, lineal and collateral, in all degrees of kinship.]

[12] [*Editor's note:* Prior to the arrival of Soviet government on Sakhalin and the Amur in 1925, Gilyaks bore only single, one-word names. After 1925, officials began giving Gilyaks Russian names, patronymics and surnames. Paradoxically, at the same time as the Soviet government denied Gilyaks use of their personal names, it introduced formal use of the autonym Nivkh.]

[13] [*Editor's note:* Petr Ivanovich Suprunenko was a doctor for the Sakhalin prison administration living in the village of Korsakovka, outside Aleksandrovsk, and later, Korsakov. Between 1881 and 1891 he collected ethnographic and zoological materials on the island. His work is discussed in Boris Polevoi, "Sakhalinskaia kollektsia P. I. Suprunenko," *Vestnik Sakhalinskogo Muzeia* 2 (1995): 144–155.]

On February 6, 1891, on two sledges harnessed with dogs—one for myself with provisions for a month and another for my interpreter—we started on our first voyage over Sakhalin Island. Our expedition created an alarmed sensation among the Gilyak. The fear that the census might have fiscal significance in connection with yasak [fur] taxation,[14] or the recruiting of soldiers, shut the mouths of the natives and immediately caused a hostile attitude toward us. The eloquence of my interpreter, however, overcame all these obstacles: He introduced me as a friend of the Gilyak who wished to find out all the needs of the people in order to help them.

As the news about "the friend of the Gilyak" spread and overtook us with the speed with which all news spreads among the natives, we met with friendly confidence and a willingness to answer all our questions throughout the rest of our voyage. The census gave me an opportunity to investigate their kinship terminology and to make many interesting observations of other aspects of the life of these people. During the winter, the Gilyak live most intensely. Life in the settlements of northern Sakhalin, where living conditions are more favorable, presents the most interesting field for observations.

The success of my first census inspired me to undertake in 1891 a similar investigation among other tribes of Sakhalin. I selected the Tym' River and the eastern shore of Sakhalin, from Cape de la Croyere, a territory inhabited by Gilyak, Tungus, and Orok. The most fantastic legends circulated among the Russians and the Gilyak of the western shore about the Gilyak of the eastern shore. They were called the "black Gilyak," and all kinds of vices were attributed to them. It was said that they were wild, thievish, inhospitable, and inclined towards cannibalism, that whenever they caught a vagrant they shut him into a hovel, fattened him with dried fish [iuko-la], and then killed him and arranged a feast. I believed there was little truth to these legends. Constant communication existed between the Gilyak of both shores, and the "black Gilyak" whom I saw during my census did not differ in any way from their "white" fellow tribesmen [soplemenniki]. Furthermore, the territory of these Gilyak had been visited before by several travelers. But at the time the legends were so strongly rooted that when I departed, the news spread that I had been killed. When I returned to Aleksandrovsk, the governor of the island was about to send a detachment to the scene of the crime.

The fact is that my journey was most successful. In the beginning of June, as soon as the flow of spring waters of the Tym' began and navigation on that mountain river became possible, I set out in the usual Gilyak dugout boat made of poplar,

---

[14] [**Editor's note:** Yasak (from the Russian, *iasak*) was a levy imposed on indigenous Siberians by Russian imperial overseers. On paper, it was the obligation of every native male aged 15 and older to provide a fixed number of designated fur pelts or the ruble equivalent once a year to the Russian state. Whole communities often shared yasak debts collectively, as well as inherited them. Although some peoples such as the Chukchi rebuffed their yasak burdens, the overall toll was enormous. In the 1640s alone, almost a third of the entire revenue of the Russian state came from the fur trade. For more on yasak see Grant, *In the Soviet House of Culture,* 42–44; George Lantzeff, *Siberia in the 17th Century: A Study of the Colonial Administration* (Berkeley: Univ. of California Press, 1943), 19–24; 96–99; Marc Raeff, *Siberia and the Reforms of 1822* (Seattle: Univ. of Washington Press, 1956), pt. 2; and Yuri Slezkine, *Arctic Mirrors: Russia and the Small Peoples of the North* (Ithaca, NY: Cornell Univ. Press, 1994), 7–90 (*passim*).]

in company with three Gilyak youths who, for a small payment, consented to act as my fellow travelers and guards. I did not have my old interpreter with me, but as I already had some experience with the natives, and since I had heard that the eastern Gilyak knew about me, I hoped to inspire their confidence.

The banks of the Tym', one of the largest rivers of Sakhalin, once so lively were now quite solitary. The Gilyak population, which moved at the end of the winter to the seashore to hunt seals, had not yet returned, so that during the 4 days of our journey we passed through completely deserted country. Only towards the end did we begin to meet the dugout boats of Tym' River Gilyak who were returning to their homes in time for the first salmon run. Fatigued, they looked like beached salmon themselves.

The first meeting with the "black Gilyak" in the settlement Nyivo completely dissipated whatever fears I had about them. After 2 days in the village we quietly started making the necessary preparations for the sea voyage. The territory settled by the natives is very limited. Summer navigation along that shore was not very convenient. The Sea of Okhotsk is so stormy at that time of the year that the Gilyak will not risk launching their shells. North of Nyivo communication is carried on through lagoons, but the latter are so shallow that traveling is possible only at spring tide.

Southerly travel is possible only on foot or on deerback. It is interesting that in this small area of Sakhalin, Gilyak fishermen and the majority of the reindeer-herding Orok live side by side. Traveling the entire month, partly by water and partly on deerback, I was able to visit all the inhabited parts of the territory and take a detailed census of the population, while continuing my observations on their life and beliefs. With the appearance of salmon [keta][15] and the season of continuous rain, we started homeward along the Tym'. It took us 11 days full of hardship and privation; our provisions were exhausted and the banks of the river were full of bears. But the endurance and patience of my companions overcame all difficulties, and we finally returned to our Russian Palestine.

The winter of 1892 was passed in quiet, sedentary [statsionarnaia] work. I was visited by the Gilyak from neighboring settlements and through discussions with them I gradually completed and corrected my previous observations. During that winter, I grasped for the first time the intricacies of the Gilyak language. In spite of these two trips and a long association with the people, my knowledge of their language was rather poor. I had learned to ask some questions and to control the answers to the interpreter to a certain extent, but a thorough knowledge of the language seemed impossible to acquire; the grammar and phonetics seemed so difficult that I gave up all hope of ever learning it. During my first trip, I collected material through an interpreter with great difficulty because the interpreter himself knew very little Russian, and it was necessary to explain the meaning of every question. I was fortunate, however, for soon after I met an exceptionally intelligent Gilyak interpreter in

---

[15] [**Editor's note:** Shternberg refers to the general Russian word *keta*, or salmon, in the AMNH Russian typescript. The dominant species found off the shores of northern Sakhalin are *Oncorhynchus gorbuscha* and *Oncorhynchus keta*.]

FIG. 8. A Gilyak man and woman in the tunics worn by both sexes up to the Soviet period. The bear fur worn by the man would have been worn in winter during bear festivals. Photo by Lev Shternberg. *Source:* AAN f. 282, o. 2, d. 162, l. 88.

the person of Gibel'ka. Possessing natural gifts which were sharpened in constant barter with Russians and other natives, he was made, as it were, for this difficult role.

Gradually, by translating short stories, I began to understand the phonetics and etymology of the Gilyak language. I was able to write down a considerable number of their poems, which gave me an opportunity for objective analyses of the psyche and beliefs of these primitive people.

During the winter lull I also decided to go more deeply into Gilyak grammar. Applying the most recent methods of self-instruction in foreign languages, I wrote down a short tale and, gathering several Gilyak men who were familiar with Russian, asked them to make a literal translation for me. And so a key was found. In spite of the great phonetic difficulties the obstacles were gradually overcome.

In 1893 I decided to make another trip. This time I wanted to see that part of Gilyak territory I had not visited before, south of Aleksandrovsk toward the Ainu region. It stormed continuously throughout the trip, but towards the end of the month I finally reached the southernmost Gilyak settlement at Cape Saturnai. My efforts to reach the nearest settlements of the Ainu were frustrated at that time because a typhoon suddenly arose and swept away our tent with all provisions. I was forced to return to Aleksandrovsk.

Thus I visited all the Gilyak settlements on Sakhalin and took a general census. Now I was ready to settle down and assess my material, but a study of the Gilyak people without any knowledge of the life of their neighbors seemed useless. During the next summer I carried out my original plan and visited the Ainu.

We started in a dugout boat along the Poronai River. On reaching the sea I turned first eastward and took the census of the Orok and Ainu in the region of Toroiki Lake. Then gradually returning in a southwesterly direction towards the Bay of Patience, I traveled from settlement to settlement close to Tunaichi Lake. From Naibuchi, I traveled by land to Korsakovsk. From here I again went to Naibuchi and then to Port Manue; crossing to the western shore I reached Port Kosunai. Then I proceeded to Mauko, after crossing the ridge, arrived on a raft at the mouth of the Litogi, and along the latter traveled down to the Russian settlements of the Korsakov district.

In the summer of 1894, I traveled once more along the western shore to Cape Mariia. My goals were to check up on my census to find out the rate of mortality during the past few years, investigate the question of the salmon run, and find out whether there had been a stone age on Sakhalin. The last days of that trip almost ended in calamity: the motorboat sent to me from Aleksandrovsk was caught in a typhoon and almost sank in the waters of the Tatar Strait together with all my collections, which included a particularly large collection of stone age implements gathered on the sand dunes of the northern shore.

After I had finished my work among the Gilyak and their neighbors on the island, I decided to move to the continent in order to familiarize myself with the Gilyak of the mainland shore and Amur region, as well as with their neighbors of Tungus origin. For this reason I undertook three expeditions during 1895: first a general excursion along the Amur and Ussuri, then the territory of the Oroch in the bays of Imperatorskaia Gavan' and down the Tumil River, and finally the continental Gilyak along both banks of the Amur from the mouth to the gulf and northward along the seashore to the settlement of Kol'. After that, I returned to Sakhalin to continue my study of the Gilyak language and folklore.

On the first two voyages, I became familiar with the Gilyak of northern Sakhalin and with the Orok and Tungus scattered among them. On the next trip I studied the Ainu of the whole southern shore, and also the Tungus and Orok around the mouth of the Poronai. Investigating every phase of the life of these tribes, I was particularly interested in the religious and social organization, language, and folklore of the Gilyak.

Learning first the grammatical construction and phonetic peculiarities of the Gilyak language, I recorded many texts in various Gilyak settlements. The majority, however, were written down in the region of Aleksandrovsk and the settlement of Rykovskoe. Consequently these texts are written in the Tym' dialect, which is most primitive and especially important because the people speaking it are the most isolated of the Gilyak tribes and have therefore preserved much more of their original creativity.[16]

Among the Gilyak there were many storytellers, but generally they could only repeat stories that they had been told. Real poets who improvised were rare. They were usually exceptions—shamans or children of shamans—mostly persons of great sensibility and imagination to whom creativity was an absolute necessity. They recited their poetic improvisations while in a trance, at the end of which they would fall into complete exhaustion. Not only were there few such individuals, but still fewer enjoyed the good health and patience for dictating word by word epic poetry of anywhere from two to three hundred stanzas. On meeting such an individual I naturally tried to get as much material from him as possible.

I was very fortunate in finding one such poet improviser, a youth called Koinyt, the son of Ada, a deceased shaman of the Tym' region.[17] He was as poor as Job, alone, and homeless, rich only with the hopes of a future life. He claimed to have inherited two souls from his father, who had had four, and was entirely obsessed by his calling. He saw visions, had bouts of hysteria, improvised, and sang his songs. The Gilyak were very eager for his poetry and would listen to him through whole nights. They would present him with dry fish and other foods. The youth lived with me for several months, pleased with a warm corner and abundant food, singing his poems and dictating them to me.

In the spring of 1897 I returned through Siberia to European Russia. Once more in 1910, from May to September, I visited Sakhalin and the Amur region.[18] What follows are my studies based on these two sojourns.

---

16 [**Editor's note:** Today most Gilyaks (Nivkhi) refer colloquially to the "Eastern dialect" and the "Amur dialect," where the Amur dialect includes West Sakhalin speech (here, the "Western dialect"), since before the establishment of Soviet administration on North Sakhalin in 1925 many Gilyaks traveled between the Amur River delta and the northwestern coast of Sakhalin, which directly faces it. The two dialects are intelligible to each other, but not greatly so. Some linguists recognize two other dialects: the "Tym' dialect" of the Tym' River valley, which Shternberg refers to here, and the "Schmidt dialect" of Sakhalin's uppermost northern Schmidt Peninsula. For more on Gilyak/Nivkh linguistic terms, see the works in the bibliography by Robert Austerlitz, Bernard Comrie, Erukhim Kreinovich, Galina Otaina, and Vladimir Z. Panfilov.]

17 [**Editor's note:** Shternberg's high praise for the young, shamanically inclined Koinyt echoed that of Bronislaw Pilsudskii (1886–1918), the Polish exile ethnographer and younger brother of the Polish leader Iuzef Pilsudskii, who also worked with Koinyt as a young man. Such character references held little sway 40 years later when the first Gilyak language literacy primer, *Cuz Dif* [Gilyak, *New Word*] singled out "the kulak shaman Koinyt" for persecution in the USSR of 1932. See Grant, *In the Soviet House of Culture*, 88, 93, 95; Kreinovich, *Cuz Dif* (Leningrad: Gosudarstvennoe Uchebno-pedagogicheskoe Izdatel'stvo, 1932); Bronislaw Pilsudskii, "The Gilyaks and their Songs," *Folk-lore* 34 (1913): 483. Although references in the Russian versions of this passage are to "Koipyta," this appears to have been either a pseudonym (not used for other Shternberg informants) or an error in transliteration.]

18 [**Editor's note:** During this second 1910 stay, Shternberg spent 2 weeks on Sakhalin and the remaining time on the Amur. From the archive of Kreinovich, SOKM, Iuzhno-Sakhalinsk.]

Introduction: Family and Clan[1]
[1–3; 1–4; 129–131; 60–62][2]

THE STRUCTURE of the Gilyak family and the norms of their sexual relations seem on superficial acquaintance to be so simple and so similar to our own that they mislead even a serious observer. The famous Academician Leopold von Schrenck lived with the Gilyak for more than 2 years and left us his well-known multivolume monograph on that tribe.[3] Yet he was firmly convinced that the Gilyak family belonged to the normal patriarchal type, and he countered the opinion of Phillipp Franz von Siebold, who, following the reports of Mamiya Rinzo [1776–1844], a Japanese traveler of the 18th century, asserted that, "The northwest coast of Sakhalin (that is, Gilyak territory), is the only part of the world where by force of law or custom polyandry is practiced."[4] Von Schrenck regarded his own presentation of the facts as unquestionably correct. Not being able fully to accept the accuracy of Mamiya Rinzo's communications in general and believing him to be an excellent observer, von Schrenck could but attribute the statement about the polyandric practices of the Gilyak to the

---

[1]   [*Editor's note:* Although the AMNH English typescript translated this title as "The Family and the Gens," I follow Shternberg's December 1, 1912, recommendation to Boas in a letter archived in the AMNH that "Clan" is more suitable.

   Beginning with this chapter, numbers in bold at the ends of paragraphs track the corresponding page numbers in Shternberg, *Sem'ia i Rod.* While they are intended to allow specialist readers to quickly locate the same material in a Russian edition, it should be stressed that the considerable variation among all earlier versions of the Shternberg manuscript makes these indexings approximate only. Unmarked footnotes, such as note 3 below, are Shternberg's.]

[2]   [*Editor's note:* Page numbers for the AMNH Russian and English typescripts restart here at 1.]

[3]   Leopold von Schrenck, *Reisen und Forschungen im Amur-Lande, 3 vols.* (St. Petersburg: Eggers and Co., 1860–1900). [*Editor's note:* von Schrenck's works were also published in Russian under the title, *Ob inorodtsakh Amurskago kraiia, 3 vols.* (St. Petersburg: Imperatorskaia Akademiia Nauk, 1883–1903). Shternberg's references are to the German edition published in St. Petersburg. These references are not found in Shternberg, *Giliaki,* and Shternberg, *Sem'ia.*]

[4]   Siebold, *Nippon,* vol. II, 169. [*Editor's note:* The full reference is: Philipp Franz von Siebold, *Nippon. Archiv zur Beschreibung von Japan und dessen neben- und schutzländern Jezo mit den sudlichen Kurilen, Sachalin, Korea und den Iukiu-Inseln,* 2 vols. (Wurzburg: L. Woerl, 1897). The AMNH English typescript curtailed this quotation; the longer version here was restored from the AMNH Russian typescript, Shternberg, *Giliaki,* and Shternberg, *Sem'ia.* Von Siebold (1796–1866) was a Dutch explorer expelled from Japan by Japanese authorities after accusations of spying. For more on von Siebold, see Harumi Befu and Josef Kreiner, eds., *Othernesses of Japan: Historical and Cultural Influences on Japanese Studies in Ten Countries* (Munich: Iudicium, 1992).]

"personal motives" of the Japanese traveler—namely, to his resentment toward Gilyak women who made him do common work on a par with other men [60].[5]

"Among the Gilyak, both on Sakhalin and on the continent," concludes von Schrenck, "polyandry does not exist." Von Schrenck was right in his own way: It was almost impossible for him personally to note the polyandric character of the Gilyak family, for it is quite true that open, public polyandry is not found among the Gilyak.[6] Mamiya Rinzo's data in turn are rather vague. He noted the factual frivolity of sexual relations, but his ignorance of the Gilyak language prevented him from grasping the true nature and normative character of what he observed [61].

In order to discover the polyandric nature of Gilyak marriage, we must penetrate deep into the most intimate features of Gilyak life, know their language, and spend considerable time among them in their yurtas. Rinzo's prolonged stay as a dweller and working man in a Gilyak house enabled him to see what escaped the attention of von Schrenck, who observed Gilyak life as an outsider. Acquaintance with the nomenclature of relationships is necessary for a correct understanding of the form of the Gilyak family. Here again von Schrenck failed on account of a deficient knowledge of the Gilyak language.[7]

To an outside observer, Gilyak marriage fails to present any striking peculiarities. To all appearances, the wife or wives of the Gilyak (the polygynous marriages of one man to two, three, or four wives are customarily permissible) are his own individual property. The man very often buys his wife from her agnates (father or brothers) for a very high price. The woman comes to live permanently in his house, follows him in his travels and migrations, and is considered before the world to be his wife and the mother of his children. The children belong exclusively to the father and inherit from him following his death.

After the birth of the first child, the father and mother give up their former names, and are henceforth addressed by the name of the child as "father of so and so," or "mother of so and so" (teknonymy). The exclusive rights of the husband over his wife seem to be publicly sanctioned; he is allowed to take reprisals against, or even kill [krovovaia rasprava], anyone who infringes upon his marital rights.

The clan is based on the agnatic principle; marriage is exogamous. The traveler may visit the entire Gilyak territory, live in the dwellings of the natives, carefully observe their family life, and yet fail to notice anything unusual. In the large win-

---

[5]   Von Schrenck says, "Having no cause to suspect Rinzo of intentional misrepresentation, we cannot refrain from supposing that he was influenced by personal motives; the resulting obscurity in his statements gave rise to diversified interpretations . . . . It is not improbable that vanity and the fear of losing the respect of the Government (on account of his slave-like position) prompted the traveler to explain his humiliating position among the Gilyak as due to a custom of their country" (i.e., to polyandry and the ruling position of the women). *Reisen,* vol. III, pt. II, 19–20.

[6]   [*Editor's note:* Lydia Black has rightly observed that while "polygyny" might better capture Shternberg's intent, polyandry likely resonated more fully with Shternberg's emphasis on women participating in group marriage.]

[7]   The few data contributed by von Schrenck on that subject are highly misleading. Thus, for instance, he wrongly asserts that a Gilyak calls his mother and his father's sister by a common name, *imk* (see von Schrenck, *Reisen,* vol. III, pt. II, 6). Von Schrenck's informant probably meant the mother's sister, and not the father's sister.

ter houses, residents are grouped by families, each with its own concerns. During the summer every family lives in a separate yurta, often far from neighbors and relatives. The relations between husband and wife or wives and their children are peaceful and tender. Married couples frequently give evidence of great affection for each other; when one dies, the other may commit suicide or seemingly die of grief.[8] Thus we seem to deal with a typical individual family commonly called patriarchal, and certainly anything but polyandric.

Such were my own first impressions. But no sooner had I gathered some information about kinship nomenclature than grave doubts began to arise in my mind, prompting me immediately to undertake a detailed study of that side of the problem. A systematic census of the population seemed to me the best way of studying kinship terminology. With this goal in mind, I undertook, in the course of the winter of 1891, my first census of Gilyak settlements of Sakhalin's northwestern coast, the result of which was my discovery of their complex classificatory kinship system and unique form of group marriage.[9] Subsequent censuses taken in different Gilyak regions (1891–1894) gave me a full and rich, multifaceted picture of kin nomenclature and sexual relations with their attendant variations by clan and dialect.[10] During the same period I also studied the southern neighbors of the Gilyak, the Ainu, and found among them a system quite different—one representing typical features of endogamy and maternal succession without any trace of group marriage. Among the Tungus [Evenki] of the Amur region, especially among the isolated Orochi on the coast of the northern Sea of Japan, I discovered a fully developed classificatory system of relationship connected with group marriage roughly similar to that of the Gilyak but differing from it in many important points. In this way I accumulated sufficient material for this general comparative survey of kinship terminology, as well as family and clan organization among all the representatives of the Amur region.

In light of both the great importance of kinship terminology for understanding the Gilyak family and clan structure, as well as the recent scholarly debates that surround classificatory kinship systems and their meaning generally, we find it necessary now to consider Gilyak classificatory nomenclature in its fullest detail [**62**].

---

[8] [***Editor's note:*** The Polish scholar Bronislaw Pilsudskii, who began his ethnographic career while in exile with Shternberg on Sakhalin Island, recorded several such instances. See Robert Austerlitz, "Ten Nivkh Erotic Poems," *Acta Ethnographica of the Academy of Sciences of Hungary* 33, nos. 1–4 (1984): 33–44; "Two Gilyak Song Texts" *in To Honor Roman Jakobson— Essays on the Occasion of His Seventieth Birthday, 11 October 1966*, I: 99–113 (The Hague: Mouton, 1967); Alfred E. Majewicz, ed., *Collected Works of Bronislaw Pilsudskii. Vol. 1: The Aborigines of Sakhalin (1)* (Steszew, Poland: International Institute of Ethnolinguistic and Oriental Studies, 1992); and Bronislaw Pilsudskii, "The Gilyaks and their Songs," *Folk-lore* 34 (1913): 477–490. A recent, excellent volume exploring the relationship between Pilsudskii and Shternberg is: Vladislav M. Latyshev, *Dorogoi Lev Iakovlevich* (Iuzhno-Sakhalinsk: SOKM, 1996).]

[9] A report on this subject entitled "The Gilyak of Sakhalin" was in due time presented by the author to the Moscow Anthropological Society; in 1893 it appeared in the Society's journal, *Etnograficheskoe Obozrenie [The Ethnographic Review]* (1893, II). In the foreign press two notices of the article appeared: one by Mr. Th. Volkov in *L'Anthropologie* (V, 341), the other in *Die Neue Zeit* (1893) by Mr. Friedrich Engels.

[10] [***Editor's note:*** Koshkin discusses Shternberg's Sakhalin censuses in Shternberg, *Giliaki*, xiii.]

ONE

The Gilyak Kinship System[1]

[10–26; 5–32; 132–149; 68–75]

THE GILYAK SYSTEM OF KINSHIP has no distinct terms to indicate affinity.[2] According to the basic principle of Gilyak marriage laws, affinity must coincide with kin ties. The Gilyak distinguish two main categories of kinship which may be designated, respectively, agnatic and cognatic. The first term comprises all persons bound by

---

[1] [*Editor's note:* Of all the chapters in the Shternberg text, the reader might appreciate that this is perhaps the most difficult to follow. On receiving the first drafts in 1912, Boas wrote to Shternberg to say he found it "very hard reading." The reader is urged to refer closely to the glossary and table 1 where necessary. For useful English language guides, see Claude Lévi-Strauss, "Internal Limits of Generalized Exchange," in his *Elementary Structures of Kinship* (Boston: Beacon Press, 1949), 292–309; and Lydia Black, "Relative Status of Wife Givers and Wife Takers in Gilyak Society," *American Anthropologist* 74, no. 5 (1972), 1244–1248.

This chapter demonstrates the greatest variation among the four main earlier versions of this work—the AMNH Russian and English typescripts and the two 1933 Soviet editions—in both form and content. In the three Russian versions, chapters 1 and 2 of the present edition are reversed. Specifically, in the AMNH Russian typescript, the section titled "Ch. 1: The Classificatory Kinship System," 4–9 (which corresponds to sections in Shternberg, *Giliaki,* "Terms and Forms of Kinship," 132–136; and Shternberg, *Sem'ia,* 62–68) precedes the material beginning this section. In the AMNH Russian typescript they are two separate chapters, whereas in the 1933 editions Koshkin collapsed them into one chapter. This edition follows the sequence of these chapters outlined by Shternberg in an undated memo to Boas in the archive of the AMNH.

It should be stressed that table 1 is found in the AMNH English typescript only. The AMNH Russian typescript and 1933 Soviet editions contain truncated versions (AMNH Russian typescript, 23–26; Shternberg, *Giliaki,* 147–149; and Shternberg, *Sem'ia,* 74–75). This is likely the table Boas suggested to Shternberg in their 1912 correspondence, and may have initially drafted himself (appendix A, letter of October 26). In the 1940s, Lévi-Strauss worked from this new table in his chapter on Gilyak kinship, *Elementary Structures of Kinship,* 292–309. With the introduction of Gilyak kin terms in this chapter, reconciling the four separate systems of transliteration used in the two AMNH typescripts and the two 1933 editions involved much consultation with Gilyak (Nivkh) readers on Sakhalin in 1995. In this edition, Gilyak words follow Shternberg's AMNH Russian typescript, except when Sakhalin native speakers strongly recommended revision. Hence, in this section, *xal* became *khal, tuvn* became *tuvng, ymgi* became *imgi, nae* became *nats, ymk* became *imk, angey* became *ang'rei, aek* became *atsk, jox* became *iokh, ogla* became *og'la, ranr* became *ranrsh,* and *irx* became *irkh.* Please see the Note on Transliteration in the frontmatter. Lydia Black's comments have improved many parts of this book, but I am particularly grateful for her close attention to translations throughout this chapter.]

[2] [*Editor's note:* This first sentence is found in the AMNH English version only.]

ties of common descent from a male ancestor, in other words, all persons born or adopted into one or another patrilineal clan. A woman, in marrying, passes to the clan of her husband. Cognatic kinship is of two kinds. The first kind comprises the clan or clans into which the agnatic kinswomen of a particular clan have married; the second kind encompasses the agnatic clan or clans from which men of the same particular clan have taken wives [**68**].

All persons related agnatically are known as *khal-nigivin*,[3] or simply as *khal*, *khalbekh*, "people of the clan" (from *khal*, "clan," and *nigivin*, "man"). In relation to the first group of cognates (that is, to the members of the clan or clans who take or have taken wives among the *khal-nigivin*), the latter with their entire clan are called *akhmalk* (X,[4] "fathers-in-law" [in Russian, *testi*]), and reciprocally, *imgi* (XI, "sons-in-law").[5] On the other hand, in relation to the second group (that is, to the clan or clans among which the *khal* themselves take wives), the latter are called *imgi*. Both groups in relation to the first cognatic set, and all three in relation to one another, bear the characteristic name *pandf*[6] (from *pandind*, "to be born"), that is, consanguineal kin bound by ties of common descent (through women).[7] Thus we see that "affinity" and "cognatism" are converging among the Gilyak. How this came to be will be apparent from the discussion of marriage norms. Let us now discuss each kinship category.

AGNATIC KINSHIP WITHIN THE CLAN

Within the clan the Gilyak distinguish only three lines of agnatic relationship: (1) the *tuvng*, collateral branches, encompassing classes of brothers and sisters (own and

---

[3] Here as everywhere in the text I have used the terms of the Eastern dialect [E.D.]. Whenever the Western dialect is given, it is preceded by the initials W.D. The terms of relationship are given in table 1. [***Editor's note:*** This footnote is found in the AMNH English version only. The intention to include synonyms from both of the Gilyak main dialects was expressed by Kreinovich in a 1930 letter to Shternberg's widow (AAN f. 282, o. 5, d. 27). Kreinovich's handwriting is found in a number of places in the AMNH Russian typescript, which Boas received in part through Shternberg's widow, and many of Kreinovich's editorial suggestions can be found incorporated in the AMNH English version.]

[4] Roman numerals in parentheses occurring after key kinship terms refer to table 1. [***Editor's note:*** This footnote is found in the AMNH English version only.]

[5] [***Editor's note:*** For Russian language equivalents, Lydia Black noted that Russian distinguishes between two kinds of father-in-law: *test'*, the wife's father, and *svekor*, the husband's father. Shternberg explains that among Gilyaks, "wife-givers" are "*testi*" (Russian, wives' fathers) to the "wife-takers" (in Russian, *ziat'ia*, daughters' husbands). See Black, "Relative Status." This edition employs "father-in-law" and "son-in-law" in general circumstances, except when context demands the more precise "wife's father" and "daughter's husband."]

[6] Von Schrenck is wrong in asserting that relatives on the father's side (i.e., agnates, members of the same gens) call themselves, as a group, *ngafk* (correctly, *nafk*, *navkh*), and those on the mother's side *amal*. In reality, both terms—*amal* (X, *akhmalk*) and *ngafk* (XIII, *navkh*)—indicate exclusively the fact of relationship through either mother or wife, but never on the father's side. The latter group of relatives, the agnates, bears the name indicated above: *khal*, *khal-nigivin*.

[7] [***Editor's note:*** While Shternberg gives the literal translation for *pandf*, 1995 Gilyak (Nivkh) readers agreed that the broader understanding of *pandf* designates the ancestral point of origin of a clan.]

collateral), within one's own generation;[8] (2) the ascending generation, *nerkuns'vakh* ("my fathers' generation"), without distinction of direct and collateral lines, because a father's brothers, own and collateral, make one class (only the ascending generations are distinguished in order as *nesvakh, mesvakh, s'esvakh, nisvakh, tosvakh,* and so on, meaning the first, second, third, fourth, etc., generations); (3) the descending generation, *nekhlunkun s'vakh* ("my children's generation"), where the term "children" includes not only the descendants of a man and of the entire class of his brothers (own and collateral), but also of all the descending generations of these persons. In each generation of kinspersons, classes of husbands and wives are distinguished [**68**].

(1) A MAN'S OWN GENERATION.[9] For a better understanding of what follows, we shall begin with the class of brothers and sisters (I, *tuvng*) (W.D. *ruf*). The special significance of this term is that it refers to persons of both sexes indiscriminately. It designates:

1. One's own brothers and sisters (i.e., children of one father).
2. Children of all the father's brothers, own and collateral (that is, all male and female cousins of all degrees in the male line).
3. Children of one's mother's sisters, own and collateral (that is, all male and female cousins in the female line).

Thus, in one's own clan, all agnates, male and female, of the same generation—brothers and sisters and cousins in the male line—are his *tuvng*; a man may also have *tuvng* born in other clans, if they are children of his mother's sisters, own and collateral. Thus the Gilyak clan organization permits one to have true agnates (brothers and sisters) outside his own clan.[10]

The wives of all male *tuvng* constitute a separate class of *tuvng*, addressing one another by the same terms as real agnate sisters and cousins.

The class *tuvng* has two important divisions, which greatly influence both the whole terminology and sexual norms. This division is into persons older and persons younger than the speaker or the one spoken of: namely, (I(a)) *akand, aki* (older male or female *tuvng*); and *askhand, askh* (I(b)), younger male or female *tuvng*). For an older *tuvng* another term is also used (namely, (I(c)), *nanakh, nanak*), and it is remarkable that the same term is applied to one's paternal aunts, the reason for which will be duly explained in connection with sexual regulations. In addressing one another, the *tuvng* use exclusively the above terms for "elder" and "younger" in the vocative form—*aka, askha, nanakha,* and so on. Certain other terms are used for designating the subdivisions of the class *tuvng*, such as *ranrsh* (I(d)), "sister" in relation to brothers), *kivung* (I(e)), "brother" in relation to sisters). Descriptive terms are employed

---

8   [**Editor's note:** A collateral "brother" or "sister" in this context is the common equivalent of a cousin.]

9   [**Editor's note:** The AMNH English typescript here and elsewhere in this chapter lacks several lines later used in some of the Russian editions. Where possible, I have added lines from the AMNH Russian typescript and the two 1933 Soviet editions to clarify.]

10   [**Editor's note:** This last line of the paragraph is found in the AMNH English version only.]

for distinguishing real brothers and sisters from cousins in the male line, such as *oskir tuvng* (real [*rodnoi*] brother or sister) in contrast to *tukhor tuvng* ("male or female cousin"). All these terms, however, are outside of the general series of classificatory terminology and are used only when necessary to specify certain individuals. If two of the most remote agnates of one generation are asked what they are to each other, the answer will be either simply *tuvng*, or *aki* (elder *tuvng*), or *askh*, according to the ages of the speaker and his companion. The seniority of brothers (in our terminology "cousins and third-cousins") is determined not by the places of their fathers in the ascending line, but by the actual age seniority of the cousins, doubtful cases being decided by the male elders.

(2) THE ASCENDING LINE WITHIN THE CLAN. In respect to terminology, we find in this line only two grades for each sex: (1) fathers and grandfathers, on one side; (2) mothers and grandmothers, on the other side. Outside of the ascending line stand only the paternal aunts (fathers' sisters), who are classed as we have seen above with one's elder female *tuvng* and designated by one and the same term, *nanakh, nanakhand* [**69**].

(a) Grandfathers and Grandmothers. Within the clan, the class of grandfathers (IV, *atk, atak*) embraces all males in the ascending line of one's father, in direct as well as indirect lines: that is, not only grandfathers, great-grandfathers, and so on, but also all the *tuvng* of the latter (grand-uncles, great-grand-uncles, etc.). Among the Gilyak speaking the Eastern dialect, this class includes also older brothers of one's father, that is, all paternal uncles older than one's father. All the wives of the "grandfather," and all sisters of the latter (that is, all paternal grand-aunts, of a male or female, are one's grandmothers (V, *atsk*; W.D. *itik, itsik*).[11] Whenever a person of that category must be more precisely defined, the Gilyak use descriptive phrases similar to our own. To designate the grandfather's younger brother, for instance, they will say *ri er atk pilan* ("my father's younger uncle"), etc. These expressions, however, are but rarely used, for in matrimonial questions relationships of these degrees play no part whatever [**69**].

(b) Fathers and Paternal Uncles within the Clan. Here two forms must be distinguished, reflecting, as it seems, two consecutive stages in the development of marital and sexual norms. The Gilyak speaking the Western dialect (that is, those of the continent and the western coast of Sakhalin, especially northward from Pogibi) use identical terms (III, *itk*, etc.) for "father" as well as for all their male *tuvng*, that is, for all brothers, one's own and collateral. Another group, which speaks the Eastern dialect, makes a distinction between *tuvng* ("father's juniors") and *tuvng* ("father's seniors").[12] Among these Gilyak the class of fathers embraces the real father and his younger *tuvng* only, while the elder *tuvng* are designated by the same term as the

---

11 [***Editor's note:*** In the AMNH Russian typescript, Shternberg handwrote *aѕ̀k* and *aek* in the text; the 1933 Soviet editions typeset the same word as *asx* or *ack*. Following the transliteration table Shternberg filed for Boas in the AMNH archives, I have rendered the term here as *atsk*.]

12 [***Editor's note:*** None of the AMNH or 1933 Soviet editions distinguish these two terms of the Eastern dialect.]

grandfathers—(IV) *atk, atak.* But even here, among this group, in the spoken language as well as in the texts, the term "father" (III, *itk* and its synonyms) is also used indiscriminately for the father and all his "brothers" (*tuvng*). This fact is clearly revealed by the customary use of "father" in the plural. For instance, *nitkkhyn* (pl. of *itk,* "father"; literally, "my fathers") means "the father and his 'brothers' (*tuvng*)," without distinction of age. Hence, we may conclude that the first group, with a common term for "father and his *tuvng,*" is the more ancient one; though formerly dominant, it has receded before the gradual changes in sexual norms, probably (as will be shown below) as a result of Tungus influence. Other evidence for this conclusion may be drawn from the term "*tuvng*" applied indiscriminately to children of all brothers without regard to their relative ages, and from the term "mother" to be discussed next.

(c) **Mothers within the Clan.** In connection with the preceding class, whereas some differences have been shown to exist between the terminologies of the eastern and western Gilyak, the two groups completely coincide in their terminologies for the class of mothers. Each Gilyak, male or female, applies the term "mother" (II, *imk* and synonyms) not only to his or her own mother or stepmother, but to the wives of all his father's *tuvng* [**70**].[13]

(d) **Wives within the Clan.** The most common term for "wife" in both dialects is *ang'rei* or *ankh.* This term is also a classificatory one, but it differs in scope as used by the eastern or the western Gilyak. Among the latter, especially among those of the Amur, the term "wife" includes not only one's actual wife, but all the wives of all his *tuvng,* without distinction of age; among the other Gilyak, only the wives of one's elder *tuvng* are termed his actual wives, whereas the wives of his younger *tuvng* are designated by a different term, *iokh,* signifying "daughter-in-law." The wives of the *tuvng* address one another as "elder sister" and "younger sister."

(e) **Husbands within the Clan.** The terminology of this class corresponds to that of the preceding class of "wives." Within the clan of her husband, a woman applies the term "husband" (IX, *pu, ivn, okon,* etc.) not merely to her actual husband but also to his *tuvng.* The western Gilyak make no distinction between elder and younger *tuvng,* but among the eastern Gilyak, only the younger *tuvng* of a woman's husband are termed her "husbands" (*pu,* etc.), the husband's elder *tuvng* being designated by the same term as that used for "father-in-law" (X(a), *atk*).

(3) **THE DESCENDING LINE WITHIN THE CLAN.** For this class there exists but one term for both lines, direct as well as indirect, and for all generations—*og'la* or *eglan, ola.* The term *og'la* is applied by a man within his own clan, not only to his own children born from his actual wives but to all children of his brothers (*tuvng*). Similarly a woman uses the term *og'la* for her own children as well as for the children of all her husband's "brothers." The term *og'la* is applied not to the first generation alone, but to all descending generations of the speaker and of the entire class of *tuvng.* Thus

---

[13] I came across a single exception in my census of the village Kol', where in one case the wife of a father's senior brother was called by the Tungus term *ivei,* a fact accounted for by the presence in the village of Tungus clans.

FIG. 9. Gilyak women and children during winter, 1890s. Women's clothing was often ornamented with Chinese coins on the lower hem. Photo by Lev Shternberg. *Source:* AAN f. 282, o. 2, d. 158, l. 2.

the Gilyak designates as *og'la* not only his own children and agnatic nephews but all the latter's descendants as well (that is, grandchildren, great-grandchildren, etc.). In that use of *og'la* we recognize the same phenomenon as in the terminology of the ascending line, where one term, *atk,* designates all generations higher than father and mother.[14] Besides the above normal cases, the term *og'la* is frequently used as a term of endearment, in quite different connections. Thus a woman calls her husband's sister's son by the term *og'la,* and a man, his wife's brother's son, though, as a rule, quite different terms are used for those persons. For a more specific definition, two additional special terms are used. One term, *oskip og'la,* is descriptive, and applies to a "related" descendant (one's own child, son or daughter); the other term, *ykye,* indicates primogeniture. However, neither of these terms is of any importance in

---

[14] [***Editor's note:*** In the AMNH Russian typescript, Shternberg penned the rather confusing line, "Tut my vidim to zhe iavlenie, chto v terminologii voskhodiashchei linii, gde odnim termi-nom 'atk' and 'ark/ask' opredeliauts'ia vse pokoleniia vyshe ottsa i materi." The 1933 Soviet editions eliminated the second term probably because Shternberg framed the sentence around only one; I have deleted the second because neither of the versions ("ark/ask," handwritten by Shternberg) were included correspondingly in table 1. The 1995 Gilyak (Nivkh) readers did not comment here because we worked with the published 1933 Soviet edition of *Sem'ia,* which does not contain the alternative wording.]

either the general terminology or the sexual norms. For indicating the sex of the *og'la*, the words *sankh, umgu* ("woman") or *asmits, utgu* ("male") are added, for instance, *sankhekhlan*, "girl," or *asmitsekhlan*, "boy."

COGNATIC KINSHIP

Let us now turn to the terms used for persons outside the clan—in other words, to cognatic kinship—the key to the entire system. We have already drawn attention to the fact that in the Gilyak system of relationship affinity and consanguinity are identical; that is, their classificatory system does not recognize relationship by affinity. In order to grasp this strange fact with greater clarity, we shall begin our survey of kin links outside the clan with the relationship (through the mother) to the members of that clan or to the entire clan from which came the mother of a given individual [71].

"I" being male, my maternal uncles and their male *tuvng* are to me and to all my male *tuvng*, "wives' fathers" (X, *akhmalk*), and the daughters of these persons are our wives (VII, *ang'rei*); reciprocally, I and all my *tuvng* are sons-in-law (XI, *imgi*) to our maternal uncles, and husbands (IX, *pu*) to their daughters. This same relation exists between all other generations of my own clan and the clan of my maternal uncles. All female *tuvng* of my mother's brothers—in other words, all sisters (own and collateral) of my mother—are "wives" of my "fathers," and consequently my "mothers." On the other side, the daughters of my maternal uncles' sons are wives of my maternal uncles' own sons and of the sons of my "brothers," and so in every generation all males of my own clan, and all females of my mother's brother's clan, are husbands and wives. Thus both clans are at the same time bound by ties of affinity and consanguinity. In the clan of my mother, I (being male) and my clansmen have, on the one hand, cognatic and even agnatic relations—maternal uncles, aunts, grandfathers, grandmothers, cognatic cousins, and even mothers (sisters of my own mother). On the other hand, we also have fathers-in-law and mothers-in-law, wives, and daughters-in-law. My father-in-law is at the same time my maternal uncle, my wife is my cross-cousin (daughter of my mother's brother), my daughter-in-law is the daughter of my maternal uncle's son, and so on.

Because of this double relationship, a double terminology has been formed for some categories of the clansmen of one's mother's clan. While for a man's mother's clansmen the general term for two generations older than the speaker is *akhmalk* (X, the term of affinity and consanguinity at the same time), there exists also another term, *atk* (X(a), "grandfather," "uncle"), because they are really grandfathers (fathers of the speaker's mothers or uncles (mother's brothers)), whereas for those of the speaker's own generation, or the younger one, an additional term, *navkh* (class of cognatic cousins), is used.

The position of clanswomen in regard to their mother's clan is quite different. In the latter they have no husbands, no fathers-in-law, no mothers-in-law. They have only consanguinei. They call all males of this clan by one and the same term, *atk*; the males' wives and all clanswomen of the generations older than the mother are called *atsk*; the mother's "sisters," *imk* ("mothers"); all other clanswomen of the mother are called *navkh* ("cousins").

The terminology used by the clansmen of my mother to me and my clansmen also shows clearly the double relation of affinity and consanguinity. I being male, all the clansmen of my mother call me *imgi* ("son-in-law" or "man"). Those mother's clansmen of my own generation or younger further address me as *navkh* ("cognatic cousin"). In turn, independent of generation, they call me and my clansmen's wives *tuvng* ("sisters"), *nanakh* ("agnatic aunts"), *og'la* ("daughters"), or *atsk* ("great-aunts"); my clanswomen are to them either *atsk*, (more simply, aunts) or *nern* ("cousins" on the female side). On the other hand, the daughters of my mother's "brothers" call me and my "brothers" their *pu* ("husbands"); my wives, *tuvng* ("sisters"); my fathers, *atk* ("uncle" and "father-in-law"); my "mothers," *nanakh* ("aunt" and "grandmother"); my grandfathers and grandmothers, *atk* and *atsk.*

From what has been said above, it is clear that the relation of a man to his mother's clan extends throughout both clans.

Let A be my clan, and B that of my mother's brother; the latter as a whole will be wives' fathers (*akhmalk*) to A, who in turn, will be sons-in-law (*imgi*) to B. Importantly, this correlation of the two clans remains fixed once and for all. Under no circumstances can clan B become sons-in-law (*imgi*) to A. This may be gathered from the mutual terminology of the two clans. As was demonstrated above, clan B owes its name *akhmalk* to the fact that the members of clan A have a class of "wives" (*ang'rei*) in clan B; while the men of clan B have among the women of clan A either "sisters" (*tuvng*), or "daughters" (*og'la*), or aunts (*atsk*), or "nieces" (*nern*), but no "wives" (*ang'rei*). Therefore clan B cannot become sons-in-law (*imgi*) to A.

The terminology of relationship through the mother determines yet another form of cognatic relationship—that through the father's sister. While I call her by the agnatic term "elder sister" or "aunt" (*nanakh*), she refers to me as her "younger brother" (*askh*). At the same time she and her husband's clan assume towards me and my clan the same relation as that in which I and my clan stand to the clan of my mother's brother; that is, my father's sister's husband and his brothers (*tuvng*) call all my father's sisters "wives" (*ang'rei*), and are called "husbands" (*pu*) by them. My sisters and my other female *tuvng* become "wives" (*ang'rei*) of the sons of my father's "sisters," and "daughters-in-law" (*iokh*) of all ascending generations of my father's sister's husband. Hence, my "daughters" become wives of the sons of my "sisters." On the other hand, my clansmen, according to their generations, become either *atk*, *akhmalk*, or *akhmalk navkh* to the clansmen of my father's sister's husband, while the latter become *imgi navkh* to us. The women of the other clan are to us either agnates, "aunts" (*nanakh*), "sisters" (*tuvng*), "daughters" (*og'la*), or "nieces" (*nern*), but in no case can they be our "wives" (*ang'rei*). In brief, my clansmen and I are *akhmalk* to the clansmen of my father's sister's husband, who are *imgi* to us.

The terminology of this group (that is, a man's relations to his mother's brother and to his father's sister) is the key to the entire terminology of relationship. The entire nomenclature of marital relationship in general is fashioned after it.

When a Gilyak marries, the terminology adopted between him and his clan, and between his wife and her clan, is the same as if his wife was his mother's brother's daughter, and when a Gilyak marries off his sister, the terminology of relationship between the two clans is the same as if his brother-in-law was the son of his father's sister. That is why the Gilyak system of terminology knows no special relationship by affinity. To a Gilyak male his father-in-law is the same as his mother's brother or his grandmother's brother's son; his son-in-law is the same as his sister's son; his son-in-law's father is the same as his grandfather's sister's son; his daughter-in-law is the same as the daughter of his mother's brother's son, etc.; the members of the two clans thus constitute a quasi-consanguineous group.

If we keep in mind the nomenclature of relationship in the mother's brother's group and in the father's sister's group, we have a ready scheme of relationship for any marital combination—between the husband and his wife's clan, between the wife and her husband's clan, or between a man and his married sister's clan [72]. Accordingly, we can observe the following general rule: My father-in-law and his kin in ascending generations, and the corresponding classes of their *tuvng,* are to me *akhmalk, atk.* Their male descendants I call *akhmalk navkh* while they call me *imgi navkh.* The wives of all my *akhmalk* I call *atsk.* The sisters of my father-in-law and his female *tuvng* are my "mothers" (*imk*); their husbands, my "fathers" (*itk*), while I am the son (*og'la*) of both. Similarly my wife's "sisters" (*tuvng*) are "wives" (*ang'rei*) to me and to my "brothers" (*tuvng*); their children call us "father" (*itk*) and "mother" (*imk*) and are "brothers" (*tuvng*) to one another. My sisters and daughters, on the other hand, are merely nieces (*nern*) of the men of my father-in-law's clan; therefore, no one of that clan can become "son-in-law" (*imgi*) of my clan. On the other hand, I being *female,* my husband's father and all his *tuvng* are to me uncles (*atk*), being sons of my grandfather's sisters; all the ascending males of my fathers-in-law are also *atk,* being my great-uncles; my mothers-in-law are to me *nanakh* (my father's sisters); my husband's brothers (*tuvng*) are to me husbands (*pu*); their wives are to me elder or younger sister (*nanakh* or *askh*), and to their children I am mother (*imk*); all my "sisters" are wives (*ang'rei*) to my husband and to his "brothers," just as my paternal aunts and great-aunts are wives or my fathers-in-law and their "fathers"; all the clanswomen of my husband are to me either aunts of great-aunts (*atsk*) or cognatic female cousins (*navkh*).

NEAR AND REMOTE AKHMALK. We have seen that the interrelation of the *akhmalk* B and *imgi* A clans is a permanent one, but the members of clan B must, in their turn, have another clan C which is *akhmalk* to them, while the members of clan A must have their separate *imgi* clan D. In terminology, these clans are distinguished by the additional terms *khanke* or *mal* ("near") and *tuyma* ("remote"). Thus clan B is *khanke akhmalk,* or simply *akhmalk,* to A and *tuyma akhmalk* to D, and so on. But beyond these general terms (*tuyma akhmalk* or *imgi*), the terminology of relationship between the members of the remote *akhmalk-imgi* clans does not extend.

There is a growing complication in the *akhmalk-imgi* terminology. From what has been said above it is clear that the construction of this terminology requires that every clan have one single *akhmalk* clan. At the present time, however, clansmen may take wives from several clans; in this way each marriage from or into a new clan establishes, in regard to the two newly related clans, the entire chain of the *akhmalk-imgi* terminology. As a matter of fact, nowadays almost every clan has several *akhmalk* and several *imgi* clans.

It is easy to realize the great complications that have arisen through this order of things in the terms of relationship and, as we shall see further on, in the sexual relations of these people. For this reason a change is now being contemplated to check the growth of the *akhmalk-imgi* relationship in two directions—first, by not applying every new *akhmalk* relationship to the entire clan of the marrying man, but to his individual family only; and secondly by limiting this relationship to individuals of the first two generations. This change, however, has not yet had the sanction of public approval and the old rule holds sway over most clans.

AGNATIC RELATIONSHIP OUTSIDE THE CLAN. We have seen that one calls by the term "mother" (*imk*) not only the wives of his father and his paternal uncles but also the "sisters" of his mother, and that the children of one's maternal aunts are to him brothers and sisters (*tuvng*). It may happen, however, that the sisters of one's mother may be married to men not belonging to his own clan; nevertheless, the terminology and the sexual norms remain the same as if his maternal aunts were married to his father or to his father's brothers. Thus, according to this terminology, a man can have agnates, both male and female, outside his own clan. In discussing sexual norms we shall see how this apparent anomaly may have originated [**72**].

CLASSIFICATORY AND SECONDARY SUBSTITUTE TERMS

Besides strict classificatory terms corresponding to the norms of marriage and sexual relations, there are terms used in address or for designation which have nothing to do with kinship in the strict sense of the word. There are secondary substitutive terms used either metaphorically or as terms of endearment, reverence, or familiarity. Thus the term *mam* (literally, "old woman") is often used in the sense of "mother" and "wife." Similarly *irkh* (literally, "old man") is often used in the sense of "husband"; *umgu sankh* ("woman") is used in the sense of "wife"; *azmec, utgu* ("male") is used for "husband"; *ola* ("child") is sometimes used by a woman in relation to her son-in-law; and so on. As terms of reverence we find *nats nivukh* for *akhmalk*; *rak nivukh, poskhp* for *imgi*; and many others. Such secondary terms have many times puzzled investigators, leading them to the conclusion that the classificatory terminology has no significance.[15] It is necessary, therefore, to bear in mind the important distinction between true class terms and secondary metaphorical terms. The Gilyak themselves and all other tribes I have studied understand very well how to distinguish between these terms, and when relationship or matrimonial questions are under discussion, the secondary terms are never used.

DESCRIPTIVE OR CIRCUMSTANTIAL TERMS

Since the classificatory system does not suffice in cases where the relationship of a singular person is concerned, descriptive terms are used, if need be, as in European

---

15 Such a puzzling term might be one already mentioned, namely *mam*, used familiarly for designating "mother," "wife," and generally "old woman." It would be absurd to assume that such a term is a classificatory one, or to draw any conclusion from it regarding sexual norms.

TABLE 1.

LIST OF COMBINED AGNATIC AND COGNATIC KIN TERMS[16]

The following is a classified list of the agnatic and cognatic terms of relationship combined. The terms in this list are given in the two main dialects: the Eastern dialect, spoken mainly by the Gilyak on the Tym' River and on the eastern coast of the island of Sakhalin, and the Western dialect, spoken on the continent and on the western coast of Sakhalin, especially northward from Pogibi. The Western dialect terms are indicated by the initials "W.D."; otherwise the terms given are in the Eastern dialect. When the meaning of a term is given without special mention of the sex concerned, it is to be understood that the term is used by or for both sexes indiscriminately [74].

    I. *Tuvng* (*tuvn, ruvn, ruvun*) (W.D. *ruf*). Not used for direct address.

        Brothers and sisters:

           1. Children of common father and mother.
           2. Children of brothers (own and collateral).
           3. Children of sisters (own and collateral).
           4. Children of common father.
           5. Children of common mother.
           6. Wives of all male *tuvng* reciprocally.

    (a) *Akand, aki* (W.D. *ikind, iki*). Vocative forms: *aka* (W.D. *ika*).

        Elder male or female *tuvng*.

        Seniority in the side lines is determined not by the father's seniority but by the age of the persons concerned. The same rule holds for the younger *tuvng*.

    (b) *Askhand, askh* (W.D. *as'khanzh, as'ik* or *as'i'k*). Vocative forms: *askha* (W.D. *as'ika*).

           1. Younger male or female *tuvng*.
           2. Wife of the husband's younger *tuvng*.
           3. Brother's (*tuvng*) children (speaker being female) (see also VIII).

    (c) *Nanakhand* (or *nanakh, nanak*) (W.D. *ninkh, nink*). Vocative forms: *nanakha* (W.D. *ninikha*).

           1. Elder female *tuvng* (additional term to *akand* (Ia)).
           2. Sister of the father and all his *tuvng*.
           3. Husband's mother and all her female *tuvng*.

        (In one instance in the village of Viakhta, I heard this term applied to a mother's sister; generally, however, she is not *nanakhand*, but *imk*, mother.)

    (d) *Ranrsh* (or *rankr*) (W.D. *ranzh*). Not used for direct address.

        Sister in general, without distinction of age. Used exclusively in relation to brothers.

---

[16] [**Editor's note:** The AMNH English typescript preceded this table with a short note: "Pleonastic Possessive Pronouns in Terms of Relationship: As in the Dravidian and some North American languages (Seneca, for instance), Gilyak terms of relationship are always used in combination with possessive pronouns. For instance, instead of *itk*, the Gilyak always says *nitk* (*ni itk*) and so on. In the table, for the sake of simplicity, the terms are given in their pure etymological form." The placement of the table at this point in the chapter follows the AMNH English typescript.]

TABLE 1. CONTINUED

(e) *Kivung.* Not used for direct address.

Brother in general. Used exclusively in relation to sisters.

II. *Imk* (or *imik*), *im* (W.D. and E.D.). Vocative forms: *imka, imika, ima.* Other terms: *irn, zhizn* for designation. Vocative forms: *mam* (*mama'*!) (W.D. *oma*).
1. Real mother.
2. All actual or class wives (*ang'rei*) of the father.
3. Wives of father's *tuvng.*
4. Father's wives' "sisters."
5. Father's *tuvng*'s wives' "sisters."
6. Mother's "sisters" (female *tuvng*).
7. "Sisters" (*tuvng*) of wife's father.
8. Sisters of brother's (*tuvng*) father-in-law.

III. *Itk* (*itik, it, it,* rarely *utk*) (E.D. and W.D.). Vocative forms: *itka, ita.* Designative term: *er.*
1. Real father and all actual or class husbands (*pu*) of my mother.
2. Father's elder and younger "brothers" (*tuvng*), among Gilyak of W.D.
3. Father's younger male *tuvng,* only among Gilyak of E.D.
4. Mother's sisters' (*tuvng*) husbands and their male *tuvng.*
5. Wife's father's sisters' (*tuvng*) husbands.
6. Brother's wife's father's sisters' husbands.

(a) *Pilan* (E.D. and W.D.). Designative term: *pila nigivin* (W.D. *pil nivukh*).

Used as an alternative term with the term *itk* for father's younger male *tuvng,* mainly among the eastern Gilyak. This term signifying "elder" must be of a later origin, formed perhaps after the Tungus term *aga* (elder), and also applied to one's father's younger brother.

IV. *Atk* (W.D. *atak*); sometimes *app, appik.*
1. All ascending males of the father in the direct as well as indirect lines (that is, grandfather and his male *tuvng,* great-grandfather and his male *tuvng,* and so on).
2. Father's senior *tuvng,* among the eastern Gilyak only.

Other meanings of this term, used alternatively with the term *akhmalk* will be given below (see X).

V. *Atsk, atskh* (W. D. *itik, itsik*; west coast of Sakhalin *asi*).
1. Grandfather's and great-grandfather's wives and sisters (on father's and mother's side).
2. Mother's brother's (*tuvng*) wife and all his clansmen's wives.
3. Wife's "mothers" and all her clansmen's wives.
4. Wives of an *akhmalk* and all his clansmen.
5. Husband's grandmothers and great-grandmothers.
6. Husband's paternal aunts and great-aunts.

VI. *Oglan, eglan, ekhalun* (W.D. *og'la, ola*). Vocative form: *ola.* For designation of sex the following terms are added: *azmits* (W.D. *utgu*) for males, and *sank, sankh, sanikh* (W.D. *umgu*) for females. Example: *utgu ola* (boy), *umgu ola* (girl).

TABLE 1. CONTINUED

---

    1. Son or daughter (children of either sex).

    2. Children of one's "brothers" (*tuvng*), speaker being male.

    3. Children of one's "sisters" (*tuvng*), speaker being female.

    4. Wife's sisters' (*tuvng*) children.

    5. Children of one's brothers' (*tuvng*) wives' sisters, speaker being male.

    6. Children of maternal uncles' daughters, speaker being male.

    7. Son or daughters of one's male oglan.

(a) *Ivi* (or *iv, iv, ivei, evei*). Used in many localities of the W.D., especially on the Amur, formed under the influence of the neighboring Tungus tribes. Used by males for designating the following categories of class wives:

    1. Wives of one's *tuvng* (without distinction as to seniority).

    2. Sisters of one's individual wives.

    3. (Exceptionally) wife of father's younger "brother" (in one case, in the village of Kol', among clans of Tungus origin; among the Tungus even now the wife of my father's younger brother is my wife).

As a term of endearment this term is applied sometimes by a man to his sister's son and by a woman to her brother's daughter (the reason for which will be given later on) and in general by old men to children and young men.

VII. *Ang'rei* (E.D. and W.D.) for designation and direct address. One part of the Amur Gilyak bordering the Ul'chi have only a designative term *ankh* ("wife"), while they address their class wives by name.

Speaker being male:

    1. Actual wife.

    2. Wife's sisters, own and collateral (*tuvng*).

    3. Senior *tuvng*'s wives.

    4. Every *tuvng*'s wife's "sisters."

    5. Daughters of mother's brothers and of his *tuvng*.

VIII. *Iokh* (E.D. and W.D.). Vocative forms: *iokho, iokho'y*. Designative term: *erak-hand*.

    1. Daughter-in-law.

    2. Actual wife of my younger *tuvng* (speaker being male).

    3. Bride (speaker being male) [75].

IX. *Pu, if, iv, ivn* (E.D. and W.D.), *okon* (vocative *okono*), rarely *ora* (only in W.D.).

Speaker being female:

    1. Actual husband.

    2. Sisters' (*tuvng*) husbands.

    3. Husband's brothers (*tuvng*), among the Amur Gilyak and in the northwestern part of Sakhalin; husband's junior brothers (*tuvng*), among the other Gilyak.

    4. Father's sisters' (*tuvng*) sons.

Among some few families in northern Sakhalin, the actual husbands have been termed *pu, ivn*, even *navkh* (in address); and the husband's *tuvng, okon*. Especially for husband's junior *tuvng*, two terms have been used, *okon* and *ora*.

TABLE 1. CONTINUED

This confusion in the terminology, however, must be ascribed to Tungus influence. The term *ora* itself is of Tungus origin.

X. *Akhmalk* (W.D. *amalk* or *amal, amaln*). Used mainly for designation, but also for direct address. Applied by male and female clansmen (speaker being male) as a general term for:

1. All clansmen of my mother.
2. All clansmen of my own wife or of the wife of anybody of my own clan.

Besides this general term, the following differential terms are used for different categories of *akhmalk*:

(a) *Atk* (W.D. *atak;*) of Tungusian origin (*appik, app*); used more frequently in the W.D. Vocative forms: *atka ataka, appaka, a'ppo*. Designative terms: *arir, erir, aritskh, ariritskh, edr, er*.

Speaker being male:

1. Mother's brother, his male *tuvng*, and all his ascending clansmen (that is, my uncles, grandfathers, and great-grandfathers, and maternal great-uncles.
2. Father-in-law, his male *tuvng*, and his ascending clansmen.
3. Every *akhmalk* of the generation older than my own.
4. Sometimes the elder brother of my wife.

Speaker being female:

1. My father-in-law, his male *tuvng*, and his ascending clansmen.
2. The senior *tuvng* of my husband, only among the eastern Gilyak.
3. For the *akhmalk* of the generation older than my own, the term *atk* is used; the terms *arir, edr*, etc. are applied by women to their husband's clansmen.

(b) *Navkh* (*navkh*) (E.D. and W.D.).

1. All *akhmalk* of my own generation (speaker being male) and their descending clansmen.
2. Alternative term: *atk* is used for the *akhmalk* of the generation older than my own (speaker being female).

XI. *Imgi* (*umigi, emgi*) (E.D. and W.D.), *ora, okon* (mainly among the Amur Gilyak).

I, being male, and all my clansmen and our wives apply this term for:

1. My son-in-law and all his clansmen.
2. My sister's son and all his clansmen.
3. My sister's husband and his clansmen.
4. My father's sister's husband and all his clansmen, etc.
5. Generally for the husband of every clanswoman and his clansmen.

The following differential terms are used for different classes of *imgi*:

(a) *Navkh* a familiar term for *imgi* of my own generation and their descendants (clansmen).
(b) *Okon* (only among the Amur Gilyak bordering the Ulchi), used for my (speaker being male) senior sister's (female *tuvng*) husband and for my father's sister's (female *tuvng*) husband.

TABLE 1. CONTINUED

(c) *Ora* (only among the Amur Gilyak), used for my (speaker being male) daughter's (own or class daughter's) husband and the husband of my junior sister (female *tuvng*).

XII. *Oraiu* (plural of *ora*), a collective term for the *akhmalk* clansmen and *imgi* clansmen together (used only among the Amur Gilyak).

XIII. *Navkh.* Used for designation and direct address. Besides cases X(b) and XI(b), where this term is used alternately with other terms, it is applied:

1. Between a woman and her husband's sisters (*tuvng*).
2. Between a woman and her father's sister's (*tuvng*) daughter.
3. In some localities on the Amur, between the wives of brothers (*tuvng*), strictly corresponding in this case to the Hawaiian term *punalua*, also used between brothers' wives, and having the same meaning (partner or colleague). With the same meaning *navkh* is also used as term of address between persons not related, who are marrying from one and the same clan.

XIV. *Nern* (*nern, nirn, negn* (E.D. and W.D.).

Speaker being male:

1. My sisters' (*tuvng*) or daughter's husband's sisters (*tuvng*).
2. My sister's (*tuvng*) daughters.
3. My father's sister's daughters.
4. Sister of every *imgi* of my own or descending generation.
5. The younger sister of my wife (if exceptionally she is married to one of my class *imgi*).

Speaker being female:

1. Husband's sister's daughter.
2. Husband's paternal aunt's daughter.

---

languages. Thus, while the class term for a paternal great-uncle will be *atk*, if it is desired to define the given *atk* more circumstantially, one may say *ner itk askh* or *ner itk aki* ("my father's father's younger or elder brother") and so on. For the same purpose sometimes personal names are applied: For example, instead of saying "my father's elder brother's wife" (my mother as a class term), one may simply say "Kat's mother" (the mother of one called Kat), and so on. More instances of this kind are given above in connection with relationship within the clan [73].

THE TERMS "GREAT," "GRAND" (*pilang*).[17] In the spoken language as well as in my texts, the adjective "great" or "grand" (*pilang*) often appears in combination with

---

[17] [***Editor's note:*** Although Shternberg's intention was to work through the Eastern Dialect, which would render this adjective *piland,* throughout the text with few exceptions the Western Dialect variant of *pilang* is used. Up to four transliterations of the adjectival form are given in Shternberg's handwritten insertions to the AMNH Russian typescript alone, e.g., "pilang," "piland," "niland," and "pilang." Soviet editors reproduced "pilaṅ" in the 1933 publications.]

one or another of the terms of relationship. Among some other peoples the addition of the adjective means the shifting of relationship by one degree in the ascending line (father, grandfather). In Gilyak, however, *pilang* is never used in this sense. Usually it is added as an adjective to a term of relationship to indicate the mature age of a given representative of a classificatory term. This peculiarity is readily accounted for when we consider that in the classificatory system even such terms as "father," "mother," "grandfather," "grandmother" do not, as in European languages, sufficiently determine age in relation to the speaker; in fact, in Gilyak these terms have no relation whatever to age. Not only the "father" and "mother," but the "grandfather" and "grandmother," may be younger than their "son" or "grandson." Whenever it becomes desirable to indicate that the person spoken of is an adult representative of one or another category, or is older than the speaker, the adjective *pilang* (*pila, pil,* "big," "mature") is added: for instance, "adult younger brother" (*pilan askh*); "my old father" (*n vilan itk*); "my old mother" (*n vila nimk*); "my adult elder sister or aunt" (*n vila nankh*); "my old uncle, father-in-law, grandfather" (*n vila natk*). In such cases *pilang* is often used also as a term of reverence or even as a mere pleonasm. *Pilang* is used in some cases, too, when it is desired to designate more exactly the relative position of persons of the same class. Thus the general term for one's father's brothers' wives is *imk* ("mother"). But if one wants to indicate definitely the wife of his father's elder or younger brother, he says *pil aimk* ("big mother") or *matka imk* ("little mother"), just as he says *pil itk* ("big father") to indicate that the given person usually called or addressed simply as *itk* ("father") is older than his real father. In the same descriptive sense these terms are used for distinguishing different mothers, wives of one's own father. Thus *pila imk* signifies "father's wife older than one's real mother," and *matka imk* the younger one. In a single instance (namely, in the substantive form *pilan* or *pila nigivin*), *pilang* becomes a term of classificatory relationship, signifying "father's younger brother," synonymous with *itk* ("father"). The Tungus term *aga* is probably responsible for the development of this peculiarity [73].

PLURAL OF TERMS OF RELATIONSHIP. The classificatory system has favored the frequent use in the plural of such terms (strictly singular in our own languages) as "father," "mother," "wife," "husband," "father-in-law," and so on.

The common use of such plural terms has a rather curious result. The plural is often used even in cases where only one person is spoken of: for instance, *tserkun saktokh vind?* (literally, "Your fathers, where did they go?") instead of *tser saktokh vind?* ("Your father, where did he go?"), or *er erkun itin shankh* ("the woman indicated by the fathers," plural instead of singular).

Here is a characteristic example taken from one of my texts.[18] The hero of the tales says to his wife, "I my fathers, my mothers, to seek shall go"; and when he finds them,"his *mother* on the left-side couch was sitting, his *father* behind the mother

[18] Shternberg, *Materialy po izucheniiu giliakskogo iazyka i fol'klora* (St. Petersburg: Imperatorskaia Akademiia Nauk, 1908), vol. I, 107, 108, 120, lines 85, 120, et seq.

was sitting, his uncle (father's brother) on the right couch was sitting, there the young woman would be sitting" (probably his mother's sister).[19]

The plural is sometimes used as a collective term for relatives of different categories: For instance, *tserkun* (literally, "your fathers") is used in the sense of "father and mother" or "the father and his agnates"; *ni itkuntokh vind*, "I go to the fathers" (that is, to the village where my father and mother live or lived); *nakhmalkkhuntakh*, "to my fathers-in-law" (that is, to the village of my wife's relatives); *neorankkhyn* (literally, "my women," "my wives"), in the sense of "a beloved one and her male companions"; *ingikhyn* (literally, "sons-in-law"), in the sense of "son-in-law and his wives." A similar phenomenon seems to occur among the Yukaghir. I gather this from an instance cited by Mr. Iokhel'son, where a man says *mat atsiananin* ("my fathers") instead of *mat atsi-ianin* ("my father").[20] Mr. Iokhel'son believes that in this case the plural may have been used to show respect for the father; but as it appears from the context ("Friend, to my fathers let us migrate"), the father was not present and there was therefore no necessity for exhibiting special respect.

TERMS OF RELATIONSHIP USED FIGURATIVELY. The terms of relationship reflect in a curious way on the terms used by lovers not bound by marital ties. In their vocabulary we often find terms borrowed from the matrimonial terminology. Thus a woman calls her lover *azmits*, "man," "husband" (W.D. *okon*, "husband"); *ivn* (applied to fiancé); or *navkh* (from the terminology of the son-in-law and father-in-law group). The last term as well as the term *akhmalk* is sometimes used by the wives of "brothers" (although they may be strangers to each other) and for fun by men who have a nonmarital liaison with one and the same woman. In everyday life the terms *navkh* among the eastern Gilyak, and *amaln* among the western Gilyak (vocative forms *navkha* and *amala*), are used very often for addressing even persons not related to the speaker. In daily life, *navkh* can mean simply "companion," "partner in common enterprise." In this way *navkh* coincides with the well-known Hawaiian term *punalua*, derived from its own local family groupings [**74**].[21]

---

[19] In Old-Turkic monuments (namely, in the Koshko-Laidam inscriptions) V. O. Radlov [Radloff] found traces of a similar use of plural terms, although at the present time all traces of a classificatory system excepting the terms "elder brother" and "younger brother" have completely disappeared. Accordingly, when he encountered the expression "my mother, the queen, and the mothers" he translated the last word in the text as "step-mothers." Since he has become acquainted with the Gilyak classificatory system, he is inclined to interpret the expression "mothers" as "class-mothers" in distinction from the real mother, that is, the mother and her sisters.

[20] Vladimir Il'ich Iokhel'son [Waldemar Jochelson], *Materialy po izucheniiu iukagirskago iazyka i fol'klora* (St. Petersburg: Imperatorskaia Akademiia Nauk, 1900), 48, 50.

[21] [**Editor's note:** The AMNH English version dropped the last sentence regarding *punalua* from its translation. It is found in all three Russian versions.]

TWO

GILYAK KINSHIP IN A SIBERIAN FRAME[1]

[4–9; 33–44; 132–136; 62–68]

IT IS INTERESTING to see what relation the Gilyak system of nomenclatures has to those of neighboring peoples such as the Ainu, the Tungus of the Amur region, the northern Paleo-Asiatics, and the Ural-Altaic group of peoples in general. During the long-standing process of communication between the Gilyak and their neighbors, some borrowing must undoubtedly have taken place [63].

Comparing the Gilyak terms of relationship with those of the so-called "Ural-Altaians" and "Paleo-Asiatics," we find the following groups of analogies.[2]

1. The largest of these groups shows forms which often occur in the terms for "parents." I refer to the combinations *pa, ap, ta, at,* for "father," and *ma, am, na, an,* for "mother." From the time of Buschman onwards these have been held to have

---

[1] [**Editor's note:** Earlier titles for this chapter include: "The Classificatory Kinship System" (AMNH Russian typescript) and "Kinship Terms and Forms" (Shternberg, *Giliaki,* and Shternberg, *Sem'ia*). The AMNH English typescript called it "Relations between Gilyak Terms of Relationship and Those Used by Neighboring Tribes." I have simplified this last version. While I verified the use of Gilyak words in this chapter and elsewhere with Gilyak (Nivkh) speakers, the difficulties of confirming the additional 19th century terms of address from the many languages here has meant that I have deferred to both Shternberg's handwritten insertions to the AMNH Russian typescript and Shternberg, *Sem'ia*. It is hoped that the reader will forgive any errors. Ethnonyms are those used by Shternberg, with Library of Congress terms shown in brackets at first usage.

In this chapter, as elsewhere, earlier versions differ widely. A shorter version of this chapter, containing no tables, is found in the AMNH Russian version, 4–9, complete with handwritten insertions by Shternberg; Koshkin followed this in *Giliaki,* 132–136. The AMNH English typescript, by contrast, devises a series of lists to present more extensive linguistic terminological comparison; these are closely, but not exactly, reproduced by Koshkin in Shternberg, *Sem'ia*. I defer to the content of the AMNH Russian typescript and the form of the AMNH English typescript for their extra detail.

This version does not include four opening paragraphs found in Shternberg, *Sem'ia,* 62–63 (corresponding to the three opening paragraphs in *Giliaki* 133–134), comparing Gilyak kin terms to Ainu and Tungus (Evenk) analogues. That both 1933 editions list Koshkin (Al'kor) as editor, yet contain these and many other divergences, suggests that the work of Shternberg's posthumous editorial commission was truly a collective enterprise.]

[2] This comparative study is founded partly on my own studies among the Tungus [Evenk] and Ainu, partly on the works of Radlov, Castren, and many others, as well as on personal information kindly given to me by many reliable investigators of different Siberian tribes. The material on the northern Paleo-Asiatics is taken mostly from the works of Messrs. Bogoraz and Iokhel'son.

31

sprung up everywhere independently from the language of children, and are called by him "natural sounds" (German, *Naturlaute*).[3]

Since there are many languages that do not have *Naturlaute*—as for instance the Gilyak—I regard the analogies as due rather to mutual interaction than to a spontaneous origin from the language of children.

In the Gilyak language we find the following phonetic combinations of Buschman's scheme:

(a) *at* in the terms *atk* or *atak, atik, adr, edr* (*k* and *r* are suffixes), meaning "uncle," "grandfather," "father-in-law;" *it* or *itk* (rarely *ota*), meaning "father," "paternal uncle"; *ik*, "old man."

Analogous terms occur in Tungus languages. It is suggestive that they have also the same suffix *k* [**64**].

> *atki* (northern Tungus), "father" and "elder brother."
> *etk* (Amur Tungus), "uncle," "elder brother of father."
> *itki* (Amgun Tungus) [Negidal], "father-in-law."
> *idiki* (Ulchi) [Nanai],[4] "husband's junior brother."
> *adi* (Gol'd) [Nanai], "husband."
> *ide'k* (Turukhansk Tungus), "uncle."
> *itsi* (Amur Gol'd) [Nanai], "paternal uncle."
> *atki* (Orochon), "wife's father."
> *otki* (Transbaikai Tungus), "father-in-law."
> *at-anga, anga* being a suffix (Ulchi, Orochi), "grandmother."

In Turkic and Finnish languages we have, all with the meaning "father,"

> *ata* (Kyrgyz) [Kirghiz].
> *atsa* (Altaic).[5]
> *Ati, ata* (Ostiak)[Khant].
> *atte* (Chuvash).
> *atai* (Votiak) [Udmurt].
> *aca* (Cheremiss) [Mari].
> *äcci* (Old Turkish, "paternal uncle" (cf. Gilyak *ik*).

In the Mongol language, belonging to this group, is the term *otok*, a division of the clan.

In the Paleo-Asiatic languages we find

> *a'te* (Chukchi), "father."
> *athak, adak* (Aleut), "father."

---

[3]   Buschman, *Über dem Naturlaut* (Abhandlungen der Academie der Wissenschaften zu Berlin, 1852).

[4]   [***Editor's note:*** The Library of Congress references Ulchi, who the 1989 Soviet census listed the nationality of 3233 people as Nanai.]

[5]   [***Editor's note:*** Shternberg, *Sem'ia*, lists only "Altaitsy" (Altai), but I have switched this to Altaic to recognize the many different peoples who identify themselves under this rubric. For more on the Altaic family, see Ronald Wixman, *The Peoples of the USSR: An Ethnographic Handbook* (Armonk: M. E. Sharpe, 1984), 9–10.]

atsa (Ainu), "uncle."
etsi'e (Yukaghir), "father."
atsitse (Koriak), "grandfather."

(b) *ap* in the term *app* (*appak, appik*). In Gilyak this term is a synonym of *atk* (see above), and should be regarded as borrowed directly from the Tungus language because it is mainly used by those Gilyak bordering closely on the Tungus tribes. Similar terms are found in all Ural-Altaic and Paleo-Asiatic languages:

Tungus

apa (Amgun), "uncle."
apanga', -nga being a suffix (Orochi, Orok, Ulchi), "uncle" (father's senior), "grandfather," "wife's brother," "husband's elder brother," sometimes "father."

Turkic

apa, aba (Altaic), "father."
abaga (Yakut), "paternal uncle," "maternal grandfather."

Mongolian

aba (Khakhass), "father."
abre' (Buriat), "paternal uncle."

Paleo-Asiatic

apa (Ainu), "father."
a'pa (Chukchi), "father."
apats (Kamchadal), "father."

It is noteworthy that *appa* with the meaning "father" occurs also in northwestern America (Athabaskan) and among the Dravidians, the classificatory system of which stands very close to that of the Gilyak.

(c) *na* occurs only in the term *nana* (*nanak*), "elder sister," "paternal aunt." Among the neighboring nations an analogy is to be found only in the Ainu term.

nana (Ainu), "mother."

(d) *im, um, om*, in the Gilyak terms *imk, uma, oma* ("mother"), *um* (*ga*) ("woman"), find analogies in

uma (Birar Tungus), "elder brother's wife."
imkhi (Gol'd), "wife's sister."
ama, in some Tungus dialects "mother"; in others, "father."

Turkic

yimik (Chuvash), "younger sister."
amakh (Yakut), "old woman."

Mongolian

omok, "a division of the clan."

Paleo-Asiatic

ama (Koriak), "grandmother."

(e) *an* in the Gilyak terms *ankh, ang'rei* (female, "wife") has analogies in

Tungus

ine, "mother,"

Turkic

ana', ina (Yakut), "female," "mother."
yinge' (Chuvash), "senior brother's wife," "paternal junior uncle's wife"
    [65].

Finnish

ana', "mother."

Paleo-Asiatic

anak (Aleut), "mother."

2. Among the terms that have no relation to Buschman's *Naturlaute*, I mention, in the first place, the Gilyak terms

(a) *aki* (adj. from *akand*, vocative *aka'*), "elder brother" or "elder sister." This term is familiar to all Ural-Altaic languages. In many cases the similarity covers not only the root (*ak*), but also the suffix (*i, n, nd*).

In the Tungus language we find the following analogies, all meaning "elder brother" or "paternal uncle" (more frequently the junior paternal uncle):

akha, aki (Ulchi).
akhi (Amgun) [Negidal].
aki (Orochon).
aki, akan, akin (northern Tungus).
akind (Birar).

In Mongolian we have:

akee' (Buriat), every person older than the speaker.

In Turkic:

aga, aka, axi'n, asu'n (common forms), "elder brother."
ara (Yakut), "elder," "father."
akka, ara'i, "elder sister."

In Finnish:

aki (Vogul) [Mansi], "paternal uncle." In the Ainu language we find the
    same term *aki*, but with the meaning "younger brother."

(b) *er*, a designative term meaning "father," bears a striking similarity to the Turkic *ar* and Mongolian *er, ere*, both signifying "male," "man," "hero" (Turkic), and "male adult" (Mongolian). There is good reason to suppose that this term has been borrowed, because in Gilyak *er* with the meaning "father" is but a subsidiary term of reverence, whereas the original term in all dialects is *itk.*

(c) *yirk, izn,* "mother." This term, like the preceding, may be supposed to have been borrowed, for it is a subsidiary term to *imk.* In the Mongolian we find a similar term, *izi,* also meaning "mother."

(d) *oglan, ola* ("son," "child") coincide with the Turkic *o'glan ogli* ("young man," "boy") and *ol* ("son").

(e) *kivung* ("brother" in relation to sister) may well be related to the term *khibun* ("son," "young man"), so far found by me only in the Buriat language. It is likely that we shall find similar terms in other Ural-Altaic languages.

(f) *askh* (W.D. *atsik*), "younger brother," is analogous to the Tungus (Birar dialect) *atskha'* ("father's younger brother").

(g) *tuvng* may be analogous to the Chuvash term *tuvan* (Kyrgyz, *tugan*), "relation."

(h) *atsk* (*ar*, root; *k,* suffix) or *asi*[6] (dialect of the eastern coast of Sakhalin), "grandmother," "maternal uncle's wife," "mother-in-law," recalls the Tungus terms *atki* (Orochon), "husband's mother;" *asi* (Amur, Transbaikalia), "wife"; *asi* (Turukhansk), "wife."

(i) *pilan* (*pi* root, *lan* usual suffix for adjectives), "father's younger brother," "elder," may be related to the term *piy* with the same meaning in the Yakut and Chuvash languages and with the meaning "elder," "chief," "superior," in other Turkic languages.

3. The following Gilyak terms have undoubtedly been borrowed from neighboring Tungus tribes:

> *okon,* "husband."
> *ivi, ive,* "brother's wife" (speaker being male).
> *ora,* "son" or "brother-in-law."

These terms are in use exclusively among the western Gilyak, who are neighbors of the Ulchi, and who have intermarried with them. But these Gilyak have conserved at the same time the corresponding original Gilyak terms *pu* and *imgi.* It is interesting to note that the term *okon* ("husband") occurs also in the Ainu in the form *oko* with the same meaning. At the same time there is no reason for thinking that this form has been borrowed, for the Ainu terms are completely isolated from those of their neighbors.

Summarizing the data just given, it appears that the Gilyak terms which are analogous to those of other languages may be grouped into three categories. The first is the category of Buschman's scheme—terms originally covering the idea of "father"

---

[6] The change from *s* to *ts* is very common in the Gilyak dialects; for instance, the term *askh* ("junior") in the Eastern dialect changes to *atsik* in the Western dialect.

and "mother." Against the general opinion that such terms are always independent spontaneous formations derived from the language of children (especially that such terms must be the most ancient and original elements of every tongue), I am inclined to think that during the long process of migration and diffusion, they with many other terms may have been transmitted from tribe to tribe, undergoing (at the same time) manifest changes in the process. Abundant illustrations of such a possibility in the most striking forms are very often furnished through linguistics. In the Osman language, for instance, such fundamental terms as "father" and "mother" have foreign origin: "father" (*peder*) from the Persian and "mother" (*valide*) from the Arabic. In another Turkic language (Taranchi) [Uighur], one single term is borrowed from the Persian: "sister" (*khvar*). We see the same phenomenon in the Finnish languages, where also the single term for "sister" (*sisar, siessa,* etc.) is of Aryan origin. Another example is still more instructive. In a tundra clan of the Yukaghir, which has been in close contact with the Lamut [Even], we find that the four most fundamental terms of relationship—"father" (*ama'*), "mother" (*ana'*), "elder brother" (*aka'*), "elder sister" (*aka'*)—have been borrowed from the Tungus. The majority of all the other terms have remained pure Yukaghir. Mr. Iokhel'son, who has described these facts, is quite right in seeing the explanation of this strange case of partial borrowing in the circumstance that the borrowed terms correspond in meaning to the Yukaghir ones, while in all other respects the Yukaghir system of relationships is sharply distinguished from that of the Tungus [66].[7]

So much for the first group of similarities of Buschman's type. The same may be said with still more reason of the second group, especially about such terms as *aki, og'la, kivung,* etc. To deny the common origin of these similarities would be very difficult, for the explanation of the fact lies on the very surface. There is sufficient historical evidence to show that all the nations of the Ural-Altaian group (the Turk, the Tungus, the Finn, the Mongol) were in close connection in former times and influenced one another extensively. The Tungus tribes, the nearest neighbors of the Paleo-Asiatics, were the mediators between the Ural-Altaian group and the Paleo-Asiatics, especially the Gilyak, to whom they were nearest. As for the third group of similarities (*okon, ora,* etc.), nothing can be added to what has been said above. They are used only by a small part of the Gilyak and are undoubtedly borrowings of relatively recent origin, brought about through intermarriages with the Amur Tungus. Thus in the general system of relationship of the Gilyak, only the first two groups should be taken into consideration for purposes of comparison. Nevertheless, whatever the origin of the similarities between the Gilyak and the Tungus-Turkic terms of relationship might be—whether accidental coincidences or the result of ethnic interaction—the number of unquestionable borrowings is so small that the complex nomenclature of relationship remains essentially independent not only in content but in its lexical character as well. When we consider that the process of amalgamation of the Gilyak with their neighbors has been continuous, it really seems remarkable that the various terminologies of relationship should have so little in common. The originality of the Gilyak terminology is attested to

---

[7] Iokhel'son, *Materialy*, 240.

by the etymology of the Gilyak terms of relationship, for the majority of them can be traced to their original roots, which indicates their stability through long periods of time.[8] Here are a few examples:

> The group *itk, ittutk* ("father"), *ut-gu,* W.D., *gu* being a suffix ("man"), *atk* ("grandfather," "maternal uncle"), *itik, atsik* ("grandmother," "aunt"), *itskh* ("old man, " "husband"), has the common root *ut, it* ("body"). The group *imk, uma, oma* ("Mother"), *um-gu,* W.D. ("woman," "wife"), *imgi* ("son-in-law," "sister's son"), has the common root *um.* Then we have *ang'rei,* "wife" (from *ankh,* "female"); *azmits,* "beloved one," "husband," "man" (from *ar,* "male"; and the verb *mits,* "to be, to become"); *sank, sankh, rankh,* "woman"' and *ranrsh,* "sister"; etc. [**67**].

A few words must be said regarding the differences in dialect for kinship terms. These differences are of secondary character. In the primary terms there are either no differences at all (the terms *itk, imk, pu, ivn, ang'rei, nanakh, ranrsh, imgi,* etc., are quite the same in all dialects) or they show differences of slight phonetic character (as, for instance, *atak-atk; itik atsk; ruf-ruvn' ola-og'la, eglan; amalakhmalk;* and so on). In those cases where the terms are quite distinct phonetically, this is due either to borrowing from the nearest neighbors, as in *app* and *ivei* which were mentioned before, or to the derivation of the given term from different synonyms common to all dialects. Thus, for instance, *sankh* ("women") in the Eastern dialect has been derived from the common word *ankh* ("female"), while in the Western dialect *umgu* ("woman") is a derivative of the common word *im(k), uma, oma* ("mother"); similarly, *utgu* ("man") in the Western dialect is of the same root as *itk, utk* ("father"), while the corresponding term in the Eastern dialect, *azmits,* is associated with *ar* ("male").

We are now ready to consider the question of the relationship of the Gilyak nomenclature to that of the neighboring tribes. The latter, to judge from the bulk of the Gilyak terminology, must be looked upon in general as original and independent. As for the similarities in some of the terms, they relate almost exclusively to the Ural-Altaic peoples, especially to the Tungus tribes, whereas with Ainu terminology the Gilyak has almost nothing in common. The few similarities indicated above may certainly be regarded as merely accidental. This statement corresponds fully to historical data, as well as to the data on family organization and system of relationship of these people. The Gilyak are by origin a continental tribe, later moving to Sakhalin, where they first met the Ainu in relatively recent times. Up to the present time, intermarriage between the Gilyak and the Ainu has been very rare. The differences in the social organization of the two tribes is very great. The Ainu, in contrast to the strict agnatic principles of the Gilyak, count their relationship through the mother and are imbued with principles of matriliny. Their sexual norms are strictly individual, group

---

8   This stability is unusual among many historic peoples. Thus V. V. Radlov, the well-known student of Turkic languages, tells me that according to Orochon and Uighur monuments, the Turkic kin terminology, excepting one or two terms, has undergone a complete change since the beginning of the 10th century, with even such terms as "father" and "mother" being affected. It will suffice to compare the Old-Turkic *kan* ("father") with the modern *aba.*

marriages being wholly unknown. Thus since their kinship systems are diametrically opposed, the borrowing of terms could not easily have taken place.

However, the situation changes completely in relation to the Tungus. The Gilyak have from the oldest times lived in close contact with them on the continent. Intermarriage, especially on the borders of the Gilyak territory, is a common occurrence; most importantly, the Tungus have an agnatic clan, a classificatory system, and norms of group marriage similar in many respects to those of the Gilyak. Lastly, almost every Gilyak speaks a Tungus language. Under such favorable conditions, it is but natural that some borrowing takes place, which in every case must have been easier than between the Gilyak and the Ainu, wholly divided by their language and social system.

The influence of the Tungus extended itself not only to the mechanical adaptation of terms, but psychologically as well. In the Gilyak terminology there are some terms etymologically of true Gilyak origin, but formed in accordance with Tungus norms of sexual relations. Thus, according to the Tungus norms, a man has marital rights to his junior paternal uncle's wife. Therefore, I (being male) call my junior paternal uncle by the same term (ara, "elder") as my elder brother. On the other hand, according to the Gilyak norms, I must call my paternal junior uncle "father"; but under the Tungus influence, among one part of the Gilyak, besides the term itk, an additional term has been invented—pilan ("elder")—a literal translation of the Tungus term aga'. Or to take another example, the Gilyak have two terms for designating "elder sister," aki and nanakh. The latter is not only superfluous but leads to confusion in terminology, because nanakh is at the same time a term for one's father's sister. This strange fact can only be explained as due to the influence of the Tungus, with whom one's father's sister and one's elder sister stand to a man in the same matrimonial relation as his potential mothers-in-law.

THREE

Norms of Sex and Marriage in Light of Classificatory Kinship[1]

[26–35; 45–61; 149–161; 75–82]

LET US NOW EXAMINE the extent to which the classificatory kinship system corresponds to modern norms of sexual intercourse and marriage. Among the Gilyak,
at the present time at least, there is no question of any general prohibition of extramarital sexual intercourse. Sexual intercourse with a woman is to the Gilyak a natural act, as insignificant morally as any other natural act answering the well-known
needs of man. Prohibitions and limitations extend only to definite groups of persons
bound by agnatic or cognatic relationship. Outside of these groups, sexual intercourse
is not subject to any regulation, nor to religious or public condemnation [75].

Besides the prohibitions determined by relationship, extramarital intercourse
knows only one restriction, the reactions of the concerned persons. The young men
of a clan who have access to the women of a certain locality, when displeased with
a usurper, may give full vent to their resentment for his trespassing. Such cases are,
however, very rare. The consequences are much more serious when a married woman
is the source of trouble. A stranger caught in *flagrante delicto* with a married woman
is killed by the husband on the spot. Such at least was the custom until recently. The
fear of Russian criminal law has of late somewhat curbed these impulsive murders,
so that they have been replaced by duels and ransoms. The woman in such cases suffers much less. Although she is badly beaten, murder is never committed because she
is always considered her husband's cognate; having sometimes cost her husband a considerable sum, she represents an object of great value as a working hand. However,
all this refers exclusively to cases where a married woman is in question. Sexual intercourse with an unmarried woman or a widow, when it takes place with the woman's
consent, evokes no reaction even on the part of her father or brothers although they
are much interested in the bride-price received when the woman marries. I have
never heard of reprisals being taken in such cases. Action is taken by the woman's
kin only when a duel or a ransom may be expected. Nor are there at present any prohibitions against the marriage of persons not bound by any kin ties.

This attitude changes completely in regard to persons connected by the
classificatory terms of relationship. Then an elaborate system of restrictions and

---

[1] [**Editor's note:** Earlier titles for this chapter include "The Classificatory System of Relationship and the Norms of Sexual Intercourse and Marriage" (AMNH English and Russian typescripts, and the 1933 Soviet versions).]

prohibitions appears which coincides fully with the nomenclature of relationship. Only those persons have the right to sexual intercourse and marriage with each other who, according to the established class terminology, belong respectively to the classes *pu* and *ang'rei*, that is, the persons who from birth are "husbands" and "wives" to each other. All other classes are covered by an absolute prohibition.

But who are these prohibited classes?[2] In the first place, the large class *khal*, that is, the persons born to a common agnatic clan. Among the agnates, as shown above, there are no classes which stand to each other in the relations of *pu* and *ang'rei*. The Gilyak clan is absolutely exogamic; marriage and sexual intercourse of agnates within a clan is impossible. In this connection we must categorically contradict von Schrenck's statement that the Gilyak clan is endogamous. "The fact of belonging to a clan," says von Schrenck, "plays no part whatever in the most important aspect of their life, namely marriage; . . . the Gilyak fully sanction marriages between members of one and the same clan."[3] In another place he expresses this still more definitely: "Marriage is prohibited only to real brothers and sisters and to the children of real brothers."[4] This entirely erroneous assertion, emanating from an investigator who spent 2 years among the Gilyak, would be incomprehensible were it not for the fact that von Schrenck did not speak the Gilyak language and therefore needed the assistance of an interpreter. My own dealings with the Gilyak for many years, and my intensive study of their language and matrimonial laws, make it possible for me to contradict categorically von Schrenck's assertion that among persons born in one clan, marriage and sexual intercourse are allowed. During my long sojourn among the Gilyak and my intimate communication with them, I never saw or heard about even an exceptional infringement of exogamy. The abhorrence of sexual intercourse among clansmen, even the most remote, is as great among the Gilyak as the feeling in our own society against intercourse between brothers and sisters or father and daughter [**76**].[5]

Let us now consider in detail the classes between whom sexual intercourse and marriage is forbidden.

ASCENDING AND DESCENDING GENERATIONS. These are persons who call each other *atk, atskh, itk, pilang, imk, nankh,* and *og'la*—grandfathers and grandmothers, fathers and mothers, agnatic and cognatic uncles and aunts, on the one side, and their descendants, on the other. Intercourse is thus prohibited between persons of ascending and descending generations in the direct and most remote collateral lines. Sexual inter-

---

2   [**Editor's note:** Shternberg follows Morgan's use of "classes" to describe intermarrying divisions. "Sections" was later more commonly adopted in analyses of Australian and other kinship systems to avoid the connotations of hierarchy. Richard Lester Hiatt, *Arguments about Aborigines: Australia and the Evolution of Social Anthropology* (Cambridge: Cambridge Univ. Press, 1996), 42.]

3   Von Schrenck, *Reisen,* Vol. II, 23–24.

4   Ibid., 6.

5   I once saw among the Golds on the Amur a village inhabited by ancient Gilyak colonists who were now for centuries true Golds by culture and language. They had never seen their clansmen from the lower Amur, but they preserved carefully the tradition of their clan, mainly in the fear that they might eventually contract marriage with their clansmen.

course is thus impossible between uncles and nieces, aunts and nephews, the same applying to their *tuvng* classes, in the agnatic as well as in the cognatic lines. The interdict in these lines and in general to persons of different generations is not limited to persons of both sexes inside the above groups, but extends to those who are married to these persons, and also to those who, according to the nomenclature of relationship, stand to them in the relation of *pu* and *ang'rei*. Thus for instance my (I being male) paternal uncle can have no sexual intercourse either with my wife or with my wife's most distant collateral sister, even if the latter were married to a man from a strange clan, for I call her *ang'rei* (wife). Similarly I cannot have sexual intercourse either with my paternal uncle's wife or with his wife's sister, even if married to a stranger, for she is my *imk* ("mother").

To realize the full range of this prohibition, it should be borne in mind that the sisters of a man's father's wife, as well as their husbands, belong to that man's ascending generation, for they are his "mothers" and "fathers." It must therefore be understood that the above prohibitions between persons of ascending and descending generations is not really limited to persons of different generations. The distinction of generations is purely nominal. We have seen that in the classificatory system, the same terms—*it, imk, atk, atsk* ("father," "mother," "grandfather," "uncle")—are used in reference to persons of the first ascending generation (the actual father and mother, etc.) as well as to their "brothers" and "sisters." In such a system the significance of generations and that of real age must obviously be obscured. The father's brother or sister may be younger than the person speaking, but they are nevertheless his "father" and "mother." The prohibitions imposed by the classificatory system must hold.

TUVNG. This class consists of two groups: the descendants of agnatic brothers and male cousins, and the descendants of agnatic sisters and female cousins. Within each of these two groups, in all generations, sexual intercourse and marriage are absolutely prohibited. In neither of these groups are there persons who call each other *pu* and *ang'rei*; they are in every generation all *tuvng*. I have noticed only one exception among the descendants of sisters (and that only in a few clans, namely, if the sisters are married to men who are strangers to each other): The prohibition extends only to the first two generations. But this is merely a local deviation due no doubt to the fact that when women are very scarce, it is difficult to carry out the letter of the law. As a rule, however, it is strictly followed [77].

The sex taboos within the above group have entered deeply into the life and thought of the Gilyak.[6] They are adhered to even in the most distant degrees of relationship, such as the so-called *tilgund tuvng*, "the traditional agnatic cousin." The Gilyak, in fact, believe that these conditions are so completely in accord with nature that they even extend to their one domestic animal, the dog. They believe that among dogs, brothers and sisters do not copulate. The rare exceptions are ascribed to the influence of *milk* (evil spirits). Therefore, when a Gilyak happens to witness the

---

6   [***Editor's note:*** Shternberg uses the Russian *tabu* in the AMNH Russian typescript; while the milder *zapret*, prohibition, is used in the 1933 Soviet publications.]

incestuous act, he must kill the dog, or the guilt will fall on himself. The killing of the dog is a religious ceremony—he is strangled and his blood is sprinkled towards the four quarters of the world. For the dog, however, this procedure is merely punishment for incest. It is curious to note that incest between dogs of ascending and descending generations is tolerated by the Gilyak. May we not see the reason thereof in the fact that this prohibition is of later origin than the one between persons of the same generation?[7]

COGNATIC COUSINS (MALE AND FEMALE). Only cognatic cousins [cross-cousins] will be considered here, that is, a brother's children in their relation to a sister's children, and vice versa; for the brothers and sisters are *tuvng* to each other, and the categorical prohibition within these groups has already been discussed. We know from the kinship terminology that the terms applied by cognate cousins to each other depend on whether they are the sons or daughters of the mother's brother or of the father's sister. For example, I (being male) call my mother's brother's daughter *ang'rei* ("wife"), and am called by her *pu* ("husband"), but my sister calls my mother's brother's son *akhmalk* ("mother's clansman," German, *Gevatter*) or *atk, navkh* ("uncle," "cousin") and is called by him *nern* in return, the terms used not being matrimonial at all. Thus sexual intercourse and marriage between a sister's daughter and her brother's son, the same applying to their *tuvng*, are strictly prohibited. On the other hand, marriages between a sister's son and a brother's daughter are not only allowed, but are considered the only orthodox ones. In that case, as in all other instances discussed, the terms "brother" and "sister" are class terms, that is, the norms applied to the children of brother and sister extend to the children of brothers and sisters of the most distant degrees of kinship. Therefore exchange marriage between the children of "brother" and "sister," as practiced among the Tungus, cannot take place here. For all *tuvng* classes, a sister's sons have a right to her brother's daughters, but a brother's sons are prohibited to his sister's daughters. As we shall see in the following section, the above norms, which seem to be of special character, referring only to brothers and sisters, in reality play a dominant role in regulating the sexual relations of entire clans.

THE AKHMALK AND IMGI CLANS. Special attention must be paid to the remarkable fact that the sexual norms regulating the relations between the children of a "brother" (own and collateral) and a "sister" (own and collateral) extend not only to their own children but to both clans in their entirety. The rights and prohibitions relating to the children of a brother and a sister extend to all generations of both clans, that is, the clan of the brother and the clan of his sister's husband. Thus in each generation all men of the *tuvng* class in the sister's husband's clan, and all women *tuvng* in the brother's clan, are from birth *pu* and *ang'rei* to each other and actually have the right of sexual intercourse and of marriage; whereas, on the other hand, the men of the brother's clan, and the women of the sister's husband's clan, including the wives of his clansmen, are in all generations absolutely prohibited to each other. This strict-

---

7   [**Editor's note:** As Lydia Black has suggested, this becomes more compelling if we speculate on the possibility of every Gilyak having a canine alter-ego. For more on dog symbolism among Gilyak (Nivkh), see Lydia Black, "Dogs, Bears and Killer Whales: An Analysis of the Nivkh Symbolic System," Ph.D. diss., Univ. of Massachusetts, Amherst, 1973.]

ly corresponds to the kinship terminology. The men of the sister's clan (*akhmalk* clan) have among the women of her husband's clan (*imgi* clan) either *nern* or *atsk nanakh, tuvng* (the latter three among the wives of the *imgi*), but never *ang'rei* ("wife"). Thus it suffices for one woman to be married into a given clan, and that all women belonging to that clan become prohibited to all her clansmen [78].

Let a man of clan A marry a woman of clan B. Then, although the woman and her clan may be strangers to clan A, the same relations are established between the two clans as if the bridegroom's father-in-law were his mother's brother. The entire class of female *tuvng* in each generation of the father-in-law's clan are the "wives" of the male *tuvng* of the son-in-law's clan. Conversely, all women of the latter are prohibited to the former. Thus *atk, akhmalk* applies to mother's brother as well as to wife's father in general, while *imgi* ("son-in-law") also means "sister's son" or any man from the sister's husband's clan.

The above norms often lead to very complicated situations. Let us suppose as is so often the case that individual members of clan A take wives from several different clans and, in their turn, give the women of their own clan to men of different clans. Then clan A and all those other clans become subject to the same prohibition as applied when only two clans intermarry. All women of clan A are prohibited to all clans from which the members of clan A have taken wives; and, conversely, all women belonging to the clans who have taken wives from clan A are prohibited to the men of clan A. The situation is further complicated by another restriction. Clan B, from which clan A takes wives, takes wives from clan C. Then clan C has become *akhmalk* ("wife's father") to B as well as to A. Therefore the women of A are prohibited not only to B, A's direct *akhmalk,* but also to C, which as we have seen is called, in distinction from B, *tuyma akhmalk* ("distant wife's father"). However, there is another aspect to this very severe rule. The number of clans prohibited to A increases with each new clan the members of which take wives from A. But with each new clan from which the members of A in their turn take wives, a large class of accessible women (*ang'rei*, "wives") is added to the other clans. In spite of this, the extension of prohibitions to many *akhmalk* clans leads to considerable difficulties among a people numbering scarcely four and a half thousand. This extension resulted in a partial modification. If a man takes a wife from a strange clan and not from his old *akhmalk* clan, the restrictions are often limited to only two generations; in cases where the wife dies childless, the restrictions are dropped even in the second generation.

THE CLASS IOKH. There remains one more class to be discussed, the class *iokh*. As we have seen, the term *iokh* applies to two quite distinct classes of women: (1) the wives of a man's descendants (*og'la*), and (2) among the eastern Gilyak, the wives of his *askh*, that is, younger brothers (*tuvng*). The restrictions in regard to the first class have already been discussed under those of the ascending and descending generations. Prohibitions relating to the second class are less absolute. As we have seen in our list of terminologies, different localities use different terms to designate the wife of a junior *tuvng*. In several places on the Amur, on the continental coast, and on the northwestern coast of Sakhalin, only one term is used for the wives of the younger and older brother, namely *ang'rei* ("wife"). In those localities sexual intercourse is permitted with all "wives" of "brothers." In all others where the term *iokh* is used to designate the wife of the younger male *tuvng*, sexual intercourse with the latter is strictly forbidden. For the present we must consider this prohibition as dominant. However, there is good reason for believing that the terms as well as the norms of sexual intercourse were originally the same for all "wives" of "brothers." This conviction is also supported by the fact that even in those localities where sexual relations with "wives" of younger "brothers" are not prohibited, children call the "wives" of all father's "brothers" *imk,* the term used also for their own mother. In many places they call all father's brothers *itk* ("father"). Hence, we must conclude that in olden times sexual rights extended to the "wives" of all "brothers" without distinction [**79**].

THE NORMS OF LAWFUL SEXUAL INTERCOURSE. We know from the nomenclature of relationships, which corresponds perfectly to actual conditions, that entire groups of men call entire groups of women their "wives" and vice versa. In our own nomenclature such groups of men and women simply stand to each other in the relationship of marriage. Before examining more closely a type of marriage which seems so strange to us, it is necessary, to avoid misunderstandings, to carefully analyze the meaning of the term "marriage."

The three main factors of marriage are sexual intercourse, the production of offspring, and common economic activity. It is obvious, however, that only the first of these factors, sexual intercourse, may be considered essential. The other two factors, of course, play a highly important part in the marital union, but they may also be entirely lacking. Marriages occur which remain without progeny; there are also marriages which do not aim at economical considerations. But neither does sexual intercourse, however continual it may be, constitute marriage. Sexual intercourse, in order to become marriage, must in some way or other be sanctioned by the social milieu. It must have social or religious sanction; in a word, it must be lawful. The lawfulness of sexual intercourse thus constitutes the essential factor of marriage. This point at least is peculiar to the institution of marriage among the most diverse peoples and in the most diverse stages of development. If differences exist we have to look for them in the concrete forms assumed by sexual intercourse within marriage among different peoples. These forms often strongly differ from our own standards, a fact which tends to obscure greatly the concept of marriage whenever we have to deal with various forms of sexual intercourse among primitive peoples. Our interpretation of primitive marriage is most frequently vitiated by the modern concept that marriage necessarily presupposes permanent cohabitation and the regular exercise of marital prerogatives.

As a matter of fact, among many primitive and historic peoples this element was not considered at all essential. Among the Spartans, for instance, the women lived separately from the men, and married couples had to arrange secret meetings.[8] Similar conditions still prevail among many primitive people who have the so-called *Männerbund,* where the male members of the society, including the married ones,

---

8   [***Editor's note:*** Shternberg, *Giliaki,* and Shternberg, *Sem'ia,* end the paragraph here. The AMNH Russian typescript contains one additional line by Shternberg, "O nekotorykh amerikansk. indeitsakh razskazyvaet Lafiteau." It is not clear who produced the Männerbund and Lafiteau references.]

FIG. 10. Gilyak men, center and right, meet Russian officials at a bank in Aleksandrovsk, 1890s. Photo by Lev Shternberg. *Source:* AAN f. 282, o. 2, d. 161, l. 10.

live in communal dwellings. Such is the case, for instance, on the Fiji Islands, where man and wife are permitted to meet only secretly in the night. Says Lafiteau concerning several American Indian tribes, "Ils n'osent pas aller dans les cabanes particulières ou habitent leur épouses que durant l'obscurité de la nuit" [80].[9]

Among other people such as the Ainu, a woman often remains for years in her father's house after she is married, while the husband, who lives in another remote village, visits his wife only during certain seasons of the year.[10] Among the Kirghiz a husband will for years visit his wife only at night, and without the knowledge of her parents, until the bride-price is paid in full. Nor do we find more regularity among polygamists of the Moslem type. A Turk may have women in his harem with whom for years he has had no sexual intercourse, but these women are nevertheless considered his wives. Permanent cohabitation, however, and regular sexual intercourse become all but impossible among people whose social organization requires that entire groups of men consider entire groups of women their "wives" and vice versa, and where a man can do no more than exercise his rights whenever he has a chance to do so. In one of the Australian tribes, the Dieri, each *kumi* (a term corresponding to the Gilyak *pu*, "husband") finds his *kroki* ("wife") within the entire extent of his territory, no matter to what village he goes. A *kumi* may never have occasion to see one or another of his innumerable *kroki*, but she is nevertheless his wife; for if he chances to visit her village he may exercise his rights without laying himself open

---

[9]   "They dare not to enter the special huts of their mates except during the cover of night." Westermarck, *Geschichte der menschlichen Ehe* (Jena: H. Costenoble, 1893), 151–152.

[10] [***Editor's note:*** By contrast, Shternberg indicates that Ainu do not have men's associations. Shternberg, *Sem'ia,* 180.]

to the criticism of the community, the wrath of the gods, or the resentment of the individual husband of his *kroki*.[11]

Such relations, notwithstanding the absence of permanent cohabitation and of regular sexual intercourse, have a lawful character and must hence be recognized as marital relations. After Morgan, the current scientific designation for such relations is "group marriage," the distinctive feature of which is the potential for sexual relations.[12] This potential assumes various forms among different peoples. Sometimes they are of a strictly obligatory character, where neither party may refuse sexual intercourse to anyone who may lawfully demand it. Among the Chuckchi, a woman may not refuse her favors to a man who stands with her husband in the relation of "exchange marriage" [*peremennyi brak*]. Among others full sway is allowed to individual preferences, as, for instance, among the Dieri, the Tungus, and the Gilyak, where the consent of both parties is required for sexual intercourse. As soon as such consent is given, intercourse becomes lawful. This phenomenon is really the same as in pure polygamy, where the husband may favor or neglect one or another of his wives without in any way affecting the status of marriage. The same holds true of group marriage. Notwithstanding the disparity of habitat of the persons within a marriage group, as well as the merely potential character of their marital rights, sexual intercourse within that group is lawful; hence it is marriage.

Of course, permanent cohabitation and regular sexual intercourse must be admitted to be the most normal conditions for marriage. We find a tendency towards that direction, in varying degrees, among the most diverse peoples. This tendency, however, must be clearly differentiated from the pairing instinct. Sexual selection and sympathy between individuals may be the basis of some unions of greater or lesser duration. But such unions do not necessarily involve either individual possession or permanency of cohabitation. We have already cited the case of the Ainu whose wife often remained with her parents, sometimes several days' journey away from him, although marriage among the Ainu is strictly individual. Even more natural is the absence of these conditions among people who have group marriage. For in group marriage the number of persons among whom sexual intercourse is permitted is large, and hence cohabitation as well as the regular exercise of the right to sexual intercourse with all the members of the group can seldom be realized. Cohabitation and regular intercourse are determined not so much by the sexual side of marriage as by the development of a household. Wherever economic conditions necessitate the cooperation of a group of individuals and permit cohabitation, group marriage may assume the form of a regular communal union; but such conditions are rare in primitive communities. They may at times be realized among brothers. Here group marriage is in fact associated with cohabitation and the regular exercise of marital rights. We can find such cases among the Gilyak, among some of the Tungus tribes, in Tibet, and in India [**81**].

Contrary to the old view that the life of primitive man is largely communistic, I find that the primitive household, insofar as it provides for shelter, as well as the

---

[11] Lorimer Fison and K. W. Howitt, *Kamilaroi and Kurnai* (Melbourne: George Robinson, 1879), 340.

[12] [***Editor's note:*** The first two sentences of this paragraph are found only in the AMNH English typescript.]

preparation of food and clothing, is in the main an individual one. Only at certain periods of the year do cooperative enterprises such as hunting expeditions arise, later to disappear again when circumstances change. A typical example of an individual household we find among the reindeer-breeding Tungus, who congregate for a short period, perhaps twice a year in small kin groups. Most of the time they live far apart from one another, each one selecting his own particular territory for pasturage and hunting.

Among nonpastoral people who live more closely together, the household remains more or less individual. Under such conditions each individual householder would naturally desire to have a woman who would, according to the natural division of labor among the sexes in her tribe, share with him his daily toil. Regular cohabitation between one man and one or several women thus arises naturally. In societies where group marriage exists, such individual unions do not in the least affect general conditions. The individual wife lives permanently with her husband in the same house, works with him, helps to educate his children, and follows him wherever he chooses to go. But she may also extend her favors with impunity to an entire group of individuals who lawfully request them. Individual unions are favored by economic considerations as well as the potent factor of sexual selection, the mutual attraction between two individuals. In such a way there arise, on par with irregular marital group relations, individual unions which are sanctioned by the community. Here we have—to use an old but excellent definition from Howitt—"the most frequent modification of group marriage, in which the woman is specially possessed by one man, with the co-existence of potential possession by all other men of the same class."[13] Persons united in individual marriage are bound to each other not merely by regular sexual intercourse and coresidence, but by a common household economy and children. At the same time each of them is permitted to have sexual intercourse with individuals of his or her own marriage-group.

Such sexual relations—although irregular in character and taking place in secrecy, sometimes requiring for each sexual act the consent of both parties or a consideration of the preferential rights of the individual husband—must be classed as true marriage. They are sanctioned not only by society in general but also by the individual husband. This is not only theoretically the case but is in harmony with the legal worldview of these people. It is this ideology which brought forth the classificatory terminology which designates the individual spouse by the same name as the group spouse, and imposed on both of them the same marital obligations. If for instance an individual husband dies, a member of his marriage-group must take his place and provide for the widow, even if she is no longer fit for sexual intercourse. He must provide for her children, who are considered as belonging to all the members of the group. If a man's wife dies, her group-sister takes her place at the widower's hearth [**82**].

The above considerations will help us interpret the Gilyak marriage classes *pu* and *ang'rei*, to which we now turn.

---

[13]   Fison and Howitt, op cit., 340, 341. [**_Editor's note:_** This expository reference to Howitt is found in the AMNH English typescript only.]

FOUR

HUSBANDS AND WIVES[1]

[41–50; 62–71; 161–168; 82–86]

As INDICATED BEFORE, a Gilyak is permitted, at least presently, to have sexual intercourse or to marry a woman of his tribe who is not related to him in any way. In regard to such unrelated women, however, he has no rights whatever. Sexual intercourse occurs at the risk of bloody retaliation on the part of certain groups of men while individual marriage becomes merely a civil pact accompanied by payment of considerable purchase monies [82].

Quite different is the position of a man towards all those women who stand to him in the relation of *ang'rei* ("wife"). As we have seen, this category contains (1) all mother's brothers' daughters; (2) all his wife's "sisters"; (3) the "sisters" of his "brothers'" wives; (4) the individual wives of all *aki,* that is, wives of senior "brother" among the Gilyak of the Eastern dialect; (5) wives of all "brothers" without distinction of age among the Gilyak of the Western dialect; (6) every woman of his own generation belonging to his *akhmalk* clan. Every woman in her turn applies the term *pu* ("husband") to (1) all her father's sisters' sons; (2) all actual husbands of her "sisters," and the "brothers" of those husbands; and (3) all actual husband's junior "brothers," or in some localities, all her husband's "brothers." All these categories of "wives" and "husbands" are by no means nominal; they stand for two important and real rights: the right to sexual intercourse and the right to individual marriage.

As a rule the rights of a *pu* or an *ang'rei* belong to the individual from birth, but they may also be acquired through one's own or a clansman's marriage with a strange woman, that is, one completely unrelated to them. Thus a man may acquire a new *ang'rei* in the "sisters" of his own wife or his "brother's" wife and their sisters, who may have been until then complete strangers to him.

THE RIGHT TO INDIVIDUAL MARRIAGE. In the first place, the classes *pu* and *ang'rei* are united by their mutual and exclusive right to marriage. In other words, out of the entire

---

[1] [**Editor's note:** The title for this chapter in the English and Russian AMNH and 1933 Soviet versions is "The Pu and Ang'rei Classes." The AMNH Russian typescript organizes this as two separate chapters, the second being "The Right to Individual Marriage"—here a subheading, as in Shternberg, *Giliaki,* and Shternberg, *Sem'ia.* The two Soviet 1933 publications run this material as a subsection of the longer previous chapter, "The Classificatory Kinship System and Norms of Sexual Relations and Marriage."]

number of individuals covered by the kin terms, only members of these two groups have the right to individual marriage. All other classes are strictly forbidden to marry one another. Here the mnemonic-adjudicating significance [*mnemonisticheskii-razreshitel'noe znachenie*] plays a key role, for when the proper kin relations can become confused, a firm knowledge of the marrying classes serves as the only guarantee against transgression. Such mnemonic significance exerts more than a legal influence.[2] Marriage prohibitions, as we have seen, are also absent among individuals who are complete strangers to each other in the sense of formal kinship; yet to consider such people *pu* or *ang'rei* prior to their marriage is impossible. Indeed, the right to individual marriage between persons of the *pu* and *ang'rei* categories is not a simple *nudum jus.* It is a right, as well as an obligation and a debt, for both interested parties. This sense of obligation is seen most vividly between brothers and each other's wives, who stand in relation to each other as *pu* and *ang'rei.* As a rule, widows of "brothers," one's own and collateral, cannot leave the clan but become the wives of their husband's surviving brothers, sometimes even notwithstanding the surviving brothers' wishes. None of them can refuse the widow presented to them.[3] It is not, however, in levirate that we find the most typical trait of the juridico-matrimonial relations of the *pu* and *ang'rei.* Levirate marriage is a more or less exceptional phenomenon and comprises only one small category of the entire marriage class. The most characteristic functioning of the matrimonial rights and obligations of the *pu* and *ang'rei* must be looked for in the conditions of normal marriage [**83**].

The obligatory character of the bonds between the *pu* and *ang'rei* have been shaken in recent times by many causes of which we shall speak later. Although the modern Gilyak may marry a strange woman from a clan not related to him, it is not the orthodox form of marriage but instead is a mere purchase, for such a woman must be paid for. Modern custom and ancient lore bear witness that marriage between the classes *pu* and *ang'rei* was obligatory and acknowledge it to be the only form of orthodox marriage. To quote a characteristic Gilyak expression, only such marriage is *sik urlaf urlaf parkin* (pure, holy), truly in conformity with the dictates of their religion. If a man hesitates to give his daughter to a *pu* who is wooing her, the father of the young man rebukes him, saying,

---

2   [***Editor's note:*** The two preceding sentences abridge the original Russian language from the AMNH Russian typescript and the 1933 Soviet editions, which used double negatives to express the same ideas.]

3   [***Editor's note:*** In place of the above paragraph, restored from the AMNH Russian typescript, 43, the AMNH English typescript excluded the interesting discussion of the mnemonic-adjudicating function of kin terms by presenting the more curt:

> Towards all the individuals of these sanctioned groups one has obligations as well as rights. The mutual obligations of these classes stand out most clearly among "brothers" and their individual wives. At the death of a "brother," the widow is by a general rule prevented from marrying outside of the clan. She is allotted, by a decision of the clan, to one of the surviving "brothers" as an individual wife quite independently of her own sentiments in the matter, and no man belonging to the category of the widow's *pu* has the right to refuse her.

By contrast, however, the AMNH English typescript is the only edition to include the Gilyak-language imprecations in the next paragraph, which may have been added by Shternberg or Kreinovich.]

*Ti pekhlan nekhian kim khavrkhai brolv tor sik pikizndra'! Sik urlaf urlaf
parkin khunivmugnate! Nekhlankunu petslanzunu vara vara, akhmalk-
mugnate!*

("If you refuse to give your child to my child the old law will be wholly
lost! We must all stay pure! Your children and my children are alike our
common children, our common blood. Let us preserve the clan of our
fathers-in-law!")

To illustrate how imperative this type of marriage seems to the Gilyak I shall cite an
instance from one of their traditions. In this story a fight takes place between a young
Gilyak and a mysterious transformed shaman.[4] The fight ends by the shaman being
mortally wounded and retiring to his hut. On his deathbed the shaman learns that
he is a remote *akhmalk* ("wife's father") of the murderer, hence, the clan of the
shaman is obliged to give wives to the clan of his murderer. The shaman immediately sends for the young man, against whom blood-vengeance is imperative even if
the murder were unpremeditated, and whom to admit into one's house would be the
gravest offense. In the presence of members of his clan he solemnly declares,
"Although this man has killed me, give him my daughter! Be sure not to forget my
word!" Such is the power of the ancient law of marriage between the *pu* and the
ang'rei. It still retains its vitality.

The true extent of this institution of obligatory marriage is fully reflected in
the terminology of relationship. Let us review some of the key facts: (1) The wives
of clansmen call each other, according to their generation, either younger and elder
"sisters," "aunts," "great-aunts," and "nieces"; (2) all clansmen of an individual's wife
are "wife's fathers" (*akhmalk*) to all clansmen of that individual; (3) a sister of a
man's wife's father [when a man is speaking] is called "mother"; and (4) a daughter
of a man's mother's brother is called "wife" (*ang'rei*). Such terminology could obviously only be formed under the following conditions: The wives of all the members
of a clan must be taken from one and the same clan, and hence these women are in
every generation agnatic sisters. This clan is for each man his mother's clan; his wife
is his mother's brother's daughter. These principles notwithstanding, the destructive
tendencies of later times are still all-pervading in the psychology of the Gilyak. The
ideal is for all clansmen to take wives from one and the same clan, that is, the clan
from which their fathers and forefathers used to take wives; while for each individ-

---

4   The shaman had the power to change his human form into that of an animal or some other
    form. [**Editor's note:** Shternberg's 1904 monograph, "Giliaki," *Etnograficheskoe Obozrenie* 28,
    no. 2, 19–55, and Shternberg, *Giliaki*, 49–81, contain his cardinal essay "Religiia giliakov," dis-
    cussing Gilyak shamanism. A recent, excellent book exploring shamanism among neighbor-
    ing peoples of the Amur region is Anna Vasil'evna Smoliak, *Shaman: Lichnost' i funktsii*
    (Moscow: Nauka, 1991). For broader perspectives on shamanism in the former Soviet Union,
    see Marjorie Mandelstam Balzer, ed., *Shamanism: Soviet Studies of Traditional Religion in
    Siberia and Central Asia* (Armonk, NY: M. E. Sharpe, 1990); Roberte Hamayon, *La Chasse à
    l'Âme: Esquisse d'une Théorie du Chamanisme Siberien* (Nanterre: Société d'Ethnologie, 1990);
    Michael Henry, ed., *Studies in Siberian Shamanism* (Toronto: Univ. of Toronto Press, 1963);
    and Anna-Leena Siikala and Mihàly Hoppàl, *Studies on Shamanism* (Helsinki: Finnish Anthro-
    pological Society, 1992).]

ual the most appropriate marriage is one with his mother's brother's daughter. If for some individual that should prove impossible, preference is always given to a clan from which some one of his own clansmen have occasionally taken wives. *Pfandukh ang'rei den urdra,* "From the clan of one's birth must a man take his wife." Thus runs the maxim of the Sakhalin Gilyak. *"Pil pand os apakukh ni umgu genei furara"* (From the father-in-law of one's own birth a wife should be taken), say the Gilyak of the Amur. *"Erur taf khoro"* ("I am sick for the home of my mother's brother"), is the theme of the modern Gilyak song. The extent to which these principles are operative was demonstrated from the very beginning of my statistical investigations. Even before I had fully grasped the details of the kinship nomenclature, I was struck by the frequent occurrence in each clan of wives who had been taken from one and the same clan, calling each other, according to their husband's generation, "sisters" and "aunts" (and who really proved to be such). A great number of Gilyak men who had been married several times had wives who frequently belonged to one and the same clan, namely, to their mother's clan. One of my traveling companions, Issaika, was married three times and all his wives had come from the same clan. In a great many cases the husbands and wives were children of real sisters and brothers, or at least children of cross-cousins.

As we have seen, such marriages are the only ones reputed to be orthodox or "pure." Such a marriage echoes what Fison and Howitt have described of the Gond and Bygar tribes of Sathpuras, central India, where, "marriage between cousins is almost compulsory when the brother's child is a daughter, and the sister's child a son."[5] Indeed, the tendency towards marriage between children of "brothers" and "sisters" is so strong that the union is often agreed upon soon after the birth of the children in order to avoid accidents. Soon after the birth of a son, the mother's first concern is to do everything in her power to bring about his betrothal to the daughter of one of her brothers. The following ritual is performed: The baby bridegroom or his father ties around the bride's wrist a thread made of dog's fur and nettle, magical symbols for a household organized around fishing and dog breeding. From that moment the marriage is concluded. When the bride reaches the age of 4 or 5, she generally goes to the house of her bridegroom, and henceforth becomes his companion. The children call each other "my wife" or "my husband" (*nfu, nang'rei*) until sexual maturity is reached. Then without further ritual they become husband and wife *de facto,* dispensing with all the formalities that are generally required at marriages between strangers. This custom may account for the fact that the adult husband and wife generally call each other "old man" (*its'kh*) and "old woman" (*mam*). For at the age when most of us are about to be married, a young Gilyak couple can have been married long enough to celebrate their silver wedding anniversary. This custom is at

---

5 Fison and Howitt, *Kamilaroi i Kurnai,* 154. [**Editor's note:** This quotation is not found in the AMNH English typescript and has been restored from the Russian versions. As an example of the terminological confusion that plagues all editions, it might be noted that Shternberg's handwritten insert to the AMNH Russian typescript lists the groups as the Sands and Bygars; Shternberg, *Giliaki,* speaks of the Song and Bygar; and Shternberg, *Sem'ia,* lists the Gond and Bygor. The Fison and Howitt reference is to Gonds and Bygars, known as the Gond (Muria) and Byga (Baiga) in Library of Congress listings.]

times responsible for abnormal unions where the boy is 16 years of age and the girl 4 or 5. Not infrequently one finds such couples living in one yurta and calling each other "husband" and "wife." The explanation for such a union would be that either the wife's elder sister was dead or that the wife's mother was much younger than her brother. However that may be, such cases only tend to emphasize the binding character of marriages of this type. It is characteristic that these customs are practiced with special zeal by well-to-do families, who are generally noted for their strict adherence to all ancient customs and rituals [**84**].

The most important aspect of this primal form of marriage between the *pu* and *ang'rei* is the absence of payment for the bride, the so-called bride-price [*kalym*]. In marriage with unrelated women, which is becoming more and more widespread, the payment of the bride-price plays an all important role, being an important economic factor in the life of the Gilyak. Among the *pu* and *ang'rei*, especially when the parties are first-cousins, not only is no payment necessary, but it is strictly forbidden to mention the subject during the procedure of courting the bride. If the *pu* and *ang'rei* are distant cousins, sometimes an insignificant payment is made, but this is not the general rule. That in former times payment for a bride was wholly unknown can be clearly seen from the traditional epic poetry of the Gilyak, the *nastund*. There, while courting rituals are so often and so minutely described, there is no mention at all of payments for the bride. On the other hand, usually before sending the bride away, her "fathers" [*testi*] fill the canoe or sledge of the bridegroom with every kind of treasure.

Considering the great importance of bride-price in the economic life of the Gilyak—it sometimes being the only means of saving from ruin the household of a poor man—the complete absence of it in former times is the best demonstration of the obligatory character of marriage between these classes.

Owing to this obligatory character, undoubtedly brought about by religious motives, remarkable relations arose between individuals of the "wive's fathers" class and their "daughters' husbands." A "son-in-law" (*imgi*), even if he be only a potential one, receives at times better treatment at the hands of his "fathers-in-law" than is accorded to their own children. In some dialects the term for "father-in-law" is *arir*, which means "feeder," a term used by the Yukaghir for a man's own father. The code goes, "The son-in-law must be fed by the father-in-law." This dry formula is rich in meaning; in time of need the son-in-law, perhaps accompanied by his large family, goes to live with his "father-in-law," and without offering remuneration, stays with him for months or even years. At all times the son-in-law, even if only by name, is a favorite guest in his father-in-law's house. The young Gilyak spend entire months in boisterous recreation in the villages of their "fathers-in-law," finding in each yurta hearty welcome and the choicest food. The potential son-in-law is a constant participant in his "father-in-law's" fishing and hunting excursions and when the time of parting arrives, he carries home his share of the booty in addition to the customary presents. On important occasions such as the bear festival, the sons-in-law are the first to be invited, and upon them falls the honor of killing the animal. In time of war "sons-in-law" and "fathers-in-law" are expected to assist each other. In order to fully grasp the religious character of the strange relationship between "sons-in-law" and "fathers-

FIG. 11. The open front of a Gilyak summer house along the Tym' River in Arkovo, 1926. Rurnet, at left, and Zagan, at right, were the parents of Aleksei Churka (Zagan), the first Gilyak student to study in Leningrad. Photo by Shternberg student Erukhim A. (Iurii) Kreinovich. *Source:* AAN f. 282, o. 2, d. 313, l. 3.

in-law," we must note the wide application which the Gilyak, with a truly primitive passion for extending original taboos, give to the term "father-in-law."

We know from the kinship terminology that the clan of "fathers-in-law" is not only the clan from which an individual's clansmen usually take their wives, but also any clan from which any one clansman may take a wife. Thus every individual may have several clans of "fathers-in-law," and in every one of these clans a man finds the same privileged treatment and rights as with his real fathers-in-law.

The manner in which this complex system developed will be discussed in detail below. In the meantime, I believe, we have said enough to show that in the sphere of individual marriage the class names *pu* and *ang'rei* played and continue to play an all important role, symbolizing as they do the right to marriage—one of the many benefits conferred by the clan organization on its members [**85**].

We shall now indicate the practical bearing this institutionalized right to marriage has on the life of the Gilyak today. For the modern Gilyak, marriage is one of life's hardest ventures. Not merely in tales, but in real life, the task of finding a wife is one of uncommon difficulty due to the great paucity of women. From computations based on my census, it appears that for every 1000 Gilyak men on Sakhalin there are only 785 women, and a considerable percentage of well-to-do Gilyak keep from two to four wives. Thus, according to my census of the west coast of Sakhalin, north of the village Arkovo, there was one polygamist to every nine monogamists, and one old bachelor to every 11 married men, the total proportion of men to women being 1000 to 694. If in addition one considers the numerous marriage prohibitions, it becomes clear how limited the choice of women must be. In view of so restricted a choice, the purchase money (bride-price) paid in valuables or services extending over many years naturally reaches very high figures. Under such conditions a great many of the poorer men would have no chance to get an individual wife were it not for the right to marry, under privileged conditions, persons of the *ang'rei* class. First among these, of course, are a man's mother's brothers' daughters, followed by their collateral sisters, and, finally, daughters of the large class of men known to him as his "wife's fathers" (*akhmalk*). As a necessary resort, there is always a likely chance of marrying a brother's widow. However, given the scarcity of women, the intense rivalry within each *pu* class for their *ang'rei,* the greed for bride-price spurred by a heightened trading economy, and hence the weakening of pure matrimonial traditions, even this privilege to individual marriage often remains a *nudum jus.* This is where the other important factor of Gilyak life which supplements individual marriage steps onto the scene, group marriage. To that we now turn.

FIVE

GROUP MARRIAGE, OR, THE RIGHT TO SEXUAL RELATIONS
AMONG THE *PU* AND *ANG'REI* CLASSES[1]
[50–67; 72–93; 168–182; 86–93]

SHAKEN THROUGH THE INEXORABLE MARCH of historical and economic changes, the right to group marriage—to sexual intercourse between individuals of the *pu* and *ang'rei* classes—still persists with all its original vigor. Moreover, this right is devoid of all compulsory character. Neither a woman's kin nor individuals of the *pu* class can force a woman to have sexual intercourse. Nor do we find here, as among other peoples, the custom of hospitality or hetaerism in which the father, brother, or husband of a woman may ask that she share her bed with a guest who is her *pu*.[2] Public exhibition of sexual intimacy is forbidden. No one would dare lie down in an occupied yurta under one cover with his *ang'rei*, even if the woman's consent were previously secured. Intercourse must take place *privatim* and out of sight of the woman's individual husband.[3] Publicity of sexual relations is, moreover, not permitted even in individual marriages [**86**].[4]

If two people wish to have sexual intercourse at night in a dwelling where outsiders are present, they must lie down apart; and only when all the others are asleep can they join each other. The initiative may come from either party, but is less frequently taken by the woman. In summer, intercourse most frequently occurs outside. During the day, the most favorable spots for "catching" *ang'rei* are in the areas where berries are picked. In the evening usually some spot outside the village, such as near a

---

[1]   [***Editor's note:*** Earlier titles for this chapter are "Group Marriage" (AMNH English typescript; Shternberg, *Giliaki*), "Group Marriage: The Right to Sexual Relations among the *Pu* and *Ang'rei* Classes" (AMNH Russian typescript), and "The Right to Sexual Relations among the *Pu* and *Ang'rei* Classes" (Shternberg, *Sem'ia*). For a discussion of the concept of group marriage, please see the Foreword.]

[2]   [***Editor's note:*** Hetaerism, from the Greek *hetairismos,* or prostitution, is a recognized system of concubinage, communal marriage in a tribe.]

[3]   Compare a similar phenomenon among the Tibetans: "In Tibet, where the brothers of a family very often have a common wife, more than one is, according to Warren Hastings, seldom at home at the same time." Westermarck, *Geshichte,* 141. [***Editor's note:*** Shternberg, *Giliaki,* and Shternberg, *Sem'ia,* have this reference to, but not the quotation, from Westermarck.]

[4]   The avoidance of caresses in public by a couple in individual marriage must not be regarded as a peculiarity of the Gilyak. To accept Radlov's testimony, an Altaian will refrain in public from even touching his wife, notwithstanding the fact that among those peoples the relations between the sexes are characterized by great laxity. V. V. Radlov, *Aus Siberien, Vol. I* (Leipzig: T. O. Weigel, 1884), 314.

55

well, is chosen. At certain periods, however, group-mates are entirely free from restraint. Married men are often gone for weeks hunting on their taiga territories; summer or winter, they are constantly visiting or attending festivals. It is then that group-mates have their chance. There is only one strict requirement: The participants, as well as accidental witnesses to the intercourse, are strictly forbidden from speaking about it to anyone, especially to a person who may be closely interested. This secrecy, required perhaps to prevent possible outbreaks of jealousy, does not in any way affect the public character of the institution of group marriage. These rights are expressed in juridical formulae that have become a part of the common stock of knowledge of the tribe. All parents consider it a religious duty to impart a knowledge of these formulae to their children at an extremely early age. Group-mates not only treat each other publicly with unconstrained familiarity, but always apply to each other such tender epithets as "my little husband" or "my little wife." The publicity of group matrimonial relations becomes most conspicuous at the death of a man who was not married individually. On such an occasion, one of his group wives, normally the wife of an elder brother, mounts the burial platform just before the cremation of the corpse and publicly laments the deceased as her lover and her husband. It is curious that, amidst negotiations between *pu* and *ang'rei*, symbolic gestures such as smoking or eating, redolent of marriage ceremonies, are often employed. To suggest to an *ang'rei* woman, "*Urin tamkhtanate!*" or "Let us smoke together!" is an invitation to exercise spousal rights.[5]

The public and religious sanction of sexual intercourse between members of the *pu* and *ang'rei* is a privilege of vast importance, for sexual intercourse with any other women may lead to serious consequences. At the present time if a woman is a perfect stranger, the act does not constitute a religious infringement, but calls for bloody retaliation in case the culprits are caught in *flagrante delicto*. In any case a duel with sticks (sometimes to the death) follows and a fine may be imposed.[6] If the woman is

---

5 [**Editor's note:** The last two sentences of this paragraph were not in the AMNH English typescript or Shternberg, *Sem'ia*, but have been restored from the AMNH Russian typescript. In corresponding sections, Shternberg, *Giliaki*, 170, omitted the Gilyak-language words.]

6 There are some reasons for believing that in ancient times intercourse with strange women was completely prohibited. This supposition is supported perhaps by the following curious custom. If a woman who is not an *ang'rei* to a given man tries to seduce him, by perhaps catching hold of his leg in an isolated spot—a symbolic act for offering oneself to a man—the man, presuming he does not succumb, must either face the wrath of the gods or publicly demand a forfeit from the woman. On one occasion I became a witness to such a forfeit ceremony. It took place in the village of Tamlavo. One of my companions, an aged Gilyak, roused me one morning, and with some anxiety asked me to accompany him to the neighboring dwelling where "court" was to be held. There I found myself in the presence of a large gathering of the family heads of the village. My companion proceeded to present to them his case against one of the local women who, in the evening of the preceding day, had caught him by the leg. Accordingly he demanded his forfeit (*tkhusind*). The accused was called in. She confessed, and was made to publicly hand over the forfeit to the accuser—namely, a pup and some birch bark ware. In this case the fine imposed was insignificant unless these objects were meant to symbolize specifically female labor. But this seemed clearly due to the fact that the woman lived alone and had no more valuable objects in possession. It must be remembered that the Gilyak are very passionate, and do not like to miss a chance of playing the Lovelace whether the women be strangers or not. The above custom must be considered a survival of a time when there was a religious interdict on intercourse with strange men. [**Editor's note:** Only the AMNH English typescript contains the first three sentences of this footnote, as well as the replacement of Don Juan for Lovelace.]

a class relative within the prohibited categories (not the man's *ang'rei*), intercourse with her is followed by public condemnation as a terrible crime, and divine vengeance, remorse, and inevitable expulsion follows. In fact, though, such cases are extremely rare. Even sentiments of mere love are severely condemned and are ascribed to the machinations of an evil spirit. Suicide is a common method of atonement. Self-control towards individuals of the prohibited categories even of the remotest degree has become as instinctive with the Gilyak as it has among us towards mothers and sisters. The right to sexual intercourse therefore asserts itself more powerfully, then, to turn to the *pu* and *ang'rei* categories. In that connection, the Gilyak may be described in the terms used by Fison and Howitt, in speaking of the *kumi* and *kroki* of the Dieri tribe in Australia. In the entire extent of his territory, wherever a man may find his *ang'rei*, he also finds a conjugal hearth. He need only know the proper kin terms. Over the course of my travels across Sakhalin I had more than one opportunity to convince myself of this fact. Time and again I visited with Gilyak companions villages which neither they nor their fathers had ever seen. Nevertheless, in the course of a few sentences, bonds of relationship were discovered, and the *pu* and *ang'rei*, although complete strangers to each other, would at once set about negotiations for sexual intercourse [87].

In their group marriage rights, girls are lawfully as free as married women, but practically their position differs from the latter's. The prospect of pregnancy and child-bearing is not pleasant to thc Gilyak girl. Given the broader agnatic kinship ideology, the birth of a child by an unknown father is a dangerous situation on account of the uncertainty of the sexual, marital, clan, and especially religious rights of the child, which must be determined by its father.

The pregnant girl is severely scolded by her father, who generally insists on knowing the name of her seducer or forces her to have an abortion. If the child is already born he forces her to kill it. But however hard the moral burden of individual women in such cases may be, in practice things seldom take that turn. In the first place, many women are married as children and few remain single for a very long time. Women are so few that every girl is married by the time she has reached an age at which sexual indiscretions are possible. Finally, those women who are not married and who indulge in free sexual intercourse with men seldom restrict themselves to one lover. The extent to which such polyandric forms of sexual intercourse are carried by some girls may be gathered from the following example. The wife of my friend Pigunaika from the village Arkovo, a pleasant woman, excellent housewife, and the mother of children, had before her marriage no less than 14 lovers at the same time. They all belonged to her native village and called each other *navkh*, *akhmalk* (companion or partner). Curiously enough, *navkh* means literally the same as *punalua* in Morgan's well-known Punaluan family.[7] This woman often had sexual intercourse with all her lovers in one session. They told me in the most good-natured manner how all 14 would gather on a clearing not far from the village, and one after another would exercise their rights; and most curious of all is that one of

---

[7]   Morgan discusses the *punalua* category in *Systems of Consanguinity and Affinity*, 451–458; and *Ancient Society*, 427–428.

that gay crowd was Pigunaika himself, the present happy individual husband of this woman [**88**].

Under such circumstances the Gilyak youth naturally feels in many respects freer and more at ease among *ang'rei* girls than among married *ang'rei*. In dealing with married women he encounters various difficulties on account of the preeminent claims of their individual husbands. In his own clan, however, the youth does not find the girls whose company he is thus led to seek; for even with his remotest *tuvng* he cannot have sexual intercourse or even conversation. In his own clan he can have sexual intercourse only with married women. *Ang'rei* girls, on the other hand, live comparatively seldom in the same village with their *pu*. The Gilyak youth's mother's brother's daughters, the sisters of his brothers' wives, the daughters of his *akhmalk*, in other words, the entire clan of "wives' fathers," is the focus towards which his sympathies converge. He need not hide himself in the home of his *akhmalk*. Here he is met with open arms. For an *imgi* as we know is the closest person to the *akhmalk* and his wife, and he is a favorite hunting companion in summer as well as in winter. He is an ever-welcome guest and the choicest dishes are served to him. But there is another reason for his great popularity. The *akhmalk* and their sons may neither talk nor jest with their clan brothers. An *imgi*, on the contrary, is the legitimate partner for fun and joking to one's heart's content. In those surroundings the youth finds scores of young girls with whom he may openly talk, fool, and on occasion have sexual intercourse.

Let us now turn to the relations of men to their numerous married *ang'rei*. The married group-wives of a man constitute the following categories: (1) the wives of all his "brothers"; (2) all married "sisters" of his own wife; (3) all married "sisters" of the wives of his "brothers"; and (4) every married woman in the class of his *ang'rei*—a large category comprising many scores of individuals spread over the entire Gilyak territory. Now, in accordance with the general norms of Gilyak marriage, "sisters" as a rule marry individuals of one *tuvng* class, such that one's own wife's "sisters" and the "sisters" of "brothers'" wives come under the one rule referring to the wives of "brothers"—that these women must marry one of their *pu*. Owing to recent departures from traditional norms, however, it sometimes occurs that a man's *ang'rei*—his wife's sister or a sister of his *tuvng's* wife—is married either to a total stranger or even to one of the man's occasional *akhmalk*.[8] In such cases the norms of sexual intercourse as well as the kin terms cease to be uniform. In the majority of clans, intercourse with women who have thus married outside of their group is lawful, with the participants still calling each other *pu* and *ang'rei*. Their children are *tuvng* and call their mother's sisters and the husbands of those sisters "mothers" and "fathers," respectively. Among other clans, however, especially among those adjoining the Ainu, the rules are different. If a man's wife's sister marries one of his *akhmalk*, sexual intercourse with her as an *akhmalk's* wife is absolutely prohibited, nor is she any longer *ang'rei* to the man, but *as'kh* ("aunt," "mother-in-law"). If she marries a total stranger, her relations

---

8   I use the term "occasional *akhmalk*" to describe a speaker's relative who has opportunistically and secretly taken a wife from a clan contrary to the clan from which the speaker's relatives normally take wives. Usually the term *akhmalk* is applied to a clansman related to a person from olden times by matrimonial ties with all his clan.

FIG. 12. A Gilyak semi-underground winter dwelling, 1890s. The central room at left rises up under the snow peaking at a chimney opening. Photo by Lev Shternberg. *Source:* AAN f. 282, o. 2, d. 162, l. 32.

with him become those of strangers, that is, sexual intercourse between them is neither prohibited nor sanctioned. What is most remarkable, however, is that the offspring of the two families remain, even in cases of the latter type, *tuvng* [**88**].[9]

This undisputed and traditional right of a man to the "wives" of his *tuvng* has invariably been exercised throughout the entire Gilyak territory and persists to the present time with the one exception mentioned before—that sexual intercourse must not take place in sight of the woman's individual husband or in public. The right of the individual husband is, of course, of primary importance. The wife must fulfill her conjugal and household duties; she must, at his wish, accompany him on all his wanderings, and he also has the exclusive right to her children. But the subsidiary right of the group-husbands to sexual intercourse is equally accepted. The group-husbands must, of course, wait for favorable occasions on which to exercise their rights, as when the individual husband is absent or asleep. But such opportunities present themselves even more often than is necessary. The men spend a great deal of time outside their home, fishing on the river or going away for several weeks on hunting exhibitions, or visiting. The women, on their part, also absent themselves for entire days, gathering berries or roots in the taiga. Intercourse is also possible at night in the presence of the sleeping husband. The rights of group marriage may thus be exercised

---

[9] I shall give an instance which will illustrate the relationship between such *tuvng*, that is, of the children of sisters whose husbands are strangers to each other, as well as their respective wives. Vremgin and Gibel'ka were two Gilyak men belonging to different clans of the villages Tangi and Khoe, but their mothers were "sisters" in one and the same clan (*tuvng*). These two men, notwithstanding the fact that they themselves as well as their fathers are strangers, call each other *tuvng*, for their fathers were married to sisters and had mutual rights to sexual intercourse with each other's wife. Their wives are "mothers" (*imk*) to their children, and being the junior, Gibel'ka has the right to sexual intercourse with Vremgin's wife.

without much difficulty. The unmarried *tuvng*, of course, do so more than the married ones, unless they happen to conceive a strong passion for some particular *ang'rei*. But when away from the village and temporarily deprived of their individual wives, the married men indulge as freely as the unmarried ones [89]. It would be safe to say that the relations between *pu* and *ang'rei* are mainly determined by conditions of coresidence. Their relations must obviously be sporadic if they reside in different villages. In many cases group-mates may know of each other only from hearsay. No sooner do they meet than an understanding is reached and a passing union established. Both men and women have a great penchant for adventures of this kind without being much concerned with questions of sympathy or love. Nothing is easier than for a *pu* and *ang'rei* to reach an understanding: One need only, when accidentally encountering an *ang'rei* in a hallway or courtyard to touch a woman's breast or to make the classic proposal, "Let us have a smoke together!" (Gilyak, "*Renin tamchtanate!*"). Sometimes merely an exchange of glances will suffice [90].[10]

In cases where the *tuvng* reside in the same village, firm unions often arise between an unmarried man and the wives of his *tuvng*. In such relatively firm unions, sexual intercourse is often accompanied by an element of sympathy and attachment, which however does not prevent the woman from satisfactorily fulfilling her marital duties to her individual husband, to whom she may even feel sincerely attached. Such relations often result in highly interesting forms of cohabitation. Sometimes two or even three brothers, although quite independent economically and fully able to obtain individual wives, may nevertheless prefer to live together with one common wife. In such cases the senior brother is considered the official husband of the woman. Through marriage he has secured the rights of an individual husband, but it is tacitly understood by outsiders as well as the children of these "brother-husbands" that the wife belongs to all of them. One is likely to find such arrangements in the most prosperous and respected of families. My friend Gibel'ka, from the village of Tangi, who was my first teacher of Gilyak and the richest native of Sakhalin in his time, lived with his younger brother Pleun in this manner. Gibel'ka's younger brother was fully as able a fellow as Gibel'ka himself; he enjoyed the reputation of an excellent hunter and had managed to lay aside a great store of "valuables" so that he could have easily secured one or more wives had he wished to. Nevertheless he preferred the two-part ownership of his elder brother's wife. As a boy he had access to Gibel'ka's wife, being a younger brother. In the course of time a deeper attachment sprang up between them such that he ultimately decided not to marry, and remained permanently with his elder brother's wife, whom he really loved. Characteristically enough, the surrounding Gilyak, as well as Gibel'ka himself, considered the phenomenon a completely normal one. When I once asked Gibel'ka about the matter, a momentary shadow crossed his handsome, intelligent face, for he knew in what light the Russians regard such relations. Otherwise my question did not particularly phase

---

[10] [***Editor's note:*** This last paragraph summarizes almost two pages of Russian text as found in the AMNH Russian typescript, 56–59; Shternberg, *Giliaki*, 173–175; and Shternberg, *Sem'ia*, 88–90. As a general rule, here as elsewhere, Shternberg, *Giliaki*, is the more conservative of texts where Gilyak-language translations are concerned, omitting them when Shternberg, *Sem'ia* includes them.]

him. He spoke of his wife with enthusiasm and tenderly loved his children, although he could have no assurance as to whether they were his own or his brother's. His son, moreover, a boy of 14, was more attached to his father's younger brother than to his father. Gibel'ka, of course, was perfectly free to deny his house to his younger brother or to put him out of doors together with his wife and obtain another beautiful wife or even several wives from the best families. With his great ambition and his passionate love for popularity, he would not have hesitated to take the most determined steps to save his reputation had he felt that the least shadow of ridicule was cast upon him. It so happened that Gibel'ka outlived his brother, who tragically perished during a winter hunt alone in his hunting tent. When the deceased, amidst a large and solemn gathering of Gilyak who had come from all over the territory, was raised to the funeral platform and the ceremony of cremation was about to begin, Gibel'ka's wife, her hair loose in sign of mourning, ascended the platform. In the presence of all, she began to mourn over her "younger husband" and "beloved" in terms as pathetic and tender as if he had been her individual husband. By this public act, she emphasized better than any maxim the Gilyak view of a man's relation to his brothers' wives.

Permanent cohabitation of brothers with a common wife is not always noticed. In the first place, sexual intercourse is carefully kept from publicity. The Gilyak live in large yurtas, each one sheltering families of several brothers, so that an outsider would find it difficult to delve into their most intimate relations, especially as he would have to overcome a natural reluctance that the Gilyak have in speaking of such matters. Secondly, it is but seldom that a young Gilyak chooses to bind himself to the wife of one of his brothers, as he generally prefers the less regular relations with the various wives of his many *tuvng*. In such cases of continual cohabitation of many brothers with one wife, we have the typical form of group marriage, for, notwithstanding common possession, one of the "brothers" officially remains the individual husband [**91**].

There are cases, however, where the brothers are officially common husbands, one of them having preeminent rights over the other. Two or even more brothers choose a wife together through marriage or purchase and live with her in common possession in a common household. It is true that such cases are becoming rarer; nevertheless, during my journey in 1910 I encountered many instances, even among the Amur Gilyak (who, owing to close contact with civilized people, are more individualistic than the Gilyak of Sakhalin).

In Gilyak folklore material one finds unmistakable signs that such forms of marriage were common in ancient times. A great number of the so-called "heroic traditions" (Gilyak, *nastund*) begin with the words, "Two Gilyak brothers kept one wife" (Gilyak, *Nigvin menvin ruvn ang'rei nenkh aivund*), and in what follows, this theme is developed in detail. In one of these stories, where the Mountain Man carries off the common wife of two brothers, we find the following passage, which depicts the forms of sexual intercourse and the woman's relations to her two husbands:

> The same evening she made those . . . sacrificial cups for her husbands to
> take along to the dwelling; during the same night, having slept a little (that

unmarried daughters of his "mother's" "brothers," and finally, outside of these clans, he has a right to the married sisters of his or his *tuvng*'s wives and to the wives of his "mother's" "sisters'" sons. Moreover, as his own clansmen and members of his *akhmalk* are spread over most distant villages, there is scarcely a place where a traveling Gilyak may not find someone of his legitimate *ang'rei*. Mutatis mutandis, we can say of the *pu* and *ang'rei* what Fison and Howitt said of *kumi* and *kroki*—that a man may find a legitimate wife over the entire extent of his people's territory [93].

Thus, almost every Gilyak is a party to two forms of marriage—(1) the common individual marriage with one or several women of his *ang'rei* group (principally with daughters of his mother's brothers) as well as with no women of foreign clans; and (2) group marriage with all women of the *ang'rei* group, which may be accompanied by cohabitation in a common household with the women's individual husbands. In addition, there exists a third form of marriage which is truly communist— that of several brothers with one wife combined in group marriage.[13]

The form of group marriage we are here confronted with is a typical one, examples of which are well known and may be found among many different peoples of the world. A most curious and typical analog to our system is presented by the Dieri people of Australia, among whom the two forms of sexual intercourse, individual marriage and group marriage, are regulated by the differentiated terms *noa* and *piruari*. According to this system, each women is individually married to one man, and they call each other *noa*; but she is also married to a group of men whom she calls, and by whom she is called, *piruari*. What must be especially emphasized is that the *piruari* of the Dieri stand to one another in the same relationship of common unity as the *pu* and *ang'rei* of the Gilyak stand to each other. The *piruari* of a woman are the "brothers" of her individual husband, and the *piruari* of a man are the "sisters" of his individual wife. This principle is clearly shown by Dieri kinship terms. Thus a man or a woman calls by one and the same term (*apiriwak*) the *piruari* of their mother and the "brother" of their father, and accordingly by one and the same term (*andriwakha*) the *piruari* of their father, the sister of their mother, and the individual wife of the father's brother.[14]

Two other remarkable analogical features deserve to be noted. All the children of any given *noa* are brothers and sisters of the *piruari* group to which the *noa* belongs, and a woman becomes the *noa* of a man by being betrothed to him when she is a mere infant, exactly as among the Gilyak.[15]

The ritual distinction of the Dieri system comes when the *piruari* (that is, the partners of group marriage) are solemnly allotted to each other during the session of the great council of the people previous to the circumcision ceremony. Only from that moment does their marriage right begin. The purpose of this measure, in my opinion, seems to be twofold: (1) to strengthen the public consciousness of the legit-

---

[13] [***Editor's note:*** Alongside this passage in the AMNH Russian typescript, Kreinovich penned in, "But not quite, in the class sense." It isn't clear whether he was referring to "class" as a marriage category or a hierarchical term.]

[14] K. W. Howitt, "Australian Group Relations" [paper presented to the Smithsonian Institution, 1885], 10.

[15] Ibid., 79.

imacy of sexual intercourse between certain groups of individuals; and (2) to make public the names of these individuals. Among the Gilyak, things have not progressed so far. They are a small people, and each individual is told in early childhood by his parents the names of his group *pu* and *ang'rei.* Under different circumstances, Gilyaks would likely have advanced to this Dieri procedure as well.[16]

---

[16] [*Editor's note:* The AMNH Russian typescript and the 1933 Soviet editions conclude this section with one to two paragraphs of additional comparison between Gilyak and Dieri kin customs.]

SIX

THE MORAL AND PSYCHOLOGICAL CONSEQUENCES OF
SEXUAL NORMS

[67–76; 94–107; 182–190; 93–98]

THE UNIQUE NORMS of sexual intercourse described in the previous chapter, wide in their sanctions and strict in their interdicts, have affected the Gilyak in two diametrically opposed ways.

The wide field of legitimate sexual intercourse open to both men and women tends toward a general sexual laxity. Chastity, sexual moderation, and conjugal faithfulness are unknown concepts among the Gilyak. Occasionally, among married women we may find exceptional individuals who remain more or less faithful to their husbands. Among men, to take the testimony of the Gilyak themselves, such exceptions do not occur at all. The most respected members of the tribe discuss with great zest the liveliest of amorous adventures. A career full of romantic intrigues in no way depreciates the reputation of a gentleman (*urdla nivukh*). In my presence, and before an audience of respected old men, a young Gilyak, Laruk, told of his numerous romantic escapades amidst general acclamation and gay laughter, boasting for instance that in one village he was responsible for the birth of no less than 20 children. Such an attitude on the part of old and respectable men towards the sexual laxity of the young is possible only in a community where sexual intercourse within a group is legitimate and practiced on a large scale [**93**].

If I ever heard elders rebuke the young for sexual excesses, it was always for economic reasons, as love affairs often kept them away from work in the house. Pregnancy in girls was also censured. But here the special consideration was the fear of possible intercourse with an individual of a prohibited category and particularly the uncertainty of parenthood. As a rule, however, the love affairs of the young are open secrets and call forth no rebukes. It is the usual thing for young men to spend several months visiting the villages of their "fathers-in-law," where so many *ang'rei* girls are at their disposal. The older generation, far from opposing them, are highly satisfied, as the unmarried *imgi* ("son-in-law") is the favorite guest in every household. The women have the same attitude as the men towards what we term sexual morality. However, they must be careful where total strangers, individuals outside of the *pu* class, are concerned; for that reason they always assume an air of stern inaccessibility. In the end, women are as susceptible as the men.

To deny the Gilyak all sense of sexual morality would be unjust. In reality his conduct is well within the bounds sanctioned by his community. When it comes to

66

prohibited categories of behavior such as outbursts of jealousy before one's *tuvng* and especially sexual intercourse with individuals of forbidden groups, these categories are adhered to with a rigor quite unknown amongst ourselves in spite of the fact that these prohibitions often lack all foundation in physiological, psychological, or any other prudent considerations (as, for instance, the prohibition of intercourse between the most remote agnatic cousins). During my many years' stay with the Gilyak and after extensive inquiries, I heard of only two or three cases of open violation of sexual prohibitions. The most striking case occurred in the village Tamlavo, where a young Gilyak, after the death of his father, lived for a while with his young stepmother, whom the father had bought shortly before his death. This occurrence caused a sensation in all Sakhalin and was generally regarded as monstrous. Another well-known case was that of a young Gilyak, Pavlinka, who married a woman from his *imgi* clan, that is, from a clan which took wives from Pavlinka's own clan. Now, Pavlinka was a very Russianized Gilyak who served as policeman and looked down upon the customs of his people. Another Russianized Gilyak from Tamlavo (Allykh) forced the council of clansmen, who were as usual debating the question of who was going to get the widow of the deceased, to give her to him, although he as an *aki* ("elder brother") had no right to her whatsoever. This, however, was an exceptional case and accepted as such by the community. Nonetheless, in the first two cases the culprits were forced into voluntary exile; they had to settle outside the limits of the village, condemned to a lonely existence and deprived of all the benefits of clan life. I repeat, however, that these were exceptional cases, predicated on changing psychological attitudes transformed under the influence of foreign culture.[1]

As a rule, the mere suggestion of sex in connection with an individual of a prohibited category evokes an instinctive reaction of disgust. The rare cases where love springs up between such individuals are looked upon by the Gilyak as instigations of an evil spirit, and as thoroughly unnatural, not only among men but among animals as well. As mentioned before, even a dog that commits incest is killed. The attitude towards people is quite the same. It is not uncommon for lovers belonging to prohibited categories to kill themselves at the instigation of their relatives. In one of the songs of such an unfortunate pair the woman complains that her sister called her a bitch, and her beloved a devil (because he was her uncle); and that all her loved ones—father, mother, and sister—kept telling her, "Kill yourself! Kill yourself!" Meanwhile the object of her criminal passion may have been a remote relative of her own age, brought up in some distant place; their love, according to our standards,

---

[1] [***Editor's note:*** The AMNH Russian typescript, 69; Shternberg *Giliaki*, 184; and Shternberg *Sem'ia*, 94, include a footnote which reads, "There are also exceptional cases of a different type, when marriage norms are transgressed in favor of competing norms valued more highly by society. This can take place during times of epidemic, when a man's widow may not be able to marry according to levirate rules. In that case, in order that the woman remain in the clan of her dead husband, she can be given to any member of the clan, of ascending or descending line, by provision of the clan council." In the margins of the AMNH Russian typescript, Kreinovich's characteristic hand penned, "?" The quotation is not found in the later AMNH English typescript. Whoever later translated the AMNH Russian typescript into English, as a result of the frequent exchange of texts between Boas and Ratner-Shternberg between 1927 and 1933 (appendix A), appears to have incorporated this and other marginalia from Kreinovich.]

would be considered quite natural. The feeling of sexual repugnance in regard to individuals of prohibited degrees has become as instinctive with them as it is in our own community with respect to one's mother and sisters. We must also describe as almost instinctive the Gilyak's remarkable control of jealousy wherever the relations of their individual wives to group-husbands are concerned. In the absence of such remarkably developed attitudes, the realization of their sexual norms would have been impossible. Unbridled jealousy would have put an end to group marriage, while, in the absence of their well-developed aversion or indifference to individuals of prohibited categories, a great many of the norms would have lost their hold [95].

The question now arising is, how were these attitudes developed? One of the most important factors in this development was the classificatory kinship system. From an early age boys and girls know the terms applied to the various individuals, as well as the sexual rights and obligations associated with them. In that way, the relations between the various classes of persons are from childhood onwards established and regarded as completely natural. As in our education when we develop sexual indifference to parents, children, brothers, and sisters, so too among the Gilyak; owing to common terms and an early consciousness of the prohibitions, a similar feeling is developed, not only towards one's own mother and father but towards all "fathers" and "mothers," all father's brothers, all "sisters" and "brothers," and so on. Similarly, if the child knows the rights of the *pu* to their *ang'rei*, the mature man has learned to look with indifference on his wife's affairs with his *tuvng* and her *pu*. At the same time he is far from indifferent when an outsider is concerned. Then his wrath knows no bounds. He either kills the adulterer in *flagrante delicto* or fights a fierce duel. Moreover, if even his own *tuvng* were to permit himself in his relations with the man's wife—a breach of the customary privacy of sexual relations—his equanimity would be shaken and the culprit would be forced to leave the village.

Together with this education (and one might say the almost hypnotic effect of the kinship terms), the development of these attitudes in the Gilyak is still more powerfully stimulated by various avoidance rules. Their aim is twofold: One is designed for those individuals between whom the greatest possible reduction of jealousy is necessary, the second for those who must avoid sexual intercourse with each other. These interdicts act not only through suggestion and habit but also as strict religious taboos. To infringe on one, in the eyes of primitive man, is a terrible sacrilege. The power of the avoidance taboos and the attitudes they foster may be gathered from the following incident related by Iokhel'son. A Yukaghir approached his brother by mistake with undue familiarity. When he suddenly became aware of his mistake, he dropped dead. Below is given Iokhel'son's own account of that remarkable incident, which, however, would equally apply to the psychology of the Gilyak.

> There lived two brothers. With them lived [their brother-in-law] the husband of their elder sister, to whom it is allowed to speak. For that reason both brothers laughed and joked with him . . . . But the brothers stood to each other, as usual, in non-speaking relations. Once the elder brother, on returning from the hunt, found the youths of the village playing games and dancing. The younger brother, who happened to be in his brother-in-law's

fur coat, was among the dancers, his back turned towards the brother who had just arrived. The latter, taking the younger brother for his brother-in-law, approached him from behind and thrust his arm between the other's legs with the intention of scaring him for fun, but happened to touch his genital organs. The younger brother quickly turned around. Then the older one recognized his mistake, and "from shame" dropped dead on the spot. An autopsy was made, in accordance with custom, in order to ascertain the cause of death, and his heart (so says tradition) was found to be broken in half [**96**].[2]

Now let us turn to the avoidance restrictions themselves. The interdicts of the first category refer to persons of the same sex and are designed to reduce jealousy between all those individuals who are in the same class as regards group marriage. It is interesting to note that this interdict in many clans applies to men only, women being free from it. The reason for the exclusion of women seems to be ascribed to the effect of the regular practice of polygamy in individual marriage—polygamy itself being considered a good school for self-possession towards a woman's partner in marriage.[3] The Gilyak woman is not obliged to react against the infidelity of her husband even found in *flagrante delicto* with a woman outside of his *ang'rei* class; the man, finding himself in the same position, must wreak blood vengeance. There is, therefore, all the more need for preventative measures against jealousy amongst men.

Thus the avoidance rule applies to class-brothers (who, though they may not be related, may be married to one's class-sisters) and their children. Only on the Amur, where the old norms are decaying, is the prohibition limited to one's own brothers exclusively.[4] In other clans, be they one's own and collateral, women not related to one another but married to brothers (their own and collateral), are included under this prohibition. All these people among whom occasion for outbursts of jealousy may be found every day—nay, every hour—are separated from each other by an impenetrable wall of the strictest avoidance which begins at birth and ends at the grave, creating an attitude of self-suppression equal in its power to the strongest instincts of nature.

To the same category of avoidances must be added the interdicts between the paternal aunt and her niece, who call each other by the same terms as elder and junior sisters (*nanakh* and *askh*). The reason for this prohibition may be sought in their terminology itself, but another reason more serious may also be indicated. The paternal aunt, as may be seen from the terminology and from the rules governing marriage, is the orthodox mother-in-law of her niece. The relationship between mother-in-law and daughter-in-law is always a rather delicate affair, especially under conditions where the woman lives always in the family of her husband, often while

---

[2]   Iokhel'son, *Materialy*, XIII.

[3]   [***Editor's note:*** This reference to polygamy, while found in the AMNH Russian version, is absent from the 1933 Soviet editions, which rearrange this and the next paragraph in slightly different ways.]

[4]   [***Editor's note:*** While Shternberg, *Giliaki*, 96, mentions "one's own sister's," context suggests that the reference to "one's own brothers" found in the AMNH Russian typescript is the correct version.]

the husband is a mere infant. Although intercourse between the father-in-law and his daughter-in-law is strictly prohibited and infringements almost unknown, jealousy, though wholly unfounded, is possible. Thus the interdict barring the mother-in-law from familiarity with her daughter-in-law appears to be a safeguard against attacks of jealousy in their everyday relations.[5]

Prohibitions of the second category, as we have seen, are devised to prevent sexual intercourse between persons of different sex belonging to prohibited groups. For that reason we find no interdicts between persons who belong to the class of "husbands" and "wives" respectively, whether they form an individual union or not. Every man may freely converse with his individual wife, as well as with all his group-wives. However, even in the categories between whom sexual intercourse is prohibited, there are certain groups of individuals who, according to the Gilyak view, do not require the safeguard of an avoidance taboo. These are first of all the mother, and to a certain extent the father. With the mother, the sons as well as the daughters may speak and fool without any restrictions whatsoever. The same holds true for the entire class of "mothers" and "sons." The terms alone, acquired in childhood, are considered a sufficient guarantee of sexual indifference between these persons.

The father and his class are treated somewhat more strictly; he may speak or quarrel with his daughters, but he may not joke with them. The same applies to the whole class of "fathers" and "daughters." Grandfathers, great-grandfathers, grandmothers, and their grandchildren stand outside of any interdiction in regard to each other. Not so with other persons of the prohibited categories. Particularly strict are the interdicts referring to women of one's own clan. "Sisters" as well as paternal aunts, who are called "elder" sisters (nanakh), are strictly prohibited from speaking to them, to cast glances at them, or to indulge in obscene actions such as uncovering their bodies. This interdict extends beyond one clan, if these persons are tuvng to each other, as for instance, the children of sisters who married men belonging to different clans. Moreover, as we know, for every woman her "brother" is a potential father of her daughter-in-law; and for every man, on the other hand, a "sister" is a potential mother of his son-in-law. Accordingly, a woman is under an interdict in regard to the father of her daughter-in-law, real or potential, while a man is similarly restricted in regard to the mother of his son-in-law.

The avoidance prohibitions are operative in many clans between men and the wives of their younger tuvng, on the one hand, and between women and the elder tuvng of their husbands on the other. As is evident from the kinship terms, persons belonging to those groups apply to each other the interdictory terms iokh and atk, and sexual intercourse between them is of course prohibited. These terms are also used by daughters-in-law and fathers-in-law with respect to each other and, as persons belonging to prohibited groups, any communication between them is again forbidden, although not everywhere with equal strictness. In some localities—among the Gilyak of the Amur estuary—neither conversation nor joking is permitted. In

---

[5]   [**Editor's note:** This paragraph is found in the AMNH English version only, suggestively hinted at by a single arrow drawn by Kreinovich in the margins of the AMNH Russian version. None of the Russian versions include it. In some respects the explanation of the role of the paternal aunt, found two paragraphs down, is clearer.]

and cannot always be dispensed with. The elder brother, for instance, often takes the place of the father in a household, and it thus becomes impossible to avoid talking to him. For that reason, in extreme cases younger brothers are permitted to communicate with their elder brother. Short and direct address in the form of orders, business advice, etc. is always permitted between brothers, and between husband's father and son's wife, including even the use of the vocative. Still one generally tries to avoid direct forms of address. If a person outside of the prohibited category is present, the words are addressed to him or to her, but in such a way that the prohibited individual can hear them. He, in his turn, answers by the same method. In other cases, the address is put in the third person or in an impersonal form. For instance: "The son's wife may do this or that," instead of the vocative form "Sister's wife, do so and so," or "Thanks to my brother," instead of "Thank you, brother," etc. Sometimes the plural of the pronoun is used instead of the singular. For instance, while a man addressed the wife of his elder brother in the singular form (*ri*, "thou"), he usually addressed the wife of his junior brother in the plural (*rin*, "you"). Owing to the custom of evading direct address through use of the third person, it is often used instead of the second person. The third person is also used in addressing strangers in anticipation it seems that they might prove to be of a prohibited category. When an unknown Gilyak enters the house, he is generally greeted with "Where did the Gilyak come from?" instead of "Where do you come from?" This custom, brought about by the interdict against direct address and found among many other peoples, may be responsible for the origin of that strange use of the third person instead of the second, which we find in Italian, Polish, Tatar, etc. [97].

Another curious consequence of this interdict against direct address is that the Gilyak do not exchange greetings on meeting or leaving each other. It may well seem strange to us that a Gilyak does not utter any greetings, even upon returning home after a long absence or when leaving his family on a dangerous hunt which might last for several months. Yet the Gilyak are very ceremonious, always greeting their guests and seeing them off with solemn speeches and good wishes. The neighbors of the Gilyak—the Ulchi, Gold, and Ainu—exchange greetings upon meeting or leaving each other. The absence of greetings among the Gilyak is due to the fact that each Gilyak has in his house and village many persons whom it is not lawful to address. Habitual greetings might easily lead to involuntary infringements of the avoidance regulations. The interdict on conversation, as generally known, is found among many peoples. Recall the American Arapaho, for instance, among whom brothers may not speak to one another. The Yukaghir interdicts are of special interest to us. The avoidances between "brothers" and "sisters," between father-in-law and mother-in-law and their daughters, or between elder brothers and the wives of younger brothers, are common to both the Yukaghir and the Gilyak. In cases where address cannot be dispensed with, we again find, as among the Gilyak, the use of the third person.

SEVEN

THE GENESIS OF GILYAK MARRIAGE RULES AND KIN TERMS[1]

[77–91, 108–129; 190–214; 98–105]

OUR INVESTIGATIONS SO FAR have revealed the close parallels between sexual norms and kinship terms. Now we inquire into the origin and development of the complicated system of relationship and marriage, and search for its determinants [**98**].

It is obvious enough that so complicated a system could not have arisen artificially. Its source must lie in some one simple principle, a categorical imperative plausible to the primitive mind, from which must have sprung, as from a seed, that complex organism of Gilyak institutions on which we have dwelt at such length. On par with the genesis of the kinship system, however, we must also study its long evolution, without which a proper grasp of kinship terms will be quite incomprehensible.

Why, for instance, do the wives of even the most remote *tuvng* call each other sisters, although they may be utter strangers to each other? Why do I (a man) call my wife's father, who may be a stranger to me, "mother's brother," while a woman under similar conditions calls her husband's mother "father's sister"? Why is it that when I marry a woman who is a stranger to me and to my clan, all her father's sisters, even the unmarried ones, thereafter become my "mothers," and no man of her clan is now permitted to marry a woman of my clan?

Why may not the women of my clan marry any man of clan A, into which any of my clansmen marry, or of clan B, from which the men of clan A obtain their wives? Or how should we explain the apparently paradoxical fact that a man may have male and female agnates (sons and daughters, brothers, fathers and mothers) in a totally strange clan? The complexity and apparent incongruity of some details of the system can be explained in but one way. The originally simple and logically consistent system, like any religious norm, must have undergone inevitable changes under the stress of historical and local conditions. New categories of people must have been introduced into the chain of the marriage union, and many withdrawals must have been made. At the same time, instead of simplifying the old norms or adapting them to the new conditions, they strictly persisted in preserving the old forms and

---

[1]   [***Editor's note:*** The chapter title is taken from AMNH Russian typescript and the two 1933 Soviet editions; the corresponding title in the AMNH English typescript is "The Development of the Matrimonial Regulations and of the Terminology of Relationship among the Gilyak." This chapter and the next contain material distributed, in different order, over three chapters in Shternberg, *Giliaki*, 190–214; and Shternberg, *Sem'ia*, 98–111.]

extending them more and more over new categories of persons and new conditions. To add to the complexity of the system, kinship terminology, being a formal element of great stability, remained entirely unchanged. This is like every primitive social system in the nature and sanction of its religion.[2]

What, then, was the original system of marriage? In the course of our study we have occasionally touched upon this topic. In the following pages we propose to deal with it at length.

The detailed analysis of marriage regulations made in the last chapter has shown that these regulations tally exactly with the kinship terminology; in other words, the complicated kinship terminology appears to be nothing but an automatic record of the system of marriage. This faithful record, so stable amidst manifold changes, must therefore furnish the basis for a reconstruction of the Gilyak system of marriage in its original form.

As indicated before, the Gilyak system has no separate terms for relationship by marriage (affinity), but uses only terms for blood relationship (consanguinity). Affines, even remote ones, are called *pandf* (i.e., people of common descent, cognates).[3] The term for a man's father-in-law is the same as that for his mother's brother; the term for a woman's mother-in-law is the same as that for her father's sister; the term for husband is the same as that for cognatic cousin, father's sister's son; the term for wife is the same as that for mother's brother's daughter. Such a terminology must obviously have come into being in a social system where marriages were concluded exclusively between blood relatives on the mother's or the father's side [**99**].

The nature of these marriages is further revealed by other kin terms. In each clan the wives of *tuvng* (that is, of brothers, one's own and collateral) call each other "sisters"; they call their husbands' mothers (that is, the mothers of all these *tuvng*) "aunt" (father's sisters). On the other hand, a man calls his wife's father's sister "mother." It therefore follows that the wives of all members of a clan must be relatives taken from one and the same clan. In other words, every clan may take wives exclusively from one particular clan; no marriage outside of that clan is permissible. Secondly, marriage is regulated according to generations. Each generation of "brothers" of a clan must take wives from the corresponding generation of "sisters" of the other clan. Thus each ascending generation of "brothers" are married to the aunts of the wives of the next descending generation. Likewise the brothers of the next descending generation must marry "sisters" who are the nieces of their mothers, and so on. This is the reason why the wives of "brothers" call each other "sisters" (for such they are), while their mothers-in-law are "paternal aunts." The husbands call the sisters of their fathers-in-law "mothers."

---

[2]   [*Editor's note:* The Russian versions of this section are less critical of religion as a conservative force. The point made in the AMNH Russian typescript, 77–78; Shternberg, *Giliaki*, 191; and Shternberg, *Sem'ia*, 98, is more simply that as the social circumstances of marriage transformed and became more flexible, kinship terminology remained the same. Only the AMNH English typescript adds: "This is like every primitive social system in the nature and sanction of its religion."]

[3]   [*Editor's note:* Zoia Ivanovna Iugain, a Gilyak (Nivkh) reader on Sakhalin in 1995, added that *pandf* implies common place, the home of a clan, and only then in turn a group of people from there.]

Thus the first principle, according to which marriages must take place exclusively between blood relatives, is supplemented by another principle: The wives of clansmen must come from one and the same clan. Two clans thus become linked by mutual obligations—one must take wives from the other, the other must give women to the former. The men of the same generation in the first clan are from birth considered the husbands of the corresponding generation of women of the other clan. The terminology of relationship, however, indicates that this relationship cannot be reversed. The men of the second clan and the women of the first do not constitute classes of husbands and wives; they are strictly forbidden to one another.

These principles correspond perfectly to conditions still existing among the Gilyak. The right to marriage persists to this day, marriage with the *akhmalk* clan continues to be the only "pure" marriage, and clansmen usually prefer to marry into one and the same clan. Thus we may with confidence continue our analysis.

What, then, is the clan into which clansmen are required to marry? The answer to this question has already been given in the kinship nomenclature, according to which the mother of a man is the sister of clansmen who come from the same clan to which their brothers belonged. The members of a clan are thus seen to be related by blood through the father as well as through the mother. Each individual member of a clan must marry a daughter of his mother's brother; the daughters of a man are the prospective wives of his sisters' sons. This principle of obligatory marriage between children of brothers and sisters, so common now among many primitive peoples, will be seen later as a general stage in human marriage brought forth as a means for regulating sexual relations. It is the seed from which grew up the highly complex system of classificatory kinship, group marriage, and the clan itself.[4]

Let us now follow the dynamics of this process and consider the natural consequences: As long as a brother's daughters belong from birth to his sister's sons, it is only natural that the prospective wives should as mere infants pass to the families of their future husbands. This system is still found among the Gilyak as well as among many other primitive peoples. Thus in cases of orthodox marriages—that is, marriages between the children of brother and sister—the future wife, as when a mere infant, joins the household of her "husband" and grows up in his company.[5] The

---

[4]   [**Editor's note:** In the AMNH Russian typescript, 80; Shternberg, *Giliaki*, 193; and Shternberg, *Sem'ia*, 100, three further sentences expound on why young Gilyak boys go to live in the families of their future wives. Shternberg explains the matrifocal residence unit by its commonality with other primitive peoples, and pledges further discussion below.]

[5]   This fact stands in striking contradiction to the assertion of Westermarck, Crawley, and others, to the effect that the prohibition of marriage between brothers and sisters must have originated in an instinctive sexual aversion born of close cohabitation. Crawley refers, in this connection, to the following dogmatic statement by Ellis: "The normal failure of the pairing-instinct to manifest itself in the case of brothers and sisters or of boys and girls brought up together from infancy is a merely negative phenomenon due to the inevitable absence under these circumstances of the conditions which evoke the pairing impulse." Cf. A. E. Crawley, "Exogamy and the Mating of Cousins," *Anthropological Essays Presented to Edward Burnett Tylor in Honour of His 75th Birthday, October 2, 1907* (Oxford: Clarendon, 1907), 52. Among the Gilyak and many other primitive peoples, however, future marriage mates are required to be brought up together, and none of the consequences suggested above seem to fit. [**Editor's note:** This footnote, from the AMNH English typescript, expands on the corresponding note found in the three cardinal Russian versions.]

terminology of relationship has given permanent expression to this custom insofar as children of certain classes of persons are from birth termed *"pu"* and *"ang'rei."*

In this manner a constant supply of women was provided for the sons of sisters in the persons of their brothers' daughters. Thus every group of brothers was supplied with wives, and the problem of sexual relations was socially regulated. This measure, however, was only sufficient to satisfy the want which had created it. There was need for a corresponding system of distribution of the sexes which would ensure peace between brothers who had a group of sisters as wives.

It seems apparent that the norms of distribution could not have been exclusively individual or exclusively communal. Communal possession generally leads to continuous strife. A purely individual arrangement would, of course, have been the most satisfactory one, but it required an even distribution of the sexes, a condition not always realized, especially in the limited circle of a few families. Under such circumstances, the norms of distribution had to represent a compromise between individual and communal rights, if all the problems arising from an uneven sex distribution were to be accommodated. Under the stress of these requirements, a mixed type of individual and group marriage arose, found among the Gilyak and occurring among all those peoples for whom marriage is based on the same principles. This combined system of individual and group marriage was molded by the different combinations of sex distribution among the descendants of a brother and a sister. An inspection of such combinations will suffice to demonstrate the above proposition [100].

(a) If we were to take the simplest type of sex distribution where we have one brother and one sister, and the brother has as many daughters as the sister has sons, an individual distribution might be realized, but not unless the men and women reach marriageable age simultaneously. *À la longue*, however, the probability of such a combination becomes even more remote; for the descendants of the brother and those of the sister multiply and form several families in which a contemporaneous existence of an equal number of marriageable men and women in the two lines of descent must be highly unusual.

(b) Let us examine the same case of one brother and one sister, except that the sister has several sons, and the brother but one daughter. Here the inevitable outcome is communal marriage of the type found among the Gilyak and typically represented in all accounts of the Tibetans. The methods of cohabitation with common wives have already been given. As to the children of such marriages, they are either not at all distinguished according to the fathers, or, as among the Todas, they are so apportioned that the first is regarded as belonging to the eldest brother, the second to the next oldest, and so on.

(c) Here is still another variation of the same case. The first brother reaches marriageable age before the second. The older brother lives with his mother's brother's only daughter as an individual wife until the second brother begins now to exercise his marital rights as a group-husband. It may happen, however, that another of the sister's daughters becomes marriageable. Then the second brother takes the opportunity to get her as his individual wife; but at the same time the older brother now receives the same group-rights over the wife of the younger one, as the latter in his time exercised over the wife of the older brother.

(d) Suppose at a given moment the brother had several adult daughters, while his sister had only one adult son. The latter becomes the husband of all the daughters of his mother's brother. These conditions prevail among the majority of Indian tribes where a man who marries the oldest daughter is required to marry all her sisters. But suppose another brother comes of age. One of the women is ceded to him as his individual wife; the others remain with the older brother, who is economically better fitted to support several wives than his younger brother, who is just starting out. The latter, however, justly becomes the group-husband of all the wives of his older brother. The corresponding rights of that elder brother are not so clear.

(e) So far we have only considered the simplest variations of the one brother/one sister case. When there are several brothers and sisters the results, although similar, are more complicated. If there always were as many sisters as brothers, and if all sisters and brothers had an equal number of descendants, male and female, each pair of brother and sister could constitute a closed matrimonial group. But in reality such cases are highly exceptional. As a rule the number of brothers and sisters is not the same. Still less probable is an equal distribution of sexes among their descendants. Let us analyze a few concrete instances. Several brothers have one sister. The brothers have several daughters; their sister has several sons. In such a case not only sisters but also cousins become the group-wives of the brothers. Or take the following [101]:

(f) There are several brothers and several sisters, but the distribution of the sexes is such that there are not enough sisters for all brothers. Here the marriage group will embrace brothers and sisters as well as cousins, male and female. Finally, not all women may have had brothers, nor all the brothers have daughters. In such cases it becomes necessary to have recourse to the daughters of first and second male cousins. It will thus be seen that a matrimonial group constituted as the descendants of a brother and a sister must inevitably be extended so as to include, on the one hand, all collateral brothers (including those of the most remote degrees) and, on the other hand, all collateral sisters. When these conditions are realized, we have the Punaluan family in its purest form.

Thus the classification system, which appears to be so complex, becomes clear and simple when logically deduced from the fundamental principle that all female descendants of a brother belong to the male descendants of his sister. At first sight, it may seem strange that the term "wives" should be applied not only to one's brothers' wives but also to their sisters. The explanation, however, is quite simple. The wives of brothers cannot be anything else but sisters, and they all belong to the group of "brothers," their cousins. The wives of brothers and the sisters of those wives are the same individuals. Similarly, one's mother's brothers are called "fathers-in-law," for the reason that one's father-in-law can only be one's mother's brother [102].

The only variations possible in this system are the differences in group marriage rights between older and younger brothers. In some tribes, all brothers are group-husbands of their common wives; in other tribes, only younger brothers exercise group

FIG. 14. A Gilyak fishing team, center, prepares fish for drying on racks shown here in the village of Kul', 1893. Photo by Lev Shternberg. *Source:* Photo archives of the MAE, 2446-24.

rights over the wives of their elder brothers. Among the Gilyak we find both systems, and consequently two sets of terms for father's brothers and brothers' wives. Thus, in some groups, a man may call only the older brothers of his father "fathers"; in others, only his younger brothers. Similarly, in some groups, a man designates as "wives" only the wives of older "brothers"; in others, the wives of all brothers.

Let us again proceed with the consequences of the fundamental principle that every mother has the right to expect her brother's daughters to become the wives of her sons.[6] Suppose the mother is (a) and her brother (A); the daughters of (a) must belong to the sons of her husband's (B) sister (b). The daughter of (b), however, cannot be married to the sons of (A), for as explained before, the exchange of women between the descendants of a brother and a sister is not permissible.

Thus, on par with the two groups, the sister with her husband (a + B) and her brother with his wife (A + c), there arises a third group—the sister of B and her husband (b + X), together with their descendants. In each of the three groups, the men of all generations take wives from the group of the mother's brothers, while the women marry into the third group of the father's sister. Thus each group constitutes a perfect exogamous unit, that is, a clan which is paternal if the wife joins the husband's clan

---

6   [*Editor's note:* Here, to the end of this chapter and into the next, begin a number of key discrepancies between the AMNH English typescript, on which this book is based, and the three main Russian versions of the text (including the largest discrepancies between the AMNH Russian typescript and the two 1933 Soviet editions). For example, the section beginning with this paragraph and leading to the next subsection, "The Phratry and Its Origins," is a much condensed version of materials found approximately in the AMNH Russian typescript, 85–87; Shternberg, *Giliaki,* 190–203; and Shternberg, *Sem'ia,* 98–105. Readers can find detailed versions of these sections in chapter eight. Because all four versions take notably different directions here almost sentence by sentence, I defer to the sequencing of the AMNH English typescript. Chapter sequencing among versions resumes greater harmony with chapter nine.]

and the descent is on the father's side, and maternal if the husband joins the wife's clan and the descent is on the mother's side. Since ancient times the Gilyak clan has been patrilineal. The strength and solidarity of such a clan does not merely lie in the negative bond of exogamy (exogamy, in the sense of prohibition of marriage with relatives of certain degrees, can exist independently of the clan), but in the important positive bonds such as the common right of clansmen to the women of the clan of their mothers, the mutual rights of group marriage, and the privilege of having blood relatives as fathers-in-law and of marrying the children of one's father's sisters (members of clan which from remote antiquity had married the women of one's own clan).

The strength of the clan bond is enhanced by its very nature. Within the clan all individuals are related by blood. If the clan were maternal and the sons-in-law came to their wives' houses, all women born in the clan would remain together while their husbands would all come from one clan, being their wives' cognatic cousins, sons of their fathers' sisters. In an agnatic clan the outside women are all related to one another, while their husbands are their cognatic cousins.

This common blood relationship of the representatives of both sexes, whether original members of the clan or not, constitutes the all-important element of clan solidarity—a factor of great significance which unites all Gilyak through the bonds of a common ancestral cult [**103**].[7]

THE PHRATRY AND ITS ORIGINS[8]

We have seen that the clan is by no means an isolated entity. The existence of every clan is organically connected with the existence of at least two other clans related to it by blood: the clan from which it takes its wives, and the clan into which it must give its own women in marriage. These two clans, moreover, cannot coincide, as the exchange of women between two clans is not permissible [**109**].

With reference to every individual member in the clan, this means that in addition to membership in his own clan (A), within which neither he nor any of his descendants can marry, he must stand in a specific relation towards at least two other clans—the clan (B) of his mother's brother, from which he himself and his male descendants take wives, and the clan (C) of his father's sister, into which his female descendants marry.

We know from the kinship terminology that both clan B in relation to clan A, and clan A in relation to clan C bear the special name "*akhmalk khal*" ("clan of wife's fathers"), and are in turn called by these clan "*imgi khal*" ("clan of son-in-law"). All three clans combined are called *pandf* ("men of common descent"). As all three clans are blood relatives, each clan and each clan member, with reference to marriage, constitutes an organic part of a three-clan union of blood relatives (*pandf*). Hence this is a real cognatic phratry for in each generation all husbands and wives are cognatic cousins. The Gilyak phratry, however, has nothing in common with

---

7 [***Editor's note:*** Readers can find the discussion of destructive influences on the kinship system, which is found after this material in the three Russian versions, at the start of chapter eight.]

8 [***Editor's note:*** Approximate versions of this section and the tables are also found in the AMNH Russian typescript, 98–112; Shternberg, *Giliaki*, 209–214; and Shternberg, *Sem'ia*, 109–111.]

TABLE 2.

THE THREE-CLAN COGNATIC PHRATRY

CLAN A (ANDREI)[9]	CLAN B (VASILII)	CLAN C (STEPAN)
Clan Ancestor and Wife	**Clan Ancestor and Wife**	**Clan Ancestor and Wife**
Andrei Vera	Vasilii Sophia	Stepan Anna
Andrei, brother of Anna, who is married into clan C	Vasilii, brother of Vera, who is married into clan A	Stepan, brother of Sophia, who is married into clan B
Vera, sister of Vasilii of clan B	Sophia, sister of Stepan of clan C	Anna, sister of Andrei of clan A
Their Children	**Their Children**	**Their Children**
1. Sons marry daughters of mother's brother, Vasilii of clan B	1. Sons marry daughters of mother's brother, Stepan of clan C	1. Sons marry daughters of mother's brother, Andrei of clan A
2. Daughters marry sons of father's sister, Anna of clan C	2. Daughters marry sons of father's sister, Vera of clan A	2. Daughters marry sons of father's sister, Sophia of clan B

In succeeding generations, marriages follow the same rule: Men marry mother's brother's daughters; women marry father's sister's sons.[10]

Morgan's phratry; marriage within the Gilyak phratry is not only possible but imperative. This three-clan system is represented schematically in table 2.

At first glance, our hypothetical phratry of table 2 provides for all necessary marriages. In each clan, a man marries his mother's brother's daughter; a woman marries into a third clan, taking her father's sister's son.

However, there is a problem. Such a marital arrangement abrogates a separate marriage rule which forbids giving women to the clan of the wife's father of the second degree (*tuyma akhmalk*). If we apply this rule to our hypothetical phratry, we arrive at the following predicament.

[9] [**Editor's note:** Although Shternberg penned in Anglicized clan names to the AMNH Russian typescript, "Astor, Brandt, Clive and Danton," the use of surnames is inconsistent with the structure he uses in the same text, where clan names are tied instead to the first names of their *rodonachal'niki* (Russian for clan ancestors). Hence, I have restored the Russian equivalents that appear in the 1933 Soviet editions as well as the very early version of this table in Shternberg, "Giliaki," *Etnograficheskoe Obozrenie* 28, no. 60 (1904), 35. The effect is nonetheless much smoother in the original Russian, where the Cyrillic letter "В" represents the "V" for Vasilii, and the Cyrillic "C" denotes the "S" for Stepan. What Shternberg gained in simplicity with the use of these familiar surnames distracts all the same from the Gilyak tradition of naming clans after totemic symbols or place names, not clan ancestors.]

[10] [**Editor's note:** Tables here follow the two AMNH typescripts, which include this last sentence in the table itself. The Soviet editions put it in the body of the text.]

TABLE 3.

THE FOUR-CLAN COGNATIC PHRATRY

CLAN A (ANDREI)	CLAN B (VASILII)	CLAN C (STEPAN)	CLAN D (JOHN)[11]
Clan Ancestor and Wife	**Clan Ancestor and Wife**	**Clan Ancestor and Wife**	**Clan Ancestor and Wife**
Andrei Vera	Vasilii Sophia	Stepan Anna	John Mary
Andrei, brother of Anna, who is married into clan C	Vasilii, brother of Vera, who is married into clan A	Stepan, brother of Mary, who is married into clan D	John, brother of Sophia, who is married into clan B
Vera, sister of Vasilii of clan B	Sophia, sister of John of clan D	Anna, sister of Andrei of clan A	Mary, sister of Stepan of clan C
Their Children	**Their Children**	**Their Children**	**Their Children**
1. Sons marry daughters of mother's brother, Vasilii of clan B	1. Sons marry daughters of mother's brother, John of clan D	1. Sons marry daughters of mother's brother, Andrei of clan A	1. Sons marry daughters of mother's brother, Stepan of clan C
2. Daughters marry sons of father's sister, Anna of clan C	2. Daughters marry sons of father's sister, Vera of clan A	2. Daughters marry sons of father's sister, Mary of clan D	2. Daughters marry sons of father's sister, Sophia of clan B

In succeeding generations, marriages follow the same rule: Men marry mother's brother's daughters; women marry father's sister's sons.

Clan B gives women to A who, in turn, gives women to C. Consequently, B represents the wive's fathers of the second degree (*tuyma akhmalk*) to C, meaning that C can*not* give women to B. Vasilii's wife cannot be the sister of Stepan. As a result, the men of clan B remain without wives, while the women of clan C remain without husbands. And that would be sad.[12]

In order to overcome this obstacle, it is necessary that the phratry contain a fourth clan, from which B could take women and to which C could give theirs [**110**]. Then the schematic table of the four-clan phratry would assume the form shown in table 3.

This four-clan phratry is in perfect accord with the Gilyak norms of marriage. An analysis of the table reveals the following facts: In each clan all generations of

---

11 [*Editor's note:* Though I restored Shternberg's Russian clan names to the tables in this chapter, I make first-name exceptions for Shternberg's use of John and Mary (found in the AMNH Russian typescript as "Dzhon i Meri")—imperial and Soviet Russia's popular answer to Dick and Jane. The 1933 Soviet editions Russified them as "Dem'ian i Mariia."]

12 [*Editor's note:* In the AMNH Russian typescript, after noting the predicament of clans B and C above, Shternberg speculates on what would happen if clan B took women from clan C, representing this in a repeat of table 2. However, Shternberg then informs that his hypothetical solution clashes with the Gilyak rule that a woman must not marry into the clan from which her own clansmen take wives, and he disavows this model and moves on to the four-clan phratry (table 3). The digression is not found in the 1933 Soviet editions.]

men take wives from the clan from which their clan ancestor originally took his wife, or every individual takes a wife from the clan of his mother. While the rule holds that women of a clan marry according to their generation into the clan where the sister of their clan ancestor was married, in practice each individual woman takes a husband from the clan into which her father's sister is married.

The exchange of women between two clans is not permissible. Clan A, accordingly, takes wives from clan B, the clan of its ancestress Vera. It may not, however, give its women in exchange to that clan, but marries them off into clan C, where its clan ancestor's sister, Anna, is married. Clan B, then, might take wives either from C or from D; but clan C is ruled out, for B stands to it in the relation of *tuyma akhmalk* (the clan of wife's fathers of the second degree). Thus clan B is limited in its choice of wives to clan D, which is the clan of its clan ancestor's wife, Sophia. The women of C and the men of D still seem unprovided for, but, as the table reveals, the latter are married to the former as their mother's brother's daughters. Now the phratry is matrimonially self-sufficient, and all marital norms are accommodated.

Let us now examine the relationship between the members of different clans. Let us begin with the relationship between clan ancestors and their wives. Andrei (clan A) is a first-cousin both of Vasilii and of his sister Vera, for their father's sister was his mother. Andrei is also a first-cousin of Stepan (clan C) and his sister Mary, for their mother must have been Andrei's father's sister (clan C marries from clan A). At the same time Andrei is a second-cousin of John and Sophia, for John's clan (D) takes wives from C, who in turn take wives from A. Thus the grandmother of John must have been the sister of Andrei's grandfather, and thus John and Andrei are cognatic cousins of the second degree. Obviously the relationship between the clan ancestor toward the others is the same as in the case of Andrei; this will be true of representatives of the various clans in all generations, for the marital norms are the same everywhere [111].

Our analysis shows the following:

1.   In each generation the representatives of all four clans are either brothers and sisters or cousins, persons of common descent in the male and female lines.
2.   In each generation of the clans which stand in a matrimonial relation to each other, the group of potential husbands are cognatic cousins, usually of the first degree. This is also true of the group of wives.
3.   In clans which do not stand to each other in matrimonial relations but are mutually *tuyma akhmalk,* such as the clans A and D or B and C, the husbands are cognatic cousins to each other, and the wives are cognatic cousins to each other, but not nearer than the second degree. They are as a rule less intimately related than is the case in matrimonially connected clans. Remoteness of relationship beyond a certain degree thus appears among the Gilyak to be, as in Australia, a barrier to marriage.
4.   If I am male, my father-in-law is my mother's brother and a first cousin of my father, while my mother-in-law is my father's second-cousin and a first-cousin of my mother. If I am female, my father-in-law is a first-cousin of my father and a second-cousin of my mother, while my mother-in-law is my father's sister and

a first-cousin of my mother. In other words, husband and wife are related through their fathers and through their mothers. On their father's side as well as on their mother's, they are second-cousins; through wife's father and husband's mother they are first-cousins; through husband's father and wife's mother they are third-cousins.

5. The relationship between the clans of the phratry as such may be represented as follows: Clan A is *mal akhmalk* ("father-in-law of the first degree") of clan C, *tuyma akhmalk* ("father-in-law of the second degree") of clan D, and *imgi* (son-in-law") of clan B, to which last clan A also stands in the relation of father-in-law of the third degree, for D is the clan of fathers-in-law of B. Clan B stands in exactly the same relationship towards clans A, C, and D; the same is true of clan C with reference to clans D, B, and A, and of clan D with reference to clans B, A, and C.

Accordingly, we can now make the following statements:

1. The *imgi* clan is the clan of fathers-in-law of the third degree with reference to the clan of its actual fathers-in-law; consequently, the third father-in-law relation is a form of relationship which is quite negligible from the point of view of the regulation of marriage. As a matter of fact, no term exists for this relation, which recognizes only two forms of the father-in-law bonds—*mal akhmalk* ("father-in-law of the first degree") and *tuyma akhmalk* ("father-in-law of the second degree").

2. The relation of *tuyma akhmalk* is a reciprocal one, A being *tuyma akhmalk* of D, D being *tuyma akhmalk* of A, and so on. The present marriage law of the Gilyak requires that women shall not marry into a *tuyma akhmalk* clan; and as the relation *tuyma akhmalk* of two clans is reciprocal, no matrimonial relationship between such clans is possible. This fact is illustrated in table 3; *tuyma akhmalk* clans (A and D, B and C) are not matrimonially related. As noted above, this prohibition is not based on closeness of relationship. Quite the contrary, *tuyma akhmalk* clans stand to each other in a more remote degree of relationship than matrimonially related clans.

What may have been the origin of this peculiar institution of *tuyma akhmalk*? Whence came the fundamental interdict against giving women in marriage to a *tuyma akhmalk* clan—an interdict necessitating the formation among the Gilyak of a four-clan phratry instead of a three-clan phratry? When I first published my observations of the Gilyak phratry I deduced this interdict from the necessity of having in the *tuyma akhmalk* clan a reserve supply of wives in case of extinction of the *mal akhmalk* clan.

My prolonged studies of the development of Gilyak marriage resulted in the conviction that the origin of the above interdict must be looked for elsewhere, namely, in the preceding phase of marriage. Before we pass to a consideration of this problem, however, we must glance at the evolution undergone by the four-clan phratry and the norms of Gilyak marriage, an evolution spurred by a special set of conditions which finally brought about the matrimonial forms we know today.

EIGHT

THE EVOLUTION OF THE PHRATRY

[85–98, 107–112; 130–154; 200–209, 214–219; 104–114][1]

IN ORDER that this really endogamous system survive and discharge its functions in their full and lawful entirety, certain definite conditions were necessary. Economic, physiological, and social conditions had, of course, to be favorable. Separate families of the phratry, notwithstanding their growth in numbers, had to retain a common territory. The increase in numbers in some families had to be in excess of, or at least equal to, the loss in others, and in no cases could the dying out of entire clans occur. The people had to be more or less isolated from external influences if the imperative toward marriages within the phratry was to retain its original hold [**104**].

Among any primitive people powerful obstacles can stand in the way of the continuance of such conditions. Hence, notwithstanding the Gilyak love for their ancestral territory, the stress of economic conditions has forced individuals, separate families, and even entire clans to change their habitat and wander to places far removed from their ancient homes. In the course of a few years during my own first stay on Sakhalin, many families migrated from the Tym' valley to more remote regions of the Ainu territory in northern Sakhalin, or to the Amur. But none did so by choice.

One striking illustration was the village of Pilavo, the most southern Gilyak settlement on the western coast of Sakhalin, on the very border of the Ainu territory. Owing to a feud among clansmen, part of the clan moved 500 versts further to the north and named their new village after their metropolis—as North Pilavo. Another feud arose, and another group of clansmen went from Sakhalin to the Lower Amur, founding the larger village of Khez, which no longer exists. Finally a new feud arose and a third village was founded 1000 versts further on the middle Amur, near Khabarovsk, in the midst of the Gold (Nanai) territory. The many branches of this widely scattered clan, in spite of the breaking off of all their former bonds, have to this day remained exogamous, but they could not maintain the ancient matrimonial relations of the phratry.

The breaking up of clans in such a manner has continued up to the present time. This explains why the Gilyak, in real life as in epic tales, must so often travel hundreds of miles in search of a wife from the proper clan. Such heroic quests, however,

---

[1] [***Editor's note:*** The AMNH English typescript and Shternberg, *Sem'ia*, are the closest in sequencing of materials in this chapter. The AMNH Russian typescript and Shternberg, *Giliaki,* diverge significantly, as indicated in notes throughout the chapter.]

are not for the average man. Most frequently an individual will seek adoption into another clan and marry the widow of one of his new clansmen, thus severing all ties with his old phratry. In the case of migration, not only of single individuals but of entire families, the descendants often end up by marrying into neighboring clans not belonging to their original phratry.

Catastrophe itself has taken perhaps the greatest toll on phratry organization, not least when the Gilyak have come into contact with alien cultures, first Far Eastern and then European. Between the alcohol and the exploitation made manifest by these peoples, the Gilyak have suffered from numerous infectious diseases which play havoc among a primitive population lacking immunity. Many times before my very eyes, epidemics of smallpox, scarlet fever, diphtheria, and other diseases decimated the scanty population. Some of the smaller clans have been entirely wiped out, while among others, only one or two clansmen have survived. It must also be remembered that the population is so widely scattered that the depopulating process does not strike the different clans of a phratry with equal force; at any given moment one clan may remain intact, while another may lose the greater part of its members.

The social consequences of such epidemics can best be shown by one of my own experiences during my last trip to Sakhalin in 1910. When visiting an old friend on the Tym' River, I was greatly surprised to see many Gilyak married to women of prohibited categories. For instance, one of my friends, Churka, an old bachelor, had married the widow of his class "father" (agnatic uncle), i.e., his class mother. This was unheard of even within my memory. Nor was the Churka case the only one in the village. "What could we do?" they said, when I asked how such events could have transpired. "The epidemic (smallpox) of last year killed off many of our clansmen—what was to be done with their widows? It would be a sin to let the widows leave the clan, so the elders decided that the widows must be kept." It is easy to appreciate the havoc wrought. At once the entire kinship terminology was done away with. Such cases are the best explanation of the perplexities and inconsistencies found in some classificatory systems, and which have puzzled many very able investigators (such as Dr. Swanton), inducing them to deny the true meaning of Morgan's views on the classificatory system.[2]

The psychological effects of contact with other peoples have also been indirectly destructive. As so often happens, exposure to new opinions broadens the mental horizon and weakens the strength of religious imperatives. The representatives of a higher culture look down upon the institutions of a more primitive society, and the primitives themselves can begin to lose their unquestioning respect for their own institutions. At first, only a few will tend to transgress the law, but the few will then be followed by many. According to the Gilyak themselves, their marriage regulations have lost vigor since the advent of the Russians. But even before the arrival of the Russians, the Gilyak came in contact with Chinese and Manchu, not to mention the Tungus and Ainu. The Chinese, as we shall see later, supplied the Gilyak with wives and, together with the Ainu, furnished them with female slaves.

---

[2]   [**Editor's note:** Cf. John Reed Swanton, *Contributions to the Ethnology of the Haida* (Leiden: E. J. Brill, 1905).]

Of similar significance were traveling merchants and hunting expeditions to the territories of neighboring tribes. The Amur Gilyak would often spend several years hunting and trading in the territories of the Ainu, and would bring home with them Ainu women. In turn, isolated Tungus and Ainu would settle among the Gilyak and form matrimonial alliances with them, being adopted into Gilyak clans. Indeed, not a single Gilyak clan can be said to be free from foreign, Ainu, or Tungus blood. A great many clans even embrace foreigners as their clan ancestors [*rodonachal'niki*].

The economic relations with peoples of more complex cultures was another factor of special significance. Before contact with the Chinese and Russians, Gilyak had no incentive to amass wealth. Property merely consisted of the necessities of life. No one tried to save, and the highest ambition of the able and lucky man was to divide his share with others. Trade with the Chinese brought new material goods that could not be consumed but were highly prized, and profitable to amass. Rich men arose as fortunate possessors of wealth, and others did not enjoy but craved such possession. The rich began to be conscious of their riches and position, and began to cherish the ambition to mate among their equals. The poor, in turn, began to make the marriage of their daughters a means of acquiring valuables. Finally the rise of capitalism precipitated the growth of individual marriage. The custom for several brothers to cohabit with one wife became less and less common. Indeed, while 100 years ago Mamiya Rinzo described such arrangements as a constant occurrence, at present they are becoming steadily rarer [**105**].[3]

THE DYNAMICS OF THE DESTRUCTIVE CONDITIONS

Of all the conditions detrimental to the phratry—emigration, extinction, war, foreign immigration, hunting expeditions, and the fading of economic equality—likely the most powerful factor was catastrophe.

What effect did this have on the surviving clans? Let us recall table 3 of our four-clan phratry. We will assume that clan A, from which clan C took its wives, became extinct. What would be the result? What course would be adopted by clan C, which used to take women from A, and by clan B, which used to give its women to clan A? It is natural that the members of these clans should first look about for substitutes within the phratry itself, for outside of it no "pure" marriage is possible. But clan C cannot take women from D, because the latter supplies women to the former, and the simple exchange of women can under no circumstances be tolerated. For the same reason clan B may not give its women to D. The only way out would be for C to take women from B, and it would be best also from a religious point of view. The orthodox marriage is, as we know, with a woman of the mother's clan. Thus, after the disappearance of clan A, the most closely related clan on the mother's side for C is B, for from that clan A took its women; clan A, in its turn, supplied women to C. If that were the method adopted, the four-clan phratry would have been transformed into the three-clan phratry. But that method could be applied

---

[3] [***Editor's note:*** For a discussion of Rinzo's account of Gilyak life, see Bruce Grant, *In the Soviet House of Culture: A Century of Perestroikas* (Princeton, NJ: Princeton Univ. Press), 49–51.]

FIG. 15. Gilyak fishermen with their dogs alongside a long dugout boat used to cross the Tatar Strait, 1890s. Photo by Lev Shternberg. *Source:* AAN f. 282, o. 2, d. 98, l. 44.

only as a last resort because C is *tuyma akhmalk* to B and as such is strictly forbidden to take women from B.

This interdict is so powerful that, as we have seen, it holds full sway even to the present day. The four-clan phratry had to be saved. There were two possible ways of achieving this end. One way would be the artificial splitting up of one clan (in our case, clan C) into two parts—a process familiar in North America. However, no reference can be found to such a practice in either traditional epics or modern custom. Meanwhile another and more natural method was offered. The process of depopulation affected more than one phratry, and an isolated clan, the fragment of another phratry, could easily be found. Such an orphan clan would undergo many sacrifices to achieve adoption, and in this way the matter could be settled to the satisfaction of all parties concerned [**106**].

So far we have assumed that only one clan, A, had become extinct. However, it may have happened that a phratry lost not one clan, but two and three. This occasion would call not merely for the adoption of one clan into the phratry but for the merging of several mutually alien clans into one common phratry.

Thus it came about that the fundamental principle of marriage was seriously impaired. Men began to marry women of foreign blood. And while it is true that in the following generation things resumed their normal course again (each man could marry his mother's brother's daughter), the psychological effect of the break was irreparable. Over the course of time, marriages of isolated individuals outside of the phratry were tolerated, though not considered quite proper.

Let us now analyze what would happen if clan A were merely to decrease in numbers instead of becoming completely extinct.

As clan A takes women from B and gives them to C, it may happen that some of the men of C will remain without wives, while part of the women of B will have no individual husbands. As in the first case, the best remedy here would be to adopt into the phratry a new and also depopulated clan, E, which would join A in giving its women to C and in taking women from B. This would result in a five-clan phratry, and individuals of one clan would take women belonging to several different clans. This latter practice would tend to undermine the very foundations of the old psychology insofar as it would foster the indifference of individuals towards the ancient norm of prescribed marriage of all clansmen with women of their mother's clan. As a result we find in modern times many members of a clan married to women of several different clans.

But what would happen if the adoption of a fifth clan should prove impracticable, and it were decided that the only possible adjustment, the *ultimum refugium*, would be for those men of clan C who remained without wives on account of the depopulation of A to take some of the women of the prohibited *tuyma akhmalk* clan B, which is nearest to them on the mother's side? Thus the members of one clan would be taking women from two clans! Still another consequence would be even more disruptive, when B is the clan from which clan A also takes its wives. Thus *akhmalk* and *imgi* ("fathers-in-law" and "sons-in-law") would find themselves married to women of one clan (B), and in every generation these individuals would be married to "sisters," and as such, according to the norms of Gilyak marriage, would be group-husbands; meanwhile, their children would be brothers and sisters (*tuvng*). In the next generations, marriage would be prohibited between one part of clan C and one part of clan A, a complexity which would inevitably lead to new combinations and the further disintegration of the old system.

The sum of unfavorable conditions led to the following: (1) marriage with women of clans other than that of the mother began to be tolerated; (2) members of one clan were married to women of different clans; and (3) the ancient four-clan phratry lost its exclusiveness, being forced sometimes to adopt entire new clans. As a consequence of the irregular marriages of some individuals with women of different clans, each one of these clans came to be included under the classificatory terminology, and thus became equated to the original clans of the phratry [107].

PERSEVERANCE OF OLD FORMS

In the face of these adverse conditions, however, the ancient norms have not lost their strength but continue to dominate in Gilyak minds. Marriage into the *akhmalk* clan still remains in the eyes of modern Gilyak the only "pure" marriage. Irregular marriages appear rather as exceptional events which for the time being break the accustomed rule, only to be drawn back into the established run of things. This may happen in various ways. In some instances, a man may, for some reason or another, marry outside of his mother's clan. His descendants, however, will resume taking wives from the old *akhmalk* clan. In other instances, where the restitution of the old order is impossible, the clan from which a man has taken his wife becomes the legal marriageable clan for his descendants, who in each generation follow the old rule and marry the mother's brother's daughter. Sometimes the descendants will take wives from the new or the old *akhmalk* clan according to circumstances, and both types of marriage will thenceforth be sanctioned by public opinion. An individual or clan may also have more than two clans from which to choose wives. But each individual, when entering a matrimonial union, will try to comply by looking for a wife in its mother's clan, the mother's brother's daughter being the preferred party.

This amalgamation of an old institution with a new one, and the adoption of all the regulations and restrictions born of the old one, resulted in extraordinary complications for kinship terminology as well as for group marriage itself. Under the old order, where only marriages with one definite clan were entered into, the procedures of group marriage were clear and simple: In each generation all "brothers" of a clan were partners to group marriage with all "sisters" of the same generation of another clan. Thus the wives of "brothers" call each other "sisters," while the husbands of "sisters" call each other "brothers," for such they are in actuality.

With the intrusion of irregular marriages, "brother" clansmen may be married to women of a number of different clans. But the wives, although they may be complete strangers to one another, will cling to the old custom and call each other "sisters," as group-wives to their brother-husbands. Similarly, "sister" clanswomen may be married to men of different clans, and the husbands, although strangers to each other, will have group rights over these women [108].

The following is another striking example of the extension of the old norms. In the days of "pure" marriage within the phratry, as we know, a clan was not permitted to give its own women to the clan from which it itself took its women (the clan of one's father's sister), nor to the clan from which the latter clan took its wives, the two prohibited clans being those of *akhmalk* and *tuyma akhmalk*, respectively. At the present time, when separate individuals of a clan may take wives outside of their mother's clan, the term "father-in-law" (*akhmalk*) [or, more precisely, wife's father— B. G.] is extended to all clans from which a clansman, even if he be the only one, has taken a wife. A situation may thus arise, for instance, when five men from clan A entered into willful matrimony with women of five different clans such that all of these clans and their *akhmalk* would then become *akhmalk* to clan A and would thereby become prohibited to the women of clan A (admittedly, only to the third generation).[4] If we add the two clans already presumed *akhmalk* of the first and second generations to clan A, that makes 12 clans prohibited to the women of clan A! One can imagine the havoc this would cause. Indeed, the tendency to extend prohibitive regulations might have led to serious difficulties in the way of marriage, for each new marriage reduces the number of clans that may be married into. However, the effect of these sweeping prohibitions is counterbalanced by the tendency of the clan and its individual members not to deviate except in extreme cases from the old norms and to take wives from one definite clan, the clan of the mother. Another check on the extension of matrimonial restrictions is the rule already mentioned, according to which the restrictions apply only to those families directly involved in irregular marriages.

Still greater complexity was wrought by the extended regulations. Formerly the classificatory kinship system extended beyond the clan of an individual to two other clans, that of the father-in-law and that of the son-in-law, with the terms corresponding to actual sexual relations. If, for instance, I (being male) should call the sisters of my "fathers-in-law" "mothers," this would correspond to the actual facts.

---

4   [**Editor's note:** Gilyak marriage rules lost their sanction after two generations.]

For the sisters of my "fathers-in-law" would be the group-wives of my "fathers," while one of them would be my own mother. Or if I (being male) should call each "father-in-law" in the *akhmalk* clan "mother's brother," and his daughter my "wife," this would correspond to the actual matrimonial relations. At present when incidental irregular marriages have caused the classificatory system to be extended to a set of clans alien to the clansmen, the terms "fathers-in-law," "mothers," "mother's brother's daughters," and so on are applied to persons who have never been related to the given clan. As the number of persons drawn into the classificatory terminology continues to increase, familiarity with such relationships, once so easily attainable, becomes a feat of considerable difficulty. In view of the great importance of such knowledge in the life of the Gilyak, its acquisition has now become a real science, into which one is initiated from childhood, and which is fully mastered only on attaining maturity. It is not astonishing that the classificatory system should strike Europeans as amazingly confused and incomprehensible.

In reality, as we have seen, the complexity and the seeming incongruity of the system is due to the intrusion of the new practice of free marriage upon an old system which still clings to its ancient norms, according to which marriage must be between blood relatives and with the mother's clan [**109**].

The Place of Gilyak Marriage in the General Evolution of Marital Institutions

Since we have seen that the fundamental form of Gilyak marriage is between a sister's son and her brother's daughter, it must be regarded as a variation on the theme of cousin marriage. [We say "variation," for in the common forms of cousin marriage the children of brother and sister are permitted to marry indiscriminately. The exchange of women moreover is not only permitted but required, so that cousins marry each other's sisters—a practice strictly tabooed among the Gilyak.] [**111**][5]

How did this type of marriage originate? This leads us to the consideration of cousin marriage as an important stage in the evolution of marriage. I shall therefore take the liberty to dwell on this point.

As far back as 1900, in a paper presented to the Imperial Russian Geographical Society (subsequently published in *The Ethnographic Review* [*Etnograficheskoe Obozrenie*] and in other articles),[6] I was led to the conclusion that cousin marriage

---

5   [***Editor's note:*** The preceding two sentences are in brackets because they appear to have been added to the AMNH English typescript only, signaled in the AMNH Russian typescript by an editor's insertion arrow. While Shternberg recognizes that Gilyaks followed a form of prescriptive matrilateral cross-cousin marriage, he theorizes an earlier stage of reciprocal "cousin marriage," sometimes known as sister-exchange, after Morgan, to explain the rise and nature of exogamy. Shternberg, *Sem'ia*, 112–114, which the AMNH English typescript abridges, is the clearest source for this discussion. It is especially appropriate in this chapter to remember that page numbers in bold, referring to Shternberg, *Sem'ia*, indicate locations for what is often only similar, rather than exact, material.]

6   [***Editor's note:*** Previous versions of the text include no citations for the report to the Russian Geographical Society or the article "Theories of Clan Life." Shternberg's article "Endogamiia i Eksogamiia" was published in 1904 in the ESBE. The AMNH English typescript directs the reader to the three 1904 installments of Shternberg, "Giliaki."]

constitutes the original form of exogamy and lies at the root of the classificatory kin system of group marriage and the clan itself. I pointed out that clan exogamy is not merely a restrictive institution, but one that regulates sexual relations, the main function of which is to assure to every clan a constant supply of wives, the latter being related to the clan by ties of consanguinity—a factor which is of vast importance in the different stages of society.

In recent works (such as those of Rivers, Crawley, Frazer) as well as in the work of their predecessors in the field of Australian and Dravidian marriage (Fison and Howitt, Spencer and Gillen, Kohler, and others), one finds ample demonstration of the wide distribution of that form of marriage at the present time.[7] The Australian marriage system demonstrates conclusively that cousin marriage presented the first conscious attempt to restrict marriage between brothers and sisters, and that the entire subsequent evolution of marriage constitutes a set of progressive limitations on the marriage of first-cousins [**112**].[8]

One cardinal issue for us still goes unexplained. I refer to the question as to why cousin marriage requires unions between the children of brother and sister (cross-cousins) while prohibiting marriages between the children of two brothers or of two sisters (parallel-cousins), although the blood relationship here is just as close in the former. W. H. R. Rivers, for example, refuses even to look for an explanation of this remarkable fact. He writes,

> Cousin marriage bears every evidence of being a survival. It is very diffi-
> cult to see how such a regulation could have had any direct psychological
> foundation, to conceive any motive which should make the marriage of
> the children of brother and sister desirable, while the marriage of the chil-
> dren of two brothers or of two sisters is so strictly forbidden.[9]

Others have attempted to explain this phenomenon, but their explanations often have been purely mechanical. Kohler, for instance, sees the source of the custom in "the dual organization of society." This is a strange explanation indeed, for the dual organization is itself a consequence of cousin marriage as "an automatic result of the fact that the name of the family is inherited . . . . The children of the brother and sister may marry because by their names they belong to opposite phratries."[10] Frazer

---

[7]   A realization of this fact led Crawley to remark that "cousin marriage generally is the most favorite connection among early peoples." Cf. Crawley, "Exogamy," 57.

[8]   The best analysis of the Australian marriage in that sense is given by James Frazer in his monumental work *Totemism and Exogamy* (London: Macmillan, 1910), vol. 4. [***Editor's note:*** This note is found only in the AMNH English typescript. Shternberg, *Sem'ia*, contains a later, laconic reference to Frazer, without such praise.]

[9]   W. H. R. Rivers, "Marriage of Cousins in India," *Journal of the Royal Asiatic Society* (July 1907), 623.

[10] Kohler, *Zur Urgeschichte der Ehe*, 121. [***Editor's note:*** Although the page numbers do not correspond to Shternberg's entry, an early German edition of Kohler's work was printed in serial form as "Zur Urgescicte der Ehe: Totemismus, Gruppenehe, Mutterrecht," *Zeitschrift für vergleichende Rechtswissenschaft* 12 (1897): 187–353. For an excellent English edition see Kohler, *On the Prehistory of Marriage: Totemism, Group Marriage, Mother Right.* Translated from the German by R. H. Barnes and Ruth Barnes. Edited with an Introduction by R. H. Barnes (Chicago: Univ. Chicago Press, 1975).]

also arrives at the same conclusion. "The reason," he writes, "why both these first-cousins (that is, the children of two brothers or of two sisters) are prohibited from marrying is that they belong to the same exogamous clan, and are therefore barred by the fundamental law which forbids a man to marry a woman of his own exogamous clan."[11] The fundamental error of all these writers is that they confuse effect with cause. They regard so-called "cross-cousin marriage" as the result of the division of a group into two exogamous classes, without so much as asking themselves why this came about.

In fact, the division into two exogamous classes was the result of the new institution of marriage between the children of brother and sister which replaced the ancient endogamous consanguineous marriage. Until then the group of descendants of a single clan ancestress was indivisible; marriages took place within the group, usually between brothers and sisters. Only when these marriages had been recognized as harmful, and marriage between the children of brother and sister had become the rule, was the originally integral group divided into two exogamous halves. One half was made up of the brothers, with their wives and children; the other, of the sisters, with their husbands and children. Thus the dual division is seen to be a consequence of cross-cousin marriage. In exploring this, we must look to the well-known conservatism of primitive man, especially with reference to an institution like marriage which is so intimately governed by religious ideas and prohibitions. The main tendency is to preserve *quand même* as much as possible of the old forms, even though the essence of the institution is no longer there. Only under its old exterior can a new institution be introduced.

Keeping in mind this fundamental conservatism, let us consider the conditions under which the great transformation in the history of marriage took place. During the period which preceded cousin marriage, the favored orthodox form of marriage was between brother and sister, with marriage between blood relatives of different generations prohibited. The matrimonial formula then was that marriages were to be concluded between the children of brother and sister, while the latter themselves were husband and wife, and parents of the young couple. When it became necessary to prohibit blood marriage in the first degree (between blood brothers and sisters) and to pass to marriages in the second degree (that is, to first-cousins), the issue for the conservative mind was that these cousins should be, as before, children of brother and sister (although the latter were no longer husband and wife), but not children of brothers, or children of sisters. In preserving the old form (a fact always of paramount importance in the eyes of primitive man), the substance of the change becomes disguised from the deity—a common and pious way of deceiving the supernatural powers [**113**].

---

[11] Frazer *in* Crawley, "Exogamy," 57. [***Editor's note:*** The closest reference in Crawley's article reads, "Families of the one great family cannot intermarry because they belong to that family, and they marry into the other great family because it is 'the other side.'" However, the line, from p. 55, is not from Frazer, who does not appear in the article. The AMNH Russian typescript and Shternberg, *Giliaki*, contain no reference for this line, found in the AMNH English typescript. Shternberg, *Sem'ia*, 112, note 5, refers to Frazer, *Totemism and Exogamy* (London, 1910).]

Still, we ask: If cousin marriage is to be regarded as the first stage of exogamy, as the first restrictive movement against marriages between near blood relatives, how shall we explain its strict—nay, almost categorical—character? It seems that with the realization of the harmfulness of marriage between blood relatives and the benefits of exogamy, the most reasonable attitude to have adopted would have been to favor marriages between persons of the remotest degree of relationship. Marriages between cousins should have been tolerated, at least in early stages, as a necessary evil, *malum necessarium,* to be eliminated later as an antisocial institution. Nonetheless, among primitive peoples everywhere the reverse is the case: Cousin marriage of a certain degree is either obligatory or at least more favored than unions between more remote kin or even absolute strangers.

The best example of this strange fact is furnished by the evolution of marriage in Australia. To judge from the class organization and from statements made by natives themselves, these peoples are fully aware of the harmfulness of marriage between near blood relatives, and they have therefore exercised extraordinary inventiveness in their efforts to reduce it. So complicated an organization as the eight-class system of the Arunta [Aranda] was especially invented to prevent marriages of first-cousins. In the presence of such a system, one would think that only marriages between the most remote relatives would be favored, while marriages between second-cousins would be barely tolerated. As a matter of fact, however, even "third-cousins are too remote; beyond this relationship, marriage is forbidden."[12] Thus marriage between cousins, excluding only those of the first degree, is not only permitted, but prescribed; and the Australians are no exception. The Dravidian natives of India, so numerous and so far advanced in culture in comparison with the Australians, are no exception [**113–114**].[13]

If cousin marriage were but the first step in the limitation of unions between near blood relatives, the first stage of exogamy, then it must have given way long ago. If it persisted so obstinately, as for example among Dravidians, there must have been other essential reasons than the mere prevention of inbreeding. To my mind the strength of cousin marriage is based on two important psychological factors. The first factor is the natural tendency of every kin group, and particularly of every mother, to supply descendants with wives. In the early stages of human development, the struggle between the sexes must have played as important a part as it did in the rest of the animal kingdom. Thus one of the most vital problems of human society was to diminish this struggle by means of various regulations. The institution of marriage—prescribed marriage between individuals belonging to definite groups—was just such a sexual regulation that satisfied this essential need.

Before the establishment of exogamy, this need could be satisfied by the practice of marriages between brothers and sisters. With the establishment of exogamy, cross-cousin marriage could solve the problem most successfully. From birth on, the sons of a woman are the husbands of her brother's daughters, while the latter's sons

---

[12]   Crawley, "Exogamy," 61.

[13]   [***Editor's note:*** The additional reference to Dravidians is found in the AMNH Russian and English typescripts only.]

are her daughter's husbands. This combination is equally satisfactory to the father of the family, for his children marry the children of his sister [**114**].

The other psychological factor favoring cousin marriage is of a religious nature. In such marriages the family hearth, with its ancestral gods, unites persons not alien to each other, but of common descent through both father and mother. Thus husband and wife may equally count on the favors of their common ancestral gods—a consideration of vital importance to primitive man, to whom the securing of divine goodwill through the performance of religious rituals figures among life's most urgent deeds, the most important means in the struggle for survival. This explains why that form of marriage came to be not merely favored, but religiously enforced, as among many Dravidian peoples of India with whom marriage is quite compulsory whenever a brother has a daughter, and his sister a son. Thus with these two factors—the natural tendency to regulate sexual relations by giving the right to marriage to every member of the related group, and the assurance to partners in marriage of the help of powerful ancestral gods—we find essential reasons for the persistence of cousin marriage.

With these remarks established, we may now turn to the history of the evolution of cousin marriage itself.

NINE

GILYAK COUSIN MARRIAGE AND MORGAN'S HYPOTHESIS[1]

[113–129; 155–159, 168–185, 159–167; 219–235; 114–124]

COUSIN MARRIAGE must ultimately be deduced from the realization that close blood marriage between close blood relatives is harmful. We have seen that primitive man, for a number of reasons (be they religious conservatism, ideas associated with ancestor worship, or the desire for a peaceful organization of marriage), did not pass directly from marriage between brother and sister to marriage between remote relations or strangers. Our goal in this chapter is to trace the genetic link between the Gilyak system and that of Australia, to see how the Gilyak diverged from the Australian system at the stage when marriage between two-sided first-cousins first began to come into disrepute [114].[2]

The great transformation towards exogamous marriage took place with extreme slowness. Thus, as is the case even now among the Australian natives, the first form of exogamy adopted was that of enforced marriage between children of brother and sister. As the marriages occur uniformly from generation to generation, the group, in matrimonial order, is necessarily divided into two moieties which, following the generations, exchange their women by cross-cousin marriage. In its application to individual families, this system requires that the son of a brother marry the latter's sister's daughter, and conversely, the son of a sister, the latter's brother's daughter. In this system, husband and wife must be first-cousins, such that the wife of a man is, on the one hand, his father's sister's daughter, and on the other, his mother's brother's daughter, because the fathers of the couple are married to each other's sisters [115].

---

[1]   [*Editor's note:* The AMNH English typescript presents material from this and the next chapter in a different manner than its Russian-language counterparts. For the virtues of discussing Morgan's work first in light of the Gilyak kinship system and then in the comparative context of other North Asian peoples, I have restored the sequencing from the AMNH Russian typescript. It loosely approximates corresponding sections of the two 1933 Soviet editions, which differ in both sequence and content. Earlier titles for this material included "Cousin Marriage and the Gilyak Marital Norms" and "Suggestions" (AMNH English typescript); "Cousin Marriage and Gilyak Marriage Norms" and "The Wide Distribution of Gilyak Cousin Marriage" (AMNH Russian typescript); "Cousin Marriage [continued]" and "The Gilyak Kinship System and Morgan's Hypothesis" (Shternberg, *Giliaki*); and "Cousin Marriage and Gilyak Marital Norms" and "The Gilyak Kinship System and Morgan's Hypothesis" (Shternberg, *Sem'ia*).]

[2]   [*Editor's note:* Although this sentence is found only in the AMNH English typescript, it repeats the biological slant from the end of the last chapter and the end of this one.]

Such was the first stage in the restriction of marriage between persons closely related by blood. Further restrictions followed different lines among various peoples. In Australia these restrictions followed the most simple course. From first-cousin marriage they passed to marriage between second-cousins, and the former became prohibited.

No change in social organization accompanied this transformation. The group was still separated into moieties which exchanged women, with the difference being that a man no longer married his father's sister's daughter but the daughter of his male first-cousin, so that the descendants of brother and sister could again intermarry only in the second generation. Husband and wife were now one degree removed from each other on both the father's and mother's side. The principle of cross-cousin marriage (the exchange of women) remained intact, but the other principle—stating that marriage between the children of brother and sister was imperative, or at least the only orthodox route—was completely abandoned. In the end, it proved impossible to save both maxims.

These people, among whom the Gilyak are the most instructive representatives, also resolved to limit first-cousin marriage, believing it necessary to establish a more remote degree of relationship between the parties of a marriage union. But they were unwilling to sacrifice the principle they regarded as most important—the premise by which a mother marries her son to her brother's daughter. This principle was accordingly preserved, but in order to comply with the need for a lessening of the closeness of relationship between marriage partners, they gave up bilateral cousin marriage.[3] Among the Gilyak, as we know, the son of every woman claims her brother's daughter, while the reverse is not allowed; a brother's son may not marry the former's sister's daughter. The result was a reduction in the closeness of relationship between marriage partners; they are still first-cousins, but only on one side, that of the husband's mother, no longer on the side of the wife's mother. Thus at the same time the ancient fundamental principle, marriage with the mother's brother's daughter, remained intact, while the marriage mates were still first-cousins, if only unilaterally.

This deviation from the Australian system of limiting first-cousin marriage brought with it a radical change in the social organization: It changed the bipartite organization of the group with its classes to a pure clan organization, and in particular to the four-clan phratry we have found among the Gilyak.

In the Australian system, the restrictions of cousin marriage may extend to any degree without in any way affecting the division of the group, from the point of view of marriage, into exogamous moieties constantly exchanging women. Essentially

---

[3] [**Editor's note:** With bilateral cousin marriage, a male marries his mother's brother's daughter or father's sister's daughter so as to prohibit this bidirectional marriage reciprocity or "sister exchange." Shternberg reasons that Gilyaks moved to sanction the male's marriage to his mother's brother's daughter only, a form of unilateral cousin marriage that we would now call matrilateral cross-cousin marriage. Some confusion resulted in both the English and Russian typescripts, owing to some of Shternberg's original English insertions to the AMNH Russian typescript. Instead of "they gave up two-directional cousin marriage," he used the more general, "they gave up cousin marriage." Shternberg, *Giliaki*, and Shternberg, *Sem'ia*, upgraded this to "they gave up cross-cousin marriage [*perekrestnyi brak*]," where context clarifies the direction.]

each moiety is a real clan, as marriages are forbidden within the division. The two divisions are supplemented by a complex system of classes, but these do not alter the situation; a man, no matter to what class he belongs, always remains in the same exogamous division. The classes, without affecting a man's relation to his division, appear to be a sort of mnemonic device which limits the man individually (not his descendants) in his selection of a wife to a group of women standing to him in defi-nite degrees of relationship (in the four-class system, only first-cousins are mar-riageable; in the eight-class system, only second-cousins). As a matter of fact, the classes do not constitute an essential part of the Australian bipartite system. Among the Dieri, for instance, we find the restriction against first-cousin marriage identical to that of the Arunta (but while among the latter there are, in addition, eight class-es, for mnemonic purposes the Dieri have no classes whatsoever) [**115–116**].

The Gilyak type of one-sided cousin marriage, which becomes understandable when studied in the light of its historical antecedents, has altogether escaped the attention of investigators of primitive marriage. Some scientists even assume a skep-tical attitude and regard its very existence as improbable. Thus, almost simultane-ously with my publication on the subject (Shternberg, 1901*a*), the well-known com-parative jurist Professor Josef Kohler published an article in which he quoted his correspondent to the effect that a similar type of marriage existed among the Hot-tentots. But he hesitated to accept the account for he regarded it as improbable.[4] A reviewer in *L'Année Sociologique* (1901–1902), who summarized the article, fully endorsed Kohler's attitude.[5] The reason for this skepticism is not difficult to see. The true character of this institution has very often been overlooked by observers who, while mentioning marriages between the children of a brother and sister, will not tell whether they are one-sided or two-sided. It is not sufficient to inform us that a man is permitted to marry the daughter of his mother's brother, because in cases where sisters are exchanged, the daughter of a man's mother's brother is at the same time the daughter of his father's sister [**116**].

Therefore in general treatises on human marriage, even such as Mr. Frazer's *Totemism and Exogamy,* this type of cousin marriage is not treated as an indepen-dent form in the evolution of marriage.[6] The ethnographic literature concerning this type of marriage, already known to J. F. McLennan, contains even now abundant data bearing witness to its wide distribution.[7] Particularly numerous traces are found among the Indonesian peoples and Dravidian tribes of India, among whom Morgan

---

4   Josef Kohler, "Das Recht der Hottentots," *Zeitschrift für vergleichende Rechtswissenschaft,* no. 15 (1901), 341–342. For a full English-language discussion of Kohler's work, see Josef Kohler, *On the Prehistory of Marriage: Totemism, Group Marriage, Mother Right.* Translated from the German by R. H. Barnes and Ruth Barnes. Edited with an Introduction by R. H. Barnes (Chica-go: Univ. Chicago Press).

5   [***Editor's note:*** An equally partial reference to the *L'Anneé Sociologique* review, "11th year, p. 306" is found in Shternberg, *Sem'ia*, 116. The more likely reference is to the "2nd year."]

6   Frazer, *Totemism and Exogamy,* vol. II (London: Macmillan, 1910), 788. [***Editor's note:*** The ref-erence to Frazer and this citation are not found in the AMNH Russian typescript.]

7   [***Editor's note:*** See John Ferguson McLennan, *Primitive Marriage* (Edinburgh: A. and C. Black, 1865), as well as his *Studies in Ancient History; Comprising an Inquiry into the Origin of Exogamy* (New York: MacMillan, 1886).]

discovered the Turanian system in its purest form, and among whom (for instance the Toda) even group marriage has survived. Abundant evidence may also be found in Dr. Rivers' article on cousin marriage in India.[8] In Indonesia no less an authority than Wilken makes the following statement: "Among the Batas, Rejangs and the natives of Ambonia, a sister's son is allowed to marry a brother's daughter, whereas a brother's son must not marry a sister's daughter."[9] Their kinship terminology also corresponds to this practice. A later observer, J. S. Neumann, describes this marriage custom in Indonesia still more expressively: "If a man does not wed the daughter of his mother's brother . . . the gods are angry. On the other hand, marriage with the daughter of a father's sister is not only forbidden, but punishable."[10]

In Africa, as we have seen above, one-sided cousin marriage is mentioned among the Hottentots; and though information on the subject from other parts of the world has until now been too scanty, it is only a question of time before fuller data will be forthcoming. For example, no information from northern and central Asia existed. However, today we have good information of cases regarding clear survivals of one-sided cousin marriage among the Buriat and some other people of the Ural-Altaic family. So it may be with other people about whom we do not yet have information.

Morgan's Hypothesis and the Gilyak Kinship System

The Gilyak system of kinship and marriage fully corroborates Morgan's fundamental hypothesis that kinship terms are the reflection of corresponding sexual norms. What in Morgan's case was mere speculation based on terms of relationship, we find fully realized among the Gilyak. When a Gilyak applies the term "wives" to a group of women, they are wives to him in the full sense of the word. When a Gilyak calls the well-known group of men "fathers," then they are indeed men who have rights of sexual access to his mother. When he calls the mother's brother "wife's father," that is due to the law according to which he must actually marry that man's daughter [117].

In the Gilyak system, even universal classificatory terms, such as "older brother" and "younger brother," or "older sister" and "younger sister," are terms of great importance matrimonially. In the first place, these terms regulate individual marriage in the mother's clan. The older brother must marry the older sister; the younger brother must marry the younger sister. These terms are of importance in levirate, as the widow passes to the younger *tuvng*.

The way Gilyak kinship terminology so strikingly details the terms of relationship can best be seen in the relations of brothers to their wives. Among a part of

---

[8]   Rivers, "Marriage of Cousins in India, " 626 et seq.

[9]   Wilken, *Bijdragen,* Series V, vol. I, 148. [***Editor's note:*** I was unable to locate a comparable reference for the ethnologist George Alexander Wilken in the Library of Congress. One work by Wilken with which Shternberg may have been familiar is *Handleiding voor de vergelijkende Volkenkunde van Nederlandsch-Indie* (Leiden: E. J. Brill, 1893).]

[10] Frazer, *Totemism,* vol. II, 788. [***Editor's note:*** While it is not clear which edition of Totemism Shternberg was referring to, Frazer did not include Neumann in the index to the 1910 English edition, *Totemism and Exogamy: A Treatise on Certain Early Forms of Superstition and Society* (London: Macmillan).]

the Gilyak population, as noted before, all brothers indiscriminately have the right to one another's wives, and their terms fully represent this pact. A man applies the term "wife" indiscriminately to all the wives of his brothers; the children of brothers, therefore, apply the term "father" to the latter. Among the other half of the Gilyak, only younger brothers have a right to wives of the older ones; this is also reflected in the terminology. The wife of my younger brother, with whom I can have no intercourse, I call by the prohibitive term *iokh*, but to the wife of my older brother I apply the same term as to my own wife. Again, the children of brothers apply only to the father's younger brothers the term *itk* (father), while they call his older brothers *atk*.

The objections put forward against Morgan's hypothesis in this connection were of a purely academic character. For instance, the famous argument was given repeatedly that the class term "mother" remained unexplained, as a man always knew who his mother was. This paradox is explained very simply among the Gilyak. They call "mother" every woman with whom individuals of the "father" class have a right to sexual intercourse. We can gather from the following how well aware the Gilyak are of the significance of the term.

We have just seen that among those Gilyak who only allow younger brothers to have access to the wives of the older ones, the children of brothers distinguish between the father's older brothers and his younger brothers (and call the latter "fathers"); between the father's brothers' wives they make no distinction, and call them indiscriminately "mothers." Why? The reason is close at hand. I call the wives of my father's younger brothers "mothers" because their husbands are my "fathers"; that is, they have access to my mother. The wives of my father's older brothers I also call "mothers" because my father has access to them, and they are, therefore, his wives.

The Gilyak also applies the term "mother" to the sisters of his wife's father, but this again corresponds with the actual relationship, for as we saw, father and son take wives from one and the same clan, the father taking a man's sister, the son taking the man's daughter. One's wife's father's sister, as group-wife of one's father, is really one's mother [**118**].

Also quite unfounded is Kunov's statement that classificatory terms merely indicate age-groups. In Gilyak practice, age plays no role in kinship terminology. My class "father," even if my junior, may not marry a woman that belongs to the class of my "wives," but must marry into the class of "wives" of my real father. On reaching maturity he becomes *de facto* my mother's husband.[11]

THE GILYAK SYSTEM AND THE PUNALUAN FAMILY

This insight into Gilyak social organization serves to confirm and clarify not only Morgan's general hypothesis on the origin of the classificatory system of relationship but also his hypothesis of the development of the Turanian kinship system out of the

---

[11]   [**Editor's note:** No source for the German ethnologist Heinrich Cunow (1862–1936) is listed in any of the AMNH or Soviet versions. Shternberg may have been referring to Cunow's *Die Verwandtschafts-Organisationen der Australneger; ein Beitrag zur Entwicklungsgeschichte der Familie* (Stuttgart: Deik, 1894).]

Punaluan family. According to Morgan, the essential characteristic of the Punaluan family is "group marriage"—either the marriage of several sisters (one's own and collateral) with common husbands who are not necessarily related to each other, or the marriage of several brothers, own and collateral, with their wives, the latter again not being necessarily related (in both instances, however, they often are related). The old Gilyak family, with its obligatory marriage into one clan, represented a group marriage of all brothers, own and collateral, of a single clan with all sisters of the same generation from a specific clan, so the group-husbands were always "brothers" while their wives were always "sisters." This is evident from the kinship terminology— the wives of brothers call each other sisters.

At the present time, when marriage into different clans is tolerated, all brothers, own and collateral, continue to be group-husbands of their wives. We have shown, moreover, that even when sisters marry men of different clans, traces of group marriage persist, inasmuch as their children are considered brothers and sisters.

The structure of the Gilyak family permits us to establish the origin of the Hawaiian family on the basis of which Morgan postulated the Punaluan one. That family did not originally consist of several brothers in group marriage with wives who were unrelated to each other (or vice versa, several sisters in group marriage with husbands who were unrelated to each other). Such a family could not have given rise to the Turanian classificatory kinship system, for it presupposes the possibility of several groups of brothers or sisters, each being independently in a state of group marriage to the exclusion of the other groups. Thus the common terms for all brothers and their marital relations could not have arisen. The Gilyak family, in its pure and original form, presents a perfect picture of that primal family. It is an intra-clan organization. Each group marriage family represents a generation of men, all brothers, own and collateral, of a given clan in group marriage with an entire generation of women of another clan. These women must be "sisters" since daughters of fraternal relatives, as we have seen, are the wives of their fathers' sisters' sons. When by dint of circumstances these marriages became less orthodox, "brothers" began to take wives from different clans, and women began to marry into different clans. Sisters could find themselves in group marriage with husbands who were unrelated, while brothers could find themselves similarly united with women who were unrelated. The difference would be that whereas the aggregate of sisters would, with marriage into different clans, break up into several groups according to the different clans into which they married, as in the Punaluan family, the collective of brothers who always remain in one clan would remain intact. And as the Gilyak family represents the pure type of Punaluan family, Gilyak terminology is the most perfect form of the Turanian system. Indeed, we find there classificatory terms which must have existed in the original Turanian system but later, with the decay of the system of marriage, became obliterated. Thus, for example, in the Turanian form which Morgan in his time considered the most complete, the Tamil system, two of the most important classificatory terms are lacking—namely "husband" and "wife."

The Tamil system, according to Morgan, developed under conditions where "brothers" had common wives and "sisters" had common husbands. In accordance with this, a man in the Tamil system calls "father" not only his own father but all his father's brothers, and "mother" not only his own mother but all her sisters. He

FIG. 16. Gilyaks playing chess, 1890s. Photo by Lev Shternberg. *Source:* AAN f. 282, o. 2, d. 98, l. 48.

calls the children of his father's brothers and his mother's sisters "brothers" and "sisters." Similarly there ought to exist a common term "wife" to be applied by a man not only to his individual wife but to the wives of his brothers and to his wife's sisters, as well as a common term "husband" to be applied by a woman to her own husband, his brothers, and the husbands of her sisters [119].

In reality these terms are absent from the Tamil as well from the Iroquois systems. Thus among the Tamil a man calls his wife *en mainavi*; his brother's wife, *en anni* or *en maittuni*; and his wife's sister, *en korlunti* or *en maittuni*. The case is similar with the term for "husband" (cf. Morgan's table). Among the Gilyak the terms "husband" and "wife," *pu* and *ang'rei*, apply to all persons who are parties to a group marriage. The justice of Morgan's interpretation of kinship terms is thus strikingly vindicated.

CERTAIN ASPECTS OF THE TURANIAN-GANOWANIAN SYSTEM WHICH MORGAN FAILED TO INTERPRET

The principle of cousin marriage supplies the key to certain kinship terms occurring in the Turanian-Ganowanian system. Thus Morgan was much perplexed by the apparently inexplicable fact that I, a male, call my cousins' children, both children of father's sister and mother's brother, nephews and nieces. Among the Seneca-Iroquois, on the other hand, the opposite rule prevails. In his *Systems of Consanguinity and Affinity among the Human Family*, Morgan declares this fact to be inexplicable.

The discrimination in the relationship of cousin is a remarkable fact in the Tamil system. It is now found in the systems of but a small portion of the Turanian family. From the structure and principles of the Turanian system, as has been remarked before, with reference to the Ganowanian, it was predetermined that this relationship, when developed, would be applied and restricted to the children of a brother and sister. It was probably unknown in the primitive system . . . . It is the only particular in which it differs materially from the Seneca-Iroquois form, and in this the Seneca is more in logical accordance with the principles of the system than the Turanian. It is difficult to find any explanation of the variance.[12]

In 1877 with his book *Ancient Society*, Morgan came quite near to the solution. "This shows," he wrote, "that among the Tamil, at the time of the introduction of the Turanian system, all my female cousins were my wives, while this was not true of my male cousins."[13] As near as Morgan stood to the true cause, however, it did not prevent him from regarding the peculiarity as anomalous. He was far from the suspicion that he was dealing with a system of cross-cousin marriage, for what he thought was an accidental peculiarity was the very foundation of the Turanian and Ganowanian system. That the Turanian system resulted from cross-cousin marriage follows also from other terms which for Morgan were inexplicable, and which he did not attempt to interpret. Thus among the Tamil, if I am male, then my sister's son's wife is my daughter (as in the Gilyak and the Australian terminologies); the husband of my sister's daughter is my son (as in Australian cousin marriage); the husband of my father's sister's daughter is my brother (as in the Gilyak and Australian terminologies); my wife's father is "wife's father" and "uncle" (wife's father and mother's brother among the Gilyak; wife's father and father's brother or mother's brother among the Australians); my wife's mother is "wife's mother" and "aunt" (aunt and father's sister among the Gilyak, wife's mother and father's sister or mother's sister among the Australians); the wife of my brother is my "cousin" (that is, mother's brother's daughter or father's sister's daughter); and, finally, my father's sister's son's wife and mother's brother's son's wife are my "sister" (typical bilateral cross-cousin marriage). We encounter corresponding terms if I am a woman. All this bears witness to the fact that the Turanian system was a system of bilateral cross-cousin marriage, although the case of the Batak and tribes of central India attest that bilateral cross-cousin marriage, even in its original home, begins to give way to unilateral cross-cousin marriage of the Gilyak type.[14]

We must now interpret the variation of the Ganowanian system when contrasted with the Tamil. Specifically, when I am male, the children of all my male

---

[12] Cf. Morgan, *Systems of Consanguinity and Affinity of the Human Family* (Washington, DC: Smithsonian Institution, 1871), 391.

[13] Morgan, *Ancient Society*, 427. [**Editor's note:** The AMNH Russian typescript indicates that Shternberg was using a Russian edition. Shternberg, *Sem'ia*, cross-referenced p. 444 of an unidentified English edition. The Russian edition is not listed in the original.]

[14] [**Editor's note:** The above paragraph, abridged and redirected in the AMNH English typescript, has been modified to correspond more closely to the three Russian-language counterparts in order to emphasize Shternberg's theory of the ceding of bilateral cross-cousin marriage to a unilateral system.]

cousins, i.e., the children of my father's sister's son and of my mother's brother's son, are my sons and daughters. Contrary to Morgan's opinion, this is a real deviation from the system and permits one of two explanations. The most plausible explanation is that owing to certain circumstances, the Seneca Indians were obliged to adopt a system like that of the Aleut, according to which all cousins, agnatic as well as cognatic, were indiscriminately parties to a group marriage. The other possible explanation is analogous to the one made use of above in the interpretation of the development of the Gilyak phratry. Let us recall table 3 of the Gilyak four-clan cognatic phratry. Clan A takes wives from clan B and the latter from D. Now, suppose that the number of women in clan B became greatly decreased, and therefore, members of both clans A and B have been forced to take wives from one common clan, D. The members of A and B, being cousins, will be married to sisters of clan D; according to the rules of group marriage their children will be brothers and sisters. Thus we have the Seneca case where a man calls the children of his male cousin "son" and "daughter," and which has so perplexed Morgan [120].

Thus the Australian system, based on the principle of cross-cousin marriage (exchange of women) merely requires a division of the group into two exogamous divisions. The group presents what one might call a two-clan phratry. Quite different is the case of unilateral cross-cousin marriage, as found in the Gilyak system. Here the dual division becomes impossible. From the moment bilateral cousin marriage (that is, reciprocal marriage between the children of brother and sister) was prohibited, the dual division (two-clan phratry) proved insufficient. One clan took women from the other, but the latter had to look for women outside the first clan; on the other hand, marriages outside the particular ethnic group were not permitted. It became necessary to supplement the original dual division by a set of new exogamous divisions. The first step in that direction was the formation of the four-clan phratry which we have studied among the Gilyak. The process was a plausible one; we shall see that the four-clan phratry, in an incipient state, exists also in the Australian system.

Let us imagine a community of the Australian type, embracing two divisions which in each generation exchange women in such a way that the children of a sister marry the children of her brother, so that the wife of a man is the sister of his sister's husband. Let us further imagine, for the sake of simplicity, that each division consists of only one generation of brothers and sisters, one's own and collateral, and that they stand to each other in different degrees of cousin relationship. The group of male cousins in one division we shall indicate by capital letters, A^1 A^2 A^3 A^4; their sisters shall be indicated by small letters, a^1 a^2 a^3 a^4. In the other division the male cousins will be B^1 B^2 B^3 B^4; and their sisters b^1 b^2 b^3 b^4—each letter embracing a group of own brothers or sisters. The powers of these letters stand for the different degrees of the cousin relationship between the various groups. Consecutive groups will be first-cousins, while the degree of relationship between the other groups will be indicated by the difference of their powers. The same powers of different letters indicate that the individuals of the corresponding groups are first-cousins both through the father and through the mother: A^1, a^1 are first-cousins of B^1, b^1; A^2, a^2 are first-cousins of B^2, b^2, etc. The representatives of groups indicated by different letters and with consecutive powers will be second-cousins: thus A^1 and B^1 will be second-cousins of B^2

and b^2, and A^2 and a^2 will be second-cousins of B^3 and b^3, etc. (the difference of the powers indicating the degree of cousinship).

First Division	Groups of men:	A^1 A^2 A^3 A^4 A^5 A^6
	Their sisters:	a^1 a^2 a^3 a^4 a^5 a^6
Second Division	Groups of men:	B^1 B^2 B^3 B^4 B^5 B^6
	Their sisters:	b^1 b^2 b^3 b^4 b^5 b^6

As the heteronomous groups of the males and females with the same powers are first-cousins who must intermarry, A^1 marries b^1, sister of B^1; B^1 marries a^1, sister of A^1. Similarly, A^2 marries b^2; B^2 marries a^2, etc. Thus the arrangement of marriages can be represented in the following table.

First Division $(A^1 + b^1) + (A^2 + b^2) + (A^3 + b^3) + (A^4 + b^4)$, etc.

Second Division $(B^1 + a^1) + (B^2 + a^2) + (B^3 + a^3) + (B^4 + a^4)$, etc.

In each preceding generation the marriages occurred in the same order, that is, between the children of two women, each of whom is married to the other's brother, so that the marriage-mates are first-cousins both through the father and through the mother. This form of marriage we term bilateral cross-cousin [*perekrestnyi*] marriage.

Let us now imagine the moment when the society first became aware of the harmfulness of bilateral cross first-cousin marriage and established bilateral cross second-cousin marriage as the orthodox form. Henceforth A^1 no longer marries his first cousin b^1, but his second-cousin b^2. Similarly, B^1 marries a^2, and so on. In this new order the marriages appear as follows:

First Division $(A^1 + b^2) + (A^2 + b^1) + (A^3 + b^4) + (A^4 + b^3) + (A^5 + b^6) + (A^6 + b^5)$

Second Division $(B^1 + a^2) + (B^2 + a^1) + (B^3 + a^4) + (B^4 + a^3) + (B^5 + a^6) + (B^5 + a^6)$

It is easy to see that from this moment, within each of the two divisions, there are formed two matrimonially isolated sections, the odd-numbered members (namely, of division) constituting one section, the even-numbered members constituting the other. Thus four groups have arisen [**121**].

This four-group division may be represented as follows:

First Division	Section 1	$(A^1 + b^2) + (A^3 + b^4) + (A^5 + b^6)$ and other odd members
	Section 2	$(A^2 + b^1) + (A^4 + b^3) + (A^6 + b^5)$ and other even members
Second Division	Section 3	$(B^1 + a^2) + (B^3 + a^4) + (B^5 + a^6)$ and other odd members
	Section 4	$(B^2 + a^1) + (B^4 + a^3) + (B^6 + a^5)$ and other even members

Section 1 now may not intermarry with Section 4, because the children of these two groups are two-way first-cousins. The reason is quite clear. In case the families inter-marry in consecutive order—$(A^1 + b^2)$ with $(B^2 + a^1)$—their children will be two-sided first-cousins, for their fathers are married to each other's sisters; in other cases—in families $(A^1 + b^2)$ and $(B^4 + a^3)$—the children will not be second-, but third- or fourth-cousins, a condition avoided in the Australian system. Similarly, Sections 3 and 4 may also not intermarry. On the contrary, Sections 1 and 3 and Sections 2 and 4 are mar-riageable in the consecutive order of the families. For example, in the families $(A^1 + b^2)$ of Section 1 and $(B^1 + a^2)$ of Section 3, as may be seen from the powers, the father (A^1) of the first family is first-cousin of the mother (a^2) of the second family; and, vice versa, the father of the second family, B^1, is first-cousin of the mother of the first family, b^2. Moreover, both the fathers are also first-cousins, as well as both the mothers; there-fore their children are second-cousins both on the father's and on the mother's side.

In the Australian system, however, these matrimonial sections of the two divi-sions could not develop into real clan units as each pair of the marriageable sections remained so only in one generation. The members of the next generation were bilat-eral cross first-cousins, the descendants of brother and sister, and could not as such intermarry. Therefore these sections could not become standardized as hereditary units, but remained mere classes of generations, with the practical function of mnemonically fixing the matrimonial norms.

A very different part was assumed by the four-section division in marriage of the Gilyak type. The point of departure was the same—the realization of the harm-fulness of marriage between first-cousins. Whereas in the Australian marriage sys-tem the question was solved by the introduction of two-sided second-cousin marriage and the categorical prohibition of first-cousin marriage (with the preservation of sis-ter-exchange marriage), in the Gilyak system the transformation consisted of the prohibition of two-sided first-cousin marriage. Marriage remained imperative between first-cousins, but only between one-sided ones, that is, either on the mother's or on the father's side. Reciprocal marriage between two families was thus prohibited; two men could in no way marry each other's sisters—two-sided cousin marriage had become impossible.

Let us now see how this rearrangement led to the Gilyak type of the phratry. We remember the two-sided phratry with marriage divisions for cousins of the first degree. For ease of orientation, we reproduce our second table here [**122**].

First Division $(A^1 + b^1) + (A^2 + b^2) + (A^3 + b^3) + (A^4 + b^4)$, etc.

Second Division $(B^1 + a^1) + (B^2 + a^2) + (B^3 + a^3) + (B^4 + a^4)$, etc.

In this table the community is represented at the moment when in every group, e.g., $(A^1 + b^1)$ or $(B^2 + a^2)$ the man and the wife are two-sided first-cousins, and each pair of corresponding families with the same powers in different divisions, e.g., $(A^1 + b^1)$ or $(B^1 + a^1)$, exchange women in every generation.

Here we can imagine the moment of transition from a bilateral system of cross-cousin marriage to a unilateral one. And yet, to accomplish this immediately was not possible. For in both divisions, having already followed a system of exchanging sisters, one-sided first-cousins as such do not yet exist. Thus for the new transformation it was necessary first to take the previous steps, namely, to prohibit the exchange of sisters. The most rational solution would have been the Australian one, marriage between second-cousins. But, in contrast to the Australian case, where this could be exercised in both divisions (see above), here, as a result of the Gilyak prohibition on the exchange of women, this move could only be achieved within one division. Hence, for instance, with A^1 married to b^2, the brother of the latter, B^2, may no longer marry a^1. Therefore, B^2 has to take as his wife his third-cousin, a^4. Applying this new rule to our schematic series, instead of the table above we obtain the following table of marriages.[15]

First Division	$(A^1 + b^2) + (A^2 + b^1) + (A^3 + b^4) + (A^4 + b^3) + (A^5 + b^6) +$
	$(A^6 + b^5) + (A^7 + b^8) + (A^8 + b^7)$
Second Division	$(B^1 + a^3) + (B^2 + a^4) + (B^3 + a^1) + (B^4 + a^2) + (B^5 + a^7) +$
	$(B^6 + a^8) + (B^7 + a^5) + (B^8 + a^6)$

Now, in the following generation it becomes possible to move to this new principle—one-sided cousin marriage without women exchange—as all marriageable first-cousins are one-sided cousins, every mother being able to marry her son to her brother's daughter. It will become more evident when we subdivide each division into two sections, where one has even-numbered members and the other has odd-numbered ones. In this way we arrive at the following table:

First Division	Section 1 (odd members)	$(A^1 + b^2) + (A^3 + b^4) + (A^5 + b^6) + (A^7 + b^8)$
	Section 2 (even members)	$(A^2 + b^1) + (A^4 + b^3) + (A^6 + b^5) + (A^8 + b^7)$
Second Division	Section 3 (odd members)	$(B^1 + a^2) + (B^3 + a^4) + (B^5 + a^6)$
	Section 4 (even members)	$(B^2 + a^1) + (B^4 + a^3) + (B^6 + a^5)$

In analyzing this table, we find that in the first division, the powers of women are the same as the powers of men in the second division (b^2 and B^2 as one example). The children of these families will be one-sided first-cousins and, according to the principle that a sister's son marries her brother's daughter, the sons of the first division will marry the daughters of the second. The reverse will not be permissible.

On the other hand, in comparing the odd members of the first division with the even members of the second division, we find that in the families of the same order (for instance, in the first pairing of the first division and the second pairing of the second division, in the third pairing of the first division and the fourth pairing of the second division, and so on), the men of the first division are brothers of the women of the second division, and accordingly their children will be one-sided first-cousins.

---

[15] [**Editor's note:** This paragraph has been altered from the AMNH English typescript to more closely correspond to the three Russian-language counterparts.]

To review: The sons of Section 2 marry daughters of Section 3. Sons of Section 3 marry daughters of Section 1. Sons of Section 4 marry daughters of Section 2. This is because, for example, the women of Section 1 are the sisters of the men in Section 4, and the women of Section 2 are sisters to the men of Section 3. The resulting condition is identical with that which we found among the Gilyak.[16]

As exchange marriage between two groups is not tolerated, the descendants of the intermarrying sections, in the following generation, will be always one-sided cousins, and marriages will be uniformly concluded between the same groups and in the same order of the families. Thus the exogamous sections, unlike those of Australia, will become hereditary, i.e., real clans. Then, however, we are in the presence of the four-clan Gilyak phratry, obviously evolved from the primary dual division.[17]

We have now succeeded, I believe, in tracing an intimate genetic link between the Gilyak system and that of Australia, from which the former diverged at the stage when marriage between two-sided first-cousins first began to come into disrepute. The Australian system solved the problem by adopting two-sided second-cousin marriages and by rigorously prohibiting marriages between the descendants of brother and sister in the first generation—a prohibition which became fixed in the institution of classes, as among the Arunta. The Gilyak system prohibited sister-exchange [*peremennyi*] marriage, while preserving obligatory one-sided marriages between the children of brother and sister, and fixing its matrimonial code in the institution of the four-clan phratry.[18]

---

[16] [***Editor's note:*** The paragraph above from the AMNH English typescript has been simplified to restore the meaning in the AMNH Russian typescript.]

[17] [***Editor's note:*** In the 1933 Soviet editions, this paragraph contains three further expository sentences.]

[18] [***Editor's note:*** The AMNH Russian typescript concludes this chapter with two more short algebraic tables theorizing the rise of unilateral cross-cousin marriage.]

TEN

MORGAN'S HYPOTHESIS AND OTHER
NORTH ASIAN PEOPLES[1]

[129–141; 185–212; 235–246; —]

FORTY YEARS AGO, Lewis H. Morgan, in his *Systems of Consanguinity and Affinity among the Human Family*, paid special attention to the problem of the relation between the Turanian and the Ganowanian systems of relationship. Under the term "Turanian," Morgan designated the system of relationship found among the Dravidian nations of India. Under the term "Ganowanian," he designated the system he discovered about 60 years ago, first among the Iroquois and afterwards among the numerous different Indian tribes all over North America. Morgan found these two systems to be so alike that in his *Ancient Society* both systems merged into one Turano-Ganowanian system. The similarity of the systems seemed to him so great that he found it impossible to admit even that these systems could have been borrowed from each other. His deepest conviction was that the cause for this similarity could be nothing else but the common origin of the Asiatic and American races. The peoples of America must have brought their system of relationship from their old home in Asia.

As Morgan wrote,

> Although separated from each other by continents in space and by unnum-
> bered ages in time, the Tamil Indians of the Eastern Hemisphere and the

---

[1] [**Editor's note:** The AMNH Russian typescript includes this material, without heading, directly following the Australian kin tables as a continuation of the previous chapter. The AMNH English typescript, which located this section after the Australian kin tables, as well as after the discussion of Morgan's hypothesis and the Gilyak kinship system, titled it "Morgan's Hypothesis as to the Asiatic Origin of the American Race and the Matrimonial Forms of the Nations of Northeastern Asia." The title from the AMNH English typescript, added by earlier editors, has a decidedly more Jesup ring to it, the overall expedition having been concerned with Siberian–American cultural links. Shternberg, *Giliaki*, which follows the sequencing of the AMNH Russian typescript in this and the preceding chapter, titled it more modestly, "Aspects of the Classification System among Other Peoples of Northeast Asia." Shternberg, *Sem'ia*, does not contain this section.

The AMNH English typescript, on which this chapter is based, contains a number of significant discrepancies with respect to the AMNH Russian and Shternberg, *Giliaki*, versions. On the positive side, quotations from Morgan have been added, and geographic descriptions have at times been made more specific. More interestingly, however, especially where the question of the Asian origins of the American race is concerned, the two Russian versions do not take North Asian peoples across the Bering Strait to Alaska, a theory made popular by Boas and still held today. These seemingly Boasian additions have been marked individually throughout the text.]

Seneca Indians of the Western, as they generally address their kinsmen by the conventional relationship established in the primitive ages, daily proclaim for a once common household. When the discoverers of the New World bestowed upon its inhabitants the name of "Indians," under the impression that they had reached the Indies, they little suspected that children of the same original family, although upon a different continent, stood before them. By a singular coincidence, error was truth.[2]

Morgan has not only shown the infallibility of his hypothesis, he has vividly represented how that system passed over from the continent and spread across America. He has identified the Columbia River as the center of diffusion of the system in North America.

> A careful study of the geographical features of the continent of North America, with reference to its natural lines of migration and to the means of subsistence afforded by its several parts of the populations of fishermen and hunters, together with the relations of their languages and systems of relationships, all unite, as elsewhere stated, to indicate the valley of Columbia as the nursery of the Ganowanian family and the initial point of migration from which both North and South America received their inhabitants.[3]

On the Asiatic shore of the Pacific, Morgan identifies the Amur River as the system's point of origin, much the same as he announced the Columbia River as the means by which the Turanian system reached America and spread across that continent. No matter how one regards Morgan, his deep conviction—that traces of the Turanian system can be found from the banks of the Amur across all of northeastern Asia and including the Aleutian Islands—is slowly finding vindication in the survivals of cousin marriage found in various kinship systems. The Gilyak kinship system I lay out here is particularly useful in this context. If we follow Morgan's guide, these bearers of the Turanian system should have crossed to Alaska to reach the Columbia, and from there they would have spread across the continent.[4]

Deep as Morgan's conviction was, he missed certain important facts.[5] In Asia he succeeded in tracing the Turanian system, but only to the southern boundaries of Central Asia. From there to the outermost parts of northeastern Asia he had no information at all.

He knew nothing of the matrimonial norms of the Paleo-Asiatic peoples, such as the Gilyak, Chukchi, Yukaghir, Koriak, and Aleuts. As he remarked in the

---

[2] Morgan, *Systems of Consanguinity,* 508. [***Editor's note:*** This quotation is found in the AMNH English typescript only.]

[3] Ibid., 498. [***Editor's note:*** This quotation is found in the AMNH English typescript only.]

[4] [***Editor's note:*** This sentence is found in the AMNH English typescript only and may be regarded with skepticism, as Shternberg never mentioned the Alaska connection. I am grateful to Lydia Black for noting this discrepancy.]

[5] [***Editor's note:*** The expository material beginning with this paragraph and continuing to the start of the section on Tungus is found in the AMNH English typescript only. One can see that while earlier editors sought to furnish the reader with a prefatory understanding of the Turanian system, the additions go much further in criticizing Morgan.]

concluding chapter of his *Systems of Consanguinity*, "The systems of the Tungusian and Mongolian stock yet remain to be ascertained." In another place he complains that a dearth of materials hindered him from understanding the Eskimo system.

> In the absence of all knowledge of the forms which prevail in northeast-
> ern Asia, it is premature to indulge in conjectures, but there are features
> in the Eskimo which suggest, at least, the possibility that when traced to
> its limits it may furnish the connecting links between the Turanian and
> Uralian forms.[6]

Thus the necessary links between the Dravidian and Ganowanian systems were lacking in the time of Morgan. Now that great lacuna may slowly be filled. One missing link is the matrimonial system of the Gilyak. It represents the ideal Turanian type, in both its kinship terms and its sexual norms. In this system we also find a true specimen of the Punaluan family in a functioning state.

In tracing the Turanian system among other nations of northeastern Asia, it is necessary to bear in mind the essence of the Turanian system as presented in the light of modern knowledge. The following are the principles on which the system is based:

1. Marriage is obligatory in a certain group of blood relatives who bear certain rights and obligations towards each other, such as levirate, infant marriage, wedding ceremonies, and no payment for the bride.
2. The orthodox form of marriage is between children of brothers and sisters, both one's own and collateral, i.e., cousin marriage, cross or one-sided.
3. Individual marriage is combined with group marital rights.
4. The classificatory system of relationship is but an index of the rules of marriage.

We consider two groups of people here: those of the Amur region, the Gilyak, Ainu, and the Tungus tribes (Oroch, Ulchi, Gold, and Negidal), on the one hand; and the Paleo-Asiatics of the extreme northeastern part of Asia, the Yukaghir, Chukchi, Koriak, Kamchadal, and the Aleut, on the other. I have studied the peoples of the first group. As for the second, we will attempt to explain the facts of other investigators.[7]

THE TUNGUS. Let us begin with the Tungus nationalities [*narodnosti*][8] spread all over northern Asia, from the borders of China northwest as far as the Ob River and north-

---

[6]   Morgan, *Systems*, 510.
[7]   The Chukchi have been studied by Mr. Vladimir G. Bogoraz; the Yukaghir, Koriak, and Aleut by Mr. Vladimir I. Iokhel'son. See their publications for the Jesup North Pacific Expedition list-ed in this volume. [***Editor's note:*** This footnote is found only in the AMNH English type-script.]
[8]   [***Editor's note:*** In the Soviet period, the Russian word *narodnost'*, a nationality, ethnic group, or more literally, a small people, came to take on distinctive socioeconomic baggage, sand-wiched between "tribes" (the ethnicity of primitive communism) and "nations" (the ethnici-ty of capitalism and socialism), leaving the more ambiguous *narodnost'* "the ethnicity of every-thing in between." Yuri Slezkine, *Arctic Mirrors: Russia and the Small Peoples of the North* (Ithaca, NY: Cornell Univ. Press, 1994), 322–323. In Shternberg's prerevolutionary usage the term conveys a similar terminological ambiguity without the Marxist-Leninist trappings.]

east as far as Kamchatka.[9] I have studied marital norms only among their most isolated branch, the Northern Oroch, but I also have had occasion to get comparative and supplementary data among other tribes of the Amur region, namely, among the Orok, Gold, Ulchi, and the Amgun Tungus [Negidal]. There are, of course, some differences in the customs and terms of relationship of the different Tungus nations, as greatly extended and divided from one another as they are. But in the main, the system of relationship and marriage is the same. A brief sketch of the marital norms of the Oroch will give a good idea of the Tungus system.[10]

Like the Gilyak, the Oroch are divided into exogamous patrilineal clans. In each generation of a clan, the men and women are divided into groups of older brothers and sisters and younger brothers and sisters (classificatory terms, *aga* and *nu ku*). The children of these groups are their common sons and daughters and, with reference to each other, brothers and sisters. The class of "brothers" live in group marriage with their wives in the same way as the Gilyak of the Eastern dialect, that is, younger brothers are the group-husbands of their older brothers' wives. As among the Gilyak, clansmen prefer to take wives from one clan, and we may conjecture that formerly, as among the Gilyak, marriage into one clan was imperative.

The marriage group also embraces one's wife's sisters even when the latter are married to unrelated individuals, but by analogy with brothers' wives, this form of marriage extends among some tribes only to the wife's younger sisters.

In two respects, group marriage among the Tungus extends much further than among the Gilyak. In the first place, a man has access not only to the wives of his older brothers, but also to the wives of his father's younger brothers, to whom he therefore applies the same class-term (*ara*) as he uses towards his older brothers. In the second place, in contrast to the Gilyak rules, marriage with daughters of a man's elder sisters is permitted, and this category of nieces is thus also drawn into the circle of one's group-wives.

From what we know about the origin of group cousin marriage, it is easy to realize that the marital right of a man to his father's younger brother's wife, so unusual in the Turanian system, is but a consequence of the right to marry one's elder sister's daughter.[11] Originally niece marriage must have been strictly forbidden, while the sole form of marriage was obligatory cousin marriage combined with group marital rights of all brothers and agnatic cousins. Marriage with nieces must have arisen much later, under the pressure of extraordinary circumstances. Once this new right had arisen, however, and men had begun to take the daughters of their elder sisters (lawful wives of their paternal nephews), the latter necessarily became partners in group marriage with the wives of their younger paternal uncles. The reason why the wives

---

[9]   [***Editor's note:*** The AMNH Russian typescript and Shternberg, *Giliaki,* consider the Ainu first, and then the Tungus peoples. Rather than restoring the Russian sequence, I have retained the order of the AMNH English typescript to maintain consistency.]

[10]   My first report on the Oroch was made November 1, 1896, before the Geographical Society of Vladivostok and was published in extract form the same year. See Shternberg, "Orochi Tatarskogo proliva," *Vladivostok,* nos. 47, 48, 50, 51 (1896).

[11]   [***Editor's note:*** While the above material is an already modified version of the sections on Tungus in the AMNH Russian typescript and Shternberg, *Giliaki,* the material beginning here and ending at the section marked "Ainu" is found in the AMNH English typescript only.]

of paternal uncles older than the father are forbidden is quite clear, since these women are group-wives of the father, and are mothers to the persons concerned. This new group marriage right originally applied only to paternal younger uncle's wives when nieces of the latter gradually extended to every wife of their uncles, whether they were nieces or not. It is worthwhile to mention here that traces of this right are found in the terminology of some Turkish nations like the Karagass [Karagasi, Tofalar], Yakut, Abakan Tatars, and Mongols, among whom, I have been informed, the same term is applied to a man's elder brother and to his father's younger brothers. From Chinese sources we know also that the old Turks used to marry the widows of their paternal uncles.[12] Niece marriage in connection with group cousin marriage is in no way a particularity of the Tungus and Turkish peoples. We find this institution in the birthplace of Morgan's Turanian family, in India, and with the same details. In Mysore, for instance, a man generally marries either his niece (the daughter of his elder sister) or his cousin (the daughter of his mother's brother or his father's sister).[13] Among the Kasuba, a forest tribe of the Nilgiri, a man marries either his first-cousin (the daughter of his mother's brother) or his niece (the daughter of his sister).[14]

But niece marriage is subsidiary to cousin marriage, being a natural outgrowth of obligatory consanguineous marriage. Thus the Tamil caste of Kallans in Madurai "marry nieces, aunts, or some other near relatives, only failing a cousin."[15]

The niece marriage institution among the Tungus can be explained by their mode of life. They are roving nomads who live many hundreds of miles from one another, and even if for a short time they come together, they are always in small number and the choice of wives is rather limited. Under such conditions, the deviation from old rules can be explained as the *force majeure* of necessity, as in the case of the Tamil cited above. Another important peculiarity of the Tungus is that, in contrast to the Gilyak, they are allowed to marry one another's sisters. It is now even the most favorite form of marriage. Considering that the Tungus, like the Gilyak, prefer to marry from the same clan of their mother, it seems right to conclude that the original form of marriage among the Tungus was exchange-marriage between the children of brother and sister two-sided cross-cousin marriage.

THE AINU. Since the time of von Schrenck, the Ainu have been ranked with the Amur tribes, although in culture, language, and other ethnographic traits they belong to quite a different group of nations. In spite of the close proximity of the northern Ainu to the Gilyak, the matrimonial system of the Ainu stands closest to the nations of northeastern Asia.[16]

---

12 Cf. Radlov, *Aus Sibirien, passim.* [*Editor's note:* This footnote is found in the AMNH English typescript only.]

13 Hebbalalu Velpanuru Nanjundayya, *The Ethnographical Survey of Mysore* (Bangalore: Government Press, 1906), 1, 10, 11; cited in Frazer, *Totemism and Exogamy*, vol. II, 271 et seq. [*Editor's note:* This footnote is found in the AMNH English typescript only.]

14 *Anthropos*, no. 4 (1909), 178–181. [*Editor's note:* This footnote is found in the AMNH English typescript only.]

15 Frazer, *Totemism and Exogamy*, vol. II, 225. [*Editor's note:* This footnote is found in the AMNH English typescript only.]

16 [*Editor's note:* This short section on the Ainu abridges the longer paragraph in the AMNH Russian typescript, 130, and Shternberg, *Giliaki*, 236–237.]

THE NATIONS OF FAR NORTHEASTERN ASIA.[17] These consist of three groups: (1) the Yukaghir, (2) the Chukchi, Koriak, and Kamchadal, and (3) the Aleut. Far apart as these three groups are in language, origin, culture, and geographical position, they are unified through fundamental common traits in their matrimonial institutions, which is very important for Morgan's approach.

At first glance the matrimonial institutions of all these nations seem to have nothing to do with the Turano-Ganowanian system. All these systems seem quite different from one another. Upon closer inspection, however, we find traces of classificatory terminology, cousin marriage, and survivals of group marriage. All this does not lie on the surface as with the Gilyak or the Tungus. Here, under specific local conditions, the primary Turanian rules of marriage underwent a radical change, resulting in the Turano-Ganowanian system and acquiring typical traits of the Malayan system, so designated by Morgan.[18] This change is clearly seen in the classificatory terminology of some of these tribes. The main characteristic of the Malayan system is the merging of the paternal and maternal line into one class; among the Aleut, this class of cousins even exercise the obligatory right of group marriage.

We are dealing here with the same kind of case as found by Dr. Rivers in the Torres Straits, where the Malayan features are so justly explained by Dr. Rivers as distortions of the primary Turanian system. Indeed, here in northeastern Asia as among the aborigines of the Torres Straits, we find Turanian traits combined with Malayan. The distortion is not due, as Mr. Rivers thinks, to the natural advance of society but to disintegrating forces. The true cause of the change undergone by the Turano-Ganowanian system is due to the passage from strict exogamy to endogamous practices forced by unfavorable conditions. It is easy to see how this new practice changed and distorted the old forms of the Turanian system.

As we know, the Turanian system is based on the principle of exogamy in each of the two principal lines, among the descendants of brothers on one side, and among the descendants of sisters on the other side (in each of these lines intermarriage being forbidden). Now let us imagine what would happen when a scarcity of women occurs and the men are forced to marry in the exogamic line. Under the old principle, the daughter of my mother's brother (I being male) is my wife; if she is now forced to marry her collateral brother, according to the old rule of group marriage I become a partner in marriage with the latter, and my former cognatic cousin becomes my class-brother. Thus every distinction between cousins, on the paternal as well as on the maternal side, disappears, not only in the terminology but in the group marriage rights as well.

---

[17] [*Editor's note:* Here again the AMNH English typescript diverges from its AMNH Russian counterpart and Shternberg, *Giliaki.* Where the latter two move from the Ainu and Tungus materials straight into considerations of Yukaghir, Chukchi, and Aleut systems, the AMNH English typescript offered this longer introduction, beginning at "The Nations of Far Northeastern Asia" and ending below with the paragraph beginning "I shall now begin with the Yukaghir."]

[18] By this I do not intend to endorse the view of Morgan that the Malayan system preceded the Turano-Ganowanian stage of marriage. From what follows it will be seen that my opinion is quite the opposite. At the same time, however, it cannot be denied that the Malayan kinship system exists. [*Editor's note:* This footnote is found in the AMNH English typescript only.]

In the above case, the new endogamous practice led to the widening of the marriage group. But the actual effects may be directly the opposite. According to the old rule, all members of the clan belonging to the same generation (all agnatic cousins) have up to the present been "brothers" and partners in group marriage, with their common wives taken from another clan. But now, after the infringement of the rule of exogamy it may happen that my collateral brother may marry my own sister (I being male); consequently our husband-partnership must cease immediately. So it will be with all clan brothers.

Thus the passage to endogamous practice may in some cases bring diametrically opposed results: In one case, group marriage may be extended to all cousins of every line; in the other case, it may be prohibited to all. This is the case with the nations of northeastern Asia. Among the Yukaghir and Koriak, as well as among the Ainu, for instance, the new practice produced the abolition of group marriage altogether. On the other hand, among the Aleut it produced a further extension of group marriage, to such a degree that all kinds of male cousins, on the maternal as well as on the paternal side, became partners in group marriage with all their female cousins from both sides.

The intrusion of endogamy can be explained only as due to the unfavorable conditions of life in the Arctic regions. Marriage difficulties arise mainly from the isolation of the population, whose scanty numbers are spread over an enormous area. In some cases this scantiness is caused by the dying out of the people through degeneration, epidemics, famine, and so on; in other cases, it may be caused by their economic pursuits, such as the herding of reindeer, which necessitates several families to divide in order to have enough pasture land for their herds. The very beginning of the process of endogamy may be observed even now among the isolated Arctic Tungus tribes in the region of Turukhansk, whereas among the less isolated or more sedentary southern Tungus tribes this process is wholly unknown.

Following these few introductory remarks, it should now be easier to understand the individual traits of these tribes.

I shall begin with the Yukaghir. Their classificatory system has at the same time traits of both the Turanian and Malayan systems. This merging of the two systems becomes especially clear in the first ascending line. As in the Turanian system, so here all paternal uncles (father's brothers, one's own and collateral) are "fathers," "big" or "little," literally as among the Dravidians. Similarly, all mother's sisters, one's own and collateral are "mothers"—"big" or "little." At the same time, in complete discord with the Turanian system, we find a typical Malayan trait: namely, that the class of father's brothers embraces not only agnatic, but also cognatic, cousins. Similarly the class of mother's sisters embraces agnatic as well as cognatic cousins.

If in the ascending line we find mixed traits of both systems, the line of one's own generation becomes truly Malayan. I refer to the men of the so-called class of *emjepul* including (to use the words of Iokhel'son) "not only brothers and sisters, but also first and second cousins, and so on, on the father's as well as on the mother's side."[19]

---

[19] Iokhel'son, *The Yukaghir and the Yukhaghirized Tungus* (Leiden: E. J. Brill), 68. [**Editor's note:** While Shternberg, *Giliaki*, references this source, only the AMNH Russian and English typescripts include the quotation in the main text. In the AMNH Russian typescript, the quotation is written out by Shternberg in longhand.]

This phenomenon is in perfect accord with class VII of Morgan's Malayan system.[20] The sole cause of this mixture of terminologies is the intrusion of endogamy while the traditions and feelings of exogamic practice still persist, and the struggle between the old and the new forms of marriage goes on under our very eyes. "Wise people," say the Yukaghir, "follow the custom of *n ekhi iini.*" That is, they marry according to the norms of avoidance, and the avoidances of the Yukaghir are of a truly Turanian nature. Nevertheless, in reality, "Yukaghir marriages are closely endogamous."[21] The reasons are quite clear. The Yukaghir, numbering only a few hundred people, are scattered over an enormous area and are obliged to marry with the clan, and sometimes even into the same family. Judging from their folklore, endogamous practice among the Yukaghir has been going on from far ancient times.

The theory of the former existence of group marriage is attested to by Turanian terms of relationship which are still found among the Yukaghir. Thus, for instance, the elder and younger brothers and cousins of the father are designated by the terms "big fathers" and "little fathers." Similarly, the elder and younger sisters of the mother are called "big mothers" and "little mothers." Particularly conclusive are the avoidances (1) between elder brothers or elder male cousins and the wives of their younger brothers or younger male cousins; and (2) between the elder brother or elder male cousin and the wife of the younger brother's or male cousin's son. The first avoidance we find among both the Gilyak and the Tungus, where younger brothers and cousins have marital rights over the wives of their older brothers and cousins. Sexual intercourse is not only forbidden between the elder brothers and cousins and the wives of the younger ones, but there is also a strict avoidance taboo between them. The second avoidance is easily explained by the Tungus rule according to which the paternal nephew has marital rights over the wife of his younger paternal uncle, while the reverse is not permitted. Therefore the uncle is under an avoidance taboo in regard to his nephew's wife. The only difference between this directive and the Yukaghir rule is that, among the Tungus, the interdict relates both to the younger paternal uncle and to the elder (whose wife is forbidden to the nephew). Among the Yukaghir, Mr. Iokhel'son gives only the second case; however, it is not impossible that he has overlooked the first. In every Yukaghir case the interdict between the uncle and his nephew's wife suggests that group marriage extended not only to brothers and cousins but also, as among the Tungus, to certain categories of ascending and descending generations.

There is another avoidance which testifies strikingly to the former state of Yukaghir marriage—the avoidance between members of the class *emjepul,* which embraces brothers and sisters and cousins of both lines, agnatic and cognatic. This is salient when we consider that in modern as well as in olden times, cousin marriage (with the exception of first-cousins) was lawful. It is clear that this avoidance must originally have embraced only agnatic brothers and sisters (one's own and collateral), between whom intercourse has been forbidden, as it is now among the Gilyak and Tungus. Further, there are indications that marriage with certain blood relatives

---

[20] [***Editor's note:*** Neither the AMNH nor the 1933 Soviet editions indicate a source here for Morgan.]

[21] Iokhel'son, *The Yukaghir,* 86.

was obligatory. Until now the Yukaghir knew no religious marriage ceremonies, nor was it their custom to make payment for the bride. They do, however, have the custom of bride-service, but this, as we shall see later in the case of the Koriak, is but another proof of the old law of obligatory marriage.

Finally, the existence until now of the clan among the Yukaghir is conclusive proof that in former times the Yukaghir were a strictly exogamous tribe.

Let us now turn to the vast group of northern Paleo-Asiatics, which includes the Chukchi, Koriak, and Kamchadal. Of this group, the most typical are the Chukchi. Among them endogamous practice is far more in use than among the Yukaghir. Endogamy, indeed, is the only system of marriage. Accordingly, the classificatory system of the Chukchi has more traits of the Malayan system than the Yukaghir. With the loss of exogamy, the Chukchi also lost the clan. The usual form of marriage is between cousins, when possible, even in the same family. When this is impossible, marriage is with cousins of further degrees. Only marriages between uncles and nieces are prohibited. Noting that the Chukchi used to exchange sisters, we see here the typical form of cross-cousin marriage. Formerly cousin marriage in this tribe was undoubtedly an obligatory institution. That is the reason why the Chukchi, like the Yukaghir, are unfamiliar with bride payment and why marriages until now have been concluded during childhood. Children are betrothed by their parents even before birth. Among the Chukchi this custom is even more common than among the Gilyak. As Mr. Bogoraz said, "The majority of marriages are concluded in childhood."[22]

At the present time cousin marriage is permitted in every line, between agnatic as well as cognatic cousins. It was not originally so. This fact is clearly shown by the peculiar form of group marriage. There are two forms of group marriage among the Chukchi. One of them is expressed by a formal stipulation between several men as to their mutual marital rights over their individual wives. Such a stipulation may be concluded also between persons not related to one another, but "second and third cousins are almost invariably united by ties of group marriage."[23]

Considering that the favorite form of marriage is between cousins, the Chukchi group marriage is a union between cousins married to cousins. One detail of the group marriage stipulation shows that primarily the partners of the group marriage were cousins of the agnatic line only. "The persons concerned make sacrifices and anoint themselves with blood, first in one camp, and then in the other. After that, they are considered as belonging to one fireside, as do the relatives in the male line."[24] The children of such marriage unions are regarded as cousins, because as brothers and sisters they cannot marry each other. Such a survival is the best witness that this form of group marriage was previously exercised exclusively between brothers and cousins in the male line only, as it is now among the Gilyak.[25]

---

[22] Bogoraz, *The Chukchee*, 602.

[23] Ibid. [**Editor's note:** An excellent source on concepts of group marriage proposed by ethnographers of the Chukchi is Peter Schweitzer, "Spouse-Exchange in North-Eastern Siberia: On Kinship and Sexual Relations and Their Transformations," *Vienna Contributions to Ethnology and Anthropology* 5 (1989), 17–38.]

[24] Bogoraz, *The Chukchee*, 603.

[25] [**Editor's note:** This section abridges the longer discussions of Bogoraz' work in the AMNH Russian typescript, 134–138, and Shternberg, *Giliaki*, 240–242.]

THE KORIAK. Among the Koriak, although of the same race and linguistic stock and on the same cultural level as the Chukchi, the process of endogamization has gone further than among the latter and has taken a direction similar to that of the Yukaghir. Like the Chukchi, they have lost all feeling for exogamy; they have lost the clan and every trace of the Turanian classificatory system. Like the Yukaghir, they have passed to strictly individual marriage, but unlike the Yukaghir, they have evolved a new code of virtue—chastity among women.

Nevertheless, even here we find traces of the old Turanian system. Conspicuous among these is the institution which was aptly named by Frazer the "sororate," that is, the right of a man to the sisters of his living or deceased wife. Morgan looked for the origin of this institution in the Punaluan family, although in every case it is undoubtedly a consequence of primary obligatory marriage of blood relatives.[26]

Having abolished group marriage, the Koriak prohibited a man from marrying more than one sister; they even forbade two brothers to marry sisters or even cousins. The sororate in the case of a deceased wife became not a right but a duty, and what is particularly significant is that the Koriak sororate is of the pure Tungusian type. The duty of the sororate embraces not only sisters or female cousins of the deceased wife but also her nieces. "The widower," says Iokhel'son, "must marry the younger sister, younger cousin, or niece (daughter of sister or brother) of his deceased wife."[27]

If this institution of the sororate indicates by itself the primary right to marriage, the inclusion in the right of the sororate of the niece of the deceased wife confirms in the clearest way the fact that the deceased wife of a man must have been his blood relative. Otherwise his right over her niece would be quite inexplicable unless the niece of the deceased wife had not been at the same time the niece of the husband. It becomes understandable only in the light of the peculiar form of Turanian marriage found by the Tungus and some Tamil tribes (see above) under which a man is obliged to marry his cousin or his niece. Thus the primary Koriak marriage must have been of Tungusian type.

Mr. Iokhel'son tries to explain the institution of sororate (or as he calls it, "double levirate") among the Koriak in another way. He sees the origin of the institution in the desire to sustain religious bonds between marriage mates, and in the reluctance to admit an alien element to the sacred hearth.[28] Such an explanation might become plausible if the deceased wife had been in due time brought into religious communion with the family hearth of her husband by a special religious performance. But as Mr. Iokhel'son himself states, no religious marriage performances are in vogue among the Koriak.[29] Indeed, the absence of religious wedding performances itself shows that the mates originally must have been blood relatives, cousins or nieces of

---

[26] Morgan, *Ancient Society*, 432. [**Editor's note:** This footnote is found in the AMNH English typescript only.]

[27] Iokhel'son, *The Koryak* (Leiden: E. J. Brill), 748. [**Editor's note:** This footnote is found in the AMNH English typescript only.]

[28] Ibid., 749–750. [**Editor's note:** This footnote is found in the AMNH English typescript only.]

[29] Ibid., 748. [**Editor's note:** This footnote is found in the AMNH English typescript only.]

the husband, naturally bound by ties of common ancestral worship. The usual levirate among the Koriak is also of the Tungusian type.

At the present time only marriages with female cousins and nieces of the second degree are permitted, but these restrictions are apparently of recent origin. In Steller and Krasheninnikoff, as well as in the old tales, no mention is made of them.[30]

Two wedding customs—bride-service and the ceremony of struggle over the bride—bear witness that the endogamous practices among the Koriak are not original, but of later origin.

As may clearly be seen from Mr. Iokhel'son's description, bride-service is in no way an economic institution. All the details show that its aim is ostensibly to humiliate the groom and his relatives. Such humiliation can be explained in but one way— that it is performed *in fraudem legis* to assuage the ancestral gods for infringing on the old marriage laws. The same explanation must be given to the second ceremony, the struggle to catch the bride and tear off her clothes in order to touch her genitalia. Here again, such a struggle can only be understood according to Mr. Iokhel'son as a ceremony *in fraudem Deorum* to test the groom. However, to test the groom by humiliating his relatives, to test him after years of hard service by a symbolic struggle with the bride, the issue of which depends upon the goodwill of the bride herself, seems to have very little reason.

THE KAMCHADAL. Very little can be said about the Kamchadal. At the present time they are completely Russianized and have lost all their old culture. Steller and Krashennikoff, however, describe their customs as being very similar to those of the Koriak. Nonetheless, it is particularly interesting to note Krashennikoff's testimony that cousins commonly married.[31]

THE ALEUT. Let us now turn to the Aleut, whom Morgan regarded as the connecting link between Asiatic and American peoples. We have little information as to their marriage norms, but the little we know is of great interest from our point of view, especially as the data are furnished by the well-known Father Veniaminov, an observer who at the beginning of the 19th century spent many years among these people and who understood their language.[32] In the first place, we find that among the Aleut the common form of marriage was also cousin marriage. Veniaminov gives no

---

[30] [*Editor's note:* The reference to "Steller and Krasheninnikoff" [Krasheninnikov] is found in the AMNH English typescript only. While the Russian versions make an oblique reference to "Krasheninnikov (II, 124)" in the body of the text, the AMNH English version, citing no source, refers to "Steller and Krasheninnikoff." Shternberg was likely referring to Stepan P Krasheninnikov, *Opisanie Zemli Kamchatki* (St. Petersburg: Imperatorskaia Akademiia Nauk, 1755).]

[31] [*Editor's note:* While neither the AMNH Russian typescript, 137, nor Shternberg, *Giliaki,* 242, has more than a sentence to note about the Kamchadals, the AMNH English typescript sets it aside here as its own section.]

[32] [*Editor's note:* For an English-language source on Veniaminov, see Ivan (Ioam) Veniaminov, *Notes on the Islands of the Unalashka District.* Translation of Veniaminov, *Zapiski ob ostrovakh Unalashkinskago otdela* (n.p., 1840) by Lydia Black and R. H. Geoghegan. Edited with an introduction by Richard A. Pierce (Kingston, Canada: Limestone Press, 1984).]

details but says definitely that "the daughter of one's uncle was most frequently elected for one's bride."[33] Still more interesting is his description of polyandry among the Aleut: "A woman was permitted to have two husbands, of whom one was the principal husband, the other an associate, or as the Russians say, a half-husband" [*polovinshchik*]. Far from being censured as immoral, such a woman was respected for her thrift. The second man, while fully exercising the rights of a husband, shared the latter's obligation to work for the support of his wife and family. Erman furnished similar information, without however indicating the relationship between the common husbands, or their relations in case of the marriage of the second associate.[34] We are not justified, however, in concluding that the content of Aleut marriage was exhausted by these facts. Mamiya Rinzo, as stated before, had described Gilyak marriage in expressions almost identical with those used by Veniaminov for Aleuts, whereas we found among them a typical Gilyak form of group marriage. Such descriptions of group marriage as are given by Veniaminov and Rinzo are to be expected from nonprofessional observers. The most striking form of group marriage is that in which the second husband is not individually married, as we find for instance in Gilyak traditions: "Two brothers had supported one wife." But when several men, especially when each one is individually married, are parties to a group marriage, the fact generally escapes the notice of the nonprofessional observer.

In confirmation of my assertion, I want to adduce an example from the Todas, a Nilgiri mountain tribe. An early author, W. E. Marshall, describes marriage among the Todas in the following terms: "If the husband has brothers or very near relatives, all living together, they may each, if but she and he consent, participate in the right to be considered her husband also."[35] According to this description, cited by Westermarck (an antagonist of Morgan), Toda marriage is pure polyandry like Tibetan marriage or Veniaminov's version of Aleut marriage. But here is a description of the same marriage by Short, a trained observer. He writes,

> Among the Todas, the inhabitants of the Nilgiri Mountains, a girl, upon her marriage, becomes the wife of all her husband's brothers who, in their turn, become the husbands of all her sisters. In such cases, the first child born is regarded as belonging to the older brother; the second, to the next elder.[36]

This description reveals a typical group marriage—an ideal form of the Punaluan family. It is worthwhile mentioning that the description was made in 1869, 8 years

---

[33] [**Editor's note:** While the AMNH Russian typescript contains the incomplete reference, "Veniaminov, Zapiksi ob ostrovakh Unalashki . . . ," the AMNH English typescript refers to *Trudy Arkhiespiskopa Innokentii*, vol. 3, 323–324. The AMNH Russian typescript and Shternberg, *Giliaki*, refer the reader to *Tvoreniia Innokentiia*, vol. 3. See also Ivan Platonovich Barsukov, *O zhizni i podvigakh Innokentiia* (n.p., 1893), translated into English as Barsukov, *The Life and Work of Innocent, the Archbishop of Kamchatka, the Kuriles and the Aleutian Islands, and Later the Metropolitan of Moscow* (San Francisco: Cubery, 1897).]

[34] Adolph Erman, "Etnographische Wahrnehmungen," *Zeitschrift für Ethnologie* 3 (1871), 162–163.

[35] W. E. Marshall, *A Phrenologist among the Todas* (London: n.p., 1873), 213.

[36] John Short, "An Account of the Hill Tribes of the Nilgiris," *Transactions of the Ethnological Society of London*, n. ser., vol. 7 (London: J. Murray, 1869), 240.

prior to the publication of Morgan's *Ancient Society* and simultaneously with his *Systems of Consanguinity and Affinity of the Human Family*. Thus the writer could not have had any of the modern ideas regarding the Punaluan family.

These lines had already been written when I met the well-known ethnologist, Mr. Iokhel'son, who had just returned from his expedition to the Aleut. The data he was able to furnish me finally confirmed my suppositions. He kindly informed me that among the Aleut, as among the Tungus and the Gilyak in former times, the younger brothers were in group marriage with the wives of their elder brothers, and at the present time this institution is preserved among cousins. What is most remarkable is that this is not an optional institution but an obligatory one. To participate in group marriage is the duty of all cousins. Another interesting fact given to me by Mr. Iokhel'son is that the term "cousin" among the Aleut is used as a general term for cousins of every line. We have here, then, the same Malayan feature as we have seen among the Yukaghir and Chukchi.

The peculiarities of the Aleut marriage system are not restricted to the Aleutian Islands. In words almost identical with Veniaminov's, they are described on the northwestern coast of America down to the Columbia River, which Morgan regarded as the point of origin of the Ganowanian system. Similar marital norms we find among the Koniag [Alutiiq], inhabitants of Kodiak Island, about whom the old traveler Davydov writes,

> Some women have two husbands. The first is the real husband, who selects the second with the wife's consent. The latter also acts as a servant, carries water, fuel and executes other jobs. He may sleep with the wife only in the absence of the principal husband, on whose return he loses that right. Such husbands are called by the Russians *polovinshchiki*.[37]

In this description, which seems to be taken from Mamiya Rinzo, Veniaminov, and the Tibetan travelers, we again miss an indication of the relationship between the husbands. But we have the valuable statement that the second husband may exercise his rights only in the absence of the first, as well as the clear presentation of the inferior position of the second husband. This inferiority of the second husband is well observed among the Gilyak. Its reason, however, does not lie in any provision of the marriage contract but in the fact that the older brother usually assumes the part of the master of the house. Moreover, in view of the prohibition of conversation between the two brothers, the relations of the younger to the older may appear to an outsider as those of servant and master. This institution is more definitely described by Veniaminov among the Tlingit, who clearly states, "The second husband must be either a brother or a near relative."[38] This statement throws light upon the true nature of the institution. A similar phenomenon was noted by Ross among the Central Eskimo.

However, we shall not go into detail about America, the home of the Ganowanian system which is so closely allied to the Turanian. Our purpose has been to bridge

---

[37] Gavriil I. Davydov, *Dvukratnoe puteshestvie v Ameriku ofitserov Khvostova i Davydova*, vol. 2 (1810–1812), 50–51.

[38] *Tvoreniia Innokentiia*, vol. 3, 619. [***Editor's note:*** This footnote is found in the AMNH Russian typescript and Shternberg, *Giliaki*, only.]

the gap that separated the native land of the Turanian system from the land of the Ganowanian. And I hope, after the present review, we have the right to say that it is accomplished. The system of the Dravidian nations of India is no longer separated from its American counterpart. The connection, so strenuously sought for and ingeniously foreseen by Morgan, is now found. This connection is represented by the great Tungus family and by all the Paleo-Asiatic nations.

ELEVEN

SEXUAL LIFE[1]

[142–158; 213–228; 246–257; 124–130]

THE SEXUAL FREEDOM which group marriage offers to the Gilyak is naturally conducive to the development of great sensuality. The lifestyle of the people also contributes to this development. The main occupation of the Gilyak, fishing, leaves them time for a great deal of leisure, while on the other hand, the only occupation which might serve as an outlet for emotional energy, hunting, plays a relatively unimportant role in their life. They do not undertake distant hunting expeditions, and the seasonal pursuit of sables, squirrels, foxes, deer, and even the sporadic tracking of the rather mild-tempered local bear do not present any extraordinary dangers. Prominent hunters of the kind found among the Tungus are very rare among the Gilyak. The heroic feelings aroused by wars are also unknown to the Gilyak, especially during the latter half of the century. Even before that, their wars were only sporadic inter-clan conflicts for the sake of revenge or more often because of women. War as a profession or as the favorite occupation of youth was unknown to them [124].

It is therefore natural that all their emotional energy should turn towards sex. Their sexual life begins at the first signs of puberty. All their thoughts and leisure time are devoted to women, particularly so because not everybody has an opportunity to marry. The bachelors are not content merely with the women of their own village, nor do they restrict themselves only to the group of women towards whom they have legal rights. The only category of women before whom they stop are those of the class actually forbidden them. Neither time nor distance will phase the Gilyak in his romantic pursuits, as long as there is the possibility of finding a little more female companionship. Most willingly, of course, does a young man visit the villages

---

[1] [**Editor's note:** In the AMNH English typescript, the quality of the English translation of this chapter and the succeeding ones differed markedly from the three preceding ones prior to editing, invoking a much less literal style than found in, for example, chapter fourteen translated by Iulia Averkieva, or chapter seven, which was likely translated by Alexander Goldenweiser (appendix A). A more colorful if slightly embroidered version of this chapter can be found in Chester Chard, "Sternberg's Materials on the Sexual Life of the Gilyak," *Anthropological Papers of the University of Alaska* 10, no. 1, 13–23. While borrowing occasional phrasing from Chard's version, I have preserved the version from the AMNH English typescript. The AMNH Russian and Shternberg, *Sem'ia*, versions present this section in three chapters, "Sexual Life," "Love and Jealousy," and "Sexual Abnormalities and Perversions." The AMNH English typescript and Shternberg, *Giliaki*, use the title as above, "Sexual Life."]

of his *akhmalk* (fathers-in-law). But they also do not object to undertaking journeys to strange villages. During my travels I would often be joined by a Gilyak who voluntarily offered me his services *gratis* in the hope of encountering a romantic episode. Not a very difficult feat.

Every door is open to the newcomer because the Gilyak are traditionally hospitable and eager for gossip. Thus a Gilyak feels at home everywhere. A few hours after his arrival he usually has succeeded in visiting every house and spreading all the news. Men and women alike eagerly lend an avid ear. And at the same time he has already begun to cast glances at those he favors among the women. The rest is only a matter of erotic skill and experience. It is true that the Gilyak woman conducts herself in a most unapproachable manner. Upon the arrival of a stranger she lowers her eyes, frowns, and will scarcely deign to answer the stranger's questions. But this is merely a pretense which conceals her extreme promiscuity. Imperceptibly to others she throws stealthy and curious glances at the newcomer, which he catches at opportune moments. If the guest makes a proper impression the matter is apt to be settled rather quickly. He waylays her near the well, or in the berry patch, or will simply seize her in the entry passage. After a short symbolic dialogue on the order of, "Let us smoke together" (that is, take turns at the same pipe), or "Let's exchange news," the matter will be settled very readily. Sometimes the guest stays in the home of his *inamorata* and at night slips into her bed or vice versa. On other occasions the affair will dispense with words, merely making symbolic gestures such as touching her breast or catching her leg. If these gestures encounter no rebuff then the woman's consent is assured. These symbolic gestures remind one of those connected with marriage ceremonials. The offer to smoke together is a parody of the *conferratio* rite. The touching of the breast and the catching of the leg at present do not appear in the marriage ceremonial of the Gilyak, but they are still found among several tribes of North America. Thus Profs. Boas and Teit refer to the existence of such rites among the Lilloet Indians [125].

Married and elderly men indulge in the same frivolities as the bachelors when visiting strange villages. During one of my first journeys through the country, there was among my companions an aged and respectable man called Gibel'ka. He was known throughout the island for his wealth and intelligence. During our sojourns in the various villages, he like our youthful companions spoke with zest about the local beauties. Once he was so smitten that he asked me whether he should purchase a girl who so pleased his eye that he wanted to take her along. All this despite the fact that he had been married a long time and always spoke with the greatest enthusiasm about his wife. It is true that he did not participate in the nocturnal adventures of the younger fellow travelers, but this was due to the fact that competition was already so hot that a gunfight had almost occurred among the younger men.

The violation of women is rare because of their relative accessibility. I was told, however, of certain incidents. During the season when women are far from their homes, picking berries or gathering sarana [*Lilium tenuifolium*], gangs of boys may raid the unprotected women. If the women do not surrender, violence is used. This consists of tearing of their hip-breeches which, as among the Chukchi and the Koriak, are made without any openings.

Similar invasions and romantic excursions outside the circle of related women have a special term, *shankh nanigind,* that is, "woman hunting." This term is also used for searching for a bride. The word *nanigind* has two meanings: to hunt, and to search for something or somebody in general.[2]

The special expeditions into strange and distant villages in search of women are, of course, exceptional and amateurish adventures, particularly because in the distant villages newcomers generally meet with powerful competition from the local youths. The women have their own local admirers, not to mention their husbands. To succeed in a strange village one must therefore be endowed with special qualities. I happened to meet some of these lucky fellows. They are usually sophisticated storytellers, good jokers, and singers.

Although this type of Don Juan is rare even among the Gilyak, they have a special term for him.[3] The unmarried youths are usually content with the women of their village and those of their *akhmalk* (fathers-in-law) villages. There, as we already know, they are ever welcome.

It is difficult to depict the sexual life of the Gilyak in general terms. We must first of all make a distinction between bachelors and married men. The latter, when at home, are more concerned with the protection of their own wives from intruders rather than with indulging in extramarital flirtations. Only when away from home do they readily give free reign to their sexual instincts. The married women, on the contrary, are constantly tempted by group-husbands and strangers. Thus on every convenient occasion they violate their marital faith, the more easily because not all women marry for love or men of equal age, something compensated for by extramarital affairs. In accord with Gilyak attitudes on decorum, however, these flirtations are not abnormal because they occur mostly between group-husbands and group-wives. Rightly or wrongly, one must award the palm for excellence in the extramarital arts [*pal'ma pervenststva v otnoshenii ektsessov sredi zhenatykh*] to

---

2 [***Editor's note:*** Handwritten inserts to the AMNH Russian typescript use both *nanigind* and *nanygynd.* Shternberg, *Giliaki,* uses *nan'gynd,* while Shternberg, *Sem'ia,* uses *nang'nd.* On Sakhalin in 1995, Gilyak (Nivkh) language speakers Galina Lok and Aleksandra Khuriun advocated *nanigind.* Since the Gilyak language is written down so rarely, wide variation continues to exist between the transliteration system created by Kreinovich in 1931 using the Latin alphabet, Kreinovich's later 1936 Cyrillic system, the Cyrillic system proposed by Vladimir Sangi in 1981, and other idiosyncratic phonetic variations, such as those used in the Nivkh-language newspaper, *Nivkh Dif* (1990–1996). While Lok, Khuriun, and others occasionally argued to change terms, the more common response was to leave the AMNH Russian and English typescript variants stand by default, less for their accuracy than for the confusion caused by the Gilyak-language words used in Shternberg, *Sem'ia,* which was the edition I took with me to Sakhalin. Notably, the handwritten inserts to the AMNH Russian typescript of this chapter resemble neither those of Shternberg, unless illness had unsteadied his hand, nor Kreinovich.]

3 [***Editor's note:*** No special term was known to Nivkh women with whom I discussed the Shternberg manuscript in 1995, although the AMNH Russian typescript left a space blank for this word to be inserted. Only the AMNH English typescript and Shternberg, *Sem'ia,* invoke Don Juan for what the AMNH Russian typescript and Shternberg, *Giliaki,* denote as "the successful lover." Later in this chapter, the AMNH English typescript used "Don Juan" to replace what the AMNH Russian typescript termed, "Lovelace," after the character in Samuel Richardson's novel, *Clarissa* (Boston: Samuel Hall, 1795).]

the women. As the Gilyak saying goes, "Good men are rare, but good women are nonexistent."[4]

The real sexual excesses take place among the unmarried young. Here we find such extravagances as the case of the Gilyak woman Pigunaiko, mentioned earlier, who before her marriage had affairs with 14 lovers during the same period, including her future husband. Or to take another example from a Gilyak epic: One day a man came to the home of an elder to take the elder's daughter for a wife. The future father-in-law said to him, "Your future wife lives in that small yurta. People have been visiting her, copulating continually with her. As a consequence, she has lost her legs." The bridegroom, however, was not in the least disturbed. "Never mind," he said, "I will take her all the same!" He did not find anything extraordinary in this case, although such a tale cannot be considered as exemplary. Along with sensuality and great sexual freedom there are restraining factors such as motherhood, household duties for the married women, and love and shame among both married and unmarried women.

But in general sexual laxity plays a not insignificant role in the life of the Gilyak, having both economic and psychological consequences. Ordinarily, the Lovelaces who devote most of their time to romance rarely establish families, or if they do, their households are managed most carelessly. The sharp scolding of youths by their elders for laziness resulting from too many love affairs is encountered both in the life of the people and in their epic poetry. Childless marriages are explained by the Gilyak as due to sexual excess. The saddest effect of all, however, is on the psyche of the people. An array of nervous diseases specific to these people, such as *miarechenie* among both men and women—illnesses connected with a total loss of psychological self-control—are the result of such laxity. Among women these diseases are accompanied by serious disturbances of the sexual sphere, often leading to hysterics [**126**].

LOVE AND JEALOUSY

Together with intensive sensuality and sexual freedom, sentimental love exists among the Gilyak and plays an important part in their life. Most widespread is the term *esmund,* which designates love of children, love of friends, and sexual love. There is a special term for reciprocal love, *osmund,* and for love inmarriages, *osmurkir, vav'nd.* There are several other terms for love such as *khyivynd,* but none designating "beloved," although it is possible to say *es'mula nigivin* (person who is loved). Lovers call each other either "husband" and "wife," or else "my man" and "my woman" (*n'oz'amits, n'an'kh*).

The Gilyak consider love a normal stage of life which must be passed through by everyone in his youth. This sentiment is very well expressed in a song which I recorded on the Amur. A girl complains about her mother for scolding her because she is in love. She sings the following:

---

4   [***Editor's note:*** This loosely captures the meaning of the Russianized maxim, "*Sredi muzhchin, eshche odin-odin khoroshii naidetsia, sredi zhenshchin, ni odnoi.*" The maxim appears to contradict what Shternberg reports at the start of chapter six, that Gilyak men are the less faithful of the sexes.]

Mother, mother, mother dear,
Can you have really forgotten your own youth?

[Literally: You have forgotten your own past. Leave me alone!].

Children are never scolded by parents for their amorous passions. If sometimes they hear their elders grumbling, it is only because of economic considerations; young people tend to become careless, sloppy, and neglectful of their work when they are infatuated. In general it is forbidden to interfere in any way in the love affairs of the young people, even of young girls. Fathers and brothers can do nothing to the seducer of their daughters or sisters, not even challenge him to a duel. They are not even allowed to be angry with the girl. The infatuation of children is considered perfectly natural; the mother is often the confidante of her children. In many of the songs I recorded on the Amur, the sons always turn to their mothers with their romantic problems and ask for advice as to how and where to find a sweetheart.

Serious and active protests on the part of the parents, at times even of a merciless nature, occur only in cases of love between persons of prohibited categories. In such cases, the daughter is encouraged to commit suicide by the parents themselves. Often the parents, especially the father, are pitiless when the love of a daughter interferes with profitable marriage arrangements which had been made when the girl was a child. In such cases the girl is married off against her will to a person she does not love. Such instances are, however, exceptional.

Love among the Gilyak does not differ in character from that of civilized society. Crude sexuality is totally absent. In their love life one finds the complete gamut of this universal emotion, from the very tenderest tones of poetic sentiment and gentle anguish, to the most tempestuous impulses of heroic passions braving all obstacles, not hesitating to part with life itself. These feelings are well expressed in their love songs, particularly those of the women. Nature has endowed the Gilyak woman with a depth and subtlety of sentiment which she knows how to express in touching images and forms.

Night and day I think about you . . . . I look out for you as if for my own mother . . . . If you will go away I will think only of you . . . . Where you pass I too will pass . . . . I will drink your black shadow from the well from which we drank together . . . . As in the woods one likes the best tree, so among all the other men you are the finest and most beautiful . . . . O, take me along! . . . I want to become the pouch for flint and tinder which hangs on your belt . . . . I will be the bottom of your boat, only to be with you . . . . My left tear runs and falls like rain. My right knee weakens and becomes immobile. My legs no longer move.

In such expressions picked at random from various love songs does the Gilyak woman proclaim her love. The songs of the men sound the same sentimental notes. Comparable are frequent mentions of left and right tears knocking like rain on the knee, of anguish at parting, and of sweet dreams of a love tryst. One comes across such expressions as "I fell completely in love with you." Rarely one hears vulgarities, from our point of view, such as, "The joint under the knee of your plump thigh is twitching. O, how I like it." But there is never any cynicism [**127**].

FIG. 17. Two Gilyak men, 1890s. Photo by Lev Shternberg. *Source:* AAN f. 282, o. 2, d. 158, l. 1.

The abundance of sentimental songs indicates the role love plays in the life of the Gilyak. Not everyone can tell stories or recite poetry, but love songs are known by all. It is the language of lovers. When they meet, lovers sing to each other improvised songs instead of speaking. If they cannot see each other, they send songs of their own composition through a third person, *ad hoc.* There are special terms for such songs.

The intensity of love among the Gilyak can be judged from the reactions of lovers when there are hopeless obstacles in their way. Suicide seems to be the only solution. Most of the obstacles are put in the way by parents who because of greed for a bride-price, or unwillingness to break an infant betrothal, marry her off by force. Sometimes the girl is abducted. In such cases the woman tries at first to escape from her despised husband, but in case of failure she commits suicide, sometimes long after her marriage. I remember a characteristic case which occurred in the village Nianevo, where a girl was married off against her will. Soon after, she escaped to her father. The latter turned her over to her lover, tempted by the opportunity to receive a second bride-price. But the first husband wasn't reconciled to this situation and at the first opportunity took her away by force. Half a year later the unhappy woman hung herself. There are known cases where a woman escaping from a despised husband killed all the children she had had from that marriage. The men defend their rights to women energetically. Usually they attempt with the help of clansmen to take the woman by force; however, they do not stop at killing the husband of the beloved.

In the same village of Nianevo occurred an extraordinarily heroic love affair. During my stay there, a Gilyak named Nyngun was the wealthiest and most respectable person in the village. His beloved was forcibly married to another man. He killed his rival, and was arrested and taken to Nikolaevsk. In the meantime the brother of the widow again married her off by force to someone else. Escaping from jail, Nyngun immediately started for the village of his beloved. Near her yurta he took off all his clothes, except his penis sheath, and naked, notwithstanding the winter cold, entered the yurta, which was packed with people. All were so terrified by his resolute appearance that no hand was raised as he easily carried off his beloved. He lived with her for many years. Before her death she succeeded in sewing for him four fox and four sable coats.

The most tragic of all obstacles to love is when the lovers belong to prohibited categories. Here there is no way out. The parents themselves insist on suicide. Usually the lovers go to the woods and hang themselves side by side on the nearest trees. Before dying they sing songs to each other in which they celebrate their way to another world where nobody will disturb their love. Sometimes these songs reach us, for it happens that sometimes one of the participants falls from the tree and loses the desire to repeat the experience. In this way the death songs are preserved for succeeding generations [**128**].

One such tragic instance grew into a popular legend. It occurred about a hundred years ago. A young girl had intercourse with her father's young brother. Soon after her lover left on a long trip to Manchuria to buy goods. In the meantime she was pregnant and could not keep her secret any longer. She committed suicide by hanging. When her lover returned he burned all his goods on her grave, freed the bear which he had fattened for the feast, and hung himself. The song she sang during their parting was preserved.

> Take me with you. I will become the planks on the bottom of your boat
> . . . . Now I can only think about the Land of the Dead [*Mlyvo*]. That you
> may remember me, keep the earrings hanging on your wall.

Magic means are used for unreciprocated love. The dried brain of the cuckoo is mixed with tobacco and offered to the girl to smoke, or a feather of this bird is secretly sewn into the girl's dress. But there are other charms which are not quite so innocent and often end tragically. Anyone tasting these medicaments, it is said, falls into a heavy melancholy and dies within a few days. I knew two Russianized Gilyak men who were selling these medicines for high prices and by these means had killed several women.

There are among the Gilyak, as amongst ourselves, timid persons who do not have the courage to declare their love personally. There are old women who act as intermediaries. They are given presents (*pai*) for their services. Sometimes presents are sent through them to the beloved, usually a piece of cloth with several knots tied in it to indicate the number of days that will elapse before the lover will come to visit her.

There still remain a few words to be said about the qualities which the Gilyak consider as stimuli to love. First of all, of course, comes beauty, especially that of the face. The term *pot urland*, the Gilyak term for beauty, literally means "beautiful in face." It is remarkable that beauty is judged not only from one's own racial point of view. Gilyak men and women alike admire Russian ladies. Gilyak women like even the blond and reddish Europeans. A good example is my friend Bronislaw Pilsudskii, a reddish blond, who was greatly admired by the Gilyak not only for his sympathetic attitudes towards them but for his attractive appearance. For this reason they always called him *pot urakhra*, or literally, "handsome by face." When he was leaving Sakhalin the Gilyak women dictated to him many songs confessing their love.[5]

In love songs, "skin white as birch bark," magnificent hair "smooth and braided till the waistline," graceful ("a head inclined to one side, smiling, he strides"), physical power, and stature "the trunk, a broad sazhen wide, with legs that sink into the earth to his very shins," are very much praised.

Elegance of dress plays an important part in the appraisal of a lover. In love songs, embroidered cloth with a multitude of copper pendants sewn on it (*mes'kramra watramra*) is much admired for women, as are a black dog's fur coat, a spotted seal skirt, and a richly trimmed forehead bound with squirrel skins for men. Summer dresses of black material are much admired on women, while the men show best in shirts made half of white and half of red or blue material.

Besides external beauty, moral qualities are considered. Men attract women by their bravery and solidity. A woman will say: "Your voice is like that of *urdla nivukh*" (that is, of a respectable man, an accomplished conversationalist or singer). Women captivate men by their special qualities. From early childhood the girl learns to speak melodiously and to give the face an expression of dreamlike coquettishness. The ability to sing is of great advantage to the Gilyak woman. In her songs she not only gently expresses her love but can also wickedly mock a despised suitor. Her sarcasm has no limitations: In one song she compares the nose of a despised suitor with a broken place in the ice or with an open door. She uses similar expressions to describe his clothing, dogs, harness, and so on [**129**].

SEXUAL PERVERSIONS

Many times I have asked the Gilyak whether or not they have such sexual perversions as sodomy and bestiality, but it seemed as if nobody had ever heard about such cases.[6] Only in one village on the Tym' River was I told with great revulsion of a man suffering from a psychological illness who cohabited with a dog. How the Gilyak consider such perversions is evident from the following legend, which I recorded on the Amur. The tiger, panther, and even lion were once human beings. Accidentally the God Kur saw them copulating through the anus. Then he told them in great wrath, "As long as you are copulating like beasts (*na-navarand*) you shall

---

[5] [**Editor's note:** The work of Bronislaw Pilsudskii, older brother of the Polish leader Iuzef, has been the subject of increasing study through the Pilsudskii Center at the Sakhalin Regional Museum, Yuzhno-Sakhalinsk, and the efforts of the Polish linguist, Alfred Majewicz. See Pilsudskii's works in the bibliography.]

[6] [**Editor's note:** The subject of sexual variations in Siberian cultures has recently been explored in Marjorie Mandelstam Balzer's excellent article, "Sacred Genders in Siberia: Shamans, Bear Festivals and Androgyny," in *Gender Reversals and Gender Cultures*, Sabrina P. Ramet, ed. (London: Routledge, 1997), 164–182.]

be beasts for ever more." Thus, in the opinion of the Gilyak, these perversions make man resemble beasts.

The attitude of the Gilyak towards hermaphrodites (*miskund*, E.D.; *miskii*, W.D.) is quite simple. Their peculiarities are considered as simple anomalies. They are not despised and sexual intercourse with them is accepted quite willingly. The marriage of hermaphrodites is also not considered unusual.

In view of the fact that sexual intercourse and marriage of hermaphrodites on the one hand and homosexuality on the other are very often mixed up in ethnographic literature, I will cite some of the characteristic cases of hermaphroditism among the Gilyak. I know of two cases on Sakhalin Island. One was Chubuk who lived in the village of Iamy near Aleksandrovsk. He was known to be a hermaphrodite because until a certain age he considered himself a woman; his *membrum virile* was scarcely developed and he wore women's dress. In the course of time his *membrum virile* developed properly, and he began to dress like a man and at last married. The other case I came across in the village of Myi Girk on the extreme north end of the island on the western coast. There I once saw a man and a woman sitting together on the shore who turned out to be a married couple. The woman's features appeared to me somewhat to resemble those of a man. My companions explained to me that only a year ago the woman was wearing a man's dress and considered herself a man. And she was very friendly with her present husband. Once they went fishing together; they had to spend the night there. The woman told her secret and from that time they began to cohabit and finally married, although the man was strongly urged against taking the step. Such cases could easily be the source of legends of transformed men.

On the Amur a Gilyak named Putuk once told me some very interesting details about his friend who was a hermaphrodite. This person was a girl until a certain age. Suddenly she noticed that the *membrum virile* was growing, now increasing, now decreasing, and now disappearing entirely. She told this to her lover. The latter came secretly to her at night to convince himself and on the following day he told everyone about it. Several years later, she grew a beard and a *membrum virile* had definitely developed, although a vagina was also developed and she could cohabit with men. After that he began to dress like a man, then married, and was considered to be the best hunter in the region. He lived with his wife normally but sometimes copulated with men. The latter he appreciated more. He always spoke about himself with pleasure, "I have two chances, two happinesses." All considered him to be a good man, *urdla nivukh*. I have counted five such cases among the Gilyak, the same number found by Prof. Bogoraz among the Chukchi.

PUBERTY

The Gilyak do not have any ceremonials in connection with the coming of puberty. The only sign of a girl's having passed puberty is that her hair is worn in two braids. The time of girls' maturity is reckoned from the appearance of the first menses. Usually they begin at 13 or 14 years of age, and this time is considered as the beginning of matrimonial age. The term *put indind shankh* designates a woman arrived at the age of puberty, although it literally means, "woman who saw her body," which is to say that her breasts have developed to a degree where she can see them. There is a similar term for men, *put indind nigivin*, or "man who saw his body," but in this case the word *ut* (body) designates mustaches [**130**].

Before the appearance of menses a girl is prepared by her mother for the coming change in her life. She is initiated into all the laws and taboos connected with menstrual blood. The meaning of menses as the moment of puberty is recognized by both sexes, and until that moment no sexual intercourse is permitted. Often a man marries an underaged girl and sleeps under one blanket with her, but cohabitation begins only after she tells him of the beginning of her first menses.

TWELVE

Marriage Rites Old and New[1]

[172–173, 159–162, 170–171, 173–192; 229–270;
267–268, 258–262, 268–284; 135–136, 130–132, 136–144]

As an illustration of the obligatory character of marriage to a woman of the mother's clan, some chapters back we related an episode taken from an old Gilyak poem in which a man, dying from a wound inflicted by a person who had a legitimate claim upon his daughter, calls his murderer and exclaims: "Though this man killed me, give my daughter to him. Do not go against my word." In a similar manner, Gilyak epics depict types of ancient marriage which correspond exactly with the Gilyak norms [135].

Since these marriages were obligatory, there was no talk of complicated marriage procedures such as betrothal, negotiation over property obligations, or brideprice. Nor were there any of the religious ceremonies connected with the passing of the bride into a strange clan. The bride and bridegroom were of common blood on both father's and mother's sides. Therefore in all the epics we find the same picture of marriage occurring without any formalities. A man, appearing from afar and being a candidate only from hearsay, needs only declare the purpose of his visit to receive the consent of the parents, after which he has all the material rights of a husband. On the next day he may take his wife away. Furthermore, not only does no one ask him for compensation, but usually the father-in-law provides him with generous gifts. It is true that for the sake of formality the consent of the daughter is sought, but usually the daughter obeys the will of her parents and of the law. The only rite invariably practiced is the most primitive form of the Roman *conferratio* where the married couple have to eat and smoke together.

The following is an example of a marriage ceremony taken from a poem which I recorded. An old woman, the mother of two daughters, asks a newly arrived youth, "Wherefore, my son, have you come? Did you come for a wife? Your wives live in

---

1   [***Editor's note:*** The AMNH Russian typescript presents this material as three chapters, "Means of Obtaining Wives," "The Modern Way of Obtaining Wives," and "Forms of Entering into Marriage." Shternberg, *Giliaki,* reduces this to two chapters, "Means of Obtaining Wives," and "Forms of Entering into Marriage"; while Shternberg, *Sem'ia,* further sets aside the subsections "Bride Price and Dowry" and "Marriage Pitfalls" as separate chapters. While the Russian versions slightly reorder the sections found here, I agree with the AMNH English typescript that the prefatory marriage vignettes make an effective introduction to the question of how Gilyak epics informed turn-of-the-century rites.]

that elevated yurta. Go!" Our Gilyak ascended and entered. Two women were there. He sat between them. He took a pinch from his tobacco bag and gave some to the younger sister. She smoked. He then gave some to the older one. She took it and smoked. The older sister said, "Prepare food and feed us . . . ." The three ate together. After eating, they slept. On the following morning they awoke early and ate. Our Gilyak said, "Are we going today?" His new brides said, "We will pass the day here and will start tomorrow." On the day planned, they started back in a boat.

In another poem, a father-in-law responded to the demands of a bridegroom by setting one condition: "You must go back tomorrow." He ordered his slaves to prepare food, and said to his daughter, "Go eat together with your husband." The woman then ate with our Gilyak. After eating they went to urinate. They reentered the yurta, prepared the bed, lay down under one blanket, and slept. On the following day the old man said, "In the five boats loaded only with treasures you will start."[2]

In another case, the hero of a poem visits a well-populated village. When he entered the middle yurta a woman was there. This woman said, "Guest, from where did you come?" Our Gilyak replied, "I came to take you." The woman said, "Go speak to my father, if you want to take me."[3] Our Gilyak exited and entered another yurta. An old woman and an old man were there. This old woman said, "Young man, where did you come from?" Our Gilyak said, "I came to take your daughter." The old man said to his wife, "Prepare the *mos'* and feed my son-in-law."[4] Our Gilyak then went back to his new wife. "Your father said that we both must come in the evening to eat." After sleeping they got up, ate, and departed for the husband's village [**135**].[5]

MANNER OF OBTAINING WIVES

It would be interesting to reconstruct from the data given in the epics how the Gilyak of old obtained wives. According to the *nastund* [epic poetry], obtaining a wife was by no means an easy task, as is attested to by the term used for searching for a wife, *ang'rei nanigind*. The verb *nanigind* is the technical term for hunting beasts, with many difficulties and dangers implied. The greatest task for the Gilyak hero was finding a wife. To do so, he had to undertake hazardous journeys to remote parts of the country. He had to swim stormy seas, rise to heaven, and even go down to the bottom of the sea, not to mention battling a whole series of monsters connected with such an enterprise [**130**].

Why should the Gilyak hero, a strong man, have to search for a wife so far away when there were a great many opportunities to find *ang'rei* nearby?

---

[2] [**Editor's note:** This paragraph is not found in Shternberg, *Sem'ia.*]
[3] [**Editor's note:** Shternberg's use of first-person Gilyak speech in this paragraph of the AMNH Russian typescript and elsewhere runs counter to his assertion that Gilyaks preferred third-person address even when speaking to someone in the same room.]
[4] [**Editor's note:** *Mos'* is an aspic made of fish skin, seal fat, and berries.]
[5] Shternberg, *Materialy po izucheniiu giliatskago iazyka i fol'klora* (St. Petersburg: Imperatorskaia Akademiia Nauk, 1908), 57–58, 84, 118. [**Editor's note:** This footnote is not found in Shternberg, *Sem'ia.*]

The term *ang'rei nanigind* might give one reason for thinking that violence and rape were the only means of obtaining wives in the olden times. But such was not the case; although rape and violence did occur occasionally, most men obtained their wives in a peaceful manner and without bride-price. The term *ang'rei* itself indicates a category of woman to whom the Gilyak have a legitimate marriage right. And really all evidence shows that the aim of the hero was merely to find a legitimate wife. Wherever he appears with his claims, he is called *imgi* (son-in-law) and the women he claims are his *ang'rei* (potential wives). It is quite different when a strange woman is shown as a candidate for a wife. She is called not *ang'rei* but *shankh.* The following is a characteristic example. The hero of a poem was refused by his legitimate *ang'rei.*[6] She said that she would kill herself if she were forced to marry him. Then her father said to him, "Son-in-law, the girl does not want you. Search for another woman (for *shankh,* but not for *ang'rei*)." After that the hero came to another place. In a yurta he found an old woman. She said, "My son (sons-in-law are often addressed in this way by their mothers-in-law), if you come for a wife, your wives live in that log house." The plural was used here because in the yurta lived two sisters, and both according to the Gilyak law belonged to him. Indeed, it may appear strange that the hero of this poem should have to search for a legal wife under such difficulties. It should be an easy task since usually there are many of that category and their residences are known to practically everyone. Usually they can be found in the nearest village [131].

But such is the destiny of heroes—that extraordinary adventures become their lot. Generally some catastrophe has befallen their clansmen and they are left quite alone. It might be that the nearest clan of their fathers-in-law was wiped out during some epidemic or famine. The surviving branches might have settled far away and lost all connection with their former home. Under these conditions, it is understood that the hero has to wander about in all directions and, as in hunting, reach his goal by scarcely visibly traces, questionings, and conjectures. Finally it may happen that the desirable *ang'rei* for whom the hero is searching is already engaged to a stranger. In this case the hero must apply all his imposing power and fame in order to force the father-in-law to break his promise to the other suitor. For such a violation, he is threatened by war with the clan of the offended groom, or in the best possible outcome he gets off by merely paying a heavy fine. The hero himself has to go through a whole series of wars for the wife he has obtained in this manner.

Such a case is the following, taken from a *nastund* poem. The hero arrived in the house of a woman who was to become his wife. He received the following answer from her father: "She is already betrothed (*nigivin iokhta,* that is, the technical term for a girl engaged to a non-kin). There is a clan of mountain people, and several others who will come to fight with you." The hero answered, "Still I will take her and drive away with her." The old man said, "You go back tomorrow." On the next day, after the usual meal, he not only let the girl go without any payment, but also gave an order to load two boats with precious goods as her dowry. Such cases are, of course, only possible when the girl is a legitimate bride of the groom by birthright.

---

[6]   Ibid., 118.

FIG. 18. A large group of Gilyaks and Russians surround a tethered bear during a winter bear festival marking the return of the bear kin to the spirit community in the hills. Photo by Lev Shternberg. *Source:* AAN f. 282, o. 2, d. 98, l. 192.

It is characteristic of the purest Gilyak poetry, free from any Gold-Manchurian influence, that we do not find any betrothal procedures. The whole ceremony consists in the following dialogue: The groom says, "I came to take a wife"; the father-in-law says, "Alright, take her." Thus the marriage ceremony is accomplished immediately. The only rite performed is that of *conferratio.*

The father of a bride asks the hero, "Where did you come from?" The latter answers, "I am a dweller of the village in the middle of the bay. I came to marry your daughter." Then the old man says, "My child, this guest came to take you. Go to him." The woman says, "Alright, I will go to him." The old man says, "Workmen, prepare food and feed the guest." Then our Gilyak and his new wife eat together.[7]

Occasionally there are incidents when men take their wives by force. This has often been the case when a Gilyak's *akhmalk* clans were wiped out through some catastrophe and he was forced to get a wife by any means. Such catastrophes, as we will see later, are not exceptional. The two alternatives which faced the Gilyak of olden times, either to marry a legitimate *ang'rei* or to obtain a wife by violence, with almost no mention of betrothals to strange women as a special case of marriage, prove that bride-price was of later origin. It seems to have appeared as an alternative to abduction with all its bloody consequences, in the same way that fines appeared as a remedy for the custom of blood revenge. Such were the methods of obtaining wives in the olden times, as appears to us from the traditional epics.

---

7 Ibid., 47.

ORTHODOX MARRIAGE AT THE PRESENT TIME

There is still strong feeling among the Gilyak that only the orthodox marriage from the *akhmalk* clans is pure (*urlaf narkin*).[8] Even in the Amur region, one hears the following Gilyak maxim:

> *Pi pand os anakikh pu umgu furara.*
>
> [From the fathers-in-law of the common root of your birth (origin from a common mother), one must take a wife.]

The most frequent and preferred of such orthodox marriages are those between the brother's daughter and the sister's son. These marriages are so valued that a brother and a sister arrange them even long before their children are born [**136**].

Thus orthodox marriage is still considered not only desirable but obligatory. During the match-making negotiations in one of the *akhmalk* clans, the first words were, as usual:

> *Tsi naf nakhmalk nekhlin kunu tsekhlankunu vaza vasa akhmalk gun nate. Tsi nakhlan kim khavrkhaimrolf torsik pikizndra. Sik urlaf pazkund khunivmugnate.*
>
> [You are my *akhmalk*. Let our children also be *akhmalk*. If you will not give your daughter to my son you will break completely the old law. Let us live according to the law. Let us live cleanly.]

After such a reminder, it is seldom that anybody shirks his duty, although it is accompanied with the loss of a certain amount of property because in such marriages there is no bride-price, and even when there is, it is very small if the *akhmalk* clan is not very old [**136**].

Mothers usually negotiate early on, when the children are 3 or 4 years old. When the consent of both sides is obtained, a public ceremony is held in which the fathers and grandfathers participate. The father of the groom brings a male dog and the mother spins two threads from its hair with the aid of a nettle. She ties one thread around the girl's hand, while the father does the same with the boy's hand. All this is performed in the presence of the oldest members of the clan, who consider it to be an inviolable bond. From that moment the children are considered husband and wife and they address each other by these terms. A Gilyak friend of mine who had betrothed his son in this way told me proudly, "All of Sakhalin knows about this betrothal" [**132**].[9]

Usually in these cases, the underaged wife moves to the house of her husband, sleeps with him in one bed, and they spend their childhood together. With the com-

---

8   [**Editor's note:** Shternberg used the Russian word *ortodoksal'nyi* in the sense of "proper" or "traditional" Gilyak marriage, rather than Russian Orthodox church rites.]

9   It is curious that among the Haida the ceremony of betrothal, which is accompanied by the presentation of blankets instead of dogs, bears the technical term "putting a string on." Apparently in olden times this ceremony was executed by the tying of a thread, as is practiced among the Gilyak and the Tamil of India. Cf. Swanton, *Contributions*, 50. [**Editor's note:** The AMNH English and Russian typescripts place this footnote here, while the 1933 Soviet editions place it several paragraphs hence in a like context.]

ing of puberty, they begin their matrimonial life. This haste in marriage between minors could be explained by many factors, but the fundamental reason seems to be to find a legitimate marriage partner before another comes along, such as another sister's or cousin's son. Further, there might be a change in the economic standing of both parties. The bride's father might become impoverished and be tempted by the bride-price offered him by a stranger.

On occasions when children of very different ages are married, the betrothal procedure is the same. One of my acquaintances, Pletun, a lad of 20, was married to his cousin who was only 5, the daughter of Iksus. He took her to his house and they slept together, but their matrimonial life did not begin until her first menses. Sometimes the underaged wife lives in the house of her parents and with the first menses transfers to that of her husband. There is no formality connected with moving into her husband's house because the former agreement is considered a public act well known to everyone. "All the island knows about this," another Gilyak told me with pathos after he had betrothed his underaged daughter to his sister's son.

Betrothals between children of first-cousins are made with the same simplicity, although even in some cases a small bride-price is incurred [132].

NONORTHODOX MARRIAGES

Various factors have caused the dissolution of the orthodox forms of marriage in the *akhmalk* clan. The dwindling of some clans has forced marriages with women from newer, strange clans. Plus, Gilyak contact with civilized peoples of the Far East has wrought havoc with ancient marriage norms. This contact brought about a development of trade; sable pelts, fox pelts, and other articles previously having no value have become trade objects for which Gilyak can exchange luxury items—expensive textiles, precious arms, ornaments, and foodstuffs such as rice, cereals, alcohol, and tobacco. By contrast, the memory of a time when sables and foxes walked around Gilyak houses is still fresh, for Gilyak long preferred to dress in dog skins. Suddenly it became possible to obtain the most desirable things from the skins of these smaller animals. Inevitably an enormous change occurred in the psychology of the Gilyak and in their relations to one another. If before, the ideal of a Gilyak was to gain the reputation as a good man—*urdla nivukh*, that is, a prominent hunter who shares his game with his kinsmen—now the expression *urdla nivukh* is synonymous with a rich man, whose ambition it is to accumulate wealth. On the scene appeared greed, boasting, and the desire to surpass one another in wealth, even if one's wealth consisted only of a few pieces of silk and some Japanese sabers [136].

A tendency towards differentiation also appeared: The rich wanted to associate and intermarry only with the rich. A new element in marital selection appeared: The bride had to be the groom's equal in wealth as well as distinction. One frequently hears nowadays, and even in the ancient *tilgund* (legends), such expressions as, "He or she is not my equal." Wealth gave one the right to demand a wife of great beauty, homemaking abilities, or skill in sewing. Thus, once marriage between strangers became a frequent practice, the old simplicity of the marriage ceremony disappeared.

Bride-price introduced into marriage an element of barter and marriages between strangers requiring numerous negotiations expressed in new procedure of betrothal. To this matchmaking institution we now turn.

TERMS OF MATCHMAKING

The various elements of matchmaking are expressed in Gilyak terms such as *utguela tigid* or *iokhpurid* (W.D.), *iokh gagandtakhund sagund*, meaning literally, "to consent, to negotiate for the bride"; hence also, *takhir nigivin*, meaning matchmaker or negotiator; *iokh orang'rei munind*, "future wife"; and *pu munind*, meaning bridegroom or future husband. The expression *nigivin iokh ta* means to be betrothed (when applied to women). The last terms for bride and bridegroom are of special interest. In the case of orthodox marriages there is no special term for bride or bridegroom, because by the very right of birth they were called *pu* (husband) and *ang'rei* (wife). The term *iokh* for bride in the orthodox type of marriage is impossible, because as we saw it is a term applied to a category of women with whom sexual intercourse is prohibited. Thus the terms themselves prove that the procedure of betrothal originated after the orthodox type of marriage was on the wane. There is a special term for designating infant betrothal—*tkhagund* (E.D.), *tignid* (W.D.).

The participants of the betrothal on the bridegroom's side are his father and mother, the father's brother, the bridegroom's older brother, and the husband of the father's sister. The role of the latter can be explained, it seems, from the norms of orthodox marriage according to which the husband of the father's sister is the father of the husband of the bridegroom's sister. As his daughter cannot marry the brother of the daughter-in-law, the husband of the father's sister considers it his duty to help the marriage of his nearest *akhmalk*, that is, of the brother of the daughter-in-law. If the father is dead, one of the *urdla nivukh* (respected men from among his kinsmen) takes his place. Besides these persons, several respected clansmen take part since marriage is considered a clan affair. It is especially considered as such when the betrothal is between very rich and prominent people, and the girl is of outstanding reputation. In such cases, the people arrive in several boats, bringing with them articles of the bride-price. Often, if such representation and the bride-price make a proper impression, the girl is taken immediately after the negotiations. The bridegroom is present during the matchmaking proceedings. If he is absolutely alone or, on the contrary, rich and prominent, he can attend to the betrothal himself. In one song a girl sings to her beloved, *nrmkiabiz nsagia*, "holding my hand woo me." Betrothal is dispensed with if a married man takes another wife. He then goes to the clan of his former wife to choose a second one, or often enough his wife goes herself to her own or another clan to select a new wife for her husband [137].

On the bride's side, her father and mother are usually present. But the final decision is made in the presence of clan representatives. These clan representatives of both sides play a rather passive role in spite of the fact that they take part in the discussions. The wishes of the bride's brothers are also considered in the marriage arrangements, and in many cases they prevail. This tradition is a relic of an earlier matrilineal organization. The role of brothers is especially emphasized in the

FIG. 19. Four Gilyak women play a specially toned wooden beam during a winter bear festival, 1890s. Photo by Lev Shternberg. *Source:* AAN f. 282, o. 2, d. 162, l. 96.

epics. In one tale, a son informs his father that he intends to marry off his sister. The father answers, "Consult your younger brothers and then decide." It is remarkable that in the marriage arrangements, the mother plays a role no less important than that of the father, in spite of the fact that women do not as a rule openly participate in public affairs. This curious fact is only true of Sakhalin. In the Amur region, the girl is not consulted at all, though the marriage negotiations are carried out in the presence of the bride, who sits silently among her dowry chests and awaits the decision on her fate. Her role commences after the decision has been made and all she can do is obey. If she has no lover and the suitor is more or less acceptable, she says laconically, "Once you want it, how can I object?" But often, upon the arrival of the matchmakers, the girl escapes from the house and does not return until the matchmakers have departed. In such cases, the matter often comes to nothing.[10]

I do not think that the neglect of the daughter's wishes is the result of the modern type of marriage, with its temptation for a big bride-price. Rather it is a survival

---

[10] It is interesting that I found some differences among the Negidal, whose customs are usually the same as those of the Gilyak on account of old matrimonial relations existing between the two. The bride is absent during the betrothal and the mother has absolute right of veto, while the kinsmen have no voice in the arrangements. The bride appears on the scene only at the last moment when the bridegroom comes to take her away.

of the old orthodox marriage when a girl was predestined to a definite person or group of persons from birth. Under such circumstances, there could be no question of freedom of choice.

Betrothal Procedures

The current betrothal procedure of the Gilyak is very much the same as found all over the world. It is carried on with a great deal of strategy and amounts almost to a diplomatic war. In important cases, when the girl in question is very rich and prominent, the matchmakers try to catch her side unawares. Appearing in her house, they say that they are merely passing through. As if by accident, vodka is produced. The host drinks willingly, and when everyone is in good humor the matchmakers recall what good friends they have always been and that their host has never refused them anything, and that in the future they hope he will continue to do so. The host, unsuspectingly, promises to help them by all available means. He is caught up on this and brought down to business. He cannot refuse because he has given his word. In order that he should not refuse, the matchmakers see to it that there are witnesses on hand (though that is not necessary, for there are always plenty without invitation—the arrival of strangers becomes known immediately and the yurta is crowded with neighbors). Going back on one's word is a very serious affair potentially leading to threats of lawsuits involving heavy fines (*naing vad*) "to cover the face" [**138**].

Even when matchmakers do not wish to hide their purpose, etiquette does not permit them to get down to business at once. The most remote things are spoken of without any intimation of the real purpose of the visit. During the conversation they drink, and after they have spoken enough about news (*kier*), little by little the matter is approached. It is done carefully and by circumlocution, in order to find out how favorable the chances are. If the girl's father does not consent beforehand, he immediately cuts short the conversation by an absolute refusal. But such cases are rare because only those whose chances are good make the proposal. Usually "equals go to equals" say the Gilyak, since they all know each other well, notwithstanding the distance which separates them. They know everything to the smallest detail, even to the number of sables one has caught during the past season.

The main thing for the girl's father is not to give one's consent too quickly, in order to procure the largest bride-price. Etiquette demands that the father of the bride must pretend as long as possible that he does not understand at what the matchmakers are driving. And when it becomes impossible to pretend any longer, he will devise all kinds of obstacles and excuses—that the girl is ugly, that she is inept at household duties, that she is quarrelsome, and so on. But the guests are prepared for such tricks and have answers ready. "We do not hunt for beauty," they say. "As for her ignorance of household duties," they respond, "She is young yet, she will learn. Anyway we have enough able women without her. Her quarrelsomeness is not a calamity; with years she will learn to live with people." Or he is cut short by, "This does not concern you, that is our work. If she is bad, we will teach her." This unconditional praise for the bride is the thing sought by her father, for then he can name the most advantageous price and the matchmakers are forced to accept. If the matchmaker refuses the bride-price demanded by the bride's parents, he risks being hailed before a court to pay a large fine—*nivkh tsguzkhl nain vanidra.* The fine often consists of a silk gown, a kettle, and other treasures.[11] If it happens that the father is not satisfied with the matchmaker's proposals, when all objections are exhausted, he will suddenly utter a word usually used when the Gilyak want to stop an unpleasant conversation. *"Ta'arai"* ("I do not know anything"), he mumbles through his teeth, clamping his pipe. After a pause he angrily says, "Ask my wife what she wants. It does not concern me." Then the mother is approached and after many excuses she in turn ends with the laconic phrase, *"Ta'arai.* Why do you ask me? I am only a woman. Let the men decide."

Finally the conversation turns to the matter of bride-price and dowry. These procedures differ between Sakhalin and the Amur region. On the Amur, where the people are more shamelessly commercial, the bride's side enumerates every single article of the bride-price. On Sakhalin only the most valued articles are mentioned, after which agreements are made about the less valued articles. But the negotiations in both regions are carried on in a heated manner [**139**].

During this stage the conversation reaches its climax, and the word *ta'arai* begins to play an exceptional role. I happened to witness such negotiations in the village Pilavo in Sakhalin, where a friend of mine, Isaika, was wooing for his son the daughter of an old woman. The old woman had no relatives in the village, either on her own or her husband's side. Therefore all the respectable men of the village were invited by her. On the bridegroom's side was Sofronka, who was considered *khlainivukhin,* the best candidate. At first it appeared that the matter would be settled soon, because the woman was in great need and because she herself had pressed the proposal. But when the question of bride-price arose, Sofronka fought with her the whole day. In vain did he use all his eloquence and asked the witnesses to help him induce the old woman to accept his conditions. She endlessly repeated *"Ta'arai."* And the *khlainivukhin* replied, "It is a sin to interfere, for we are foreign people." Finally, after a day's painful discussion, when the old woman felt that she had shown enough character and had observed the proper protocols, she made a condition which was acceptable to the other side from the very beginning, namely, that the bride-price be paid at once.

BRIDE-PRICE

The term used by the Gilyak to designate bride-price is very striking. It throws light, it seems to me, on the origin of that institution itself. Bride-price is designated by the word *askh izind,* that is, literally, "to bequest." The word *az, azr* literally means "a gift" given by the bridegroom's family or clan to the bride's clan. The following will show that this term did not come about accidentally. In all cases when compensation by payment is obligatory, such as a fine for murder, ransom for abduction, and so on, the Gilyak use the term *iuskind,* "to pay" [**140**].

---

[11] So the Gilyak explain the reason for the father's deprecation of his daughter. I think therefore that Iokhel'son was wrong in explaining this custom among the Koriak as a warding off of possible complaints in the future. Iokhel'son, *The Koryak,* 739.

It is of interest that the word *iuskind*, "to pay," itself originated from the word *uskind*, which is both an intransitive verb and a synonym for *ikhinund*, "to fight" or "to resist." The active form of this verb, *iuskind* or otherwise *ekund*, formerly designated revenge, which was afterwards replaced by ransom. This evolution can still be traced in Gilyak epics. In one poem the hero is asked upon his return from the scene of revenge for the death of his father, "*Pitk uskind?*" ("Did you accomplish *uskind* for your father?"). The hero answers, "*Sik khukhra*" ("I killed them all"). Here the term *uskind* is used to denote the act of blood-revenge. But in another poem the same word is used to express ransom: *ivn navkh uskind*, "they received ransom for their comrade who was killed."

All this shows that bride-price was not so much a payment for the bride but a gift, although of an obligatory character. This is also evident from the fact that the gift is not one-sided, for besides the dowry, the giving of a postwedding present [German, *Morgengabe*] on the part of the bride's father was also obligatory.[12] These presents continued for years in the form of clothes and various other valuables, which frequently amounted to as much as the bride-price itself.

The following example is illustrative. An elder from the Gilyak settlement of Pomr, not a rich man, received for his daughter a bride-price which consisted of two Chinese kettles, one Japanese saber, and five dogs. In return, the father-in-law sent to his son-in-law two Chinese gowns, and in the course of 2–3 years he regularly sent him rice, tobacco, and tea. In addition, he also gave a big dowry consisting of clothes, furs, and ornaments. It would have been considered disgraceful had he not returned the equivalent of the bride-price in gifts to the bridegroom. The man who disregarded this would become the butt of his village's jokes.

So it is clear, at least among the Gilyak, that bride-price is by no means a form of marriage by abduction as has been suggested by many, even today.[13] Marriage accompanied by a bride-price is not an act of buying or selling in the minds of the Gilyak. This is proven by the fact that it is absolutely prohibited to buy wives from one another.

Still we must ask: Why is the bride-price not found in orthodox marriages? That is because an orthodox marriage consists of persons of common blood on both the mother's and father's side, and the marriage is sanctioned by social and religious considerations. But when marriages are made between members of strange clans, the exchange of gifts is a symbol of friendship and a mutual guarantee against untoward magical influence. It corresponds to the exchange of gifts during the procedure of fictive brotherhood.

The Gilyak lending of religious and social significance to this symbolism is seen from the rites observed upon the entrance of the bride into the husband's house. It is quite possible that the concept of bride-price was introduced not only as a magical element but also as a religious one. Marrying into a strange clan was at one time taboo. Every violation of the taboo, according to the primitive mind, must be paid for if not by blood then by valuables. The bride-price from this point of view becomes a tribute

---

12 [***Editor's note:*** The German variant is found in the AMNH English typescript only.]

13 Among Turkic peoples as among the Shoshone, where marriage is characterized as buying or selling, the reciprocal gift to the bridegroom is also obligatory.

to the ancestors offended by the violation of the clan taboo. Only this can explain why Gilyak have the same strong feeling against an unpaid bride-price as in cases of the murder of a kinsman. The obligation to wreak vengeance in such instances, as with murder, is a duty weighing on the clan until the third generation. For the sake of a bride-price, the people are ready to undergo the same dangers and suffering as in the carrying out of a blood revenge. The heroic deeds of a person engaged in such hazardous expeditions to distant places are the most common subjects of Gilyak epics.

The articles of bride-price are valuables of a particular character (called *sagund* [E.D.] and *sigid* [W.D.]) and are usually acquired through trading with the Chinese and Japanese. These include Chinese silk clothes and fur coats, jade work, Manchurian spears inlaid with silver, Japanese sabers and big cast-iron kettles. Besides these, fox and sable coats and women's precious ornaments are also included. These articles cannot be traded in; they are *extra commercium*. Only in extreme cases of poverty or in the absence of relatives is one allowed to dispose of them. For instance, the poor widow who had sold her only daughter answered my question as to what she would do with her *sagund*, "A part I will sell and the rest I will take with me in the Land of the Dead (*Mlyvo*)." They are kept only for extraordinary occasions during a lifetime, such as the payment of a ransom, payment of bride-price, or as dowry for a daughter, while after death they accompany one to another world. In olden times, it seems that adzes of stone and later of iron were articles of *sagund*. There is a fine legend to this effect. In the middle of Sakhalin there is a mountain known among the Gilyak as *Krius Pal*. Beside it is another smaller one, which is the wife of the former. She escaped from her husband and hid her *sagund*. Three littoral cliffs are the various articles of this *sagund*. One is named *va-ul-sif*; it is the place where the Japanese saber is buried. The second is *vin-ul-af*, where the kettle is buried, and the third is *kizokhmi*, where the head of an ax is buried [**141**].[14]

The objects just enumerated are usually used in the bride-price of rich people. That of the poor consists of valuable articles for everyday use such as boats, guns, and dogs. The rich man hunting for a big bride-price is stirred mainly by ambition, for the receiving of a big bride-price is the best proof of his own wealth. For the poor man the bride-price is the only chance of establishing an independent household of his own. On the other hand, it is almost impossible for a poor man to maintain a family and an independent household. The only salvation under such circumstances lies in the right of group marriage and the establishment of a common household with brothers. Nevertheless, it is the dream of everyone to establish a family life of one's own. Generally a poor man is helped by his wealthy kinsmen, but not every clan has rich people, and there are persons whose clan is entirely extinct. The only way to obtain a wife is through bride-service. Such deals are usually made by families who have no male descendants. A son-in-law is proclaimed an adopted son, although he cannot be a real heir for he is a stranger.

In principle bride-price is considered clan property. In serious cases, such as when a kinsman has to pay ransom, all the kinsmen have to participate in its payment

---

[14] [**Editor's note:** While the paragraph sequencing here follows the AMNH Russian and English typescripts, the legend from this paragraph is contained in a footnote in Shternberg, *Giliaki*, 278, and Shternberg, *Sem'ia*, 141.]

with their *sagund*. But usually bride-price is divided among brothers, however unequally. The youngest brother, as heir of the house, receives the smallest part. Besides his inheritance, however, his elder brothers usually buy a wife for him so that the youngest brother does not need the *sagund*.

Together with the family division of *sagund*, a curious custom has survived, vividly showing the old orthodox type of marriage. Often a part of the bride-price is given to the old *akhmalk* clan from which the family used to take wives. For example, if for several generations family A took wives from family B, every time family A married off one of its daughters (who are prohibited to family B on account of the one-sided cousin-marriage) the entire bride-price or a part of it was given to the oldest member of family B. It is interesting that this form of bride-price was generally given by the bridegroom's family to the old *akhmalk*. Sometimes this custom is performed in an even more striking fashion. A minor sister is given to the mother's brother, or one's daughter is given to the wife's brother, in order that these persons should receive a bride-price. It is not allowed, however, to demand a share in such a bride-price. "It is better to offer a daughter or a sister to an *akhmalk* than to wait for a request for them," the Gilyak usually say. Furthermore, if the mother has several brothers and a nephew has several sisters, a sister has to be given to each uncle [**142**].

What is the explanation for this custom? We might note that a similar one is found among the Tamil of India. There, a mother's brother also gets part of the bride-price for her daughter. But among the Tamil exists a bilateral form of cousin marriage. Therefore if the sister gives her daughter into a marriage that is not with a brother's son, she violates the law. But among the Gilyak, where we have only matrilateral cross-cousin marriage and the sister's daughters are prohibited to the brother's sons, why would such a privilege be given to the mother's brother? Two explanations are possible: first, that it is a survival of a matriliny when the role of the mother's brother was so important; or second, that a bilateral cousin marriage when every girl had to marry the sons of the mother's brother once existed in Gilyak society, such that this custom is a survival of a more ancient form of marriage.

DOWRY

Let us now consider the dowry that accompanies every marriage. Dowry in the Gilyak language is designated by the term *iokh sond* (E.D.), literally "being brought by the bride or by a woman." The dowry consists principally of a variety of clothes and ornaments. The rich bride brings rich fur coats of fox and sable, silver bracelets, expensive earrings, Chinese pipes, and carved and ornamental dishes and plates, including an assortment of artistically ornamented birch spoons. A mother usually gives the daughter her ornaments and sometimes her bed, but for some unknown reason, it is not permitted to give the pillows.

The accumulation of the dowry begins when the girl is a child and continues until her marriage. It is designated by the following expression: *iokh vakh vakhind*, "to prepare a bride." The dowry together with the family treasure is packed in trunks. The value of the dowry must be proportionate to that of the bride-price. When gossips comment about someone's wedding they generally speak of "a rich or poor dowry," *iaskand mangand iokh* and *sandy iaskand.*

The greatest pride is taken in giving a slave as part of a daughter's dowry. It may be either a man or a woman. In one clan of my acquaintance, a part of the girl's dowry was a female slave supplied with a Japanese saber to clean the mud from the boots of her mistress. Particularly ambitious Gilyak reserved a separate house for their daughter and a slave, which later became part of her dowry.

Although the dowry may be a compensation for the bride-price because it liberates the husband from large expenditures on his wife, it is nonetheless entirely the personal property of the bride, to which the husband has no right. She is free to sell it or to give it as dowry to her own daughter. After death it is transferred to her daughters, and if there are none, it is passed to her brothers or anybody else according to the wishes of the deceased.

After the two main aspects of the bride-price, its quantity and the terms of payment, are settled, the marriage contract is considered complete and the couple are called to eat and smoke together. A small feast is arranged, and at night the bride's mother orders the bridegroom to lie in the bed of his wife. After the wedding night the bridegroom takes his wife home. However, these cases are rare, only occurring when both sides are so poor that the small bride-price is brought at once and the dowry consists only of the most essential things for the bride's wardrobe. In such cases, there is no need for preparations. Among rich families, the immediate departure of the bride takes place when the bridegroom lives far away or when the marriage is so esteemed on account of the distinction of the bride's parents or the prominence of the bride that the suitors are afraid to postpone the marriage lest a richer rival appear. In such cases, the bridegroom arrives with several boats containing his bride-price and the payment is made promptly. A short ceremony is followed by a small feast and the bride is taken away. But we repeat that such cases are rare [**143**].

Usually the marriage is delayed and the bride-price is paid in installments. Generally only one item, such as a kettle, is given immediately after the agreement. The rest of the bride-price is paid before taking the bride, or if the bride-price is large, a part is paid on a fixed date after the bride is taken. Sometimes the marriage is postponed also on account of the dowry. Although the dowry has been accruing since the girl's childhood, depending on the bride-price it may be necessary to add things to it. The marriage date is the last thing decided in the marriage negotiations. The date is considered very important, for the dowry must be gotten ready by the day of the groom's arrival; also, numerous dishes of food must be prepared in sufficient quantities for the wedding feast and for the bride to take along with her as a gift for the family of the bridegroom.

The agreement made between two families is considered an agreement between two clans. From that moment the bride is considered a member of another clan. In case of subsequent refusal by her parents or herself, she is demanded by force. The agreement is obligatory on the bridegroom's side too, but here no sanction is necessary, for in case of refusal, usually half of the bride-price which has been paid is retained. Sometimes it may happen that the bridegroom asks for one sister instead of another. This is absolutely prohibited. In such cases the answer would be:

Nevin ckhazkhai menimin okhoia, stsanin akhai tsi urian agkikhai tsikh mukhna un ngtakhai nugi garnon tsi sik inkharkhai, enand saprindra.

[If you do not like one, you do not like both of them. When it is a question of dogs, and you desire the good one, I give you a good one. But if one is bad, then both are bad. When you are being treated and when you have finished the first dish, I'll offer you the second one.]

In other words one can ask for two sisters, but one may not ask for one instead of another.

When the agreed upon date arrives, the bridegroom, together with his relatives, comes in boats or on sledges if it is winter, bringing along the stipulated part of the bride-price and food for the feast. Protocol does not permit coming on foot, even if the bride may live in the neighborhood. The articles of the bride-price are hung outside for examination by the clan and the feast is arranged for the elders of both clans. The women attend the bride, soothe her, and give her advice on how to conduct herself in a strange place. If she is displeased with her marriage, they cajole her. During the farewell feast the bridegroom and bride sit together and eat from the same dish and smoke from one pipe. But during the day they do not speak to each other. The bridegroom must behave quietly and be silent. Late in the evening, after the feast, the bride's mother sends the bridegroom to the bride's bed. The bride appears later. And so the marriage is consummated. On the following morning the bride brings food to the bridegroom and calls him "husband"; then they depart. During the last feast, the relatives of the couple exchange good wishes and blessings. In the Amur region they say,

> If God so wills, people live their life in happiness.
> If God so wills, life is passed unhappily.
> Oh God, make the life of our children happy.

After that the bridegroom's father exclaims:

> Oh God, make the days of our children happy,
> so that we will live in happiness together.

Vodka is splashed to the sky and in all directions during these blessings. Just before the departure of the bride and groom the ceremony *nits sitsivind*, "stepping in the kettle," is performed. A big Manchurian kettle with five handles, generally used for feeding dogs and brought as part of the bride-price, is placed near the threshold inside the yurta. Another one belonging to the bride's parents and smaller in size is placed near the threshold on the outside. On leaving the yurta the couple, first the bride and then the bridegroom, each place one foot in the big kettle and the other in the smaller one, so as not to touch the threshold. The big kettle is taken by the bride's father and the smaller one is given to the bridegroom. This ceremony, interestingly, establishes a symbolic union of mutual feeding and friendship before the two female penates: one, *limizm,* an old woman who is the spirit of the threshold, and another, *kel gelnani,* an old woman who is the spirit of the door's cross beam.[15] A simi-

---

15 [**Editor's note:** Penates, from the Latin word *penus,* meaning provision of food, is a term borrowed from Roman mythology meaning household deities, especially those in a storeroom.]

FIG. 20. A Gilyak man in a Chinese scarf, canvas tunic, and sealskin skirt, 1890s. Photo by Lev Shternberg. *Source:* AAN f. 282, o. 2, d. 161, l. 27.

lar ceremony is practiced among the Negidal under the name *odilavi.* These people have been intermarrying with the Gilyak for a long time and probably borrowed the ceremony from them.

A year after the wedding, the couple, already with a child, come to visit the bride's family. When they depart for home the same ceremony, *nits sitsivind,* "treading upon the kettle," is performed, but in this case cups are used instead of kettles.

MARRIAGE PITFALLS

As in our society, Gilyak marriages are not always happy. This is very likely because women are not consulted in the choice of mates. It is very seldom that a girl disobeys her parents' will, and the parents rarely submit to the daughter's protests, even when she threatens suicide. Thus, postmarital life ends in tragedy. A woman escapes to her lover or goes back to her parents. Such refuge is a common form of escape when a woman is badly treated by her husband. In such cases the husband attempts to take the fugitive by force or demands his bride-price back. As nobody likes to give up things which have already become one's property, the resulting lawsuits are endless [**144**].

During my various trips across Sakhalin, Gilyak often looked upon me as an official, and almost in every settlement I had to listen to complaints about the return of bride-price. Generally, however, the men preferred to ask that their women be brought back by force. This latter request was often executed by the Sakhalin administrators with the help of Russian Orthodox clergymen.

Very often persons who fell in love with or captured other men's wives went to a clergyman and asked to be baptized in order to be married by church rite. This was done in order to protect the wife from being taken back forcibly by her husband. Missionaries willingly fulfilled such requests and gave the suitors their marriage certificates, which gave the man, when the woman was forcibly taken from him, the right to have her brought back with the help of public authorities. Very often this resulted in tragedy. The following is a case which I think should be immortalized. The wife of a Gilyak called Tis', aged 22, from the village of Mkhil on the Amur, was stolen by another Gilyak, Urgain, from the village of Vaida. Urgain immediately went to Russian Orthodox missionary Moskvitinov. Tis' overtook them and implored the missionary not to perform the marriage ceremony. But the missionary, for a fee, sanctioned Urgain's request. After that Tis' called his relatives and took back his wife with their help by force. However, Urgain presented his marriage certificate to the police, who in turn took another fee and issued an order to return the woman to her legitimate owner. Tis' shot her and then himself. The bride-price is returned without dispute when, soon after marriage, the wife dies without having produced children or when the wife escapes because the man is so poor he cannot support her. Finally, bride-price is returned when the wife betrothed in infancy dies while still a minor.[16]

---

[16] [**Editor's note:** The AMNH English typescript ends with the story of Tis'. Thanks to Lydia Black's observation, the last lines are restored to comply with the AMNH Russian and the 1933 Soviet versions.]

THIRTEEN

Marriage Terminology and Traces of Matriliny

[163–169; 271–277; 262–266; 132–135]

THE TERMINOLOGY used by the Gilyak in connection with marriage is very distinctive from a sociological standpoint. The Gilyak language, like ancient Aryan and modern Russian, does not have a term which corresponds to the general English term "to marry," the French *se marrier,* or the German *heiraten,* which are used for both sexes. The Gilyak, by contrast, have distinct terms for each sex. When we speak of a Gilyak man, we join the verb *gend* or *khg'end* (*g'e* being the stem) with *shankh* (woman) or *ang'rei* (wife), we arrive at *shankhg'end* or *ang'rei g'end.* But when a woman is the subject, a different verb *avind* (*av* being the stem) is used, with the corresponding addition of *nigivin* (man) or *pu* (husband), or without any addition, as simply *iavind* (*ie* ("him") + *avind*) [**132**].[1]

The following is a typical example taken from an old poem of the strict distinction which the Gilyak make between the terminology of the different sexes. The hero says to the father of his future wife, "*Iekhlun keil psindra*" ("I have come for her"). At that the father says to his daughter, "*Khun antkh psindra, iava*" ("This guest came to marry you—go to him"). The daughter answers, "*Khinka iavindra*" ("All right, I will go to him").[2]

What is the essential meaning of these individual terms *g'end* and *iavind*? The meaning of the man's term, *g'end,* is quite clear. It is a verb most often used in the Gilyak language for designating the taking or buying of something. In connection with marriage it has several meanings: receiving a woman as a legitimate wife; buying a woman by paying a bride-price; and lastly, in the sense of the Roman term *uxorem ducere,* the transfer of the woman to one's own abode, as is commonly practiced by Gilyak today.

At first glance, the meaning of the woman's term *iavind* is not quite so clear. In this form it is used in connection with marriage only; it simply designates the marriage of women. But it is not difficult to clarify the original meaning of the word from etymological forms close to it. First of all, we have *p'avind* (*pi + avind*), which means to support oneself, and "to live" in an economic sense. Here is a characteristic example:

---

[1] [*Editor's note:* As in previous chapters, I employ the Latin alphabet transliteration of Gilyak words used in both the AMNH English and Russian typescripts. Gilyak words in this chapter most often, though not always, correspond to those found in Shternberg, *Giliaki,* rather than those in Shternberg, *Sem'ia.*]

[2] [*Editor's note:* This paragraph is found in the AMNH English and Russian typescripts only.]

149

"*Nigivin n'enin pyrk pavra,*" that is, one Gilyak man lived by himself. If several persons are spoken of, this term means to live together, that is, to feed themselves together, to carry on a common household. From this originated the adverb *p'avind,* meaning "to be together." Further, a derivative form of the active case, *avind,* means to support somebody, to accept somebody in one's own care, or to adopt and feed them. It may also be used to designate feeding oneself, or grazing for one's self (*iavind e'khan,* literally, "a grazing cow"). Finally *iavind,* or *iavend,* means to warm somebody (by a fire) or to give refuge. Thus the term *iavind* applied by a woman to a man with the meaning "to marry him" formerly seems to have meant to take a man on her own support, to accept him into her house [**133**].

If this etymology is correct, and it is hard to doubt it, then it follows that formerly Gilyak were a matrilineal society like their nearest neighbors, the Ainu. As the terms seem to indicate, the husband moved to the wife's house. It is exactly the same with the man's term *g'end,* which means "to take for himself," indicating the modern patriarchate, when the wife moves to the husband's house.

At present the former meaning of *iavind* has disappeared so completely from modern memory that often people add to the verb *iavend* another verb, *vind,* meaning "to go away." As a result of this combination the expression *avind vind* literally means, "go away to take a husband on your own support." But this is an evident *contradictio in adjecto* because the verb *vind* signifies transition to the husband's house and consequently his support.

In the old Gilyak language, all terms for compatible matrimonial life were derivative forms of *iavind* (the woman's marriage term). The fact serves as a linguistic relic of the olden type of marriage. *Iavind* means to be married to somebody, the compatible marriage of two persons. For instance we have the expression, "*Itk amnakh vavin kuil itind*" or "Father ordered us to marry" (literally, "Father ordered us to support each other").

Even in the present-day life of the Gilyak we find a few traces of this matriliny. One of the formulas of a marriage right is an expression we mentioned earlier, "*Imgi arind iagnindra*" or "The son-in-law must be fed" (although the son-in-law takes his wife and lives separately from his father-in-law). Evidently this formula could only have emerged when the son-in-law moved to the wife's house or visited her regularly for a definite period of time, as is the practice among the Ainu. Among the latter the husband visits his wife regularly for a certain length of time, and the family of the latter has to feed him on the same basis, as now the family of a husband has to support his wife.

This formula has nonetheless preserved its vital meaning today. It is a set rule, for example, that gifts of food and a share of all catch must regularly be sent to the son-in-law. Furthermore, the *imgi* are ever-welcome guests in the village of their fathers-in-law and participate in the most important hunting enterprises. On distant hunting expeditions for sea mammals, the owner of the boat, also the head of the undertaking, issues a special invitation to all his *imgi* to participate in the hunting.[3]

---

[3]   We find a similar phenomenon among the Haida Indians, a purely matrilineal society. Here, as Swanton relates, a man calls together all his nephews, who are his potential sons-in-law, when undertaking a war. Cf. Swanton, *Contributions,* 69.

During that time the *imgi* are not only fed but on leaving they take along an equal part of the game and even presents. The attitude towards these youths is sometimes even more tender than toward one's own children. After all, since the *imgi* are the male children of a man's sisters or daughter, they are his nephews, who under a matrilocal organization would live with him. At the same time, the man's own sons and grandsons would go away to the homes of their wives, and would be quite alienated from him.

This obligation to feed nephews in the maternal line is a common characteristic of matriliny. Among several tribes, for example, as among the Polynesians, the right of nephews to property of the maternal uncle took an unusual form when nephews were permitted to rob their uncles without any penalty. This curious custom of a matrilineal society still exists among various tribes which switched to a patrilineal organization. Among the peoples of the Caucasus, the nephew has a right to steal his uncle's horse if the latter refuses to give it to him. Among the peoples of the Altai there is a proverb, "A nephew is worse than seven wolves" [**134**].

The role of the brother in marrying off a sister is even more typical. In many cases he, and not the father, plays the principal role in the marriage arrangements. He is the one who has to give the consent and he receives the bride-price.

There are many other traces in language and customs which could be considered as survivals of a matrilineal organization. When a Gilyak wants to say that he is married he says, "*Ni umgarvo ivra,*" or literally, "I have the wife's village" (*ni* I + *umgar* wife's + *vo* village + *ivra* is). This expression corresponds to the Ainu mode of living as well. Among the Ainu, a husband and wife often live in separate villages. The former visits her for several months of the year and then returns to his own village. Besides his own village, then, a man has the village of his wife.

The term *pandf* is used for designating the origin of a man and means literally "birth's root." The term designates the place from where a man's mother comes, but not the clan of the man, nor the place of his birth, which is natural to expect in an agnatic organization. It is of interest to note here the veneration a Gilyak expresses towards the birth places of his mother and all her female ancestors. No matter how far away this place may be, every Gilyak finds an opportunity to make a pilgrimage. During my travels I was surprised many times to see the tenderness with which Gilyak approached the village where one of their ancestresses once lived.

In some places the Gilyak, on being questioned about their origin, still indicate the birthplaces of their mothers and wives. For instance, the inhabitants of the village Nyivo on the east coast of Sakhalin at the mouth of the Tym' River always insisted, "We are from Nyi-ur," that is, they originated from the village of Nyi-ur, located at the extreme northern end of the island. When asked to explain they replied, "It is because we take our wives from Nyi-ur." Evidently these people considered their origin from the birthplace of their mother because the wives of the Gilyak are taken from their mother's clan.

Still another fascinating survival is that, although children are generally given the names of their fathers' kinsmen, in some places children are still named after maternal uncles and various relatives of their mothers. In Nianevo on the west coast of the island the names are taken from the mother's kin as though the children entered into the mother's clan [**135**].

All these survivals are strange given the present agnatic organization of Gilyak society, but not so in the psychology of the Gilyak themselves. To the Gilyak, these are not survivals. This is due to marriage norms which ensure that the wife and the husband are cousins, children of a brother and sister, with men of one clan taking wives preferably from one and the same clan. The psychologies of the matriliny and the patriliny are hence interlocked. In principle there is no gap between paternal and maternal lines, as exists in those societies where marriage norms of the Gilyak type do not operate.

Finally, we might also entertain an influence over Gilyak matrimonial psychology being exercised by the Ainu, who according to legends continually made inroads into Gilyak life, as seen by their influence, for example, on religious institutions. Nonetheless, it would seem that their influence over marital rites was highly limited, as few similarities can be found between the two peoples' kinship terminologies or marriage norms.[4]

---

4   [*Editor's note:* This final paragraph, not found in the AMNH English typescript, has been modified to correspond more closely to the three Russian versions.]

FOURTEEN

THE CLAN[1]

[193–223; 278–316; 81–109; 34–49][2]

IN OUR DISCUSSION of Gilyak marriage, we have touched on many aspects of the clan system. Now we intend to examine the clan as an institution which regulates the entire life of the people. Here we could do no better than to follow the definition used by the Gilyak themselves when they formulate their own understanding of the clan [34].

The term which is used to designate the clan is fascinating in itself. It is *khal*, or literally, "sheath."[3] It seems a very good term for designating the unity of origin—the common womb, or common origin.[4] On the subject of clan alliances the Gilyak are surprisingly concise, all the while making clear how deeply fundamental their attitude is to this most important aspect of their social organization. If you ask a Gilyak why he considers this or that person as his relative, you inevitably get the answer, "We have one (common) *akhmalk*, one *imgi*, one fire, one mountain man, one sea man, one heaven's man, one earth's man, one bear, one devil, one *tkhusind* (ransom, or clan penalty), and one sin." An analysis of this formula will help us more deeply understand the nature of the Gilyak clan alliance.[5]

---

[1] [***Editor's note:*** Archival correspondence between 1929 and 1932 indicates that Iulia Averkieva was the translator for this chapter. She assisted both Boas, in New York, and Sarra Ratner-Shternberg, in Leningrad, in the posthumous editing of the Shternberg *Social Organization* manuscript (appendix A).]

[2] [***Editor's note:*** Shternberg published a version of this chapter nearly identical to the AMNH and the 1933 Soviet editions in Shternberg, "Giliaki," *Etnograficheskoe Obozrenie* 28, no. 63 (1904h), 66–97.]

[3] [***Editor's note:*** While *khal* signifies sheath in the Eastern dialect, it signifies the body more generally as a container or covering in the Western dialect.]

[4] It is extremely interesting that the closely related term *khala* exists also among neighboring Tungusic tribes—Orok, Oroch, Gold, and Negidal—with whom the Gilyak have some shared kin terms, such as *aki* (Gilyak, older brother) vs. *aga* (among Tungusic tribes), notwithstanding the considerable divergence among the languages of these peoples in both lexical and grammatical senses.

[5] [***Editor's note:*** In the AMNH English typescript, Averkieva deleted the sentence beginning with "On the subject of clan alliances."]

ONE *AKHMALK* AND ONE *IMGI*: ONE WIFE'S FATHER AND ONE DAUGHTER'S HUSBAND[6]

As we know, securing a wife was one of the hardest tasks which faced a Gilyak man, for the number of men generally exceeded the number of women. And since women had to be paid for, the rich men usually grabbed most of the women for themselves while the poor men were left out entirely. Their efforts to acquire wives often involved great risks and even loss of life. Thus the marriage norms of the Gilyak clan gave everyone the right to a woman of the *akhmalk* clan, particularly to their mothers' brothers' daughters. This was not only a right but a religious obligation. The bride-price, in such cases, if not a mere formality, was shared by the entire clan, for the clansmen were also interested in marriage operating through one particular clan. At worst, until a man was able to establish a family of his own, the families of his brothers were his families, and his brothers' wives were his wives, for he had legitimate matrimonial rights to them. In turn, clansmen did not have to worry about the lot of their wives and children after their death. During his lifetime, his wife and children are legally and often *de facto* the wife and children of his younger brothers. So they will also be after his death. According to the decision of the clan, one of the younger brothers of the deceased will substitute for him in the rights and obligations of husband and father. If there are no younger brothers, one of the oldest men in the clan will become the breadwinner for the family of the deceased. This is an immutable law [36].

Such are the advantages the clan alliance bestows upon its members. Being born to a clansman is the only required *justis titulus* for belonging to a clan. If a man is born *itk khavrid* (that is, out of wedlock, without knowledge of his father), he is effectively without clan, a pariah, and a burden to himself and to others. Since he does not know his father, he does not know what clan he belongs to and which women are his potential wives and who is forbidden to him. Under these circumstances he could unconsciously violate sexual norms and bring down innumerable misfortunes upon himself and his relatives. Fortunately, instances of people without knowledge of their fathers do not exist. If a girl becomes pregnant out of wedlock, she is pressured to reveal the identity of the father. Having learned this, her family can force the man to marry her, an obligation he may only embrace, since this implies a greatly reduced bride-price. In the event of the girl's refusal to expose the father, the child is killed, and the clan is saved from sin and misfortune.[7]

---

[6] [***Editor's note:*** The AMNH English typescript shortened this subheading to "One *Akhmalk* and One *Imgi*," and omitted six lengthy paragraphs found in the AMNH Russian typescript, 193–195; Shternberg, *Giliaki*, 82–84; and Shternberg, *Sem'ia*, 35–36. While the paragraphs largely review principles of clan unity discussed in previous chapters, they make for an uncharacteristically lengthy discrepancy between the English and Russian versions. Judging from the seemingly uncontroversial content of the discrepancies and a May 5, 1909, Boas letter to Bogoraz, it may have been that Boas or Averkieva was trying to economize on space (appendix A). Throughout this chapter, the spirit of translation is abridgment. Efforts have been taken to restore key passages or indicate omissions where it seemed appropriate.]

[7] [***Editor's note:*** The last four sentences of the this paragraph, not found in the AMNH English typescript, have been restored from the AMNH Russian typescript.]

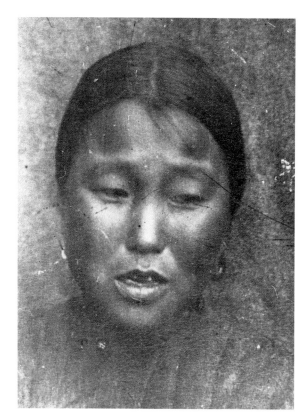

Fig. 21. A young Gilyak woman, 1890s. Photo by Lev Shternberg. *Source:* AAN f. 282, o. 2, d. 162, l. 108.

The Gilyak clan, however, like the clans of so many other tribes, has not been able to preserve its purity and exclusiveness. It has been forced into retreat and compromise by the adoption and acceptance of strangers.

This has happened in many ways, either through epidemics (which decimate the clan) or a war in which most of the men are killed. When such a clan can find another in an equally helpless condition, and which is *akhmalk* or *imgi* to them, a union may willingly be sealed by both clans. Usually the adopted persons married the widows of the clan into which they came and thereby joined the clan hearth and clan alliance.[8]

---

[8] [***Editor's note:*** While adhering to Shternberg's basic points, this material is found in a slightly different sequence in the AMNH Russian and the 1933 Soviet versions. In her translations, Averkieva deftly omitted references to "our previous chapter on religion," which are mentioned in each of the AMNH Russian and 1933 Soviet versions, despite the fact that only Shternberg, *Giliaki*, 49–81, actually contains the chapter, "Religiia Giliakov."

Shternberg, *Giliaki*, more closely followed the ordering of Shternberg's shorter 1904 monograph (Shternberg, 1904f–h), where "Religiia Giliakov" also precedes this chapter. What this helps us understand is the piecemeal nature of the manuscript Ratner-Shternberg came across among her husband's papers. While Shternberg's handwriting in the AMNH Russian typescript presented a full text to the reader, it is less clear how the chapters themselves, each separately paginated, originally came together. Of more immediate significance for this chapter is that a number of religious implications of the discussion have been omitted, having less weight here without the preceding religion chapter.]

Adoption has played an important role in Gilyak life. Indeed, when a clan has suffered the near mortal blow of the loss of most its members, newcomers are often a much-needed energetic element, more steadfast in the struggle for existence than the original members of the clan, who may have already been weakened and are gradually dying. Such may be the law of racial energy, which finally becomes exhausted under unfavorable conditions (the same fate may be shared by the descendants of the newcomers, who are replaced, in turn, by new invaders, providing, of course, they survive that long). It might appear strange that a clan composed of old members as well as the descendants of newcomers consider the former as the founders. The old kinship ties continue their influence even when the clan embraces strangers. The descendants of both sides do not necessarily merge when performing their obligations as clan members. They can continue to be in separate groups and count their relationship according to the old traditions of their clans. I happened to witness such a process. The population of the village of Tangi consisted of members of one clan which divided into two parts: the more flourishing group claimed its origin from a newcomer, an Ainu; the other group considered itself the clan founders. When the latter become extinct, signs of which are already noticeable, the former will be the only representatives of the clan and will likely call themselves the founders. The same process has been repeated many times [37].

Such wholesale adoption is, however, exceptional. Generally the adopted stranger is a person who has run away from his own clan and settled down elsewhere. He may not remain a stranger for long, since an extended sojourn normally creates a certain sympathy among members. The stranger sometimes assists at the celebration of clan holidays, and eventually his marriage to a widow of the clan will lead to his adoption. Very curious cases of adoption have occurred. Sometimes two men of different clans marry two sisters (ordinarily this only happens to two brothers). The influence of the principle of common father-in-law is so strong that children of such marriages are considered brothers and sisters. They call their aunts "mother" and marriage between them is prohibited. This appears as a fictitious clan relationship. However, if conditions are favorable and they continue to live in the same village, and one of them is separated from his own clan, they will come together to help each other in arranging clan festivals, and so on. Finally, in the second or third generation the union of these clans is an actual fact.

But usually the composition of a clan is uniform. The cases of adoption in general are rare. The past influence of endogamy and exogamy has long ago disappeared into the dim legendary past, and does not have any effect on the clan's kinship ties.

ONE FIRE

Fire is a symbol of the unity of the clan. Among the Gilyak, as among all primitive tribes, fire is a clan deity. As one Gilyak told me, an old woman who is the spirit of the fire sits within the hearth; another told me that it is an old man and an old woman with their children who sit within the hearth. The role of these "master owners of the fire," however, extends beyond the simple influence of warmth. As the divine ancestors of the clan, these spirits are respected both by living clansmen and by those who have departed to another world and who have become the deities of other elements—the forest, the sea, and the mountains. Through the fire-spirits, the latter can exercise a strong influence upon the well-being of the people. So the masters of the fire are not only deities who warm and guard the people from every kind of misdeed or evil spirit, but they are also the mediators between their clansmen and the multitude of deities who control the fortunes of the people.[9]

For important events such as illness, hunting, or departure on perilous journeys, the clansman throws into the fire his modest offering—a leaf of tobacco, angelica, or a tipple of vodka—and prays to the old woman to answer his prayer.[10] If it is out of her range of influence, she will direct his invocation to the appropriate deity.

In order to understand the attitude of the clan towards the fire-spirit one must bear in mind the following facts: (1) Deceased persons are cremated, that is, given up to the common fire spirit, who accepts its favorites into its own clan; hence, they can become masters of the clan fire. (2) All those who perish by lightning or fire also become fire-spirits.[11] (3) The representation of the fire-spirit as an old woman instead of a man is a survival of a matrilineal organization of the clan. (4) The universality of the fire, its ability to spread rapidly, and the multiplicity of its tongues which are understood as real by all primitive tribes—all these are qualities which lend to the fire a special advantage over other deities, namely, the ability to transmit prayer faster and more eloquently than any other medium. (5) Fire warms and purifies and drives away the evil spirits [**38**].

Only clansmen can make fire in each other's houses, and only clansmen have the right to take fire out of each other's houses. A stranger who lights his pipe from the clan hearth cannot leave the yurta until he finishes his pipe. Any violation of these principles on the part of a stranger brings serious consequences to the clan and to the offender.

Every clan has its own flint for striking fire, and it is kept by the oldest member of the group. Only with this flint may a Gilyak make the fire to cook bear meat for the bear festival (an all-important event in Gilyak life). When a clan is forced to separate, the oldest member breaks the flint and gives half of it to the oldest member of the departing group. Not until this formal action has taken place is the clan considered divided.

As the representative of the *akhmalk* clan, the mistress of the hearth plays a key role in relations between clans, using her patronage to tie the clan among whom she lives and raises her family to the clan from which she came, and from which, generation after generation, she has brought her brother's sons and their children.[12]

---

9   In the Vedas the fire Agni also plays the role of a mediator between men and deities; he intercedes on behalf of others as a herald [*gerol'd*] and a priest [*zhrets*].

10 [***Editor's note:*** While the AMNH typescript translated the reference to angelica in this sentence as a "sweet root," the Russian reference to "*sladkii koren'*" is a formal name denoting an aromatic plant, *Archangelica officinalis*, also known in Europe as "root of the Holy Ghost," which has long been cultivated for its medicinal and culinary qualities. I am grateful to Lydia Black for this observation.]

11 The same belief is found among the Buriat, where those who perish from lightning become powerful and benevolent spirits who preside over sacrifices and prayers.

12 [***Editor's note:*** This paragraph, not found in the AMNH English typescript, has been restored from the Russian versions.]

One Man of the Mountain, One Man of the Sea, One Man of the Sky, and One Man of the Earth

The spirits of the mountain, sea, sky, and earth are clan deities who play a most important role in Gilyak life. They are of particular interest because from them we can trace the genesis of primitive religion so widely spread all over the world. The deities of the Gilyak are supernatural and mythological beings, as among the Greeks and Romans. They are clansmen transformed into deities by a special happening or accident, such as being killed by a bear while on a hunt, being drowned, murdered, or burned, subsequently passing into the clans of the mountain spirits, water spirits, or fire.[13] In this way, they become small spirits themselves and patronize their living clansmen. These are not the fantastic heroes of classical clans, but close relatives of a living generation.

The favorites of the master spirits pass after death to the clan of their particular spirit for quite a long time. Among the mountain people, for instance, this period lasts "until second death" (that is, for two generations), during which time they patronize their clan. Mountain people send beasts to their living clansmen—sea people send fish and sea mammals, and so on. When a Gilyak speaks of some mountain or sea person who feeds him, he means one of his relatives who has become a spirit, either within his own memory or that of his father and grandfather. But as the reign of such favorites is not long, two generations being the furthest reach, there was often not time enough for proper communication with the deity because of the many deaths from wild beasts and by drowning. Thus the relationship between the clan and their divine protectors is very real and active. Special memorials erected by grateful clansmen are daily reminders of them [39].[14]

The ties of a clan to its divine ancestors are not confined to piety and grateful memories but are rooted in the real and powerful instinct of self-preservation. For the Gilyak there is no more positive truth than that everything he wrestles from nature in the desperate struggle for existence is the voluntary gift of the gods who patronize him, and that without their benevolence all his efforts would fail. As we know, the ancestor deities are the real supporters of the clan and are most interested in benefiting it. Hence no obligation is more important to a Gilyak than to encourage this benevolence in all possible ways. That is why the clan offerings and the festivals regularly honoring various spirits are such important occasions in clan life. That is why everyone considers active participation in these festivals a divine duty. It would not be amiss to say that in general all the social activity of the Gilyak is centered on preparations for solemn offerings. The poor and rich alike give everything in their power in order to make the offering plentiful and diversified.[15]

---

13 [**Editor's note:** While the start of this paragraph follows the AMNH Russian and English typescripts, notably the 1933 Soviet editions stress the opposite, that the spirits are not the ethereal figures of mythology but the products of simple, special human events.]

14 The hut where the remains of a man killed by a bear are preserved serves as a memorial to the deceased. Drowned people are cremated, and on the spot where this is done a boat is placed with all the equipment for sea and river enterprise [**Editor's note:** "Enterprise" is taken from the Russian *promysel'*, which includes both hunting and fishing]. The paddles are placed upright so that they meet at an angle in order to be visible.

15 [**Editor's note:** This paragraph abridges longer though similar material in the AMNH Russian and the 1933 Soviet editions.]

Indeed, there is a communal interest in clan offerings. Even in purely personal affairs such as illness, when an offering has to be made, a Gilyak invites all his relatives even from great distances in order to have them enjoy the benevolent results of his offerings.

The Gilyak consider it a duty to offer hospitality not only towards newcomers or the hungry but also towards those who, from our point of view, may not deserve this hospitality at all. Regardless of the number of visits paid by a neighbor, every time he appears in the home of a Gilyak, he is treated to the best food and the inevitable handful of tobacco for his pipe. If there is not enough tobacco in the house, then the host and guest smoke in turns from one pipe. This custom is especially striking when delicacies are available. If, for instance, a glass of wine is given to the head of the yurta, he would never drink it alone but would merely take the smallest sip and pass the glass on to everyone in the yurta, including the children. Otherwise, "It would be a great sin for which it is possible to die." It is a sin not to share food, and the reason for this is quite clear: A man is fed by his deities and his deities belong to the entire clan. Therefore to eat and not to share with one's clansmen or not to feed them at all is the greatest sin and entails the loss of the goodwill of his deities. The role of the hearth is important here. In the hearth lives a man and a woman, with fire spirits who are the clansmen or ancestors of the house never taking their eyes off all that happens within it. They are, as we saw above, the mediators between the clan and its deities. Therefore it is quite natural to believe that the deities of the hearth are the guardians of the principle of hospitality.

Besides all the ties which bind the clan together, there is the common ownership of all earthly goods. If this is not expressed in a purely communal form, it is only because there is no need for it. Life is so simple, the conditions for getting food are so easy, and the goods of nature so widely distributed, that there is no need for communal forms of production and distribution. But the principle exists nevertheless, as can be seen in communal hunting and fishing expeditions. Sometimes an expedition will set out in one boat to hunt sea mammals, and the owner of it, usually the most skillful hunter, will not get a larger share of the game than the youngest boy paddling the canoe; in addition, the owner will give a part of the game to families who did not even participate in the expedition. Dried fish, the main food of the Gilyak, is considered almost common property. Anyone whose provisions are gone takes fish from his neighbor without any remonstrance on the part of the latter. In all cases, nobody starves while some clansman or another has provisions. The hungry person has but to settle in the yurta of his richer kin, or merely to visit two or three times a day, and everything will be shared.

More individualistic ownership is recognized in connection with articles of luxury such as costly swords, textiles, fur coats, and so on. But this is only due to the fairly new development of exchange. In really important affairs such as the buying of a wife, payment of ransom, or burials, everybody considers it his duty to offer his property for the benefit of the clan.

The same principle of communal property is the basis for hereditary laws. The guiding principle is that the property of a clansman should not go out of the clan. The well-known saying "*Si sui heredes non habent gentilicium habento*" acts among

the Gilyak with all its force. In the absence of an appropriate inheritor in the immediate clan group, property goes to agnatic kinsmen, notwithstanding the fact that they
are very remote relatives and there are nearer cognates. The latter can receive, through
the will of a deceased person only, certain articles of *sagund*,[16] that will inevitably
be brought back to the clan. Therefore, if the deceased is from the *akhmalk* clan, he
gives those articles to his *imgi* clan which the latter will return as bride-price. Thus
iron *sagund* is given, for it is always part of a bride-price. If the deceased is from the
imgi clan then his agnatic relatives, that is, *akhmalk*, will be given fur *sagund* because
that is generally contained in the dowry of the bride [**40**].

ONE BEAR

The fattening of a bear and the participation in bear festivals are common clan duties.
The Gilyak expression *"Khalgu, utgu nandkh muve,"* which means "Clansmen, be
the guests," is used by adolescent youth as they walk from yurta to yurta calling the
kinsmen to taste the sacred meat of the bear and other foods commonly prepared by
the clan for this occasion.[17]

     Two main points characterize the bear festival. First, Gilyak celebrate of the bear
as a personality, as a potential clansman of the master of the mountain and also of
one's own clansman or his descendant (since his death transferred him to the clan of
the mountain people). Second, through the bear's spirit, various offerings are transmitted to the mountain spirit and its clan, and consequently to the kindred deities,
the clan benefactors. Hence the bear festival has greater significance for the clan's
well-being than any other clan offerings. That is because the offerings during the bear
festival go to the highest mountain deity, who is the greatest and most powerful con-
troller of all the wealth of the forests. The sacrificial bear, well-fed and honored, will
be a daily defender of his clansmen before that great mountain deity. Notwithstanding the presence of outsiders, the festival is strictly a clan affair. Only clansmen can
participate in its arrangements. Only sons-in-law can be invited as guests. They have
to be fed, which means that they are persons to whom the benevolence of the deities
of the clan also extends.

     The bear festival is a very important facet in the social solidarity of the clan.
The obligations to participate in the preparation of food, in numerous expenditures,
and in the reception of the guests create a background of well-coordinated activities

---

[16] *Sagund*, precious goods *sui generis*, are used only on important occasions such as the payment
      of the bride-price, dowry, ransom, or burial. They are divided into three categories: (1) iron
      sagund, such as big kettles, spears, armor, expensive Japanese sabers, and so on (these articles
      in the main comprise the bride-price); (2) fur *sagund*, such as fur coats and other fur articles
      which are included in the dowry; and (3) silk *sagund*, such as Chinese silk cloth and clothing
      which are used only on very solemn occasions and as burial dress.

[17] [**Editor's note:** This is another point where Averkieva omitted expository references to the
      "preceding" (Shternberg, 1904f–h, and Shternberg, *Giliaki*) chapter on religion. Although the
      ethnographic literature on bear sacrifice is considerable, A. Irving Hallowell's "Bear Ceremo-
      nialism in the Northern Hemisphere," *American Anthropologist* 28: 1–175, remains a classic.
      For more on the bear festival among the Gilyak, see Erukhim A. Kreinovich, "La fête de l'ours
      chez les Nivkh," *Ethnographie* 74–75 (1977): 195–208.]

FIG. 22. A Gilyak couple, 1890s. The man at right wears the emblem of Russian imperial officials bestowed upon Gilyak overseers. Photo by Lev Shternberg. *Source:* AAN f. 282, o. 2, d. 98, l. 25.

for the common welfare of the clan. The periodical meeting of clansmen, scattered sometimes over great areas, helps maintain the traditions and ties of the clan alliance. Finally, the character of the festival itself—the cheerful preparations, the triumphal reception of the guests, common noisy feasts, discussions, dances, songs, races, fencing, and religious ceremonials, in short, all that refines and adorns life—give the clan alliance the highest value as the source of all spiritual and social happiness.

ONE DEVIL

In some cases a dead kinsman passes to the clan of a benevolent deity. In other cases the opposite may happen: a kinsman who has been embittered in his lifetime and left the clan, or a kinsman who was not avenged or did not receive a proper burial celebration, cannot go to the land of the dead. He may pass only into the clan of evil deities or he will avenge his kinsmen on his own. The same can happen on the part of an offended or murdered stranger. The propitiation of such clan enemies is as important to the clan as the gratification of the benevolent deities, so there appears to be a common obligation to reward a shaman for the work and pain of struggling with such enemies, or to meet the expenses for propitiation, etc. [41].

ONE *TKHUSIND*

In the Gilyak language, *tkhusind* refers literally to the ransom received or paid by the clan in cases of vengeance. But it has come to be more widely used in the sense of a fine or penalty that compensates a range of transgressions. For instance, *tkhusind* is demanded for an abducted woman, for offense against a woman's chastity, or for profanation of holy things (such as the spoiling of the hearth, the violation of taboos during the bear festival), for theft, and so on. In all these cases the collective responsibility rests upon the clan; that is, they are obliged to defend the rights of their clan against a stranger and to take responsibility for all violations by their clansmen. But ransom is only a later substitution for the more important principle of "an eye for an eye."

Among the Gilyak, murder within the clan is not punished because the clan cannot spill the blood of a clansman; it is the blood of an ancestor.[18] This attitude is not due merely to religious principle, but may also be attributed to the categorical imperative of clan survival, for the strength of the clan lies in its numbers and in internal peace. Every case of vengeance within the clan would inevitably lead to another on the part of the relatives of the punished person, and thus there would be continuous strife ending in the physical and moral disintegration of the clan. Murder or any other serious violation of rights and laws by a clansman, however, is not left entirely unpunished. He suffers a political death, for it ends in the social ostracism of the offender. He is forced to leave the clan and go to a distant settlement, thereby losing all his privileges of the clan alliance, not only during his lifetime but after death as well. The latter loss is more important, for only clansmen have the right to cremate the dead. Murder within the clan is very rare, for the numerous avoidance taboos between clan relatives reduce the chances for disagreements; the broad communal marital rights allay jealousy and make the abduction of women unnecessary (this being usually the most frequent cause for bloodshed).

It is quite a different matter when bloodshed occurs between strangers. The law that "the bones of a clansman have to be lifted" is inexorable. "To lift the bones" is a technical term for blood revenge. Blood must be atoned for by blood, and only in extreme cases can compensation be substituted for revenge. This obligation is colored more by a religious element than by an emotional one. Revenge is obligatory not only to the contemporaries of the victim but rests as a burden on the following two generations of the clan as well. Vengeance is obligatory in cases of unintentional, accidental murder, even when linkage to a person is tangential. One Gilyak provoked vengeance on himself and his clan when his gun went off accidentally as he was lifting it from the bottom of his boat and killed the steersman. Vengeance is even considered obligatory in connection with animals. It is no less severe against a bear who has killed a man than it is against a human being [42].

This ritual of vengeance is very important for an understanding of the psychology that underlies this institution. Here we begin our analysis. As soon as the people learn that a man has been killed by a bear in the forest, they start out to catch the murderer. If they cannot find the actual murderer, they have to kill three other bears in its stead (the kinsmen of the murderer). If they fail to accomplish this during the winter, it has to be done in the summer. Above all, the mountain men must give to the Gilyak *tkhusind* in the form of plentiful game.

---

18 [*Editor's note:* The AMNH Russian and the 1933 Soviet editions inserted the following footnote here: "After a murder within a clan that has intermarried with Ainu (a people who still practice matriliny) the mother's brother and a close agnate of the victim collect the ransom and divide it among themselves."]

But if the bear who killed the man, or a kinsman of the bear, is caught, it is subjected to great wrath. At first its teeth are knocked out with an axe. It is then skinned and pricked constantly with knives. The most extraordinary curses are addressed to it. After the skin is removed, it is wrapped around the man who was killed; if there is nothing left of him, a wooden image is used instead. Then it is seated in the sledge with the head of the bear under the seat. This is taken to the settlement accompanied by loud cries mixed with many exclamations in honor of the killed man and in defamation of his murderer.

If the bear is not found, then a wooden image of its upper torso is placed under the seat of the murdered man, whose body is wrapped in a cloak made of shavings.[19] A hut resembling a bear's cage with two openings for the offerings to follow is erected not far from the man's native village. On the outside at each corner of the hut are erected four planed trees, while the interior is decorated with sanctified *inau* (ritual wooden shavings). The remains of the murderer and victim are placed here in the same position as they are brought from the forest.

Next to the hut, a feast from the bear meat is arranged. The kinsmen, with big pieces of the bear's meat in their hands, sit on both sides of a long fire. Everybody cuts the meat into small pieces and throws it over the fire to the person sitting across from him. The slice is caught and roasted on a knife over the fire. It is the greatest possible insult to the bear, as ordinarily bear meat is only boiled. Pieces of the slice are then bitten off with the greatest disgust and thrown away (generally it is a great sin to drop to the ground even the smallest of bones). After this procedure of refined vengeance a feast begins with offerings to the mountain master and to the recent victim. A lighted tinder is first thrown into the fire, then follow various foods. Two guardians are placed near the hut for the night in case the bear's spirit should come seeking revenge. Usually the guardians assure everyone that they heard cries during the night of the killed man, "Oh, the bear!"—and they rush with their spears upon an invisible avenger. In the morning there really seem to be blood traces on the blades of their spears [**43**].

The feast ends and the peace between the mountain people and the clan of the victim is reestablished. The victim has been accepted into and henceforth will live with the mountain people clan. Three generations of his relatives will make offerings twice a year partly to their deified clansman and partly to the mountain master.

We indicated above that the urge to revenge was based more on a religious motive than an emotional one. If it is obligatory up to the third generation, and in cases of accidental murder towards a friend or even a cognate, then it is more a burden which weighs upon the clan than an impulsive action inspired by anger. The first reaction is usually pity for the soul of the dead, followed by fear of the soul and the clan gods.

---

19 The shavings are considered holy objects of magical power. The cult of these holy shavings, *inau*, plays an enormous role in Gilyak religion. [***Editor's note:*** Here, the AMNH Russian and the 1933 Soviet editions refer to the religion chapter found in Shternberg, *Giliaki.*] Those Gilyak elected by spirits are usually buried in a cloak made of shavings. For instance, women who give birth to twins or triplets are buried in such cloaks because they are considered superior beings. The poor are dressed for the funeral in *inau* cloaks instead of costly Chinese silk garments. This leads one to imagine that in olden times dresses made of shavings were in common use and that antiquity has invested them with sanctity.

The soul of a man who died violently cannot pass on to the common "village of the dead," where earthly life is continued. Until it is avenged, that is, until the blood of the murderer gives it strength to "lift the bones," it is forced to circle around in the air in the form of a bird-avenger, making horrible cries during the night and rotting gradually until it finally falls to earth in the form of dust and perishes forever. The Gilyak call that bird *takhs*. It is a gray bird with a red beak and is called "a lover of war." Probably this surname is the source of belief in the bird's power, because wars among the Gilyak are exclusively the results of vengeance. Consequently birds of prey, who are "lovers of war," are apparently the souls of murdered kinsmen. Upon the grave of such a kinsman is placed a stump with the roots upward, in the shape of a bird.[20] Sometimes the latter is shaped with iron teeth and its extremities are shaped like human legs as in some swastika examples.[21] This horrible and unfortunate bird cries for vengeance during the night, seeking rest and return to the realm of its dead kinsmen; and of course it has the power to punish its clansmen who have forgotten their obligations. Even when vengeance is substituted by compensation, it is not satisfied. The sacrifice of a dog is needed and its heart is given to the bird. Otherwise it avenges both sides brutally.

Because the soul of a victim exists for not more than three generations, as is the case with every human soul, the obligation of vengeance ceases with the third generation. But until that moment, the pitiful existence of the soul of the victim continues to torment the conscience of his clansmen and to threaten them with the horrors of the avenger. These motives prevail over the more immediate impulse for retribution. That is why the fury of avengers never extends to the entire clan of a murderer but is limited to the killing of two or three of his clansmen. The killing of women and attempts on property are thoroughly avoided.

Nonetheless the urge to avenge is exceedingly intense. The news of a murder immediately unites the clan into a unanimous body which acts with feverish energy. The offending clan, whose task lies not so much in guarding the murderer but in guarding the entire clan, has a similar reaction. Every kinsman is threatened with death from the avengers, who search feverishly for traces of the murderer. It is not important to them to find the real murderer; they will be satisfied with any male representative of that clan, even if he is a swaddling infant. That is why mothers in moments of great danger conceal the sex of their male children [**44**].

It is not hard to imagine the feelings experienced by both sides until the end of the conflict. When both clans live in the same settlement the thing is a bit easier to bear, for at least there is no suspense. The matter is sealed by an armed conflict immediately after the murder. Relatives of the deceased, followed by several armed kinsmen, run toward the yurtas of the murderer's clan and fall upon the first man. The relatives of the murderer take his side and the battle begins. After several hours it may end, and if there is an equal number of deaths on both sides, the incident is closed. Sometimes a third clan intervenes and tries to settle the conflict peaceably.

---

20 Usually the roots of stumps upon the graves of those who died naturally are turned downward.
21 A specimen of this kind, which was brought by von Schrenck from the mouth of the Amur, can be found in the Museum of Anthropology and Ethnography of the Academy of Sciences in Leningrad.

If the clans live in different settlements, however, then martial law reigns. If the settlements happen to be near each other, the defenders are in a complete state of siege. There can be no question of outdoor work while it lasts. Neither hunting nor fishing is possible on account of a possible ambush in every corner. Even one's own settlement is not safe, for any night the enemy may invade it. Sometimes the remoteness of the hostile clan necessitates distant expeditions on foot or by boat. It must be a magnificent spectacle to see a crowd of warriors in their best attire, glistening spears in hand, quivers on their backs, with knives and Japanese sabers stuck in their belts, furiously shaking their weapons and overwhelming the primeval forests with their cries to the deities for vengeance.

Pal-kurn miia.
Tli kurn miia.
Tel-kurn miia.
Mif-kurn miia.

[The spirit of the mountains, hear.
The spirit of the sea, hear.
Spirit of the heaven, hear.
Spirit of the earth, hear.]

At the same time they brandish their spears and plunge them into every tree with the cry, "*Ch-khar miia*" ("O, tree listen"). This noisy excitement is soon replaced by a deep silence, and as they near the settlement of their enemies, their enthusiasm gives way to a concentrated seriousness.

The enemy, of course, has taken all the necessary precautions. He knows every strategic point in the vicinity. He waits for the attackers in places naturally suited for ambush and in specially constructed trenches, and will send a shower of arrows down upon imprudent warriors. There are many difficulties in the way of the aggressors. Any enterprise on the enemy's territory is dangerous. Among several clans, it is even prohibited to use the water from the rivers and brooks of the enemy. Provisions taken from home do not last very long, and the quick and open attack is impossible on account of the ambuscade and the lookouts of the women who are inviolable during the attack. With great patience and under much privation, they must wait for a favorable moment or resolve in desperation to take undertake extreme risk. The attacked generally prefer to wait for the attack in their settlement. The men leave the women and gather in a separate yurta. At the first sign of the approaching enemy given by sentries, they will secretly gather behind the yurtas via secret pathways, ready to meet the attack.

According to the intertribal regulations, the battle may continue for one night or at most a day and a night until there are casualties. Then the enemy leaves and the attacked count the dead on both sides. If there were more killed on the side of the attacked a *casus belli* arises. In any case the aggressors must consider themselves satisfied. But unfortunately the matter does not always end with a few victims. Entire clans have perished, except for the women.

Sometimes a clan, weak in number and unable to withstand the attack, will be redeemed by the sacrifice of a single member, expiating the common guilt. I know of a case when a youth, the cause of the conflict, upon news of the approaching enemy, begged his kinsmen to save themselves by escaping. When his kinsmen left the yurta with lowered eyes, he drank a cup of seal oil to give himself courage and rushed out brandishing his spear to meet the furious crowd of avengers. One finds many cases of chivalry exemplified in other forms. Although the attacks of the avengers are too impulsive to allow for plans, some war declarations come through mediators. The usual formula is merely, "The avenger has declared that he will wage war against you. If you are strong you will kill him; if he is stronger, he will kill you" [45].

Hostile expeditions are not always undertaken for the sake of revenge. Battles are very frequently fought for the sake of women, in fact, more frequently than for murders. The latter are quite rare and are a matter of momentary anger; "barbarians" may be easily excited for the slightest offense to vanity. But for the sake of a woman, a group of clansmen will invade in order to capture the beloved of their friend. This invasion is followed by a return incursion to recapture the one who was abducted. This second event is more serious, for it is of the same importance to the clan as revenge or ransom for a killed kinsman. Generally bloodshed is avoided by arranging the raid at a time when the men are absent from the settlement. Nevertheless, the matter is rarely settled without bloody consequences; both cases of capture and pursuit entail the necessity of "lifting the bones," that is, war with all its consequences.

Let us now discuss the *tkhusind* (penalty or ransom). At first it partly replaced the institution of blood vengeance and now coexists with, if almost displaces it. The factors which have gone into this reform are unknown. To my mind, however, it seems to lie in the peculiar form of exogamy among the Gilyak.

Every clan is united with at least four other clans by the most intimate kinship ties. From the *akhmalk* clan or clans it takes wives; to the *imgi* clan or clans it gives its women. Naturally these clans are dear to it; its mothers, daughters, and sisters unite them. The clan of a murderer might easily be a clan which takes wives from the offended clan or vice versa. As a result there appears the first mitigating condition—the inviolability of women. If the murderer belongs to the *akhmalk* clan, that is, to the clan of mothers and wives of the avengers, it cannot be expected that these women will be indifferent spectators of war against their fathers and brothers. If the murderer is a member of the *imgi* clan, the wives also do not easily consent to the death of their husbands at the hand of their fathers and brothers. In either case the interference of the women is inevitable [46].

The immunity granted to women greatly impedes the nature of the blood feud. The role of women as sentries is a unique one, intended to exhaust the enemy and weaken his spirit, far more than a simple active resistance. Taking advantage of their rights of *habeus corpus*, the women, enjoying complete immunity, patrol the vicinity day and night examining every bush and hummock in search of the hidden enemy. If the attackers lack the requisite strength for a frontal attack, they are never able to lull a vigilant and untouchable picket line. Thus, the patience of the attackers suffers by lack of food, is exhausted by the long raid and the tortures of waiting, and buckles under the forces of the weaker sex. A ground for peacemaking is thus established. The watchfulness of women wins out.

Such a settlement occurred in the following case. In 1851 thirty men from the village of Tebakh started out by land to visit vengeance upon one of the clans of the village Kol' for a murdered clansman. Their long trip was followed by a still longer period of vigilance on the part of the defending women who, poles in hand, constantly surveyed the site. When the avengers' water was gone, they were forced to abandon their aggressions, and the matter was settled peacefully [46].

Hence, it was enough to have several cases of peaceful settlement to put ransom on a legitimate footing with blood revenge. Later *tkhusind* replaced such aggressions entirely.

Tylor was right in maintaining that exogamy modified the relations between clans and brought peace, although his point of departure (namely, that the tendency toward peace caused the appearance of exogamy) was wrong. Indeed, primitive man is not so sentimental but extremely fearful of deities. His fear of punishment would be too great for the violation of such a rule even if it were obviously to his own interest. But he has found a definite means, as we already know, by which to circumvent the deities. In this instance, as in others, he resorts to a pious deceit which allows him to fulfill his religious duties and at the same time derive material benefits from the conflict. Normally this crucial religious procedure is ignored by scholars, despite the fact that traces of such pacifying rituals are found among all peoples. Among the Gilyak, as we will see later, these rites of ransom effect an imitation of blood revenge in the form of a struggle between representatives of the hostile clans, the killing of dogs, and the feeding of the spirits with the dogs' blood. Actual conflict is thus averted.[22]

The chief executor of the peacemaking procedure is the *khlai nivukh*, literally, "eloquent orator."[23] This man enjoys great respect among the Gilyak, for according to them, an eloquent individual is elected by a particular deity, who constantly dwells within him and inspires him with fine persuasive speeches. Quickness of speech and the ability to speak evenly for a long time, regardless of the content, is considered a gift of the highest order. "His tongue burns like the wings of a windmill" is the way the Gilyak extol prominent orators. The latter, in turn, consider themselves as the elect. On the continent, they always carry a wooden rod with a carved human head on the top of it, which symbolizes their patron. In excited moments they vigorously shake the rods in the air, threatening to break them if they are wrong in their arguments. Most often a *khlai nivukh* is selected for other distinguishing marks: he is usually wealthy, skillful in his occupations, experienced, brave, intelligent, and enjoys great popularity among kin. Every clan and every village has its own small *khlai nivukh*, although some are famous over all the land. They are called from great distances in case of need, as we would summon great lawyers. They execute their functions more for *honoris causa* than anything else. The usual fee consists only of a Chinese silk gown or a Japanese saber, neither of which compensate a wealthy person for the hardships of the task. The gifts of attire and

---

[22] [**Editor's note:** The AMNH English typescript omits the point made in the AMNH Russian and the 1933 Soviet editions that Shternberg saw evidence of a religiously sanctioned peacemaking ritual. I am grateful to Lydia Black for this observation.]

[23] Here we use the term of the Western dialect.

ornament are their *insignia magistratus*, which serves as the official costume during the negotiations [**47**].

When an avenging clan is sufficiently tried by their attempts at blood revenge, or when a murder happens under mitigating circumstances, the *khlai nivukh* is summoned. Naturally, the one who could gain the most advantageous conditions is sought out. He must of necessity belong to a neutral clan. It is impossible to send a kinsman because it would be a sin for him to have any dealings with the clan of the murderer, and because it might lead to still greater irritation between the two clans. The opponents also have their own speaker, who must defend their interests in the negotiations for a fine. The initiative is usually on the side of the offended clan.

One fine day the company of armed avengers, with a spokesman at their head, appears before the settlement of the murderer. In a nearby taiga location or on the bank of a river, they make a fire and camp. The spokesman in his official attire, with a spear in one hand and a small kettle in the other, goes alone to the hostile settlement. There in a yurta he is awaited by the enemy with their own *khlai nivukh* at the head. Resting on his spear, or sitting down and lighting a pipe with his own fire, he opens negotiations: "I am sent to you to say that you killed our man, and what a man he was! His right arm cost a great deal of money. If he were still alive, would he consent to take so little? His left arm cost so and so . . . etc." Then all the limbs of his body are counted and the sum of the penalty is named. If the opponents agree to this figure, they put into his kettle as many sticks as the number of ruble coins demanded. But usually the negotiations are not settled so easily. The speaker of the opposite side tries to vindicate the murderer and will propose a lesser amount. This gambit irritates the avenger's *khlai nivukh*, and he will leave angrily, threatening to stop the negotiations. His colleague will run after him with entreaties to yield. They sit down again, lighting their pipes, each with his own fire, and discuss the business until someone again gets angry and runs away. This ritual is repeated over and over. Protocol requires that the penalty should not be accepted at once, but only after resistance. These meetings and wranglings continue for 2 or 3 days [**48**].

At the end of the negotiations, the religious rites begin. They are an imitation of the bloody struggle, to hide from the soul of the deceased and the deities of the clan that the settlement has been of a peaceful character. The avengers with their spokesman proceed in the direction of the hostile settlement. A similar procession of the other clan comes to meet them. Several sazhens apart they stop, and the nearest clansmen of the victim and the murderer, armed with spears and bows, step out of the ranks together with their *khlai nivukh*. At a signal given by both spokesmen, they start shooting arrows or striking with their spears, skillfully dodging the blows. This is, of course, a fictitious duel, although it sometimes happens that the opponents lose their tempers and fight in earnest. The spokesmen, however, pacify their clients throughout the mock battle with constant reminders of the negotiations. In the meantime, the kinsmen bring two dogs, lead them between the opponents and kill them with spears—blood for blood. After that, the adversaries embrace each other and establish peace. The heart of the dog is given to the bird-avenger, while the meat is eaten at an ensuing feast. Then representatives of both sides go into the yurta of the murderer, where all the articles of *tkhusind* (kettles, spears, sabers, silk clothes, and

so on) are exposed. All kinsmen according to their means take part in the payment
of the ransom. It is considered a great sin not to put in one's share. On the other side,
the monies and goods obtained become the common property of the offended clan.
Part of it supplies the valuable goods needed by the deceased in the realm of death,
and the rest becomes a common fund for the family of the deceased and his clan.

The negotiations for ransom for the capture of a woman or offense to holy
things are carried on in the same way with the help of a spokesman, but not quite
so solemnly. The mediators discuss the matter in the presence of all the people,
whose opinions are heard. The decision arrived at is considered to be the consensus
of the entire meeting.

ONE SIN

Although the religious customs and rules of conduct are the same for the whole tribe,
every clan has a series of obligations and prohibitions all its own which apply only
to its members. The sexual norms constitute the first, and widest circle of such prohibitions. Members of every clan are forbidden sexual intercourse with particular
classes of women such as their clanswomen, the wives of younger brothers, all women
called *imk,* and all women from the clan of sons-in-law. It is enough to know which
women are prohibited in order to ascertain the clan they belong to. The restrictions
on conversation can also be placed in this category. For members of every clan, there
exist definite classes of persons with whom conversation is forbidden.

The religious norms, in a narrow sense, constitute yet another, third category.
As we have seen, each clan has its own deities, sacrifices, sacred objects, beliefs, traditions, and rituals. These numerous ceremonies and cult objects require the greatest care and respect. The entire clan is responsible for each violation, or the wrath of
the offended deities falls upon them. Therefore, the member of a clan must not only
avoid any violation of taboo, but he must protect them also from violation by
strangers. A penalty must be demanded for every offense. Hence the usual lawsuits
for an accidental spoiling of a hearth's fence, for carrying out fire from the yurta, or
for letting a bear's bone fall during the feast.

Finally, we must take into consideration that the term "sin" extends not only
to the formal prohibitions, but also the obligation to realize all the positive norms
of the clan. Then the formula "common sin" assumes a broad general meaning and
becomes the expression of shared clan obligations. The significance of this principle
is all the more simply important because for the Gilyak these obligations are not
juridical formulae observed as punishment. They are religious imperatives rigorously observed for the sake of self-preservation. To the Gilyak there is no difference in
prohibitions religious, sexual, or social in character; they are all religious. To observe
these requirements means to care about the benevolence of deities, the removal of
pitfalls emanating from all enemies in life, and so on. Not to observe these regulations means the ruin not only of the offender himself but of the entire clan. Hence
it becomes clear why these norms are the cement that binds the clan. Often contra-
dictory to human nature and requiring tremendous self-control, these norms are not
regarded as compulsory but as if by the natural demands of instinct. Notice, for

instance, with what power sexual regulations function. In general, as regards sexual instinct, Gilyak men and women act freely upon their natural inclinations. There is no chastity before or after marriage. Care is taken only to avoid becoming a victim of jealousy. There is neither mention nor sign of sexual moderation. Still, the Gilyak maintains absolute chastity in relation to persons of prohibited categories. Incest is unknown and considered a monstrous phenomenon.[24] The same restraint is exercised in regard to conversation. Even being face to face with each other for entire days, brothers and sisters endure the torments of silence, communicating with each other only in cases of extreme need in the most businesslike manner. And yet the Gilyak are by temperament far from silent. To a considerable degree, such self-control is the result of education and training, but it would never have attained such a hold were it not for the common realization of the ruin each individual violation would bring to the whole clan [49].

Such are the basic characteristics of the clan, according to which it is possible to judge its comprehensive role in Gilyak life. The clan's hold on a man lasts from birth to death, filling his entire life. It surrounds him with the most intimate ties of relationship on the mother's and father's sides. It unites the living generations with all ancestors by the closest ties. It guarantees a man individual marriage as well as marital rights outside of it, and insures his widow and children after his death. It guards the life of a man and his family from strangers. The clan is ready to rise as a single man in defense of the rights of a kinsman or to answer for his guilt towards another clan. It feeds him when he is hungry, pays his debts if he is poor, and helps him in the payment of the bride-price and ransom.

In the benevolence of the clan deities and in the clan sacrifices, a man finds complete protection and the strongest guarantee of well-being. The clan is a school of moral education, duty, social cooperation, and self-sacrifice. Within it he finds his greatest joys, consolation, and the assurance of his felicity in the world after life.[25]

---

[24] [***Editor's note:*** Although the AMNH English typescript's translation for the Russian word *pre-liubodeianie* was correctly given as "adultery," the context of sexual relations between prohibited categories renders the word more closely as incest.]

[25] [***Editor's note:*** The concluding paragraph to this chapter, found in the AMNH Russian and the 1933 Soviet versions, is transposed in the AMNH English typescript and in this edition to the start of chapter fifteen.]

FIFTEEN

WHAT HOLDS THE CLAN TOGETHER?[1]

[223–236; 316–332; 109–120; 49–56][2]

WHAT ARE THE MEANS by which this astonishing institution, the Gilyak clan, envelops the individual more completely than a modern state? The clan can demonstrate the greatest concern for its members while at the same time circumscribing their actions with the widest network of rules and "sins." Where are the outward bodies, so important to the European observer, which fulfill these functions? Is it not strange that such outward mechanisms should seem so absent? [49]

When writing about the Chukchi, Nordenskiöld wrote, "Here, as in all Chukch villages which we afterwards visited, absolute anarchy prevailed. At the same time the greatest unanimity reigned in the little headless community."[3] Nordenskiöld would probably have said the same of the Gilyak, for a number of other travelers have made similar observations about the primitive peoples they encountered. Indeed, the social organization described in the preceding chapter, which is the very soul of a primitive society, is very often hidden from the eyes of the passing observer. To the untrained eye, any deviation from European trappings of statehood, such as well-defined territory, representatives of authority, or a binding rule of law signals "anarchy," by which nonetheless, to at least Nordenskiöld's surprise, "members of these acephalous communities lived together in harmony and friendship" [50].

Gilyak social structure strikes the novice in just this fashion. Notwithstanding all the complexities of its social fabric, covering all aspects of life, all the formal outward signs of social organization, which the European hunts for everywhere as if by reflex, are either completely absent or found in the most tentative forms.

---

[1] [*Editor's note:* The AMNH Russian typescript and the 1933 Soviet editions of this chapter titled it, "The Mechanism of the Clan," while the AMNH English typescript used the title, "The Mechanism of the Gilyak Gens." I follow the AMNH English typescript in moving the first paragraph of this chapter from the end of chapter fourteen in order to take advantage of its directional focus.]

[2] [*Editor's note:* Shternberg published a version of this chapter nearly identical to the AMNH and the 1933 Soviet editions in Shternberg, "Giliaki," *Etnograficheskoe Obozrenie* 28, no. 63 (1904h), 97–111.]

[3] [*Editor's note:* The quotation is from Adolf Erik Nordenskiöld, *Voyage of the Vegas around Asia and Europe, Vol. 1* (London: MacMillan, 1881), 449.]

TERRITORY

Quite naturally, members of one clan prefer to live together in face-to-face communication with each other. There are, indeed, several settlements such as Tangi, Nianevo, and Viskvo in which the entire population belongs to a single clan. Sometimes the big winter yurtas in such settlements may contain from 20 to 30 kinsmen, yet not one stranger. Even in a village such as Kol', where a number of clans are found, the dwellings of each clan are aligned row by row, as if by long-observed tradition. Each clan has its own river areas for hunting, shared between families among whom they are passed from generation to generation, from father to son. It should be noted, however, that rights to property are circumscribed by actual use, with interludes when hunting and fishing grounds become *res nullius* and can be used by anyone, even strangers.[4]

The idea of property rights with respect to territory is absent among the Gilyak. Fifty years ago nomadic Tungus appeared in Sakhalin and began to hunt on traditional Gilyak territories. Yet it never occurred to the Gilyak to protest against the invasion, although the Tungus appeared in small groups and could hardly have defended themselves had force been used.

The surname of a clan alone likewise leaves us only partially informed. Among many primitive, so-called totemic tribes, the clan name is the most striking indication of clan unity. There is nothing like that among the Gilyak, although totemic legends exist among some clans. For instance, the clan living in Tangi considers itself a relative of the bear, because a woman of that clan gave birth to a deformed child whose traits somewhat resembled those of a bear. Similar legends exist among several other clans. In many clans there are only territorial names. If a Gilyak wants to refer to persons of a particular clan, he usually says, "The inhabitants of such and such a place." Sometimes this coincides with the actual residence of the clan, but most often it only indicates the oldest settlement of the clan in question [**51**].

For example, in Kol' clans bear the following names: Tyvli-fing, inhabitants of the settlement Tyvli; Mekhre-fing, inhabitants of Mekhre; Nenkhai-fing, inhabitants of Nenkhai, etc.; yet the members of these clans have already lived for a long time there and have lost all connection with the old habitations of their ancestors. The only clans having real clan names are those composed of Tungus emigrants, such as Tskharung and Choril'. It is of interest that among these tribes we find a definite transition to totemism. For instance, among the Negidal, almost every clan reckons its origin from some animal, such as the tiger, toad, or bear. Among the Gilyak, this occurs very seldom.[5]

---

[4] [***Editor's note:*** In the AMNH Russian typescript and the 1933 Soviet editions, a further paragraph following this continues Shternberg's argument that territory cannot ultimately be an indicator of clan strength. Even in more prosperous areas, he reasons, Gilyak clans have traditionally achieved peaceful resource sharing. An excellent study of Gilyak property and marriage rights is found in Erukhim Abramovich Kreinovich, "Perezhitki rodovoi sobstvennosti i gruppovogo braka u giliakov," *Trudy Instituta Antropologii, Arkheologii i Etnografii* 4 (1936), 711–754.]

[5] [***Editor's note:*** After Shternberg, the fullest study and listing of Gilyak clans on Sakhalin and the Amur at the turn of the century is found in Anna V. Smoliak, "Rodovoi sostav nivkhov v XIX–nachale XX v.," *in Sotsial'naia organizatsiia i kul'tura narodov Severa* (Moscow: Akademiia Nauk, 1974), 176–217.]

Let us now consider executive powers or institutions which, from the point of view of the European, should be the most important feature of clan unity. As we have seen, notwithstanding the complexity of clan life, there are no institutionalized authorities. The Chinese and the Russians attempted once to establish the institution of *starosta* among the Gilyak, not over clans but over entire settlements.[6] This institution bore no relation whatsoever to the life of the clan and proved little more than an unattractive episode. In the Russian case, imperial officials selected *starosta*s from among the most complacent Gilyak, rather than the wealthiest and the best. The old organization of the clan never knew anything like it. Patriarchal authority, which on the basis of biblical examples is usually associated with the clan organization, and which we still meet among the Buriat, Kirghiz, and various peoples of the Caucasus, is absolutely absent among the Gilyak, and in general among other tribes in a similar stage of development. It is absent even within the family, although women are subject to their fathers and brothers before marriage, and to their husbands after that.

Such despotism, however, has nothing in common with the Roman *patria potestas*. The killing or selling of women into slavery is impossible. Forcible marriages are quite frequent, but this to a large degree is connected with the religious sanction of marriages between children of brothers and sisters. In general, the attitude towards daughters is tender before as well as after marriage. The most intimate ties of hospitality and mutual aid are established between the families of the *akhmalk* and *imgi*. In cases of ill-treatment of the woman by her husband, she always finds protection among her kinsmen. As for the rest, the matrimonial relations are usually very tender. Men take counsel with their wives, and older women even participate in clan meetings.[7]

There are no signs of despotism with respect to males, as is evident from the attitudes of the older men toward their children. Indeed, a civilized person would find it hard to imagine the degree of equality and respect which rules here in relation to youths. Adolescents, those of even 10 or 12 years of age, consider themselves full and equal members of society. The oldest and most respected persons listen to what they have to say and answer them as seriously and respectfully as they would persons of their own age. Neither difference of age nor position is felt by anyone. Indeed, by the age of 10 or 12 the Gilyak boy is already an accomplished gentleman.[8] He not only knows the ins and outs of daily chores but is an expert hunter, fisher, and paddler,

---

6   [*Editor's note: Starosta* is a Russian administrative term for section head, group leader, or, in the context of a *sel'skii starosta* of which Shternberg speaks, village headman. It is noteworthy that when Russian officials on Sakhalin first allowed the exiled Shternberg to travel through North Sakhalin, they mandated and empowered him to appoint *starosta*s throughout Gilyak villages. Here and in his field diaries, he remarked on the futility of these efforts, precisely because in the eyes of Gilyaks, clan life preempted the need for state regulation. See "Dnevnik puteshestviia L. Ia. Shternberga," (1891), AAN f. 282, l. 1, d. 190, l. 48.]

7   [*Editor's note:* As a rule, these were postmenopausal women. For a fuller discussion of menstrual taboos among Siberian peoples, see Marjorie Mandelstam Balzer, "Rituals of Gender Identity: Markers of Siberian Khanty Ethnicity, Status and Belief," *American Anthropologist* 83, no. 4 (1981), 850–867. For a more general study, see Thomas Buckley and Alma Gottlieb, eds., *Blood Magic: The Anthropology of Menstruation* (Berkeley: Univ. of California Press, 1988).]

8   [*Editor's note:* The Russian language version of this sentence in the AMNH Russian typescript and the 1933 Soviet editions incorporating Shternberg's bilingual cursive reads, "Pravda, giliatskii podrostok 10–12 let obyknovenno uzhe accomplished gentleman."]

working alongside others like anyone else. He already possesses a good part of the spiritual knowledge of his clan; he knows from practice all the customs and religious rights; he remembers all the clan names, as well as the legends, tales and songs of his tribe. Moreover, the constant companionship of his elders in travel, hunting, and fishing give him a wide knowledge of the people and of life in general. From this comes his dignity, his solidity in conversation, and his ability to behave properly in society [52].

If sons choose to move away from their parents, they know they will receive a part of the family chattel such as sledges and so on. The association is quite free and one can leave whenever one pleases. However, it is more common for a number of generations to live in a common household. Every member of such a family is allowed to have individual possessions of sledges, dogs, or arms, and everyone has a right to his own earnings resulting from personal efforts. Every member shares everything with his clansmen, especially foodstuffs, even those he has purchased. This generosity is quite voluntary. Flour and rice bought in town are boiled in the common kettle for all. Communism and individualism coexist without friction.

Finally, it is notable that the head of the family of the common household need not necessarily always be the oldest member of it. On the contrary, young men who have proved themselves skillful, zealous, and clever are more often found at the head of families. The elders enjoy authority on special questions as keepers of tradition, experts on ceremonies and the history of clan relationships. They are consulted in cases of complex questions of kinship, the naming of children, and the conduct of ritual feasts. While these matters and more are under their care, this gives them no power or privilege.

As there is no despotism on the part of the family elders, so too there is none in the clan. There are no patriarchs vested with full power, nor any regular fixed authority, whether collective or individual, elected or by birthright or inheritance. However, nor is the clan a mere figment of the imagination. It is a complex organization which surrounds the Gilyak in a web of regulations, taboos, and obligations, giving him all the material and spiritual advantages of a solid social organization. In this context, we return to the question raised at the outset of this chapter: What are the powers that regulate this all-powerful organization? What holds the clan together in the absence of force?

The secret is found in two places—in the simplicity of Gilyak economic conditions, which leave wide opportunity for the fullest development of the individual personality, and in a holistic worldview which directs the will and activity of each individual toward common harmony through the cultivation of inner consciousness.

Let us consider these factors more closely. The prevalent economic system among the Gilyak is based on individual labor combined with the simplest form of cooperation. Fishing is the main source of food. The sea and the rivers are so rich with fish that everybody can supply his wants individually with the help of a few elementary tools. The hunting of sea mammals requires the cooperation of several persons, but it is so simple that there is no need for masters and workmen, nor any need for special organization. Each does what he is able. Furthermore, the work crew [artel'] usually consists of kin, and it would not strike anyone to divide the spoils of the hunt in any other way than by the number of workers. A part of it is given to those who were not even present at the expedition. After all, do clan gods give only to some but not all clan members? The hunting of land mammals is carried on in the same way [53].

Nonetheless, a hunter or fisherman can usually get along without help. In the fishing seasons, Gilyak scatter far and wide, each man to his favorite place. In the hunting seasons, everyone gets into his individual cabin and watches his traps from there without seeing anyone for weeks. Therefore, individual work is the prevailing economic form. Everyone must be able to do everything. They must possess all the knowledge of their tribe, be equal, versatile, and prepared for life.

As the gifts of nature are so abundant, free, and accessible, the well-being of a man depends only on his personal abilities and zeal. Inequality, which under more complex conditions could be the source of discord and social differences, does not manifest itself here. A wealthy man owes everything to his personal abilities and virtues. His accumulations can neither exploit nor degrade another person. Besides, whatever talents a man has are the gifts of the gods and consequently the chosen one cannot provoke jealousy or be proud of his advantages.[9] His guardians, who send him game from the forest and the fish from the waters, are the common spirits of his clan. To accumulate goods without sharing them would be to usurp things which belong to him as well as all his clansmen. The greatest ambition of such a man would thus be to manifest his generosity and benevolence toward all. Such are the economic conditions responsible for the integrity and the equality of the people, which exclude all possibilities of exploitation, creating a wholesome atmosphere where each is conscious of his freedom and self-determination.

The highest degree of integrity of a person is determined by his socioreligious outlook. The basic axiom of the Gilyak is that every man's existence and well-being depend wholly upon the deities, particularly those of his clan, who favor not him alone but his entire group. Therefore any attempt to monopolize the gifts of the deities must entail just punishment. Everything prescribed by religion and the wisdom of the clan in order to gain the goodwill of the deities is a blessing for every member; the fulfillment of these demands is a matter of self-betterment. The same applies to all clan prescriptions, be they sexual, those of vengeance, or religious ones. All social acts of greater or lesser importance, up to and including self-sacrifice in battles avenging a kinsman, are categorical religious imperatives which neither brook hesitation nor demand their own enforcement.

All instincts of self-preservation are in complete harmony with their religion. By an act of vengeance a man defends himself and performs his religious duty at the same time. He pacifies the soul of the deceased, for if not avenged the soul can punish

---

[9] The following example well illustrates the attitude of the Gilyak toward personal goods. Gibel'ka, from the settlement of Tangi, was the wealthiest person in my day on western Sakhalin. He was a prominent man because of his intelligence, skill, and energy. Moreover, his relations with the Russians helped him much, as he was a contractor of furs and [ethnographic and natural science] collections. Nonetheless, the Gilyak considered his extraordinary wealth as due only to a piece of cloth that he once found under a tree in the mountains. This was regarded as a talisman sent by the gods.

him. The person who has integrated his social and religious outlook finds harmony between his personal and social interests. He is the secret of the powerful clan. How smoothly he influences the life of all Gilyak can be found in the following scenarios [**54**].

A clansman dies. It is necessary to provide for his family, preserve his property until his heirs grow up, and decide, in order to avoid quarrels, to whom his widow should be given. There are neither judges nor authorities, but some time after the burial the nearest relatives of the deceased meet, discuss, and listen to the candidates. They will decide who is to be the husband of the widow and the father of her children.[10]

A family is temporarily in need. There is no special body to take care of them, yet this is not necessary, for even the remotest of relatives will offer their hospitality and help until hard times have passed. And nobody is the loser because almost everyone will use this hospitality at some time or another.

An elaborate and expensive clan feast is to be arranged. There are no collections, no acts of compulsion, and no committees for the reception of the guest. Everyone prepares what he can, contributes his share of the work, and a richer person takes upon himself the duty of arranging the feast. The prepared food is taken into his house, where people meet to partake in the preparations.

When a bear festival is held, dozens of people gather from all parts of the country for several days. Hosts must feed visitors and visiting dog teams alike. There is much work and many expenses; nevertheless they arrange everything simply and satisfactorily. Every guest prefers to visit those who are his nearest relatives or most sympathetic friends, where he is accepted not out of duty but by inclination. In every house, all are met with a warm if not hearty reception, because everyone is anxious to manifest his goodwill to all the newcomers in these days of festivity.

Famine falls on the settlement. All sufferers who have not left for more favorable places gather at the home of the one who has provisions. The rules of hospitality function in days of scarcity as in those of abundance.

The worst of calamities happens: A clansman is murdered. War is inevitable, and the entire population is up in arms. There is neither a permanent chief nor an elder. Nor are there elections. The only natural leader known and recognized by everybody is the bravest and most successful of the clansmen. He is the so-called *yz*, the master to whom all eyes are turned. In a single moment, an equal among equals suddenly becomes the war leader, gives orders, distributes arms, and fixes the date of the

---

10 [***Editor's note:*** Shternberg is laconic here and elsewhere on the agency of women during such negotiations, despite the fact that women emerged as such tenacious actors in the descriptions of armed conflict in the previous chapter.]

campaign. He is obeyed like a dictator. If this natural chief dies or is killed during the campaign, everyone knows another worthy person who can replace him.

In cases of discord between clansmen or with representatives of different clans, no one person decides on the disputes or lawsuits *ex officio*. Very often the claimant himself is judge and enforcer. If his debtor refuses to fulfill his obligations voluntarily, the claimant unhesitatingly takes possession of the dogs of the debtor or enters the debtor's storehouse in order to take the things owed him. Of course, such action is not always possible, but in each case the matter is settled without an official authority. It is enough if the offended applies directly or through some spokesman (*khlai nivukh*) to one or another prominent man from the clan of the offender, and the matter will soon be settled. The offender is called and will appear with his nearest kin and sometimes a spokesman. Outsiders also gather round. After both sides are heard and the opinions of those present are given, the majority opinion becomes the verdict. Usually the offender obeys it voluntarily, but if he does not, then those who settled the affair start for his storehouse and confiscate what was adjudged.

But who are these authorities? Who appears on the scene, personally or together with other clansmen, to manifest initiative and authority as if they were vested with power? What is their role in the daily life of the people? They are the so-called *yzg'u*, "the masters," who may also be known simply as the *urdla nivkh'gu*, the "good ones," or wealthy prominent men (wealthy and good are synonyms among all primitive tribes). They are individuals with much property. Their bravery, skill, power, wisdom, and intelligence place them in a favorable position in the struggle for existence. In the narrow circles of their families, such individuals are the natural household heads. On account of such an individual's talents, the management of the household is carried on with greater success than it would have been had it been conducted separately. The large family centered around him is better provided with the fruits of nature, including tobacco as well as various market commodities. That is because his wealth and associations enable him to undertake extensive trips to trade in furs and buy commodities first hand. He is the guardian of the common *sagund* (valuables) of his nearest kin and has his own, which is also at the disposal of his kin in time of need [55].

To the entire clan, he is the man in whose house one can always eat well, regale oneself with tobacco or tea, and listen to interesting conversation. He is also the man who can help in time of need. He is especially valuable in times of general calamity, such as war, or lawsuits with a stranger. He has the best arms and the best means of transportation. His name frightens the foe, who agrees to make peace more quickly. Finally, his reserve of *sagund* can be used when it is necessary to pay a ransom. Such a man is usually broad-minded, eloquent, and in possession of a wide knowledge of life and people. He is a natural spokesman in important cases of revenge and civil conflicts. He is even consulted by strangers in need of mediators. Thus these masters enjoy celebrity throughout the territory of the Gilyak, and in their likeness are conceived the deities of the mountains, the seas, and the heavens. They are treated almost with religious adoration. In other tribes with different social organizations, these are the persons who become rulers.

The Gilyak clan does not foster these ambitions. The yz is merely one person among many, and between him and his poorer relatives altercations have not yet occurred. At the same time the strongest ties of brotherhood prevail.

Such is the glue bonding all the Gilyak together. Wholesome, well-developed personalities with integrated social and religious ideas are the clan's wellspring. Organized power is completely absent. Instead we find almost invisible elements of authority with few pretensions to power. These elements appear on the scene as though they were accidental, rather than fixed elements of power encroaching on the free expression of the individual.[11]

Following from the three central elements of authority in Gilyak life—the clan itself, the principle of seniority, and the concept of the yz (master)—we might expect favorable conditions to give rise to the unique forms of power we find among many cultured peoples both presently and from the historical horizons of all civilized nations—public gatherings, councils of elders, patriarchies, tsar-priests, military leaders, dukes, Vikings, kings, and so on. Among the Gilyak, however, these elements are only in their embryonic stages, and it is unlikely that they will ever be spurred to such further development.

---

[11] [*Editor's note:* The AMNH Russian typescript and the 1933 Soviet editions conclude this chapter with four further paragraphs highlighting the most effective bodies of authority in Gilyak life. Of these four paragraphs, I have restored the last one, which follows here, reminding us of Shternberg's Morganian evolutionist spirit.]

SIXTEEN

RELATIONS BETWEEN CLANS[1]

[236–244; 264–274; 121–128; 56–60][2]

FOR ALL ITS HOLD over the lives of its members, the clan is not the sole organizing force among the Gilyak. Every clan, according to the basic principles of their matrimonial norms, is bound through marriage ties with at least four other clans of
akhmalk and *imgi*. Between all the relatives of the clan arise ties of common origin
from the mother (the first ancestors and representatives of each generation of these
four clans are matrilateral cousins to each other), which are of great importance to
primitive man. In addition, there arise ties of natural intimacy from the generations
of women entwining these clans in a continuous chain of marriages. We know that
in practice, however, these ties extend far beyond the original four clans, for every
clan which has some matrimonial relations with a single member of another clan
becomes *akhmalk* or *imgi* to the entire clan. On the other hand, every *akhmalk* or
imgi is not only related to those clans with whom they have direct relations, but also
to the latter's *akhmalk* and *imgi* clans. So every clan has, besides their *akhmalk* and
imgi of the first degree, those of the second, third, and fourth degrees. All these clans
are called *pandf*, persons of common origin [56].

Thus we discern that this clear and simple basic principle underlying the family and clan, the principle by which a man preferentially marries his mother's brother's daughter, also becomes the foundation for consanguineal ties and sympathies not
only within the clan itself but across much broader, inter-clan alliances among the
entire people. Owing to the unfavorable conditions we discussed some chapters back,
these ties could have become amalgamated into such organizations as the phratries
and tribes of the North American Indians. Instead they created an atmosphere of
social unity which has paved the way for inter-clan relations.

Let us consider more closely the ties which arise between the clans which
constitute the *pandf* and which take and give wives to each other. Not mere sentiments, these ties take quite definite form. First comes the mutual obligation of feeding and hospitality. This is essentially an extension to the consanguineal *pandf* of

---

[1] [*Editor's note:* The AMNH Russian typescript and the two 1933 Soviet editions titled this section, "Inter-clan Relations"; the AMNH English typescript titled it, "Gentile Inter-relations."]

[2] [*Editor's note:* Shternberg published a version of this chapter nearly identical to the AMNH
Russian typescript and the 1933 Soviet editions in Shternberg, "Giliaki," *Etnograficheskoe
Obozrenie* 28, no. 63 (1904h), 111–119.]

the obligation to show benevolence toward the clan deities (who as a rule are theirs through the female line). Thus the formula for inter-clan relations is that the son-in-law must be fed. This does not mean that in his household the *akhmalk* supports the *imgi* and his family continuously. It might have been so in the remote past when the husband lived in the house of his wife. But nowadays, when agnatic principles operate, the wife moves to her husband's dwelling and usually settles permanently in her husband's clan's habitation. Nevertheless the principle of mutual feeding plays an important role in the unification of the clans [57].[3]

Earlier we discussed a peculiar religious ceremony known as "stepping into the kettles" [chapter twelve]. At the last moment when the bride is about to leave her father's house, a big four-handled kettle is placed against the threshold inside the yurta, while a smaller one is placed on the outside. On leaving the house the bride and groom must step with one foot in the inside kettle and the other in the outside one. After that the larger kettle becomes the property of the bride's father, while the smaller one is taken by the bridegroom. A year after the wedding, when the couple makes a ritual visit to the father-in-law, the same ceremony is repeated but with cups. Our interest in this ceremony here lies in the objects exchanged, for they are called *nits,* or literally, "mine-yours," a symbol of mutual feeding.[4]

This important principle of mutual feeding is not restricted to periodical visits of the son-in-law, for much more serious instances may arise. In cases of real need, when a son-in-law cannot get help even from his own clan, as sometimes happens when fish change their course during the fishing season, he will pack up his family, dogs, and cattle and move to the village of his father-in-law for the entire season. Here he is ever welcome and feels completely at home. He is well fed, and everything is shared with him. Of course he is not a complete parasite, and does as much as possible for his father-in-law. But this hardly covers the expense of supporting his family, who often arrive suddenly at a time when fish have already been salted and stored for the season and getting additional provisions is impossible.

The same brotherly relations between father-in-law and son-in-law are manifest on hunting expeditions. The most important of these expeditions—for bear, sable, or sea mammals—require several men. And it is characteristic that in all such cases the Gilyak invites a young man from his *imgi* clan sooner than any other relative, for with him he feels more at ease than with someone from his own clan. He can

---

[3]   [**Editor's note:** In his 1949 chapter on Gilyak social organization, Lévi-Strauss asserted that, as in many systems featuring the generalized exchange of women, Gilyak *akhmalk* (wife-givers) were in a subordinate position to the *imgi* (wife-takers). Citing passages such as the one above from Shternberg, as well as Gilyak legends and the work of Soviet ethnographer Erukhim A. Kreinovich, Lydia Black argued the opposite case, that *akhmalk* were in the superior position. See Claude Lévi-Strauss, *The Elementary Structures of Kinship* (Boston: Beacon), 302–303; and Lydia Black, "Relative Status of Wife Givers and Wife Takers in Gilyak Society," *American Anthropologist* 74, no. 5 (1972), 1244–1248. For further discussion of relative status between local descent groups following matrilateral cross-cousin marriage, see Edmund Leach, "The Structural Implications of Matrilateral Cross-Cousin Marriage," in *Rethinking Anthropology* (London: Athlone Press, 1961), 54–104; and Burton Pasternak, *Introduction to Kinship and Social Organization* (Englewood Cliffs, NJ: Prentice-Hall, 1976), 73.]

[4]   [**Editor's note:** The AMNH Russian typescript and the 1933 Soviet versions of this paragraph include further Gilyak terms for this ceremony.]

speak and joke freely with his *imgi*, whereas between clansmen there is always the chance of some prohibition being overlooked. The *imgi* themselves prefer to be with their *akhmalk*, for all the women of their own generation in the *akhmalk* clan are their *ang'rei*, upon whom they have always had marital right in the broadest sense of that word. The local youth, in turn, find compensation in the clan of their own *akhmalk* [58].

As a result of these frequent meetings, the youths of the clans, the so-called *navkh*, create many tender friendships.[5] The custom of fictive brotherhood is very popular among the Gilyak. Usually it is expressed in the periodical exchange of gifts or in mutual aid when the need arises. One comes across many touching cases of covenant brotherhood between the *navkh*. I happened to witness such an example in the settlement Ngambevo. Two *navkh* lived together in one yurta. They were never apart, like Orestes and Pylades, and all that they had was shared. They followed each other like lovers. It is true that they were both young and unmarried; it is therefore hard to know what would have happened to their friendship later on. But such examples illustrate the type of relationship that exists between members of matrimonially related clans.

In spite of the strict agnatic principle which governs inheritance, there is one exception in regard to the *pandf*. According to the testament of wills, *imgi* inherit iron *sagund* (which goes into the bride-price), while *akhmalk* inherit fur *sagund* (which goes into the dowry). This rule makes the bride-price a mere formality of moving it from one pocket into another and is an important indication that the bride-price among the Gilyak was formerly not a price for the bride but a religious ransom. For what purpose?

The bride-price under the Gilyak form of marriage is a strange anomaly, since marriage into the mother's clan and preferentially between true brothers' and sisters' children is a religious obligation. Evidently the appearance of this institution was evoked by some change in the marriage norms. This change is well known to us. In cases where marriage with a woman from mother's clan was for some reason or another impossible, one was forced to take a wife from a strange clan. But the latter was obliged to keep its women for legitimate *imgi*, and could only consent to give their women when masking the action by some religious subterfuge, which would also result in personal profit for the father-in-law. Analogous to religious ransoms in cases of vengeance, bride-price appeared. It fulfilled both the demands of religion and the interest of the father-in-law. The *imgi* clan which violated the marriage laws covered itself by means of another legal fiction. They called the entire illegitimate clan from which they had taken a wife *akhmalk*, which at once legitimized it. In the course of time the true origins of this institution were completely forgotten, and the bride-price became a general rule even in marriages between legitimate clans. Such might be the origin of the bride-price among other peoples too.

The participation of the entire *pandf* in the bear festival was another important factor in strengthening the ties between matrimonially linked clans. It had perhaps

---

[5] [**Editor's note:** Russian editions include a footnote here that reads, "We recall that *navkh* mutually call each other '*imgi*,' and 'brothers' of their 'wives.'"]

even greater effect for clan unification than the Olympic games did in ancient Greece for the unity of the Greek tribes. The bear festival takes place every winter in one settlement or another. In well-populated settlements, it is held almost every winter. There are no difficulties in attending them; all one has to do is harness a sled and start off. Everywhere along the way, as in the settlement where the festival is being held, dogs are fed and travelers are regaled with the best of foods. But for the slight inconvenience, everything else is socially most gratifying. The festival, the procession, target shooting, and the killing and decoration of the bear are all very exciting to the Gilyak. In addition there are discussions among the cleverest and most honored representatives of the clan, wrestling contests, racing, dancing, feasting, and singing: in short, an almost endless variety of enjoyments. Against the background of a rather stark existence encompassing starvation, dangers, hardships, and general monotony, the bear festivals are about the brightest moments in Gilyak life [59].

Noisy and crowded as these festivals are, they are strictly regulated. Besides the clansmen, only *imgi* are invited there. They, in turn, may invite their own *imgi*. Fathers-in-law never participate. Thus the man who does his best to please his son-in-law is not even invited by the latter to his festival. But he in turn will be the first guest at his own *akhmalk*'s festival. So there arises a continuous chain which unites the long set of clans in their socioreligious festivals.

We have already mentioned the importance of sons-in-law at the bear festival. They are met many miles from the settlement and are the center of attention from the time they arrive to the time they leave. The most honorable function of the festival, the killing of the bear, is given to them. Led from yurta to yurta, they are fed to their content, and at their departure they are given the largest part of the bear's carcass.

All these honors and attentions are crowned by the serious religious ceremonials which sanction the fraternal alliance of the clans. At the beginning of the festival the *imgi* and their host exchange their *nits* (the symbol of economic cooperation for primitive man). These actions are not mere formalities; they strengthen the ties of relationship by the sanction of religious authority until they are fused into real kindred bonds. Upon their departure, *imgi* present to their *akhmalk* a dog which, together with the host's dogs, will be offered to the master of the mountains, the provider for the entire clan. The final ceremonial act is, once again, "stepping across the threshold." When a man has few clansmen or does not live on good terms with them, he leaves his native settlement and shifts his residence permanently to his *pandf*. That is why there are so few settlements inhabited by a single clan; everywhere the clansmen are mixed with their *imgi* and *akhmalk*. These ties are most important when the necessity for vengeance arises. In emergency cases, when a clan is weak gets involved in war, its *pandf* helps to "lift the bones" and to defend against the enemy. Only in the payment of *tkhusind* can the *pandf* not participate.

These matrimonial ties have even more significance in the reconciliation of hostile clans, especially if these clans belong to the same *pandf*. This is not a rare occurrence. We have already pointed out in our discussion of vengeance how the institution of fines and penalties arose due to the beneficent influence of women and the socioreligious ties linking the intermarrying clans.

Such are the relations between the *imgi* and *akhmalk* clans, relations which widen the horizon for the individual clan and extend its sympathies to a whole series of strange clans. It is a complete school of social education wherein one learns benevolence, hospitality and compassion, and social-moral behavior. Here are created those social habits and sentiments which finally extend over even larger tribal unions and eventually to mankind in general. Through our studies, we see that the term *navkh*, by which the corresponding generations of *imgi* and *akhmalk* address each other, finally became the ordinary term by which every Gilyak addresses a stranger.

The Gilyak show hospitality, compassion, and politeness to everyone without distinction, whether they be kin or strangers, whether they be old neighbors like the Orok, the Gold, and the Ainu, or newcomers like the Tungus, the Yakut, and even the Russians, who have done so much harm. Many times, fugitive convicts have slain entire Gilyak families after they had been shown the warmest hospitality. Yet it is very seldom that a Gilyak will refuse his hospitality to a wandering Russian. When it has been the case that Gilyaks have demonstrated cruelty to fugitives, it was considered no more than blood revenge for a slain kinsmen.[6] But isolated acts of this sort do little to change their attitudes toward strangers. Among Gilyak as among civilized peoples, of course there are national prejudices, but these arise from familiar patterns of ignorance that everywhere give rise to ideas and fears of a fantastic sort. Gilyak bear the same prejudices against even their own people living in remote locations. Hence, Gilyak of Sakhalin's northwestern shore look upon Gilyaks on the eastern shores of the Sea of Okhotsk as nothing short of cannibals, if not at least malevolent and thieving. In the same way, after the first invasion of the Cossacks in the 17th century, the Gilyak called the Russians *kinrsh* (the devil). The Cossacks gave them sufficient reason for this epithet, not only by their peculiar dress and weapons, but by their irrational cruelties and avidity for precious furs. Long after, when the Gilyak had met and lived with many peaceable Russians, they recalled their prejudices as anecdotes, and knew how to relate to their neighbors with great humanity [**60**].[7]

But we have wandered far from our main theme. Let us sum up.

The habits and sentiments we have observed among the modern Gilyak are a product of social relations worked out among intermarrying clans. They extended gradually over every tribesman, then over neighboring tribes, and finally over all mankind. But as we have seen, the source of these social ties between *imgi* and *akhmalk* is rooted in the astonishing organization of the Gilyak clan. It might be that the most instructive result of our long analysis is the evolution we have traced from the egotism of a closed clan, via the blood ties of *pandf*, to the sympathy and humanity the Gilyak demonstrate toward all, be they stranger or kin. From the moment when the right of marriage to the mother's brother's daughter was established, the foundation for the broad development of social habits and sentiments was laid.

---

6   The Gilyak regard Russian fugitives as a clan whose representatives answer for each other.

7   [***Editor's note:*** Several sentences from this paragraph, not found in the AMNH English typescript, have been imported from the AMNH Russian typescript.]

AFTERWORD: AFTERLIVES AND AFTERWORLDS
Nivkhi on *The Social Organization of the Gilyak,* 1995

BY *Bruce Grant*

BY THE ADVENT of World War II, the lives of most Gilyaks had changed dramatically. The Soviet government officially recognized the use of their self-designation, "Nivkh," and in the Soviet drive to create proletarians from primitives, the idea of "Gilyak" came to take on pejorative connotations of all things past. That the government embraced the name "Nivkh" as a hallmark of native self-determination, but simultaneously forbade Nivkhi to speak the Nivkh language, was only one of many contradictions between tradition and modernity that their belonging in the new Soviet Union had set before them.[1]

For the new Nivkh society, one of the greatest legacies of the post-World War II period was the widespread integration of women into the workforce. Before the war, efforts to recruit women into Sovietized native institutions such as clan councils foundered on the reluctance of Nivkh men and women alike. With the conscription of Nivkh and Russian men to the war front, women all over Sakhalin and the Amur had to take the work of the fishing collectives into their own hands. During my own fieldwork on Sakhalin in 1990, one woman explained to me,

> I was 10 when the war started. I had only been in school a year but our mother had no money, so I started working on the kolkhoz. There were other young girls, 13, 15, but I was 11—I was the youngest. It didn't seem so strange at the time. My mother had already been working on *Five Year Plan* [a fishing kolkhoz] hauling fish, so I worked with her. Now it's all

---

[1] For a sampling of thorough readings and surveys of nationality policy and language debates among peoples of the former Soviet Union, see Barbara Anderson and Brian Silver, "Equality, Efficiency and Politics in Soviet Bilingual Education Policy 1934–1980," *American Political Science Review* 78, no. 4 (October 1984), 1019–39; Gail Warshofsky Lapidus, "Ethnonationalism and Political Stability: The Soviet Case," *World Politics* 36, no. 4 (July 1984), 355–380; Teresa Rakowska-Harmstone, "The Dialectics of Nationalism in the USSR," *Problems of Communism* XXIII (May–June 1974), 1–22; Yuri Slezkine, *Arctic Mirrors: Russia and the Small Peoples of the North* (Ithaca, NY: Cornell Univ. Press, 1994); Graham Smith, ed. *The Nationalities Question in the Soviet Union* (New York: Longman, 1990); and Ronald Grigor Suny, *The Revenge of the Past: Nationalism, Revolution and the Collapse of the Soviet Union* (Stanford, CA: Stanford Univ. Press, 1993).

FIG. 23. World War II brought about the wide integration of Gilyak (Nivkh) women into the Soviet workplace. Here, a Nivkh postal carrier delivers the journal *Novoe Vremia* [*New Time*] in the northeastern coast village of Chaivo, 1950. Courtesy of the Sakhalin Regional Museum, Nogliki Branch.

mechanized, but back then it was hellish work. We had to pull in the fish nets by hand. Most of the times we didn't have gloves, out on the ice, pulling in nets that had been underwater. It really hurt, but if you let go you only had to pull them in again. We cried, we ran around . . . anything to keep warm. But we were pretty good.[2]

---

[2] Field quotations are taken from interviews I conducted in the North Sakhalin villages of Nogliki, Chir-Unvd, Okha, Moskal'vo, Nekrasovka, Rybnoe, Rybnovsk, and Romanovka between 1990 and 1995.

Another Nivkh woman explained,

> There were only 15 of us in our brigade, but we worked hard. There was
> another brigade of men, sailors, who sometimes tried to help, but they had
> a terrible time! They couldn't work as well as us. When the war ended I
> was only 19. That's when I became a Stakhanovets.[3] They gave us the
> award on August 31st, on the beach. Vorobev came from the *raiispolkom*
> [regional executive committee]. There were three of us from the women's
> brigade, and some men too. I still have the Stalin pin they gave me. I wear
> it on holidays.

The integration of women sped production as well as Soviet reeducation, and
the heady years after the war were marked by proclamations of economic triumph.
On the fishing kolkhoz Freedom in Lupolovo, the net intake per fisherman almost
doubled in the 3-year period between 1954 and 1957; in 1957 the kolkhoz overful-
filled its plan by 235%.[4] Projections through to the early 1960s on all North Sakhalin
fishing kolkhozes were comparably ambitious, and plans were approved to diversify
into fish processing. Whether these striking figures had any basis in fact is open to
question, but their importance here is the contribution they made to perceptions of
social development. By the time the Nivkh ethnographer Chuner Taksami hailed the
"renaissance of the Nivkh people," his work reflected the official position that
Gilyaks had made their great stride into history. Nivkh living standards had increased
by such an extent since the 1930s, he contended, that "they differed little from those
of the Russians."[5] Moreover, the new way of life had brought about fundamental
changes in Nivkh consciousness.

> New psychological characteristics developed which were typical of social-
> ist societies—political awareness, a socialist attitude to labor, Soviet patri-
> otism, trust and respect for other peoples and the feeling of civil obliga-
> tion toward the socialist homeland.[6]

The spirit of change was the order of the day, but there was still sufficient ambiguity in the implementation of the Soviet nationality policy for Nivkhi to maintain
some fundamental aspects of an otherwise familiar lifestyle: extensive fishing rights,
a seasonal work cycle, and, perhaps most importantly, residence in favorable territories. Yet despite such outward signs of change—shamans liquidated, languages
repressed, and towns relocated—most Nivkh men and women in the first decades
after the war could speak of the shadow lives they might have lived. If Nivkh women
who began working as fish processors and office clerks invariably reported that they
married for love, they could also tell you of the "men they might have married *if*,"

---

[3] Stakhanovites were members of a movement that began in 1935 to raise labor productivity.
Soviet government image makers credited Aleksei Stakhanov, the eponymous worker hero,
with record production figures in coal mining, establishing him as an icon for exemplary performance in industry.

[4] Chuner Mikhailovich Taksami, *Vozrozhdenie nivkhskoi narodnosti* (Iuzhno-Sakhalinsk:
Sakhalinskoe knizhnoe izdatel'stvo, 1959), 47.

[5] Ibid., 51.

[6] Ibid., 60.

the men to whom they were pledged by clan marriage rules at childbirth, arrangements that they later declined but did not forget.

In the late 1950s and early 1960s, many of these essential familiarities shifted in yet another round of state-sponsored resettlements, which they had been subject to since the regular arrival of the Russians a century earlier. In 1957, the Central Committee of the Communist Party and the Soviet Council of Ministers adopted Decree No. 300, "On Measures for the Further Economic and Cultural Development of Peoples of the North." The initiative was intended to redress what had been 20 years of a policy vacuum in native affairs since the dissolution of the Committee of the North. However, in practice the decree was overshadowed by a seemingly unrelated resolution introduced by Khrushchev on the strengthening of collective and state farms. The idea was that fewer settlements would mean fewer problems of coordination and distribution.

On North Sakhalin there had already been a series of village closings and kolkhoz relocations following World War II, after Japan relinquished South Sakhalin and the Soviets sought to lay claim to the new territory as quickly as possible. The scourge of the resettlements in the 1960s, however, was that in almost every case when one kolkhoz had to be selected from among many for expansion, the least profitable enterprises on the least profitable sites were chosen. Indeed, the only criteria for selecting which communities to expand and which to close appear to have been proximity to existing regional centers and the consequent ease of administration. But there was a further dimension congruent with the larger goal of reducing the difference between cultural identities across the country. As one Soviet state planner wrote,

> The creation of concentrated villages in northern native areas goes hand in hand with the raising of their social and cultural potential, the creation of new forms of housing and the mastery of non-traditional types of work: all this leads to a change in their ethnic self-consciousness. For these national minorities, life in multiethnic, multilingual villages and labor collectives is connected with the need for preserving their "ethnic identity," their roots and their cultural self-respect. In other words, the accelerated development of an international way of life and the transformation of traditional cultures into socialist ones sharpens rather than weakens the need for recognizing the diversity of national cultures.[7]

For many Nivkhi, these latest moves and village closings were the most visible and sobering indication of how much and how quickly their lives had changed. On Sakhalin's northwestern and northeastern coasts, the number of villages lining the shore between 1905 and 1975 dropped by more than 75%.

Across Sakhalin, the resettlement procedure was one of incremental withdrawal. The younger generations were usually the first to accede to the offers of better housing elsewhere, while among the older generations and the hesitant, party

---

[7]   Anatolii Panteleevich Derevianko and Vladimir Ivanovich Boiko, "Puti kul'turnogo razvitiia Sibiri," *in* V. I. Boiko, ed., *Kul'tura narodnostei Severa: traditsii i sovremennost'* (Novosibirsk, Nauka, 1986), 11.

members would be obligated to relocate. The school would be moved, thereby forcing parents with children to follow, and then the hospital, then the village soviet, then the post office, then the store, and then the electricity. As one former Nivkh kolkhoz director explained from his home in the new agrocenter, where he lived in 1990,

> Of course, people didn't want to leave. Here there isn't the same kind of fish. There you'll find everything. Those that didn't want to go stayed behind. But how can you stay behind if there is no kolkhoz any longer? No school? No store? So you move.

The same story is repeated again and again. A Russian farmer on North Sakhalin began with a list when I asked him about where he used to live.

> The 1960s were a turning point for us, when they began the closings. They closed the Shirokopadskii plant. There were five villages in that area and all five were closed. That's five villages that automatically lost their reason for existence. The Khoenskii kombinat was closed, that was another six villages.

> Here in the northwest we had the villages of Tuzrik, Viski, Astrakhanovka, Nevel'skaia, Uspenovka, Liugi, Kefi, Naumovka, Grigor'evka, Kalinovka, Valuska, Third Station, Fourth Station, Romanovka, Lupolovo, Tengi, Pogibi . . . and all the rest around there . . . all gone!

Yet, to cast the moves in a roundly negative light would not be accurate. For most of those involved, only in retrospect has the resettlement program come to be so rued. At the time, the plan met with few incidents of overt resistance. Most people interpreted the decision as official policy and assumed that it would be for the best. As one Nogliki resident remarked in 1990, "The tragedy is that nothing happened. The empty houses in Nogliki were all ready. The kolkhoz had already been built. Most people just got up and moved. That's the tragedy—that there was no tragedy."

Indeed, what sets the 1960s resettlements apart from those that immediately followed World War II was the absence of economic virtue. By 1968, Nogliki's newly reconstituted fishery *East* was palpably failing: debt was increasing, plans were not being fulfilled, and the kolkhoz recommended more expeditions further afield, namely, back to the villages of Pil'tun and Chaivo, which had been closed 10 years before.[8] At both *East* and the northwestern Sakhalin fishery *Red Dawn*, the average fish catches were four times lower than the regional average, while the median kolkhoz salaries were two and a half times lower.[9] In 1969, when residents of the defunct town of Venskoe complained in a letter to the Sakhalin Regional Executive Committee [*oblispolkom*] that they had been moved involuntarily, the *oblispolkom* claimed otherwise. "People wanted to move to Nogliki immediately," they argued; there was little interest in traditional life, and the authors of the letter, "the majority of whom were elderly and illiterate," did not fully understand its contents. Chuner Taksami,

---

[8]   GASO f. 53, o. 25, d. 3897a, ll. 101–104.
[9]   Ibid., l. 30.

FIG. 24. Nivkh (Gilyak) students at a parade in Nogliki, Sakhalin Island, 1970. Courtesy of the Sakhalin Regional Museum, Nogliki Branch.

himself an ethnographer, a Nivkh living in Leningrad, and the organizer of the Venskoe letter, was chided for his "incorrect, subjective approach . . . which, advocating the preservation of 'northern peoples as children of nature,' was only representing obsolete customs, morals and way of life."[10] The committee's response coincided with the recasting of the broader Soviet nationality policy at that time, whereby Nivkhi were to have bloomed [*rastsveli*], drawn closer to Russian culture [*sblizili*], and finally merged with it [*slili*].[11] However, the persistence of expressly Nivkh

---

10 Ibid., d. 3897, ll. 4–6.
11 For a discussion of this three-step process, see Yaroslav Bilinsky, "The Concept of the Soviet People and Its Implications for Soviet Nationality Policy," *The Annals of the Ukrainian Academy of Arts and Science in the United States*, no. 37–38 (1980); Gail Warshofsky Lapidus, "Ethnonationalism"; and *Rastsvet i sblizhenie natsii v SSSR* (Moscow: Mysl', 1981). Lapidus is right to point out that by the "time of stagnation" most Soviets had long given up the idea of ethnic merger. What interests me here are the contradictions of a policy that continued to be advocated long after it lost its salience.

cultural forms (language, dress, and diet) underlined the contradictions of the official position: traditional life was at once to be lauded (as a marker of the freedom of peoples) and suppressed (as a lingering resistance to abstract notions of Soviet homogeneity).

The resettlements, rather than representing a merger of collective interests, reduced the Nivkhi to second-class status. In the shuffle of kolkhoz reorganizations, Russians supplanted Nivkhi in the vast majority of skilled and administrative positions. In 1968, despite *East*'s status as a Nivkh kolkhoz, only 19% of Nivkhi in the collective worked in skilled positions, and few were being trained for promotion.[12] Figures show that overall kolkhoz membership dropped sharply with the moves, whereas there was a marked increase in unemployment and underemployment for the Nivkh community. Many who were unable to find work in the towns to which they relocated lost their pensions and state benefits. Despite the proposals set forth in Decree No. 300, the new *East* was in disarray. The medical clinic was not being funded, bath facilities were not functioning, and there was no work being done to address growing rates of alcoholism and illiteracy.[13] Of particular consequence was the introduction of regulations governing the amount of salmon Nivkhi were entitled to catch each year. Through the 1950s, the Nivkh diet was still heavily based on salmon: individuals consumed on the average up to 1000 kg each year (much of it in dried form), an amount far beyond that which could be afforded in local stores. In 1962, an annual limit of 200 kg was imposed, and in 1969, with concern for ever-weakening kolkhoz production, the limit was further reduced to 60 kg. If Nivkhi had joined the Soviet family of nations, it was reasoned, there was no cause for them to be treated exceptionally. In 1963, when the Russian Ministry of Education sent a letter to the Sakhalin *oblispolkom* requesting that they outline their needs for native language education, Iuzhno-Sakhalinsk responded that native languages in the region were not studied due to lack of interest.[14]

What made the 1960s resettlements so compelling was not only the attendant drop in quality of living for the indigenous community but the way in which they visually transformed the Sakhalin landscape. Coastlines that were once lined with villages every 10 km became littered with ghost towns. Between 1962 and 1986, the approximately 1000 settlements on all of Sakhalin were reduced to 329.[15] Rather than strengthening and internationalizing, the resettlements produced a spirit of absence felt on economic, social, and personal levels. Rather than moving forward, they generated a retrospective force that pulled many back. The brigadier from Chaivo remained behind when all of *East* was transferred to Nogliki. By 1970 he was the only one of 700 remaining, and to this day he visits Nogliki only a few months each year. Remaining behind in empty towns that no longer officially existed, he and others like him became icons of a "traditional" way of life that had become reified and reinforced by a policy expressly designed to diminish it. In creating a spatial dichoto-

---

12 GASO, f. 53, o. 25, d. 3897, 73.
13 Ibid., d. 3897a, ll. 72–78.
14 Ibid., d. 3584, l. 44.
15 A. I. Gladyshev, ed. *Administrativno-territorial'noe delenie sakhalinskoi oblasti* (Iuzhno-Sakhalinsk: Dal'nevostochnoe knizhnoe izdatel'stvo, 1986), 79–106, 125.

my between past and present, the resettlements divided allegiances by obliging people to choose (and in most cases making the choice for them).

The fortunes of both *Red Dawn* and *East* continued to decline, with the worsening ecological situation and growing bureaucratic regulations causing a drop in fish catches. Before the collapse of the former Soviet Union, both kolkhozes had "national" status, meaning they received special incentives and allowances as largely indigenous enterprises, but by 1982, Nivkhi comprised only 120 out of the 336 members of *East* and only 127 out of 400 members of *Red Dawn*.[16] In 1980, a further decree, "On Measures for the Further Economic and Social Development of the Peoples of the North," was enacted by the Soviet Council of Ministers. The government spent an enormous amount of money in the implementation of the decree—31.2 billion rubles by 1990, or 169,125 rubles for every indigenous representative in Siberia,[17] over a period when monthly salaries averaged 500 rubles. However, the Nivkh writer Vladimir Sangi, who helped draft the decree, noted ruefully that the funds intended for the cultural and economic development of the Nivkhi were spent by local authorities to purchase oil pipes, automobiles, thousands of pairs of plastic skis, typewriters, calculators and compact toilets.[18]

By the late 1980s, the retrospective assessment for Siberian peoples as a whole had little to say for the virtues of internationalization.

> The results of sixty years worth of development are not very comforting: from highly qualified reindeer herders, hunters and fishermen, native northerners have been transformed into auxiliary workers, loaders, watchmen and janitors.[19]

Public health statistics from recent years indicate the extent to which decades of required self-congratulation obscured considerable problems. In 1988, the life expectancy for Siberian indigenous peoples was 18 years lower than that for the USSR as a whole—45 years for men and 55 years for women. Social problems such as alcoholism and suicide were four to five times as high as in the rest of the country, and few native communities had acquired the trappings of much-advertised convenience: The housing base had changed little since the 1950s; only 3% of native homes had access to gas mains; 0.4% had running water, and only 0.1% were connected to district heating systems.[20] By the late 1980s, the population of Sakhalin had grown to 800,000, with Nivkhi making up a diminutive group of some 2200 fishermen, farmers, clerks, and service workers (2800 Nivkhi live on the Amur delta). Yet for all the

---

16 Igor' Krupnik and Anna Vasil'evna Smoliak, "Sovremennoe polozhenie korennogo naseleniia severa sakhalinskoi oblasti" [dokladnaia zapiska po materialam poezdki s sentiabria 1982 g.] (Moscow: Institute of Ethnography), 7.

17 Zoia Petrovna Sokolova, "Narody severa SSSR: proshloe, nastoiashchee i budushchee," *Sovetskaia Etnografiia* 6 (1990), 19.

18 Aleksandr Ivanovich Pika and Boris Borisovich Prokhorov, "Bol'shie problemy malykh narodov," *Kommunist* 16 (November 1988), 81.

19 Pika, "Malye narody severa: iz pervobytnogo kommunizma v real'nyi sotsializm," in *Perestroika, Glasnost', Demokratiia, Sotsializm: V chelovecheskom izmerenii* (Moscow: Progress), 306.

20 Ibid.

transformations Nivkhi took part in, their image as the most famous primitives who passed up cave life for Communism is one they encounter still. While I was sitting with a Nivkh family watching television one night in Okha in 1990, a Russian official being interviewed on television in Moscow looked back on the history of Soviet medicine and said, "You have to understand the difficulties posed by a country as diverse as ours. In 1917, Nivkhi were living in caves and Russians were in palaces." The irony that cave life is the first image most Russians have for a group of people who were far more cosmopolitan, far more Asian, and far less isolated geographically *before* Russians arrived to colonize them was rarely noted in popular discourse. Though Nivkhi have never lived the lives of prosaic penury or purity that generations of writers have assigned to them, their long-standing hold on the Russian imagination as the quintessential primitives of pre-Communist life had lost little of its vigor.

* * * * *

When I first went to Sakhalin Island in 1990, it was 100 years after Shternberg had first arrived. My interests were in wanting to explore the Nivkh experience over the Soviet period, particularly from the vantage point of the state's efforts to colonize, resettle, and, in turn, proletarianize the "primitive Communist" northern peoples that had been at the heart of so much early Soviet social engineering. Despite the fact that Shternberg never wrote on Gilyak Sovietization, his presence was a milestone in conversations about lives past. A constant ritual during my field trips was to begin questions with, "Shternberg once wrote that . . ." or "What do you think Shternberg meant when . . . ?" It was, for myself, one of the few ways in which I could bring to life a seemingly previous Nivkh world recorded at the dawn of the Soviet period, a world that seemed, at least to myself, so alien to Nivkh life at the Soviet period's close.

During the first 6 months I spent on Sakhalin in 1990, my fieldwork charted the retrospection that so many Nivkhi and Russians alike found so absorbing as the USSR was devolving so unexpectedly before their eyes. During a second trip in 1992, the public mood had changed further still, where, by contrast, the past seemed to count only inasmuch as it meant something useful. The Soviet Union had become the Russian Republic, and people were scrambling to secure a position for themselves amidst the political and economic mayhem. On expressly Nivkh fronts, the past played a key role in the way people could regain their former homes. Aided by a decree from Yeltsin, Sakhalin had embarked on a system of "clan plots" for Nivkhi [*rodovye khoziaistva*], whereby Nivkh families could return to areas they once lived in to start up their own fishing and processing enterprises.[21] In most cases, the tie to clan affiliation was tenuous—the majority of Nivkhi could not identify their clan status, but consulted monographs by Shternberg and later Soviet ethnographers to iden-

---

[21] Presidential Decree No. 397, 22 April 1992, "O neotlozhnykh merakh po zashchite mest prozhivaniia i khoziaistvennoi deiatel'nosti malochislennykh narodov Severa," stipulated that free land be allotted on a permanent basis to northern native peoples for traditional land use. Peoples of the north would have a voting role in the distribution of licenses issued on this land for fishing, hunting, and other resource-related pursuits.

tify the leading clan from the village where they or their parents grew up.[22] The average allotment was 20 square hectares. Originally the land was intended to be given in perpetuity as private property, but reluctant local officials intervened and leased it on time-limited arrangements. By August 1992, 36 plots had been claimed.[23] Some families had returned to the abandoned village sites of their youth and looked upon the property as subsistence operations for their families. Others sought formal sponsors such as the Sakhalin Geological Trust to make bigger profits. In the latter cases, some had taken out colossal loans of up to 200,000 rubles only to discover by the time the money was disbursed that it was no longer worth as much as they needed. But the enterprises had drawn Nivkh men and women into a form of independent activity they had not known since before World War II. Nivkh friends in Okha, in whose homes I had once spent many long, quiet evenings, had now stepped up the usual barter trading into a frenzy of exchange: 20 kg of fish for two crates of beer, two sacks of sugar for 10 sacks of salt, 1 ton of gasoline for 50 kg of mutton, . . . cars for apartments, refrigerators for motorcycles, a case of vodka for telephone installation, . . . and on and on. At a time when money did not necessarily make someone rich, exchange could.[24]

In the drive for new clan plots, as in almost all other areas of Nivkh authority, women led the way. If one factor stood out to me the most in thinking of all the changes that had taken place since Shternberg's time on Sakhalin, it was the reversals of fortune in all matters of gender and authority. In local administration, in government, in teaching, and in economic life, Nivkh women consistently held the higher paying jobs and the positions of greater influence. History and demography could explain part of the imbalance: In the 1930s, when the Stalinist juggernaut swept across Sakhalin, officials predominantly targeted Nivkh men as opposed to women for persecution. Nivkh men who had traded widely with Chinese and Japanese entrepreneurs before 1925 became easy targets for the xenophobia sweeping the country; relatively few Nivkh women had entered the Soviet workforce at all before World War II. In 1937 alone, state police liquidated one third of all Nivkh men on Sakhalin's northwestern shore, approximately 200 from a combined population of 1200 men and women.[25] One result many decades later is that when I was looking for people who could help think through Shternberg, who knew Nivkh tradition best, I knew few Nivkh men I could ask. Wanting to see how Nivkh friends and colleagues responded to *Social Organization* 100 years later, I mailed copies of a Russian version to eight Nivkh women months before I went to Sakhalin for the summer in 1995.[26]

* * * * *

[22] The most popular handbooks were Kreinovich's *Nivkhgu* and Anna Smoliak, "Rodovoi sostav nivkhov."
[23] Andrei Vladimirov, "Rodovye khoziaistva: vozvrashchenie k istokam," *Svobodnyi Sakhalin* (9 July 1992), 7.
[24] For a look at the role of barter in Siberia during the same period, see Caroline Humphrey, " 'Icebergs', Barter, and the Mafia in Provincial Russia," *Anthropology Today* 7, no. 2 (1991), 8–14.
[25] Medvedev, "Politiko-ekonomicheskaia kharakteristika "Rybnovskogo raiona Sakhalinskoi oblasti," GASO ll. 4ob–5ob.
[26] The text was from Shternberg, *Sem'ia.*

Russia's economic problems since its reincarnation in 1992 have been well known, and 3 years later, Sakhalin Island, despite its wealth of oil, fish, and timber resources, was no exception. As across Russia, galloping inflation on Sakhalin and the turtlelike pace of most salary increases left huge portions of the population in an almost moneyless circuit of exchange. Most social programs were on the ropes, and the salary lags that began in 1991 continued apace through 1995. Many Nivkh fishermen had not been paid for over 12 months; occasional fish and flour rations were their only compensation. Financial collapse had scuttled new native land use proposals and native trading workshops, but perhaps more indicatively, even many of the best funded projects had foundered on the shoals of mismanagement. A long-awaited road construction project meant to help revive two closed villages on Sakhalin's northwestern shore expired after only 8 of its 22 km had been laid, the rest of the cash lost to theft. In many ways there was nothing new to this: State funds dedicated to the "peoples of the north" have long occasioned feeding frenzies in local Sakhalin offices, as across Siberia and the Russian Far East.[27] What seemed different was that the misuse of funds was becoming more open. Hence, for 1994, in Nogliki alone, the district executive council redirected monies that had been committed to indigenous projects, instead, to the building of a city dental clinic, a dormitory at the local hot springs, and a House of Culture for Oil and Railroad Workers.

Money—earned, begged, borrowed, or stolen—was the driving force behind most people's fates, a trend that can be broadly mapped out for most Siberian native peoples in the post-Soviet era. New political platforms abounded while financial and political resources, never broad to begin with, were a fraction of what they once were. In 1995, while one could point to promising local and federal decrees pertaining to Nivkh rights (such as the "Decree of the State Duma on the Critical Economic and Cultural Position of the Numerically Small Indigenous Peoples of the North, Siberia and the Far East of the Russian Federation" or "The Findings of the Committee of the Federation Council for Northern Affairs on the Federal Budget Plan for 1995"), these signaled the idea of an unfunded mandate more than a promise of intent.[28] While money continued to support small offices of native affairs scattered around the island, Sakhalin parliamentarians repeatedly blocked the creation of a more streamlined Native Affairs directorate.[29]

With the play of the free market and the unusually high costs of transport transforming the country, Siberian communities have been among the hardest hit by industries and suppliers no longer impelled by the ideological demands of providing services to the residents of the country's most remote corners. The small coastal settlement of Rybnoe, for example, a town of 250 people where I first based my field research, thrived for decades throughout the Soviet period with a large fishery, a store, a post office, electricity, and a handful of other amenities—though no road to

---

[27] See, for example, Vladimir Sangi in Aleksandr Pika and Boris Prokhorov, "Bol'shie problemy," 76–83.

[28] Aleksandr Pika, *Neotraditsionalizm na Rossiiskom Severe* (Moscow: Akademiia Nauk, 1994), 3.

[29] B. Osokin, "Programma predpologaet, chinovnik raspologaet . . . ," *Sovetskii Sakhalin* (July 27, 1995).

speak of, despite being only 200 km away along flat land from the regional center. Residents regularly took helicopters to do errands in town, and all other necessities came by boat.

Only 5 years later, in 1995, life was radically altered. Because suppliers refused to attend to distant communities, food stores such as the one in Rybnoe folded. Claiming penury, the government closed down phone and postal service except for the most minimal monthly mail deliveries. Schools folded for want of funds, sending Nivkh children back to the centralized boarding school system of *internaty* if they could afford it. In an age of rebuilding, the historical irony observed by many was that this new round of closures was replaying the Brezhnevian relocations gauntlet of the 1960s.

Despite these man-made changes, it was perhaps only through a series of natural disasters that the more trenchant aspects of state collapse became the most apparent. In November 1994, a pounding typhoon swept over northwestern Sakhalin. In Rybnoe, the storm leveled the kolkhoz, the post office, and the day care center, knocking over power lines, washing away the mountain of coal set to heat homes for the winter, and drowning the village's basement food supplies of potatoes and salted salmon. Potatoes immediately became one of North Sakhalin's most expensive commodities, turning almost everyone I knew into consumers of the cheaper instant mashed potato flakes newly available through Korean wholesalers.

Despite the fact that the wooden flotsam of this sea disaster lay everywhere, the government's one form of compensation to the battered coastline was to supply heating oil to all communities. In Rybnoe's case, this lasted until February, when the village *traktorist* unknowingly drove his tanklike all-terrain vehicle over the oil pipes late one night, leaving 85 tons of oil to drain onto the village square and down the beach into the Tatar Strait. As a consequence, almost all of the coastline's 1995 fish catches became heavily tainted by petroleum. To complement the instant potatoes that had replaced North Sakhalin's only vegetable source, the choice of available fish became one of excessively salted or excessively toxic, a choice that had to be made three times daily with some gravity.

Despite receiving humanitarian aid from typhoon-sympathetic Vietnam, consisting primarily of rugs and track suits, which North Sakhalin officials sold in town markets, the coast was in a state of remarkable crisis. We could see in Rybnoe a version of what was happening in much of rural Siberia and the Russian Far East: With no electricity, no transportation, no heating, and no communication, social services folded, stores closed, and schools moved.

The attendant transformations in daily life around the island were manifold. In the capital of Iuzhno-Sakhalinsk, a city of a quarter million, as well as in the regional towns of Nogliki and Okha, the exodus of people back to the mainland was a reminder of how many people had come to the island for the riches of accelerated pensions accrued from jobs in the fishing and oil industries.[30] The people who could leave were packing up, but what of the people who couldn't leave?

---

[30] V. Kozyniuk discusses related demographics in, "Ostrova teriaiut, materik nakhodit," *Sovetskii Sakhalin* (April 12, 1996), 2.

Rybnoe, diminished to 150 people, was a showcase for the obvious effects of the typhoon. Huge logs lay strewn across the buildings of the fishery. In the main work pavilion, the ventilation system lay crushed, exposed wires lay everywhere, and grass grew from cracks along the walls. As there was no longer a fishery to run, the remaining staff of the kolkhoz relocated their desks to the mayor's office, where, without light, heat, telephone, or a school, the mayor, the mayor's secretary, and the former kolkhoz director, in scenes reminiscent of *Waiting for Godot,* kept daily watch over pots of ink, subscriptions for newspapers rarely delivered, and the occasional sight of neighbors passing by the window.

Young men who once lived for their motorcycles had switched to horses for want of gasoline, and the three horses that had once wandered the shore were constantly in one's field of vision as they drew carts across the main square. Candles, which had risen in price to $1 each in a community where many had little to live on but tea, potato flakes, and tainted fish, had ceded in popularity to kerosene lamps. The daily experience of crossing the town square was enough to make one feel more like an archaeologist than a pedestrian.

What seemed so profoundly at stake with the loss of the fishing kolkhoz was the dissolution of the state's presence. For a remote community that had been largely self-policing for its 100 years of existence, the figurative and literal collapse of the kolkhoz effectively unraveled a blanket of state protection: It no longer offered technical support for home repairs, transport, and a legion of social services under its aegis, such as the school, day care center, health clinic, library, and dormitory. Likewise, in the larger neighboring towns of Rybnovsk, Nekrasovka, and Moskal'vo, fishing and shipping operations ground to a halt, and the tenor of life was coming to border on suspended animation.

The damage to the northwestern coast was enough to move most of the Nivkhi I knew to a ponderous mood, but the key event that was occurring around each of the interviews here was a much starker one. Eight months after the typhoon, shortly after my own arrival in May, some 2100 people in the North Sakhalin town of Neftegorsk (population 3000) died overnight in a jarring 7. 5 earthquake. Two weeks of efforts to relieve survivors took place amidst looting and the widespread theft of corpses, which were taken in order to qualify for funeral monies for lost family members.[31] The traffic in other people's remains and the ensuing mayhem evoked scenes from Gogol's *Dead Souls.* To put an end to the confusion, the government soon detonated the town's remaining buildings and plowed over the land, leaving empty fields 5 weeks after the quake. If Nivkhi and Russians on North Sakhalin were expecting little redress for their problems before June of that year, they were expecting even less thereafter.

What the earthquake had laid bare was something many people on the island already recognized—a state apparatus increasingly less interested in lives of its residents. It seemed in the briefest way to crystallize the process that had been taking

---

[31] *Sakhalinskii Neftianik,* May 29–June 8, 1995, *passim.* Igor Marzhetto summarizes the problems related to distribution of compensation in, "Neftegorsk krichal troe sutok," *Argumenty i Fakty* 25, no. 766 (June 1995), 5.

place across Siberia and the Russian Far East, that easterly nether zone to which so many Soviets of all nationalities, decades earlier, had been recruited to build a new frontier. After decades of the most concerted efforts to settle Sakhalin as quickly as possible, building it to a population of 800,000 by 1989, the government had changed its mind. People had to go. On May 31st, 3 days after the Neftegorsk collapse, Deputy Prime Minister Oleg Soskovets arrived to survey the damage and assert a federal presence. On television and in print interviews, he announced to local residents, "Clearly this part of the country is not fit for human habitation . . . . In the government, we are looking into every effort to transform North Sakhalin's economy onto a shift regime [*vakhtovyi metod*] in order to give priority to resource development."[32] Only 4 years previously the government had still been aggressively courting newcomers.

Thinking about Soskovets' pronouncement, I remembered Marx's line from *The Economic and Philosophical Manuscripts of 1844*, charting early capitalism's first realization about its constituents—that there are, in short, too many:

> Needlessness as the principle of political economy is most brilliantly shown in its theory of population. There are too many people. Even the existence of men is considered a pure luxury; and if the worker is ethical, he will be sparing in procreation.[33]

In an ominous turn for the Sakhalin economy, what became clear was the government's decision that the local population, which it had so ardently recruited, now constituted a hindrance to free market principles and resource harvesting. There were too many people who expected too much.

Speaking to people across the island, I realized that the policy had been in effect for much of 1995. While salaries had not been paid in most cases for 3–6 months, anyone could receive their entire docket of back pay when they handed in their resident permits [*propiski*] with the promise of leaving. And so, within a month of the earthquake, in the regional town of Okha, 50 km away from what remained of Neftegorsk, over 1000 of the town's population of 30,000, spurred by fear, faith, and finance, forfeited their residence permits and returned to the mainland.

In a strikingly grim atmosphere, Nivkhi I knew often greeted this situation with some irony, joking, "Well look, we don't have anywhere to go. This means we'll have more room." But for their own part, prospects for improving the lives of the island's residents, alleviating ethnic discrimination, or entrenching a federalist sentiment in this far corner of the state held little of their original promise from 5 years previous. The level of disaffection with the central government amidst these shifts would be difficult to overestimate. But it also goes a certain way toward explaining a daily language where worlds receded, from Gilyak pasts to Soviet pasts and the moments where they met in conjuncture, fed conversation.

[32] ITAR-TASS, *in Sakhalinskii Neftianik* (June 1, 1995), 1.
[33] Karl Marx, *The Economic and Philosophical Manuscripts of 1844* (New York: International Publishers, 1964), 152.

I. RIMA PETROVNA KHAILOVA AND ZOIA IVANOVNA LIUTOVA[34]
Nekrasovka, June 5, 1995

The working session with Rima Petrovna Khailova and Zoia Ivanovna Liutova took place in the North Sakhalin town of Nekrasovka, one of the four main agrocenters to which the government relocated Sakhalin Nivkhi in the 1960s. The Nivkh writer Vladimir Sangi once described Nekrasovka as Sakhalin's premier "Potemkin village," in the tradition of exemplary show towns that lined the route of Catherine the Great every time she traveled between Moscow and St. Petersburg. (When the Canadian Northern Affairs minister visited Nekrasovka on an official tour in 1985, Sakhalin officials used huge tarpaulins to cover more than a dozen crumbling buildings on the main street to keep them from view.) Khailova lives in Nekrasovka, editing the small Nivkh language monthly newspaper, *Nivkh Dif*. Zoia Ivanovna Liutova ran the Nekrasovka library before retiring in 1993. The conversation had begun with talk of the Neftegorsk earthquake.

GRANT: Since we are covering maudlin topics like Neftegorsk, why not take one moment from Shternberg's text, about suicide. In [*Social Organization*] we get examples of the suicide of lovers who had transgressed the rules of marriage. Did that ever happen in your lifetime, or was it something that your parents talked about?

KHAILOVA: You know . . . in my own family, I lost my oldest brother when he committed suicide at age 17. My parents said later that it was probably unrequited love, but I thought that it was just because there were no girls for him to marry. But I was only 6 at the time. This was all told to me later.

Right, he shot himself. It was in the spring, in May. He shot himself in the school, the *internat* [state boarding school]. My father had to go up to fetch him—he took the dog sled since there was still snow then. Today we look upon 17 year-olds as teenagers, but then he would have been an adult. He was already hunting and was familiar with guns. He would take care of the dogs, and have things to do around the house. He could have married.

There are women who commit suicide, so many young people do today. One of my cousins, in the 1950s, was a little off. He went down into the basement of his house and slit his wrists. No, wait, he shot himself. My relatives mostly seem to shoot themselves. It's such a horrible matter. This was so long ago and I've since grown up, but I remember it all so clearly. The village council office wouldn't even let us put a marker over the grave, or bury him along with everyone else in the general cemetery. Even Soviet officials have their superstitions!

GRANT: There was one incident in [Shternberg's] manuscript recalling a fellow who had not been properly buried by Nivkh tradition, and exacted a revenge on his living relatives for not having taken care of him properly. [Our common acquaintance] Shura told me about one fellow who was working on an oil rig in the taiga a few years

---

[34] Each of the interviews here was conducted in Russian. I have edited out sections for brevity but have retained the sequence of the discussions. Vertical spaces indicate a break in the interviews, or simply a change of subject.

ago, Sergei-someone. A helicopter dropped him off at his site, but it turns out they had left him in the wrong place, and he was never found again.

LIUTOVA: Vykhtin.

GRANT: Shura was helping me read the text aloud to work on the translation, and when we got to that part she turned white. Apparently in the year after he got lost in the taiga, his older brother drowned, and his father had a heart attack.

KHAILOVA: I can't tell you about that case, because we truly don't know what happened to Sergei. But, at the same time, of course, it surprised her. What do we know about Shternberg in the first place? What do we know about ourselves? I remember when she phoned me to say that you had mailed her a copy of [the Shternberg] book. I said "Great, let's make copies," because we have never read these things before. We would sooner be able to tell you the finer points of Russian history than something about Nivkh legends.

* * * * *

GRANT: I want to talk about spirits for a moment. Shternberg refers to them throughout the text as almost self-evident forces in Nivkh life. On eastern Sakhalin they are called *milk* and [here] on western Sakhalin they're called *kinz*. So who are *kinz*, and what do they do?

LIUTOVA: I remember so often when we were young. My parents would say, "*Kinz* are coming," and we would be so scared. They would scare us all the time.

KHAILOVA: Well, scared or not scared, the important thing was that you were supposed to conduct yourself properly so that you didn't bother the *kinz*. You know, if someone was sitting there who you couldn't see, or when you went into the forest, you would know that there would be a *kinz* there.

LIUTOVA: Or for example, children couldn't play near the water, where *kinz* also live, since that could be dangerous.

GRANT: Do you still tell your own children or grandchildren not to play near the *kinz*?

LIUTOVA: Don't forget, we've become atheists!

GRANT: Sure, but people all around the world say those kinds of things to their children in order to keep them out of trouble.

KHAILOVA: Right, and we do the same in Russian with Russian fairy tales. But there is an important idea that not everyone passes on to their children, and this is that all of nature has its own master. It's all gotten mixed up with the larger idea of there once being four Masters (*yz*), you know, of the water, and the hills, and the sky, and fire. Most often their influence is felt in a negative way—that if you trouble them, they will trouble you—but it doesn't have to be negative. The idea of a *kinz* is a simple one: Every living thing has its spirit, and that people live there. If you see your child striking a bush, you can say, "There are people living there, let them be." Better still, you feed the bush, or the fire, or the water; you go back in the evening and leave them an offering.

GRANT: What reasons would there be for *kinz* to strike out at someone?

KHAILOVA: In what sense? I mean, there are different kinds of rituals. For carelessness toward the sea, or when you're in the forest, or even with the earthquake from last week. My first reaction [to the earthquake] was, "Maybe we've done something." So I got up the next day and got my neighbor Svetlana and said, "Let's go into the forest." It was early in the morning. We went out and went behind the building into the brush and, you know, fed the land with food and tobacco. Meanwhile, there were Russian women on their way to work in their vegetable gardens. There's the difference between us!

When I went to Neftegorsk [the earthquake zone] a few days ago, I did the same thing. I went to a quiet untouched place and left an offering for the land. The land has obviously suffered terribly in ways we don't even know. It's deeply ingrained in our blood that one must do this wherever you go, especially in a new place. I did it for the land and for the people who had died, but you also do it for your children and their children, for the people who will follow after you so that they will be welcomed there as well.

GRANT: I was so taken aback when I read about the master of thunder who lives at the bottom of the Tatar Strait around Pogibi. People there tell you all the time about the famously brutal project Stalin organized, for a tunnel to be dug underneath the strait to connect the island to the mainland. The strait is only 7 km wide between Pogibi and Lazarev. The crews got almost halfway over from each side, 3 km from each shore, and then one day, "Boom." There was this enormous explosion and it all caved in. Imagine that moment.

KHAILOVA: They woke him up.

About *kinz*, I could try it a different way. At home when I was growing up, there were so many difficult times. Once my older sister tried to hang herself. She had gone into the forest, and my mother simply started to feel that something was strange. My sister was married and had two children and had gone with the children into the forest. So my mother went after her, and found my sister already hanging there, but she was still alive. She cut her down and brought her home and everything. Then they cut down the tree and sawed it right off at the base. And the path to the tree they blocked off so that she wouldn't be able to return there easily. When she wanted to even move in that direction she had trouble physically moving her legs. And my mother said, "That's the *kinz* scaring her away from there." So you see, *kinz* can also protect you from things, even if they frighten you.

GRANT: Do you know why she wanted to kill herself?

KHAILOVA: What can you say? Things weren't going that well with her husband. They had been separated. He was working not that far away on another kolkhoz, cutting hay. It was only 12 km away, but that was still a few hours' walk then. He came by to check on her after the accident, but she was already better by then.

GRANT: How do you figure out that [*kinz*] are there?

KHAILOVA: That brings us back to how you raise children. Maybe my mother was just afraid of what else could have happened at [my sister's suicide attempt]. I think of *kinz* as a way of keeping people from wreaking havoc all around.

GRANT: Like an autocensorship?

KHAILOVA: Sure, but I'm getting us off track. I mean, *kinz* still exist. I remember one time when there was a man that drowned. It was up by the fish station in Rybnovsk. This man who had been working on the pier drowned, and no one could find him. Then, someone saw a shadow far off by a track of water on the beach, and they found this man up against a bush, half underwater, washed up on shore from the night before. And everyone said that it was his *tiang* —that's not quite a *kinz*, but specifically the spirit of someone who has died—people said that it was his *tiang* that made it possible for us to find him. When people saw the shadows the old sailors said that we should look over there, and they found him.

GRANT: Were there other moments in your family where people spoke about the specific influences of the dead?

KHAILOVA: Well this wasn't even so much the influence of the dead, because it was the sea that really made it possible for people to find him, by washing him up on shore. But it was his *tiang* that enabled people to find him.

I had one experience personally, when I was younger, and we lived on the edge of the village, right by the forest. It was a lot like Romanovka, or even Rybnoe, where it's all flat, and the forest just starts. I was out collecting berries near the house, and I saw a woman in the distance. I got right up close to her, maybe 10 m away, and the closer I got to her, the more my hair started to stand on end. She looked at me, with these black eyes, and I thought, I don't know her. Eventually I went in a different direction and she fell away. When I went home I told my mother about her. My mother asked what she looked like, and when I described her, she turned pale. She told me to go back to the forest and make an offering to appease this woman who had once lived in the village but had died years before.

There are legions of these kinds of things. I had another experience when my father died. We had moved here, to Nekrasovka, and he appeared to me all the time in my dreams, making me travel with him. I had been in Leningrad when he died. I was studying there, and I came back for the funeral. When I first saw him [in my dreams] after his death, when he first started calling to me, I felt that it was just because I had been upset. But then when I went back to Leningrad, not more than a week later, he started appearing in my dreams again. And he would come to me, and take me outside, and make me go all around Leningrad with him. I was sleeping, but I was also with my father, and it was exhausting me. And he would say, "Well daughter, wait for me tomorrow." And then I would wake up. Eventually that stopped. I just figured that I had gone crazy. But then I moved back to Sakhalin at the end of the year, and he started appearing to me again. He would arrive on his sled and we would race across the taiga all night long. We would go and go.

I knew that my mother was a bit of a shaman. So I said to her, "Mama, help me out. He is always taking me away night after night and I'm tired."

GRANT: Was this just when you were sleeping or was it when you were awake sometimes as well?

KHAILOVA: Just in dreams. Just in dreams. My mother went into her bedroom and was probably in there for 20 minutes. I have no idea what she did, but when she came

FIG. 25. The Sakhalin northwestern coast fishing village of Rybnovsk, seen from the air, 1990. Courtesy of Douglas Vogt.

out she said, "He won't bother you any more." And you know, to this day, I see him only very rarely.

GRANT: And in the dreams, he would talk to you as well?

KHAILOVA: He would talk to me, about all kinds of things, and travel around. I loved him very much. My parents had married late and he was older by the time I was born.

GRANT: He was probably very devoted to you.

KHAILOVA: He was very loving. He had died suddenly, but just before he died he managed to say, "Don't forget Rima." They might not have called for me because Leningrad was so far away and it cost so much money—today it costs the earth, but even then it was a lot of money—and I took a train back, through Aleksandrovsk. I couldn't come to the funeral, because that would have taken too long, a week or more, but I came back in the summer when they were fencing off the grave, you know, in the Soviet way. They brought me to the grave, gave me a hammer and a post, and told me to drive the post in for the fence. I asked, "Why?" and they said that everyone had to help build this fence, or this house for the deceased. So that, there, he would have his own place to live, and would leave the rest of us in peace.

* * * * *

GRANT: Here's another subject from the manuscript: What about tying nettle bracelets around the wrists of young girls when they are pledged in proper kin marriage to boys? Was that something you ever saw or heard about?

KHAILOVA: That's hard to say. I myself was pledged in marriage as a young girl, but no one ever tied anything to my wrist or marked it in a way that I noticed. When I grew up, I couldn't stand to be around the boy I was supposed to marry! It was already the Soviet era by then: I could see that there were all different kinds of people around me and that I had a choice of who I could marry. My mother said, "Listen, your father has already made an agreement. He received gifts [bride-price], they gave him expensive knives and everything. It's been decided, and that's that." So time got closer, and I was studying. I was in high school. And my mother said, "Well, it's time," and I said, "Mama, what are you talking about? Don't you think I can find someone for myself?" And my mother said, "But this is so awkward. Your father's already agreed." So I said, "Well if they've agreed then they can disagree." And the most interesting thing is, no one resisted when I said no. The other parents never did take back their presents, and they always asked after me. Finally their son got married, and I thought, "Thank God!"

GRANT: So they exchanged knives and . . .?

KHAILOVA: Knives, and something else, I can't remember . . . . I was a trade object too!

GRANT: Your parents didn't resist when you decided not to marry along kin lines, but had they followed the same rules themselves a generation earlier?

KHAILOVA: You might not believe this, but my mother had first been married off to a very old man (my father was her second husband). Her family had pledged her to another family and simply gave her over to them. She must have been so young, since she remembered not being able to even reach up to the table when she first lived there. Eventually she grew up and the older man married her.

FIG. 26. In the fishing village of Rybnovsk on Sakhalin's northwestern shore, the Nivkh couple Vera Kekhan (left) and her husband Konstantin (right, background) continue to keep a team of dogs though they no longer have a dog sled. 1990. Courtesy of Douglas Vogt.

GRANT: Did she know this other family at all when she moved in there?

KHAILOVA: How could she have known them? She was too little. She said she cried all the time and wanted to go home. They let her go back home to her parents sometimes, but she lived with her new husband's family. It was a formal agreement. She eventually married him and had four children with him. Then he died in 1940, when she was still young. And then after the war she married my father. But that was such a different generation: Women were so much meeker then.

GRANT: Do you know any people in your own generation who considered clan status before they married?

KHAILOVA: Now? I can't think of anyone. But before?

LIUTOVA: Everyone knew who they were supposed to marry, even if they didn't end up marrying them.

KHAILOVA: There were rules . . . .

LIUTOVA: And prohibitions . . . .

KHAILOVA: It's only now that people feel they have to fall in love. Before, you just had to like the person a little, and you'd think to yourself, "Well, it's not so terrible. We'll work something out." I had a cousin once, Raisa, and I used to tell her, "Raisa, if you were a boy, we would be married." And we would tease each other, but in fact, it was a big problem for a lot of people because sometimes there wasn't anyone who you could marry according to clan rules.

GRANT: Was there a strong sense when you were growing up that you belonged to a specific clan, and that your friends belonged to others?

KHAILOVA: You mean, the kinship system? Of course, how could you not?

GRANT: How did it manifest itself?

KHAILOVA: Even now we know who everyone in the village is, who comes from what clan. When we were growing up it was like code when our parents referred to our "closest" relatives, who we should spend our time with, and so on. And even my children . . . .

GRANT: Would it please you if your children married according to clan rules today?

KHAILOVA: No, now it's all over. We've all become Russified, you know. I have a Russian son-in-law now—what am I supposed to do?

* * * * *

GRANT: The text also talks about cases of men having more than one wife, as well as women having more than one husband, or at least a lover. Is that something you've encountered?

KHAILOVA: Polygamy? There were cases when older men had two wives; I never heard of anyone having more than that. About women having more than one husband, I've never heard anything.

GRANT: Or at least, women having more than one lover and not being held in contempt for it?

LIUTOVA: Well, what can you say, people probably did that then as now, in secret, but you wouldn't say that they were respected for it. It would not be encouraged. Women like that were thought of as . . . crafty.

In our family, one of our cousins was left without a husband or a father, and so my father took her into our family. The other children thought it was polygamy, but for our family, it was like a responsibility to take in a relative. She was the wife of his younger brother, and so, it was accorded by law.

KHAILOVA: It was the same with the aunt I told you about. She had no children. And you probably know that fellow Pogiun in Romanovka . . . .

GRANT: Vasia Pogiun?

KHAILOVA: Right, Vasilii. He had two wives. My aunt was his older wife, his first. They brought in his second wife Lida when his first wife couldn't have any children. And Lida gave birth to a whole bunch of them. And my aunt . . . .

GRANT: Was that Katia? Wasn't she a shaman?

KHAILOVA: Aunt Katia. She died years and years ago. She considered it all to be perfectly normal. The children called her "Mama," and she treated them as her own. They still talk about her all the time today.

In our family, there was a time when my cousin died. He left behind a whole lot of children, and we already had a large family. My father came to my mother and said, "We should go take in his wife and children." My mother agreed, but while my father was at home asking my mother, another brother arrived and married her, and then he gave away his own wife to another brother. Didn't I mention this to you before?

* * * * *

GRANT: What about times when someone just had a lot of money, and was able to offer a high bride-price?

LIUTOVA: I never heard of anything like that.

KHAILOVA: Apart from Aunt Lida, there aren't very many examples.

GRANT: What about the idea of wealthy Nivkhi in general? The Soviet literature made so much of the idea of rich and poor among northern peoples, that it indicated a class struggle.

KHAILOVA: People say that my mother came from a wealthy family.

GRANT: How could you tell?

LIUTOVA: Anyone who was a successful hunter had more money than others. Anyone who had a lot of fish, or a lot of dogs, a lot of alcohol.

KHAILOVA: You're describing a kulak!

GRANT: What did your mother say about her own childhood that way?

KHAILOVA: My mother used to tease my father, "Look at what a poor sod you are! Look what a low family you came from! What am I doing here?" And my father would say, "You came from a rich family, and where's the money?" But they say that my mother's father was a merchant trader, that he had a lot of furs, and dogs too.

FIG. 27. Konstantin Agniun hunting outside Romanovka, Sakhalin Island, 1990. Courtesy of Douglas Vogt.

LIUTOVA: When a woman married into a family, she was supposed to arrive in a fox fur . . . .

KHAILOVA: And at least a few formal dresses. The furs, the iron kettle, it was all part of the package.

GRANT: Both in this text and in other works by Shternberg, there is mention even of slaves.

KHAILOVA: People had their own workers, to be sure. But it was more a question of very poor people who would come to live in the homes of their wealthier relatives.

GRANT: Did you hear of any in your mother's family?

Fig. 28. Rima Khailova and Zoia Liutova, with Liutova's granddaughter in Nekrasovka, Sakhalin Island, 1995. Photographed by Bruce Grant.

KHAILOVA: My mother never mentioned it. I read about it in Shternberg! My father was an orphan, so he never could talk about his family. But, rather than the pre-Soviet period, think of the post-Soviet period. There are so many cases now of poor people going to live with their relatives, ostensibly as guests, but really as domestic workers, nothing more and nothing less. That happens with Nivkhi and with Russians.

GRANT: Helping around the house sounds more diplomatic than saying slavery.

KHAILOVA: Sure, and if they were paid, it might differ also. There are a few cases in Nekrasovka of people hiring their own servants even today. But that's different. I mean, that's only since the country has collapsed.

* * * * *

GRANT: When you referred to Baba Olia at one point when you were talking yesterday, you said that she is *imk* to you because she is the wife of your uncle. And technically, *imk* also signifies mother. Was it something like that?

KHAILOVA: Uh huh.

GRANT: So, in the Nivkh language, is there a word that signifies one's birth mother, to differentiate?

KHAILOVA: Well, it's the same word, but of course it depends on how it is used. It can go one way or the other. Sure, everyone knows who their mother is, but it's not a transgression of rules to use the same term for someone else. It's like when my cousin took his brother's widow as wife, his children could call her mother too. Here, my uncle is my mother's brother and I call his wife *imk* because it follows along the woman's side. Moreover, I don't have a mother anymore, so I call her mother.

GRANT: And for that she will always make sure you get a portion of *mos'*.[35]

KHAILOVA: Oh, that's only because I tease her. But I do bring her things every time I collect berries or collect fiddleheads. Shura doesn't like to spend a lot of time picking berries, and I know that Baba Olia likes them.

GRANT: [to Liutova] And so, she's *nanakh* to you?

LIUTOVA: By my mother she is *nanakh*. My mother was married to her older brother. So to my mother she is *nakh*, and to me she is *nanakh*.

GRANT: So, then *nakh* means . . .?

LIUTOVA: The little sister of your husband. Or little sister generally. For example, you're married, and your wife has a little sister . . . . Wait, let me figure this out. It's so confusing.

KHAILOVA: For example, a sister-in-law can call her husband's sister *nakh*.

LIUTOVA: Therefore Baba Olia is *nakh* to my mother, because her brother married my mother, and because I am my mother's daughter, I call her *nanakh*.

GRANT: So what do you call her more often, *nanakh*, or Baba Olia?

LIUTOVA: Hmm. I say *nanakh* more often, but I say both.

* * * * *

GRANT: A history question, from the pre-Soviet period, from the time of hunger and epidemics: Shternberg mentions that the famines and confusion brought on by displacement by Russians led to the lack of marriageable relatives. Hence, the downfall of the system of marriage rules. Did your parents ever talk about this?

KHAILOVA: They talked about periods of hunger, but never of an entire village, for example, dying off, just cases of hunger among a few families. It was more often a case of people not having prepared enough for the wintertime.

LIUTOVA: My mother told me about when they had epidemics of scurvy that a lot of people died from it, but she never mentioned anything specific.

KHAILOVA: It's almost hard to imagine. I mean, things must have been bad since it seems impossible to picture even one family going hungry in a village when others had food. When I was growing up in Romanovka, I can hardly remember the number of families my father would help feed. Families didn't always set aside enough for the winter, usually. My father was a good hunter, and he could always help people get more to eat. He worked on the cutter boats too and had a good salary. It would be inconceivable to imagine one family going hungry while others had enough. People were always coming by for something, for flour here or seal fat there. We kept a cow and would often give away the milk. She would bring food to all the older women who couldn't walk anymore. I was a little girl and would help her.

---

[35] *Mos'* is a traditional Nivkh aspic prepared from seal fat, fish skin, and berries.

GRANT: The rules of hospitality among Nivkhi are famous in all the literature. Do you think that they have changed much over time?

KHAILOVA: They've changed. Of course, they've changed. We're a completely different people today. I can't even remember an occasion when my mother looked at someone's house and said, "Look at how dirty everything is!" Or if she did, she would be the first to offer to help them out and start washing the walls.

GRANT: It reminds you of that famous moment in Kreinovich's book (1973), when he walks into a woman's house in Chir-Unvd in the 20s. Everyone in the house is ill with tuberculosis, but the wife is embarrassed by the dirt and disorder. She wants to offer him tea, so spits into a cup to clean it out. He is too polite to refuse, and has tuberculosis for the rest of his life!

KHAILOVA: Kreinovich was one of the few who didn't exaggerate so much about Nivkhi. When you read Engels or Shternberg, they write as if group sex was the most common thing going, that any woman would have sex with any of her husband's brothers, whereas for us it seems impossible to believe it could apply to any generation past or present.

GRANT: Engels in particular was happy that he had found a group that corresponded to his ideas of primitive Communism. People who conducted themselves freely and without guilt, people who had morality . . . but not monogamy.

LIUTOVA: That kind of freedom, of course, never existed. At least not as a general framework.

KHAILOVA: Still, people can do anything in secret. Like in Rybnoe . . . . [they laugh].

LIUTOVA: In Rybnoe there is a spot with an old Nivkh name that means, more or less, "place where you can make love in secret"! Down past the fish station.

KHAILOVA: That's all that people can do now there anyway, rebuild the clan. Few people would have guessed only a few years ago that even the clan plots would be better off than half of the towns on the island. So many towns have been closed in the last few years alone. No roads, no gasoline, no stores. It's awful.

GRANT: A more piquant question: Shternberg wrote about both hermaphrodites and homosexuality.

KHAILOVA: There have been hermaphrodites, at least. I remember one young girl who was taken back and forth to Moscow countless times for operations. As far as homosexuals go, we've never heard of any examples; for us it has always been a great sin, probably. I think that it happens in more civilized worlds.

LIUTOVA: We must still be an ancient people. We haven't got to that yet.

GRANT: Or at least people discussed it less.

KHAILOVA: I told you earlier, I think, that my father had been head of the village council when I was growing up. Everything that took place went through him—he was the local tsar at times it seemed. He would tell my mother things and then sometimes she would pass them on to us. I know that there were a number of sexual incidents brought on by Russians from the local prison.

LIUTOVA: But that again is a question of a different epoch and civilization. In older Nivkh times, it wasn't anything that people talked about.

GRANT: The idea in Shternberg was that Nivkhi looked on these things more easily than others.

LIUTOVA: It may also have been a case of just being afraid of anyone born differently. Any time anyone was born with an extra finger, or with any physical differences, people went out of their way to treat them specially, to treat them well, in case that they might have some special powers. People felt that if someone was born differently there must be a reason. It was the same thing with twins—two bodies but just one soul—before people used to sacrifice one at birth because they didn't know what to do. Later they didn't kill them, but they would give them gifts because they were, in some way, uncertain about them.

* * * * *

GRANT: There's a moment in the text where they write about a wedding, where in the course of the ceremony, someone steps into an iron kettle, first a large one, then a smaller one.

LIUTOVA: The iron kettles symbolize the parents' agreement over the marriage. If they all want the marriage to take place, then they would exchange kettles. I think it was in Shternberg where he wrote that Nivkhi put small rocks into each pot. What do you call those tiny rocks in Russian?

KHAILOVA: Cornelian.

LIUTOVA: Cornelian. But this is all from what I read. No one ever told us about it.

GRANT: So there were no kettles when the two of you got married?

LIUTOVA: In the village soviet? Go on! We're the new generation.

KHAILOVA: For us, getting married cost 3 rubles 50 kopecks. But then again, the husband always paid. I guess that's its own kind of bride-price.

GRANT: Did your parents organize any kind of dowry for you when you got married?

LIUTOVA: Oh, something very modern. I had already been working and was independent. I had received my own apartment from the kolkhoz. My mother gave me a bed set: a mattress, a pillow, and a blanket and some kitchen things. Maybe there was a kettle in there somewhere!

KHAILOVA: Along with that, my mother left me a beautiful ring. When my daughter got married I wanted to do the same thing. Now people give whatever they can. There are some New Russians[36] that give their daughters entire European villas!

* * * * *

GRANT: I wanted to ask about the idea that Nivkhi didn't address each other formally when they came or went, that there were no words of greeting or departure. I find this so hard to picture. Is that really how it worked?

---

[36] "New Russians" is the term most commonly used for the new moneyed elite in post-Soviet Russia.

LIUTOVA: Like in soap operas: People would just walk in and immediately start saying something profound!

KHAILOVA: But that's really what people did. When someone walked in your house, you had a whole ritual. Especially if the visitor was a respected person, let's say a woman. The hostess would offer a pipe and the two women would smoke together, and only then could the woman ask how her visitor had arrived there, and what news she had heard. I remember when we first moved here, to our new apartment, one of the older Nekrasovka women came to visit my mother. She was a very elderly woman, because she was older than my mother and my mother was 72 at the time. They both started smoking, though these were cigarettes, not the kind of *Belomorkanal* plug cigarettes, but the better ones. They shared one. My mother would take a puff and then the woman took a puff. And I kept looking in, I kept wondering what they were doing. The older woman spoke in the Schmidt Peninsula dialect, while my mother spoke the coastal Amur dialect, but you know, they're similar. She was a very beautiful woman and spoke in a formal manner. And then before she left, without a word, she took out some small fish she had brought for my mother, and made her a gift. My mother just smiled, and then she left. And I kept thinking how strange this was. I asked my mother what kind of fish it was, and it turned out that neither of us knew.

LIUTOVA: When my mother would have older guests, the visitors would always use these very slow, dramatic gestures. They would take these long puffs on cigarettes, silently, and with great drama. And then they would lift their glass of tea and drink it very slowly, also in silence. It was as if it was a sign of respect to be very careful.

GRANT: All in silence?

KHAILOVA: It is such a funny image I have from my childhood. My mother's women guests would sit on the floor with their legs completely outstretched, silently smoking. I kept thinking, "What are they waiting for?"

GRANT: So let's back up. This older woman would walk into the house, and, if she didn't say anything, would she smile?

KHAILOVA: Naturally.

LIUTOVA: Or maybe not. If it was the first time they were meeting, they would each be very reserved. It would be a very short, polite smile. But if they knew each other well, they would smile broadly. So she would walk in, they wouldn't say anything, they would sit down, and then be silent.

GRANT: It sounds lovely, though maybe also difficult.

LIUTOVA: Then they would start to smoke, also in silence. And then after they had smoked, the hostess would ask the guest where they came from, maybe from another village, what was going on there, and so on. Usually they would find a mutual acquaintance to talk about.

KHAILOVA: Everyone was so connected to everyone else then by all the marriage rules that it wasn't hard to figure out how each of you belonged somehow to the other.

LIUTOVA: Exactly. You talk and talk and before you know it you find out that you are close relatives!

GRANT: What if people were really close friends, and they knew each other really well? Would they still not say anything when they walked in? They wouldn't say some kind of hello?

KHAILOVA: Nivkhi tell jokes all the time when they are with their friends. All Nivkhi love to play tricks on each other. So when my parents' really close friends would come over, they would walk in, still in silence, but then when they sat down, they would immediately start to tease each other, like pretend that they were in the wrong house, or pretend that they were different people.

It all changed so quickly, that it's hard to say it was one way or the other. Around the same time, after we moved to Nekrasovka, Aunt Katia, the woman I told you about before, came to stay with us. She was so taken aback when she went into the store. She came back and said, "What do all these strange people in Nekrasovka think? I walked into the store and no one asked me who I was or where I came from." So it wasn't as if people didn't talk to each other, as if silence was more important than talking. We used to sit around all day and talk.

GRANT: Shternberg also said that this formality, this sense of distance was built into the Nivkh language in many ways. For example, instead of saying to someone directly, "Where have you come from?" people might say, "Where has the Gilyak come from?" Is that something people you know still use, speaking to each other in the third person instead of the second?

LIUTOVA: Hmm. That sounds funny to me. I haven't heard of that. Have you heard of that?

KHAILOVA: I mean, people could say it. It would be strange.

* * * * *

GRANT: I remember reading in the book how brothers and sisters were not supposed to address each other directly in conversation, for special ritual reasons. I understood the formal logic to it when I read about it, but it's another thing to try and imagine. I mean, here are brother and sister growing up in the same house, and they weren't meant to talk to each other, or joke with each other?

LIUTOVA: My father and his sister never talked with each other. I mean, they could exchange information like, "I'm going to bed now," or "I am going to work." But they never had conversations. They just didn't.

KHAILOVA: Generally women just talked to women and men talked to men. It's only now that morals have changed so much that we talk with whoever we might happen to be with, such as a brother. When I grew up with the boys, the children from my mother's first marriage, it wasn't formally forbidden to speak to each other, but you knew that you weren't supposed to. It was nothing like children who talk to their older siblings today. I did everything within the bounds of what was normal. It also depended on age: With the younger brothers I was a little closer, but with my older brother I was very strictly reserved. I hardly acknowledged him unless I had to.

GRANT: And the whole idea is that women would eventually be part of a different clan, once they married, and were therefore more distant?

Khailova: No, I don't think so. I mean, I don't know why. That's just how people acted. In general, the men were raised by males and the girls spent time with their mothers. My mother would always say, "Don't concern yourself with the boys' affairs."

Liutova: Taboo.

Khailova: In general the rules prohibited women from all kinds of things.

Grant: Even when everyone was sitting with their legs stretched straight out in front of them?

Khailova: Exactly. As if you're supposed to fly or something. All around the house they kept guns and bows and arrows. It wasn't just that you weren't supposed to touch them, if you ever stepped over a gun, you couldn't imagine the fuss. All kinds of things were considered sinful. On the other hand, we were asked to make the bullets. When you make them yourself you start out with these tiny little squares of metal, and then you have to cut them back to make them round. It's the most picky, boring work, so obviously the men made the women do it. I could never figure out why we could make the bullets but not touch the guns.

* * * * *

Grant: Shternberg wrote that the kin system was so deeply ingrained in Nivkh minds that they even projected it onto dogs, and tried to ensure that dogs mated only with prescribed kin. It sounds so funny.

Liutova: Are you sure about that? It was probably just to maintain the breed.

Khailova: People had all kinds of ideas about what made an attractive dog. But I never heard about canine marriage! Dogs were just dogs. We fed them and played with them. But who would know so much to organize their dogs' lives?

II. Elizaveta Ermolaevna Merkulova
Moskal'vo, June 15, 1995

When I first met Elizaveta Merkulova in the North Sakhalin shipping port of Moskal'-vo in 1990, she struck me with her ability to slip effortlessly between stories of growing up in a small traditional Gilyak village with her parents, and the waves of Sovietization that eventually made that world a museum piece. Her father was a successful Gilyak hunter and trader before he died young, and her mother remarried into a pro-Communist Gilyak family, often leaving her daughter torn between two sets of relatives and two competing ideologies. One day early in our acquaintance, she told me she wanted to show me something of her mother's, and returned to the living room wearing a floor-length Chinese gown in a blinding silk brocade, the likes of which I had seen only in movies. "It's in pretty good condition," she said, fingering stray threads holding prerevolutionary Chinese coins around the hem, "considering how long it was buried in the ground." Her mother had buried the dress, along with other outward trappings of premodern Gilyak life, in a box in the sand in 1937, unearthing it in the years of Khrushchev's political reprieves, some 20 years later.

When we met again in 1995, she had retired from her job as an accountant with the shipping port and was contemplating a move to a new apartment after the earthquake.

GRANT: Gilyak group marriage was one of the themes that made Shternberg's work famous. When you read about it, did it remind you of stories you knew?

MERKULOVA: I've read those stories about how a man would offer his wife to a visitor for the night, but I can't believe any of it. When I was young, my Russian friends would even ask me about it. Everyone thinks it's what we used to do. But I can't believe it, because I remember how jealously all my mother's and father's families treated the women. They were unbelievably protective and jealous. Among [Gilyaks] at least, I mean, I just don't see it. Think of all the instances of men killing their wives out of jealousy. It used to happen more frequently when I was young, but it happens today. So to imagine that a man would just offer his wife to another under those circumstances, it seems impossible. It was all a big Russian fantasy.

GRANT: There are lots of things that are hard for outsiders to understand. I've been trying to figure out the kinship system for years now and I still only have a general idea.

MERKULOVA: You find it difficult? I don't find it difficult, but that's probably because I grew up with it. I think a lot gets lost in the translation since there are some words that just don't really have translations. Even if you take the simplest words like *imk* and *itk*: Everyone thinks that this means "mother" and "father," and that's true. But neither of those words really give you a sense of what it's like when everyone is connected to each other through formal relations. There's no context to place these words when you have to start saying "the son of my sister of my father . . ."! Whereas we would just say *pu* (you know, in the eastern dialect), and you say it knowing that everyone is connected to everyone else in some important way.

GRANT: What about standard notions of polygamy? A man having more than one wife?

MERKULOVA: It's nothing that I've ever seen, but I have heard of things like that. You can find these things here and there. My uncle, for example, my mother's brother, took on a second wife. He went from Moskal'vo to the Rybnovsk shore when I was young (I was 5), and came back with a beautiful new young wife. That was in 1938. And in 1939, she bore him a little son. So he had two wives, an older and a younger.

GRANT: Why would he want two wives?

MERKULOVA: Who can answer that? It wasn't for the children. His first wife had three children, and his second had many more though only three survived. They lived well together, the group of them. Both of the women got along well. I remember staying with them when we first moved to Nekrasovka from Moskal'vo. We lived with them for 5 years, and it was always a friendly environment. They had their own house, a big house, and my uncle was both a hunter and a fishermen. He always fed the whole family.

GRANT: How did people react to them as friends and neighbors?

MERKULOVA: Perfectly fine. But I think that people had an easy way with it since the family had an easy way with it. The women were always very kind to each other and helped each other. One would stay home and make kasha while the other went out for berries. One took care of the children while the other went to work in the garden. And the whole time my uncle kept bringing home food—fish and seals, ducks and deer. What abundance they had in their home. It seemed to be a prosperous home, so people were happy to know them.

It all lasted through the war, until around 1951, when my uncle died. Then the family divided into two. The younger wife remarried and moved out with her children. The older wife remained with her children.

GRANT: When he took the second wife, then, it was by Nivkh marriage rules?

MERKULOVA: By proper custom, sure. I remember how we sent him off from Moskal'-vo on his sled, with bells and special decorations. He went with furs and gifts. It was so exciting, and she was so beautiful looking when she came back with him. They stayed with us overnight and then went on to Nekrasovka. Their children still live there. There are two of the children, Valia and Zhenia, who were both born within 5 days of each other, but by different mothers.

GRANT: When you yourself were growing up, did your parents have plans to match you with someone?

MERKULOVA: Absolutely.

GRANT: I was remembering how Shura told me she was supposed to marry Volodia K——. What a match to imagine!

MERKULOVA: I was born in 1933, and around then an old man, Iadin Kravchuk I think his name was, on Schmidt Peninsula, knew my father, Pudin. Iadin had only daughters, then, but he had a growing family. So, despite having no sons at the time, Iadin "chartered" me in advance. Five years later when he did have a son, that became the boy I was supposed to marry.

Eventually my father died. My mother married again, and we moved to the Rybnovsk shore to Sladkoe Ozero. Iadin came to see us, and he said to my stepfather, he said, "How can you allow my little Elizaveta to marry whoever she likes?" I wasn't marrying anyone then, since I was only 13, but Iadin was concerned about keeping the agreement. My stepfather said, "Elizaveta will make her own decision. This is a different time now. This is the Soviet Union. Whatever you and Pudin agreed upon doesn't have any bearing anymore."

Eventually I saw my betrothed in Iuzhno-Sakhalinsk. I was married, but he hadn't married yet. He was studying to become an engineer, while I was studying accounting. We laughed about it then, but I still in some ways think of being connected to him.

So there you have it. I had a betrothed and I had an uncle with two wives. I am a witness to these Nivkh traditions. My uncle was such a strict man—there were all sorts of rules he insisted on, especially with women. If you were a woman, there were all sorts of objects you weren't supposed to step over, guns or nets or anything to do with growing things, catching things. But the difference in all these things for me, as I told you, was that my stepfather was a big Communist. He was a very dedicated Communist . . . .

GRANT: Who rushed to the defense of his new daughter?

MERKULOVA: Communism was good for a lot of things! Who knows what would have happened? If my father had remained alive, they would have tried to give me away and I would have refused. Why would I need something like that?

GRANT: Did other Nivkh families react strangely that you weren't planning to marry your betrothed?

MERKULOVA: We didn't live close enough to other people to matter. There were only three families on Sladkoe Ozero. Vera Khein was working there, as a teacher, and I was studying there.

GRANT: Was there a reason for why you were supposed to marry that one son in particular? Did it matter which clan he was from?

MERKULOVA: He was from a totally different clan. I don't really know why it was him. But the rule was pretty straightforward. My father had a sister, and she had three sons. And I had the right to marry any of these three sons. But, for example, if she had a daughter, and my father had a son, then they wouldn't be allowed to marry.

GRANT: There is mention in the text of stories of lovers who were forbidden to marry and then met tragic ends. Was there anything like that from stories you heard?

MERKULOVA: Maybe because I never knew anyone like that it seems hard to imagine. Women literally almost never had lovers. They married the man they were supposed to marry and that was that, especially during early Soviet times.

GRANT: Well, what if there was just someone that they liked and wanted to marry, instead of their betrothed?

MERKULOVA: I can't even imagine it, but it must have happened sometime.

GRANT: What about your friends that you grew up with? Did they have to go through similar situations as yourself?

MERKULOVA: Of all my friends—this was in the 1950s—I was the only one who was betrothed in the Nivkh tradition. The single one. Everyone else did as they liked.

GRANT: Was there any special way of concluding the agreement, when Pudin and Iadin decided that you would be betrothed?

MERKULOVA: There's nothing formal that I know about. All I can tell you is that my parents were very concerned that they had so few children. My mother kept having more and more children, and so few survived. When I was born they wanted to make sure they kept me. I was born in September right at the time when the whales were running. They took me to the village soviet and registered me, but in order that I survived they had a special ritual where they put me under the doorway of the house and covered me over with refuse. My mother told me about it but I don't know all the details. Then they swept out the house as if they were sweeping out evil spirits and pretending that there was nothing in the house to steal, since the spirits wouldn't see me under the pile of refuse. Then they carried me outside and pronounced special incantations, or maybe called a shaman. But I know that they went to all sorts of lengths to keep me. My mother had had 13 children, and I was the single one to survive, so maybe the spells were what made the difference.

GRANT: When your mother remarried, and married your stepfather, was that by Nivkh tradition?

MERKULOVA: No, in fact, she remarried against the will of her brothers. Technically, she should have married one of my father's younger brothers, but both of them had died. And if there weren't any husband's younger brothers, she should have either remained a widow or perhaps married someone else of her family's choosing. But it was more difficult than that, because my stepfather was also a dyed-in-the-wool Communist. He was such a believer that even when he was arrested in 1937, and escaped from the [Stalinist labor] camps, he still believed. My mother's family didn't trust him because he was a Communist, but they also didn't trust him because he had been to prison. In the end, they wouldn't even speak to each other. My mother's relatives never exchanged a word with him.

For me it was difficult at times. On the one hand, my stepfather gave me a very modern education. He wanted me to be as educated as possible, while my mother's family didn't trust formal schooling. They weren't happy that I wasn't observing traditions in the way I should. So, I grew up superstitious, but not believing in God.

GRANT: What does it mean to be superstitious?

MERKULOVA: Well, for example, when you go into the forest, you should never take a shovel to the land: That's a sin. The same thing goes for an ax or a knife. The ground is like a skin, and you can wound it. Everything was a sin. This was a sin, that was a sin. But in the end, you could see: Men could do almost everything while women couldn't. And my stepfather would say, that's all deception. Do what you like! So I grew up of two minds.

Not all of the traditions were so imposing. My mother's family insisted that every time you went out into the forest you should take a cigarette or some food and leave it in the forest as an offering. And the same thing with the sea. Every time you go fishing you have to give the sea something back. And I still do that today. My stepfather would have said it was all nonsense.

* * * * *

GRANT: Did your mother's family ever talk to you about *kinz*?

MERKULOVA: There are all kinds of *kinz*, and mostly they scare you. It's hard to know where to start describing them. In one sense, they are just like any bad spirits that you don't want to be around. I am moving across the street into a new apartment, for example, and I'm nervous because there was a murder in the apartment last year. That's why it's being sold. A husband killed his wife and the blood ran all over the floor. But people tell me not to be afraid. We're going to have cats walk around the apartment first, like Russians do, to scare away the *kinz*.

So that's one example. You might think it's odd that I should have followed so much of what my mother's family said, but you have to realize what it's like in those kinds of situations. My stepfather was only one person, and in my mother's family there were dozens and dozens of people who felt exactly the opposite as he did.

GRANT: Have you ever felt that Nivkhi were more inclined to extrasensory phenomena than other people?

MERKULOVA: I couldn't say so. I mean, I've never met any Nivkhi who I thought had talent for that kind of thing. People say there are shamans, but I've never believed in shamans. Do you believe in them?

GRANT: As an anthropologist, I believe in almost everything.

MERKULOVA: They say there's a young boy in Nekrasovka who can see things, but I've never met him. You should ask. I think he knows Galina Fedorovna.

GRANT: When you were growing up, did your family ever have you wear a kind of bracelet around your wrist?

MERKULOVA: Absolutely, either just a few cords, or sometimes something out of wool. Sometimes you wore it around your wrist, and sometimes they would give you something to wear around your neck. What it was for, I'm not sure, either to protect you or to heal you. I remember though, I was always wearing one or the other.

When I'm afraid of spirits, I still have something tied. I have an older Russian woman do it for me, like last month when I went to go see that new apartment. I went to this woman's house and she tied a red thread around my wrist, and I made sure I was wearing it before I went inside. Whenever I'm afraid of what might happen, I'll have her tie my wrist to protect me. Who knows what it means. What did Shternberg say?

III. NATAL'IA DEM'IANOVNA VORBON

Nogliki, June 18, 1995

For my first two trips to Sakhalin in 1990 and 1992, Natal'ia Dem'ianovna Vorbon was someone I always met in the company of her two sisters, Lidiia Dem'ianovna Kimova, who had first invited me to Sakhalin from Moscow, and Galina Dem'ianovna Lok, a Nivkh ethnographer who ran a small museum in the central Sakhalin town of Nogliki, where they all lived. In the early 1990s, Natal'ia Dem'ianovna supervised a Nivkh crafts workshop, one of the early native cooperatives to come out of perestroika. When we met on Sakhalin in 1995, she had read through the Shternberg manuscript more thoroughly than anyone, and our conversation moved from kinship algebra to ways of reviving the workshop, which had recently closed because of funding problems.

* * * * *

GRANT: Shternberg talks in the manuscript about the Nivkh tradition of hospitality to guests. I am almost constantly a guest in people's homes, but I didn't realize until recently that according to tradition you can not only stay for a long time, but that you could request food for the road when you were leaving!

VORBON: People could do that, and they did. When guests were getting ready to leave, it was almost as much work as when they were arriving, since you had to prepare all sorts of extra food for them to take with them. But you can't say that everyone did it. It really depended on the woman who ran the household, because if she didn't want to take care of the guests, then the whole affair could go by the wayside.

It also depended on the strength of the bond between the two clans, if one family was from one clan and the second was from another. By certain rules, you had to feed certain clansmen, the men in particular, depending on who had married whom. So, for example, whenever we see Baba T——, she always prepares some dried fish for us, just to show that she still observes the marriage rules from decades ago.

GRANT: How is she related to you?

VORBON: Wait a second, let me try and figure this out. I'm not sure. I know that she is some kind of relation to my father, and . . . let's see. That means, she is supposed to make offerings to us because we are his children. It's more complicated than that, but I don't remember.

GRANT: So, what does she call you?

VORBON: She just calls us, *og'la,* "children."

GRANT: So I'm wondering, in terms of clan, why is she obliged to feed you? Not because you are children.

VORBON: No. How can I describe it to you? If my son Andrei or Iura were to marry . . . Wait, I've lost the thread.

GRANT: Well, why just men, for example? Why wouldn't she be just as obliged to feed the women?

VORBON: There used to be the idea that men were the providers, and therefore they deserved more attention than the women. But that was a hundred years ago, really. People don't think the same way anymore.

GRANT: I'm thinking of an example that Rima Petrovna mentioned to me, which was that every time she meets Baba Olia, who is at least 30 years older than her, Baba Olia prepares food for her, because of someone who married someone . . . .

VORBON: Wait. Wait. I know. Let's see. It's because Baba Olia is the sister of Rima's father, and remember that it all goes through the male line. The female line is different. So, if you are talking about the sister of your father, or someone from their family, we call them *nanakh*. But if it's by the mother's line, if we are talking about the sisters of our mother, we call them *machk-imk*, not just *imk*, meaning mother, but *machk-imk*, that is, younger mother. And if it was my older sister, then my children would be obliged to call her "older mother." I've seen in books that everyone called their aunts "mother," but it's much more specific than that. Naturally there was one word for your mother, and the rest followed in relation to where someone stood to your mother and father.

GRANT: When you see older Nivkhi today, is there a sense of clan ties in a way that you don't experience maybe with your peers?

VORBON: Well, in what sense? I mean, I sometimes still use the formal kinship terms when I see people like Baba Olia because I want to show respect, or simply because she is just related, as the wife of our uncle. But it's not deeper than that. I don't think that the clan system tells us that much about each other anymore.

★ ★ ★ ★ ★

GRANT: So when you got married, did you know the clan of your husband?

VORBON: Oh, probably, but I don't even think I could tell you today. I got married on the mainland, in Nikolaevsk on the Amur, and my parents were here [on Sakhalin], so there weren't the same kind of connections. My husband—that was Andriusha's father.

GRANT: So at least at one point you knew his clan?

VORBON: I did! I can tell you that our father was Cheivin, but you have to remember that women are clanless. When we marry we take the clan of our husbands. So we are from a clan when we are born, but we are never really of that clan. We were always for sale.

GRANT: Do you have any feeling about the way the position of women has changed over the years? When you read books like Shternberg's you realize how much of a man's world it was for Nivkhi at the turn of the century. But today, Nivkh women are not only the only people who can remember much about traditional Nivkh life, but they are also the community leaders. The Nivkhi who are active politically and economically are almost all women. I mean I can think of one or two men who are exceptions, but they seem like exceptions.

VORBON: You know, Bruce, you should also try to talk to my younger cousin, Kostia. Do you know him? He knows a lot. He remembers a lot too.

GRANT: I haven't met him. I should. I guess I am so struck at how few Nivkh men there are over the age of 40, period. Over the age of 60 is almost unimaginable. And yet there are older Nivkh women, relatively, everywhere.

VORBON: Yes. Some people say that men react differently to their environment, more markedly than women do. Do you know what I mean? It's as if women are more flexible because they take things into greater perspective, whereas Nivkh men . . . they look around at Soviet life, at the landscape and its horrors, and all they can do is drink.

You know, emptiness is really the word for it. I can think of all kinds of things I would like to do, or that I would like to see, to resurrect Nivkh traditions. But without men around, either to help, since so many formal public traditions were led by men, or even just to be there—it seems so incomplete. It's so sad.

GRANT: Probably the only person I can think of who really inspires me is Tolia Ngavan—he's energetic, smart, resourceful.

VORBON: The other person who remembers a lot is Leonid Iugain, also one of our cousins on our mother's side. He's an expert at boat-making especially, although he recently became an invalid. I've never been sure why we feel so much more tied to our mother's side of the family. There has never been the same pull on our father's side. With everyone on our mother's side, we socialize more. When our mother died, for example, Tania Agniun took so much care of us. She almost became our mother. We could always go see her as if we were going home.

GRANT: Can you tell me about the rule I've read about, where brothers and sisters were not supposed to speak to each other, have conversations with each other at home? I find it something so tricky to imagine. I think—but they're brothers and sisters.

VORBON: I don't even have to look far for an example, because our own father almost never spoke to his sisters. His younger sister was Vera. And his older sister—I'm not even sure what her name was, but I'm not surprised. She was Vova Kekhan's mother, the shaman. She and my father never spoke to each other. When we were young, we used to go visit them on sleds, sometimes, but we would visit his brother much more often, to go see Baba Olia. It was somehow improper when we went to go visit his sisters.

GRANT: But when he did visit them, did he really not talk at all?

VORBON: Not at all.

GRANT: At all?

VORBON: My father would in fact only communicate through our mother. If he wanted his sister to pass something to him across the table, he would ask my mother to ask her first.

GRANT: Did you ever ask why?

VORBON: It's strange, but I never asked. I mean, as a child—this was in the 1950s—I always assumed that they had had an argument. It was such a strange thing for us because we were already living in a modern fashion. We talked and played and joked with our brothers all the time, just like people do now. It never occurred to me that people wouldn't. It's strange because our father never mentioned it to us, but he observed it so strictly with his own sisters. It was only when I was older that I heard it was a rule.

* * * * *

GRANT: Let's take an example. What about Arselan? Your nephew. Lidiia Dem'ianovna's son. Who would he be supposed to marry? The daughter of his father's sister?

VORBON: Wait a second. Try Oleg, the son of our older brother. He should marry either Veronika, or Soiana—that is, the daughter of his father's sisters. Do you get it?

GRANT: Wait. Sorry. I meant, the daughter of his mother's brother.

VORBON: Wait. Right right right. Arselan should . . . wait.

GRANT: Mother's brother's daughter, right?

VORBON: Hmm.

GRANT: Like, the daughter of Evgenii, or Leonid or Aleksei, I think. Because it's the brother of the mother.

VORBON: So that would be Olia, or Ella. I guess that's it. Are you sure?

GRANT: No. I thought you were supposed to know!

* * * * *

GRANT: You know, you read a lot about what the rules were, about what people were and were not supposed to do. But you hear less often about the consequences. What would happen when a spirit did punish someone? Were there times when your parents looked at a misfortune and said, *"Kinz"*?

FIG. 29. Zoia Ivanovna Agniun, who remained behind in the closed village of Romanovka after it was closed in 1972, modeled a Gilyak salmon skin dress outside her home in 1990. Courtesy of Douglas Vogt.

VORBON: The most common examples are from hunting or fishing. If fishermen didn't properly feed the sea or the river—with tobacco, or vodka, or whatever—then *kinz* would take revenge.

GRANT: Have you thought about the recent earthquake the same way?

VORBON: Sure I have. Everything is possible. But let me give you another example.

FIG. 30. Elizaveta Merkulova retrieved this Chinese brocade dress from her mother in the late 1950s, only after it had been buried underground in sand for 20 years so that it couldn't be used by local police during Stalinism as evidence of her family's ties to foreign elements. Moskal'vo, Sakhalin Island, 1990. Photographed by Bruce Grant.

In Romanovka, about half a kilometer to the south, on the cape, is the place where our grandmother used to live. That's where her house used to be. I never saw it, but Lidiia Dem'ianovna remembers it. Baba Olia told us about it, because Baba Olia was raised by our grandmother, she was practically her favorite child. Anyway—do you know that old guy Izgin?

Grant: I know Shura Izgina, she's around 40.

Vorbon: She must be his daughter. Anyway, he was a mean old guy. He resolved to build a *nyo* there, a Nivkh summer house, the kind on stilts, right on the spot where our grandmother used to live. Everyone told him he couldn't. It wasn't just the place where our grandmother lived and died, but she had even raised a bear there, and that was it. There was no way you could build a house there without causing havoc. But he ignored everyone and said they were lying. He built the house but then went back to Romanovka, and his wife stayed there by herself. Apparently even the very first night, she was going to sleep and heard this "tok-tok-tok" sound in the house, as if someone was knocking. But she decided it didn't mean anything. So she went to sleep. Then there was a sound as if someone was crawling along the roof. The front door opened . . . . She saw something black and big, and that was it. She didn't remember anything after that.

Early in the morning, when she woke up, it was already light. It was summer so it got light early. She woke up and ran into the village. She found her husband, who had been drinking and was hung over, and she started to shout at him, "I told you that building there was forbidden. *Kinz*!" But he put her off and accused her of being a coward. "What are you carrying on about?" he said. So she said, "Fine. Go and sleep there yourself. I'm not sleeping there anymore."

He went to the house and had the same thing happen. He saw an enormous dark apparition and fled from the house in fright. That was when he became convinced that, indeed, it was sinful to have built there. It was the place of the bear.

Grant: So in the end they took the house down?

Vorbon: Yes, they took it away and put it up somewhere else.

Grant: I remember once when I was in Chir-Unvd with Galina Dem'ianovna [Lok] and I wanted to go look at the cemetery, but Galina Dem'ianovna said we shouldn't. Was that because of *kinz* as well?

Vorbon: Right. But also, Chir-Unvd was the site of old Nivkh settlements. It's not a good place to be since there are a lot of *kinz* there. It's really like that.

Grant: It's not that hard to believe, not just because of the forlorn quality there, but knowing about the Nivkh villages that were burned down to make way for the one that is there now. New lives for old.

Vorbon: I don't know if you know the two-story wooden house in the old part, where Lidiia Romanovna lives. She was raised entirely in modern ways, she's even younger than me, but even she has trouble with the *kinz* that are there. I went there once with Masha because we had to pick up money for the elementary school. When we got there we went to go see Lidiia Romanovna, and I can't begin to explain to you what it felt like. There was this tremendous feeling of gravity, weight bearing down upon me. I felt like I would fall asleep even before I got there. It was nightmarish.

When we got there, I couldn't even eat, I wanted so much to sleep. Lidiia Romanovna laid out the couch for me in the living room. I lay there and dreamt, lay and dreamt, lay and dreamt. But it wasn't sleeping—it was more of a haze. I remember that they went off to the bathhouse, and then came back. It was starting to get dark. And the whole time I was in this strange, dark space. When they came back from the bathhouse, I told Lidiia Romanovna that I had to go to sleep for the night, so she got out blankets, and I laid down. So, the living room is laid out with doors that kind of open toward the kitchen—the kitchen is more like down the hall. Have you been there?

GRANT: Uh huh.

VORBON: Well, then you know that you can see a corner of the kitchen from the couch in the main room. I could see them and heard them talking quietly in the other room, thinking I was sleeping.

Then suddenly, I felt something bearing down upon me, as if it had me in its grip. But I couldn't for the life of me cry out. I tried and tried. "Galia! Galia!" I tried, but nothing came out. It was one of the most terrible feelings I've ever known. "Galia!" I finally cried. But they kept sitting there, drinking tea and talking. I was really awake now, but couldn't move. I couldn't even sit up. So I had to wait for them to talk themselves out and come into the room. Finally Galina Dem'ianovna came into the room and lay down. I couldn't move, but I still felt better that someone was there, and I fell asleep.

When I woke up in the morning, I looked down at my wrists. They were practically blue from bruises, and you could see the outline of someone's hand's around them. I showed Lidiia Romanovna and she said that it wasn't the first time something like this had happened, that even she was afraid to live there. She said that some nights she would lock up the whole apartment, and then hear all sorts of sounds of doors opening. So she would jump up and look, but everything would be in place. The whole building is like that. They think people must have been buried there before.

GRANT: Does it matter, I mean, all the Nivkhi who weren't buried in a traditional way under Soviet power? I mean, they don't cremate people any more.

VORBON: I don't think that matters as much. It's one thing whether people get buried properly or not; but it's another to build on top of ritual sites. That gets punished severely.

IV. GALINA DEM'IANOVNA LOK

Iuzhno-Sakhalinsk, June 20, 1995

Throughout my fieldwork on Sakhalin, Galina Dem'ianovna Lok was the most central guiding figure. She grew up with her large family on the northwestern coastal town of Tengi, moving to Rybnovsk and later the Amur in her teenage years when her parents died young. After marrying a Buriat man and living in Ulan Ude for many years, she returned to Sakhalin in her 40s to run the Nogliki branch of the Sakhalin Regional Museum. In May of 1995, we sat together for several days reading the Shternberg manuscript aloud to each other for review. Some weeks later, we sat down to record this conversation.

* * * * *

FIG. 31. Natalia Vorbon (center row, third from left), in a family photograph with her sisters, Lidiia Kimova (center row, third from right) and Galina Lok (center row, center place), Nogliki, Sakhalin Island, 1990. Courtesy of Douglas Vogt.

GRANT: I think that most people could pick up [Shternberg's] book and more or less get the idea behind the Nivkh kinship system, however complicated—that people were organized into categories that underwrote marriage and exchange and 100 other things. But in reality, was it something natural that everyone you knew understood and accepted, or was it something that some Nivkhi themselves ever had trouble grasping?

LOK: It wasn't difficult. There wasn't anything you had to "know," or study, or introduce. It's not like today when we all sit around and read it as if it was about Africa. When a Nivkh child grew up, he immediately knew which clan he belonged to, and what his rights and obligations were. He knew immediately how he stood in relation to the category of *akhmalk*, how he stood in relation to the category of *tuvng*, and so on. That's because from the earliest years, his parents would tell him, "Those are the uncles you have to maintain a distance from, and those are the ones who you can be closer to." He knew it from the very beginning. When a girl was born, she knew from as early as 5 or 6 what clan she would marry into. There never used to be such confusion like we have today, where we have to dig around in books to figure out who is *pu* and who is *ang'rei.* Today, we study it like science, but before people knew it automatically.

GRANT: One of the strangest parts for someone outside the system, I think, is the use of one word to describe both one's biological mother as well as a line of women connected by clan.

LOK: But of course people knew. I mean, it's your mother!

GRANT: When we're talking in Russian though, like now, we rely on adjectives like blood [*krovnaia*] or birth [*rodnaia*] to indicate a biological mother. Were there similar auxiliary words in Nivkh to make that distinction?

LOK: There were a lot of ways to do it. One was just to refer to one's mother (*imk*), and then "one's big mother" (*pila-imk*), meaning, your mother's older sister, or "one's little mother," (*machk-imk*), meaning your mother's younger sister.

GRANT: What kind of personal reaction do you have when you read through this kind of material and realize how much of it has gone by the wayside? Is it a strange feeling?

LOK: That's hard to answer because I feel like I am reading about Nivkhi, but the Nivkhi I read about don't exist anymore. It was such a different world only 50 years ago. Today I can't really point to anyone who I consider to be a real representative of

FIG. 32. Galina Lok in Romanovka, Sakhalin Island, 1990. Photographed by Bruce Grant.

that world. How can I tell you that I'm sorry it's on its way out when it passed away such a long time ago?

GRANT: Where is the good nationalist in you?

LOK: As a good nationalist, I would say, sure, what a shame. Like any poor animal that is the last of its kind and is quickly on its way to extinction. Or like some rare plant that is about to die off because it no longer has the environment to support it. Of course it makes me feel bad. We're talking about an entire culture, an entire way of looking at the world which was different from all others, and which we are never going to see again. Poof. It's gone. But what else should I say? As a modern person, I know that times change. It's hard to avoid. Whether it's bad or not, it still happens.

GRANT: When you get together with your own brothers and sisters, do you still use [Gilyak terms of address] to refer to each other, or particularly, your older relatives?

LOK: If we were talking about before WWII, I could say, there would still be some of these traditions left. But no one I know addresses each other the way Shternberg describes in this book. If we held on to the language, that might have been one thing. But we didn't even hold on to the clan itself, which was the thread that ran through all of Nivkh life and held it together. I mean, I could go back to WWII, but I really want to go back to the 1860s, when the island was colonized by the Manchu because the Manchu mostly left us alone. Once the Russians and the Japanese started settling the island in the second half of the 19th century, it was already difficult to talk about people living the way Shternberg described in the book. Even Shternberg says this, that he was describing a system rather than a whole way of life for people who had already started to suffer economically and had begun to move from place to place in search of a way to support themselves.

GRANT: What about someone like Baba Olia, who was an older female clan member, *pila-imk*?

LOK: Baba Olia is an exception. We just call her "Mama," *imk*, because she raised our youngest sister after our parents died.

GRANT: Natal'ia Dem'ianovna told me about how Lidiia Dem'ianovna was supposed to marry, at one time, Ivan Khein. How difficult to imagine.

LOK: But that's how it worked.

GRANT: That's how it worked, but in what way? Does that mean you always knew it wouldn't quite happen, or, you somehow grew up thinking you were to marry someone in particular and then one day you realized that it wouldn't happen?

LOK: I think we always had a sense that there was a way things were supposed to be. I mean, we joked about it, that Lidiia would marry Ivan, but it was such a different time then, the late 1950s. We were going to school, and we were all living in different towns. There was never any serious conversation that these marriages would actually take place. Maybe if we were still living the same antediluvian way of life we might have married by the rules. Why not?

GRANT: How did your parents react? Were they both in agreement that you should all do as you wanted?

LOK: Of course they weren't happy about it, but what could you say? I mean, Lidiia Dem'ianovna was really smart. She excelled in everything at school, she never had any problems, and everyone knew that she could go to Leningrad to study some more. We were in school in Kirpichiki at first, and then in Rybnovsk. Then Natal'ia Dem'ianovna went to Nikolaevsk to study. Then our older brother Evgenii Dem'ianovich went to forestry school and Lidiia Dem'ianovna went to Leningrad. We all effectively lived outside this social system.

GRANT: So your parents weren't disappointed that it didn't work out the way they had planned?

LOK: Well, they died early, but they wanted good things for us, and that's why they let us go.

* * * * *

GRANT: I was curious about the tradition of raising other people's children. Was that a tradition that happened more among Nivkhi than among Russians, by your experience?

LOK: If we're talking about situations where children lost their parents during the war, or to illness, then, no, you couldn't say that Nivkhi were different. Nivkhi were different in the sense of the marriage rules that encouraged young girls to grow up in the family of their intended husbands. For example, I was supposed to marry Volodia Kekhan, and all the time I was growing up, his parents would always tell me that I could go and live with them any time I wanted. I was going to school so I didn't leave my family, but I always knew that there was another kind of school I could go to, which would just be Nivkh life. If I had gone to live with them I wouldn't have studied, but I would have got up in the morning and gone down to the beach with the whole family while the men went out fishing and the women worked on the nets or dried the fish. It was a whole pedagogy of its own. From early childhood, that's how a child knew when to put out a net, what you could do while you were between tides, when you were supposed to check the nets. It was all second nature. It also makes you laugh when you look at all the Soviets did to make us real proletarians. Before, maybe one fishermen officially had access to land here, and access to water there, but everyone worked together all the time. Children would eat at anyone's house any time. Relatives would spend whole seasons together and help out. Now we are Communists and all we do is sit inside by ourselves and watch television!

* * * * *

GRANT: There is a lot in the text about matchmaking, agreements, and contracts on the part of men. You get the impression that women had no choice in the matter. I guess I want to ask two things: Was it really the case that women had little choice? And, more generally, how is it that 100 years later, we can barely point to 2 or three Nivkh men who are in any positions of responsibility? Nivkh women are at the head of almost every family.

LOK: Let me answer the first question. I think that the exceptions are always more sensational than the general rule, and my impression is that women didn't live all that badly. The things about which Shternberg writes, here and in other books, are true: When a woman ran away from her husband, she got punished. But in other respects the clan relationships protected her. We have to remember that the clan was about much more than marriage. It was a whole system of interrelationships that were social and economic and political. And the woman's position in this system was monitored on all sides.

The second question. Why do we have so few men? I think we have to look at Sovietization. We know that it was full of good intentions, teaching literacy and sharing a Russian way of life with Nivkhi. But on the other hand, there were restrictions at every turn. From the very start the Russians hounded Nivkhi from the places where they had lived from the beginning of time. Naturally Nivkhi lived in the best spots for fishing and hunting, whether it was a question of summer villages or winter villages. So, either they chased them out altogether, or they just crowded them out and established kolkhozes. You have to think this through. Imagine—the fishing waters are now the property of the kolkhoz, state property. The average older Nivkh fisherman can literally no longer go out in his boat and fish because he would be violating state property, almost everywhere. He can catch 60 or 100 kg of fish each year, though that is all of 30 or 40 salmon, which he could catch with his own net in one good day. So he is penned in. Soviet medicine insists that eating raw fish is dangerous, that eating seal is dangerous, that killing animals generally is not ethical and that hunting bears or eating them is not attractive. In short, we have a heap of laws that forbid an entire way of life. That's it. The Nivkh man is degraded. But even that is overly simple. Remember that in 1937 hundreds of Nivkh men were sent off to labor camp after labor camp for merely having hunted bears or having spoken their native language. So you're not allowed to hunt. What are you supposed to do? At the same time, you have Russian passersby offering you vodka every 15 minutes to go catch fish for them, or go hunt a bear for them. What nonsense.

* * * * *

GRANT: Going back to Shternberg for a moment, I wonder when, or whether, we can talk even about kinship systems like this one working as efficiently as people describe it. Even Shternberg, writing in the 1890s, makes it clear that he was describing an ideal type. We know that the island had been colonized in one way or another for a long time when he arrived.

LOK: When Shternberg got there, all the epidemics had already started. It was a different kind of colonization by the Russians and the Japanese because Nivkhi never had such close contacts with the Chinese. Or at least, we don't have the same kind of record for the Chinese. When Shternberg arrived, there was already smallpox, scurvy, and syphilis. You can just imagine. There are all these Nivkh villages in the middle of the taiga and "Boom," a completely different world comes upon them. People died off by the family, one after another, from smallpox especially.

GRANT: It's not hard to see from archives that at the turn of the century Nivkhi lived like other peoples; they traded and exchanged with the Chinese and Japanese and others. When the Russians arrived, I mean, we always just say "Russians," but which

Russians? We're really talking about a penal colony set up on the island and peopled by a desperate class of exiles.

LOK: The most barbarous kind you can imagine.

I feel I always take Shternberg's work with a grain of salt because the people he was working with were different then. Most of his informants weren't very serious. Nivkhi were different then. I mean, I'm helping you today, like Shura or Zoia Ivanovna did when you were up in Nekrasovka, because we have a plain interest in preserving a culture, in making sure that people understand what Nivkhi are about. But, by contrast, the best Nivkhi of past times were always very laconic. They rarely talked with anyone just passing through. Nivkhi were always very closed people. You had to draw everything out of them, then ask one person, then ask another person. And even when you would ask them something, they would give you 2 or three words and that's it. You would have to be on the ball enough to know which of the 2 or three words you heard from any number of people were actually useful or true. I think so.

You know, not long ago, I listened to Alla Viktorovna's recordings from the 1970s. She used to travel around the Amur for her dissertation and record Nivkh songs. She's had them for 20 years, and we asked her if we could write them up for a book of Nivkh songs. I listened to hours and hours of tapes. The people she spoke to—you can hardly imagine. All the good singers she could have found, all the normal, smart people . . . not one of them was on tape. Everyone was drunk, every single one. God knows how she found them. I can hardly describe it. They would sing, and wheeze, sing, and wheeze. And then start with the wildest profanity. I couldn't believe it. She would say in Nivkh, "*Syk?*" (OK?), and they would say "*Syk! Syk!*" and then start singing songs in Nivkh that were complete mockeries, completely profane, nothing but the crudest jokes, completely uncensored, usually about her, all while she sat there with her tape recorder. I tried to translate it and I thought, what a loss all of this was. But I knew it would be like that.

So then last year Mamcheva called me and said she got a copy of Shternberg's tapes from 1910, from when he was on Sakhalin. I said that I would be over right away.

GRANT: That was the second trip he made for writing up this book.

LOK: Right. He used one of those old phonographic recording cylinders. This Nivkh man was speaking. The first few lines were brilliant. I had never heard such beautiful Nivkh speech, and from so long ago. But then Shternberg asked him to start singing. He began . . . and it was exactly the same as with Alla Viktorovna in the 1970s. Total profanity from top to bottom.

GRANT: But, if we're talking 1910, could we say that Shternberg at least had better luck?

LOK: You really can't. They were absolutely the same. I was even amazed at how the people they found played more or less the same tricks on both ethnographers even though they were 60 years apart. It should be funny, but it was just so sad. They were so drunk. It was complete mockery.

GRANT: Well, what is an ethnographer anyway? I mean, in the classic tradition you say to someone: "Please take me in, please feed me, and please answer all my questions about your personal life . . . ." So you think of Shternberg, arriving on Sakhalin 100 years ago, a prisoner, and Jewish among Russians at that.

LOK: I don't think it's unusual that he ended up with the less pleasant Nivkhi, but it does make me think how important it is for me to try myself. I think of Grigorii Pakskun, who you met and who died a few years ago. I asked him to help me record some songs, and he knew I knew the language. There are so few people that do, he knew he couldn't get away with fooling around. The material he gave me! The songs he sang were like entire epic poems. I had never heard anything like it in my life. I should go around and record everything all of these people know, but no one has a dime. On the Amur, for example, there are two people I know who would be staggering to talk to. I might find them today, but tomorrow they might be dead. These people—they are from a different planet.

The odd thing is that I think what Shternberg wrote was fine. I am more interested in the moments where he got the point than the times when he didn't. There are moments when he is trying to describe Nivkh culture proper, and others when he is more interested in broad, sweeping comparisons with all Tunguso-Manchurian peoples. That's when he starts to flag. Once in another article he said that Nivkhi would chew each other's food so that others could eat it. As if everybody did this! I mean, I could understand if he was talking about penguins. Or if he said that a few people did this for older Nivkhi who had no teeth, or for babies. But to say that everyone did it all the time is just a misunderstanding. His books are full of things like that.

GRANT: Shternberg wrote once that Nivkh women frequently have an expression on their face of being angry. I laughed when I saw it. What do you think?

LOK: [laughs] He's right, of course.

APPENDIX A:
SOCIAL ORGANIZATION IN THE ARCHIVES

GIVEN THE LONG ODYSSEY of Shternberg's manuscript, as well as the influence of outside editors on the text since Shternberg and Boas' original agreement, excerpts from the more salient correspondence are included here.[1]

1904

JANUARY 25. Boas writes to Russian academician V. V. Radlov, saying he is pleased with the work of Bogoraz and Iokhel'son and hopes to meet Shternberg soon [AAN f. 282, o. 2, d. 29, l. 1].

1905

MARCH 2. Boas writes to Shternberg, inviting him to New York for 3 months in the summer to work on the AMNH's Amur collection together with Berthold Laufer [AAN f. 282, o. 2, d. 29, l. 2].

MAY 7. Shternberg writes his wife, Sarra Ratner-Shternberg, on AMNH letterhead. In his letters over the next 3 months he writes that he has visited her relatives in New York and has had intense meetings with local Jewish activists. He makes an agreement with Boas to submit a volume on "Gilyaks and Their Neighbours" for the Jesup publication series [AAN f. 282, o. 5, d. 64, l. 80–105].

1906

AUGUST 11. Shternberg writes to Boas, explaining that 1905 was a difficult year for him because of anti-Jewish incidents in Russia. He pledges to send Boas the manuscript by August of 1907 [APS].

---

[1] Correspondence from the American Philosophical Society in Philadelphia [APS] is found in the Boas Collection (B/B61) organized alphabetically by name. Correspondence from the American Museum of Natural History [AMNH] is found in the Boas and Shternberg archives in the Department of Anthropology. Correspondence from the Russian Academy of Sciences Archive in St. Petersburg [AAN] is indicated according to Russian file codings, *fond, opis', delo,* and *list.* All correspondence was in English unless otherwise indicated; letters between Lev Shternberg and Sarra Ratner-Shternberg were in Russian; most letters between Boas and Ratner-Shternberg were in German. All emphases are original. The original spellings of names such as Bogoras, Sternberg, Jochelson, Averkijewa, and Winnikow have been retained when directly quoted. I am grateful to Alexandra Volin for translations of correspondence from the German.

1907

FEBRUARY 15. Boas writes to Shternberg that he hopes to print Shternberg's text by the end of the year [AAN f. 282, o. 2, d. 29, l. 21].

MARCH 16. Shternberg writes to Boas, "On the political horizon, we are now expecting a new hurricane of massacres" [APS].

AUGUST 9. Boas writes to Bogoraz, "I have written once or twice to Mr. Sternberg, but without receiving any reply. I am exceedingly anxious . . ." [APS].

AUGUST 16. Boas writes to Bogoraz, observing that illustrations have been made for Shternberg's book; Boas hopes to receive the Shternberg manuscript by the end of the year [APS].

AUGUST 28. Shternberg writes to Boas, having heard of Boas' impatience through Bogoraz. States that he has responded to each of Boas' letters but has not heard from Boas in 5 months. Notes that he had written earlier to Boas about the necessity of paying for illustrations he commissioned in Vienna [not found—B. G.]. Financial difficulty had obliged him to undertake other "literary work" for money; for the same reason he had not been able to travel to Vienna or Berlin as he had hoped. He was planning to write further on Gilyak marriage and social organization [APS].

SEPTEMBER 27. Boas writes to Shternberg, suggesting that Boas have the manuscript translated into English in New York [APS].

1908

JULY 17. Shternberg writes to Boas, pledging three chapters pending revisions [APS].

SEPTEMBER 19. Shternberg writes to Boas, apologizing for delays. Sends him one chapter [APS].

OCTOBER 2. Boas writes Shternberg, requesting a bill for the illustrations for the manuscript, as they agreed upon in Vienna. Shternberg's files include a handwritten invoice reading, "By order of Dr. Sternberg, I have made 62 drawings for the volume, 'The Gilyak and their Neighbours . . .'" [AAN f. 282, o. 2, d. 29, l. 25].

OCTOBER 21. Shternberg writes to Boas that he has been suffering from cholera and that his physician has sent him to Finland to recover [APS].

1909

APRIL 7. Boas writes to Bogoraz, sorry to hear of Shternberg's long illness of that year [APS].

MAY 5. Boas writes to Bogoraz explaining how AMNH funding obliges Boas to condense materials at his own discretion; this applies to Shternberg's forthcoming manuscript [APS].

OCTOBER 16. Boas writes to Shternberg, "I received your letter a few days ago, and today your ms. . . . came into my hands. I am sorry to learn that you have been ill again during the summer, but I trust that your recovery is complete, and that it will be permanent . . . . I shall have the material that you have sent me translated at once, and then I shall have the translation copied and sent to you for revision" [AAN f. 282, o. 2, d. 29, l. 28].

1911

SEPTEMBER 19. Shternberg writes Boas apologizing for delays. "I am working now hard and in a month I send you the continuation and perhaps the end of the first part (family and gens). That part is one of the most serious for the Jesup Expedition. It would be of no interest to you to speak about my difficulties . . ." [APS].

1912

FEBRUARY 16. Shternberg sends Boas "the continuation of the manuscript containing the last chapters on the construction of Gilyak marriage. That part was for me the most difficult one, because it need a great deal of preparatory and compensatory work and—last not least—very much of considerations and over and over changing. The concluding chapter of the manuscript treats on one side the connections of the Gilyak system with cousin marriage and classificatory system in general, and on the other side—the connections with forms of marriage and all other peoples of the Pacific coast of N. Asia and partly North America. The next chapters will treat the everyday life details and rites of marriage and the organization of the gens and social relations" [APS].

APRIL 4. Alexander Goldenweiser writes to Boas, informing him that he received "the Shternberg manuscript . . . a 19,250 word chapter [on] . . . a genetic interpretation of the classificatory system of relationship among the Gilyak" [chs. 3 and 9 of this edition fit this description—B. G.]. He later sends the translation to Boas on October 14, 1912, and is remunerated for that one chapter in a letter from Boas on November 8, 1912 [APS].

OCTOBER 22. Boas writes to Shternberg, "We need for your paper which I am about to send to the printer an explanation of the alphabet. You will greatly oblige me by sending me a list of all the terms of relationship in English transcription, that is to say, the way you want to have them printed in English. I am very much afraid that there is a great deal of confusion between 'n' and 'p' and 't/m,' 'p/r' etc. Please do this if possible by return mail" [AAN f. 282, o. 2, d. 29, l. 35].

OCTOBER 26. Boas writes to Shternberg, "I was about to send your manuscript to the printer, but before doing so I have to ask a few questions, which [I ask you to] please answer at the earliest moment. I find the description of the study of the system of relationship very hard reading; and I have tried to make the matter clearer to me by introducing a few English terms which, as it seems to my mind, are really the equivalents of the Gilyak terms, but I want to know whether I am right. These terms are:

Gens woman
Gens woman's husbands
Gens man
Gens man's wives
Gens men

In trying to lay out the system it troubles me whether the woman has not a term for her brother's prospective wife before their marriage, or whether they are always called tuvn even before marriage. Also does a man use the same term for the wife's brother and the wife's brother's daughter? You might expect, according to the parallelism with the terminology used by a woman, that there might be a separate term for the male of this group, although this is not necessary on account of the different treatment of the male and female lines. Then I am not clear on how a woman calls her prospective husband's brother's daughter. I mean, of course, the whole class of men of her gens we call nern. Furthermore, how does a man call his sister's prospective husband's brother's sons? I believe the whole system is set forth correctly in the enclosed diagram [not found—B. G.], but I beg to ask you kindly to look it over and correct it, and , if there is any way of filling the gaps to which I referred, to fill them in. The point that needs clearing up particularly is the nomenclature of the prospective degrees of affinity before marriage . . . . also, confusion about the alphabet! is husband *ny* or *pu*?" [APS].

NOVEMBER 7. Shternberg cables Boas, "As for your notice that you are about to send my manuscript to the printer I would prefer you send the translation first to me that I might make all supplements, corrections and changes needed *before printing,* because in the proofs it will give me more trouble and will be exceedingly expensive. I hope you will comply with my request which is considered by me very important. In the manuscript I will correct all native terms distinctly and in the next days I send you the explanation of the Alphabet and also the list of the terms of relationship in english transcription" [APS].

DECEMBER 1.[2] Shternberg writes to Boas, "Now to your questions.

1) You propose to introduce the terms gensman, genswoman, etc. I am satisfied, but in some cases it were perhaps nicer to use terms—gensbrother, genssister, gensfather and so on. And moreover do you not think that for the english reader the term *clan* would not be more suitable?"

2) You ask:

   a) How do I (male) call my *sister's* prospective husband's brother? Answer: *imgi, navx.*

   b) [writing crossed out—B. G.]

   c) Does a *man* use the same terms for the wife's father's son and the wife's brother's daughter? Of course not: for the former he uses the term—*navx, axmalk;* for the latter *yox.*

   d) How [does] a woman call her prospective husband's brother's daughter? Answer: *ogla.*

   e) How does a man call his sister's prospective husband's brother's [word on corner torn from original—B. G.]? Answer: *imgi.*

---

[2] While this letter is dated only "1 December" (the corner having been lost from the original), it responds to Boas' request of October 12, 1912 for clarification on key terms.

You ask: Whether the woman has *no term for her brother's prospective wife* before their marriage, or they are always called *tuvn* even before marriage? From the latter part of your question, I see that the typewriter made a mistake in the copy: you wanted it seemed, to know how the woman calls her *husband's brother's* prospective wife? My answer: if under the term *prospective* wife you mean the woman, which is orthodoxally from her birth the wife of a man and is called by him from childhood angej, and there can be no other meaning of the term—then the women concerned are always called *tuvn* before marriage, simply because they are really genswomen of the same generation—gens sisters.

But if in your question (in the first part) is not [a] mistake, i.e. if you want to know how a woman calls *her brother's* prospective *wife,* then is the answer, *navx.*

As for your diagram I give it separately enclosed [not found—B. G]. I have filled up the gaps. If you find it necessary to give the diagram in the paper, do you not find necessary to make it larger, for instance to give the terms also in the second ascending line especially in the divisions of one's own gens?

I enclose here also the alphabet, but I have changed a little for to adapt it nearer to the English transcription. Then the translation used in my paper till now must be a little changed, for instead of umk—imk, instead utk—itk, instead anğej—anğej, etc. . . .

A few words more about the diagram. Filling the gaps, I have taken as granted that the terms of gensman and genswoman are used in the [sense of] gensman etc. of the speaking person, but the terms can be understood also in the meaning—gensman or genswoman of the person addressed to. I have answered in the first sense. Is that what you did want?" [AMNH].

DECEMBER 17. Boas writes Shternberg, "Many thanks for your letter . . . with the enclosed tables. Since that time I have sent the ms. and I shall not do anything in the matter until I get it back from you, which I hope will be soon. I do wish to insert a table in the ms. which I think makes the whole intricate relationship ever so much clearer" [AAN f. 282, o. 2, d. 29, l. 41].

DECEMBER 26. Shternberg writes Boas to say he has received a copy of the English translation and will examine it [APS].

1913

JUNE 23. Shternberg writes Boas, "I have corrected the greater part of the translation and inserted a great deal of new interesting [material] . . . now I am finishing the work . . . . It seems that the translation has not been made by one person and one part of the text need much work and trouble in correcting, being myself so pitiful an Englishman . . . . [In] September you receive the continuation and the end of the part concerning social organization" [APS].

NOVEMBER 18. Boas writes to Shternberg, "A few days ago I received the package containing your ms. . . . There is a little difficulty concerning the table of contents, because I do not know exactly what your further plans are . . ." [AAN f. 282, o. 2, d. 29, l. 56].

1914

MAY 26. Shternberg writes to Boas, apologizing for delays [APS].

1917

FEBRUARY 28. Shternberg writes to Boas that he is sending further material [APS].

1922

MAY 17. Boas writes Shternberg that he can propose $300 for "some subject on the Amur River tribes" [AAN f. 282, o. 2, d. 29, l. 66].

JULY 19. Boas writes to Shternberg, offering to send food packages to Petrograd since money was not being transferred safely [AAN f. 282, o. 1, d. 203, l. 19].

1924

MAY 1. Boas writes to Shternberg, "There has been such a delay in publishing your G. material that I do not know just what to do. I should like to know particularly whether the ms. which I have may be printed as it stands or whether you want to revise it" [AAN f. 282, o. 2, d. 29, l. 72].

OCTOBER 24. Boas writes to Shternberg recalling their meeting in the Hague in 1924. Boas reminds Shternberg that he has agreed to send chapters on Gilyak social organization and history in return for the $300 sent in 1922. Boas acknowledges that Shternberg has also proposed further chapters on Gilyak mythology and folklore, religion and material culture. In return, Boas agrees to pay him $2000 over 1925 and 1926" [AAN f. 282, o. 2, d. 29, l. 73].

NOVEMBER 18. Bogoraz writes to Boas, explaining that his brother, a doctor in Paris, examined Shternberg and recommended a stomach operation [APS].

DECEMBER 24. Shternberg writes to Boas, "I am sorry I have not received till now the manuscript. I am working now on the continuation of the social culture. It will not be a small task. The translation will be made here" [APS].

1926

AUGUST 14. Boas writes to Shternberg, saying that he still awaits a response to their "Hague agreement" [AAN f. 282, o. 2, d. 29, l. 79].

NOVEMBER 13. Shternberg writes to Boas, expressing that he has felt "all the time remorse for breaking my promise. I am happy to be able now to not only send the Museum my work, but also to pay my debt in cash what I hope to make from Japan or after my return" [APS].

1927

FEBRUARY 27. Boas writes to Bogoraz, "I believe you know how embarrassing it is to me that [the Shternberg manuscript] is still hanging" [AAN f. 250, o. 4, d. 25, l. 29].

AUGUST 14. Shternberg dies at his dacha in Dudergof, outside of Leningrad.

NOVEMBER 4. Sarra Ratner-Shternberg writes to Boas [in German], "In the unpublished papers of my deceased husband, Professor Leo Sternberg, is a manuscript "Family and Clan of the Gilyaks," which he checked over 2–3 days before becoming ill in order to send it to you as a supplement to the part of his work on the Gilyaks that is in your hands. Be so friendly as to tell me whether I should send you this paper. In case it is not printed, be so good as to send me the part that you have" [APS].

NOVEMBER 19. Boas writes to Ratner-Shternberg, gladly accepting her proposal. "It will always be a matter of the greatest regret that it was not possible for [your husband] to write out the most important information that he had relating to the tribes of the Amur River" [AAN f. 282, o. 5, d. 68, l. 1].

1928

JANUARY 26. Ratner-Shternberg writes to Boas, "Excuse me for not yet sending you the manuscript about the Gilyaks: your letter arrived just at the time of a fresh blow of fate that struck our family (misfortunes never come singly)—suddenly the brother of my deceased husband died . . . . Since I do not know for certain whether my deceased husband proofread all of the Gilyak words, I have resolved to ask for the help of the following people: Gilyak language specialists at the Ethnographic Department of the University; and eight Gilyak students who studied with Professor Sternberg last year to work out a phonetic Gilyak alphabet. These Gilyaks, as well as representatives of other primitive peoples of Siberia and North and East Asia, are studying at the Northern Sector of the Oriental Institute in Leningrad, which Prof. Bogoras and Sternberg founded in the year 1926. Unfortunately these Gilyaks are very busy and I can ask for their help only very infrequently. It is unlikely I will be able to send you the manuscript before two weeks from now" [APS].

APRIL 2. Boas writes to Ratner-Shternberg, "I do not need to tell you how glad I am to have [the ms.]. I hope it may be possible to publish it soon. Of course it will be necessary to have it translated into English" [AAN f. 282, o. 5, d. 68, l. 5].

1929

SEPTEMBER 27. Bogoraz writes to Boas from Leningrad; introduces and recommends Julia Averkieva for a research stay with Boas in the United States [APS]. Averkieva arrives in New York in October 1930, and later travels with Boas for 6 months to the northwestern coast of British Columbia, beginning in October 1931. During this period she works with Boas on the Shternberg manuscript.

1930

SEPTEMBER 2. Erukhim Kreinovich writes to Ratner-Shternberg, noting that he has been at work on the Shternberg Gilyak materials. He asserts that Shternberg's original Gilyak informants were from the Amur and western Sakhalin; Kreinovich would like to add examples of the eastern Sakhalin dialect [AAN f. 282, o. 5, d. 27].

JUNE 6. The typesetter in Khabarovsk preparing the printing of Shternberg, *Giliaki*, writes to Ratner-Shternberg, explaining that there is confusion over how to proceed with Gilyak transcription in the text. He asks whether she would like it all in Cyrillic, or all in Latin, with diacritics or without. In the end, both Cyrillic and Latin letters are used, without diacritics, often within the same word [AAN f. 282, o. 1, d. 117, l. 7].

DECEMBER 29. Boas writes to Ratner-Shternberg, apologizing for AMNH-related delays in publishing the manuscript [AAN f. 282, o. 5, d. 68, l. 17].

1931

AUGUST 8. Julia Averkieva writes Boas from Leningrad, asking whether Boas had a chance to see the English translation she prepared. Reports that Ratner-Shternberg is concerned that there may have been mistakes in the AMNH's Russian typescript [APS].

SEPTEMBER 4. Ratner-Shternberg writes to Boas, "Almost four years ago I sent you the manuscript of my deceased husband, L. Sternberg, 'The Social Organization of the Gilyaks,' yet up to now I have received no final answer about [its] fate . . ." [APS].

SEPTEMBER 8. Boas writes to Ratner-Shternberg, "Your lines of September 4th have just reached me. The long delay in the publication of the MS of your honored husband is as disagreeable to me as to you, but I have not been able to remedy it. Julia Averkieva doubtless told you that we worked on it last year. Now a volume of the Jesup Expedition about physical anthropology has just been finished and the Gilyak MS is the next one at hand, so that I hope to receive the permission to send it to the printer in the coming winter" [AAN f. 282, o. 5, d. 8, l. 20].

NOVEMBER 14. Ratner-Shternberg writes to Boas, "I request that you kindly send a copy of the English translation carried out by Mrs. Averkieva (you probably possess such a copy), for the entering of a few important corrections in accordance with the more exact Russian original that has been found, and also for the purpose of verifying the exactitude of Mrs. Averkieva's reproduction of the Russian original. The corrections will be carried out by [her] under the direction of Mr. Winnikow [Isaak N. Vinnikov], a student of Sternberg's in the area of social organization. The proofreading will be carried out quickly, and immediately after its conclusion I will send the paper back to you. This will also eliminate the necessity of sending over proof sheets. In case you do not possess a copy of the translation, perhaps you would risk sending the original of Mrs. Averkieva's translation over here . . ." [AAN f. 282, o. 5, d. 8, l. 19–19ob].

1932

JANUARY 20. Ratner-Shternberg writes to Boas, "I have learned secondhand that you are willing to fulfill my request—to send me the manuscript of L. Sternberg's 'The Social Organization of the Gilyaks.' I request that you kindly be careful to send it *to my address and not to Mrs. Averkijewa's** (*in order to compare it with the new-found original and to check the accuracy of the translation)" [APS].

FEBRUARY 8. Boas writes to Ratner-Shternberg, "I am going to send Prof. Sternberg's manuscript to you. We are still engaged in revising the English" [AAN f. 282, o. 5, d. 68, l. 25].

JUNE 2. Boas writes to Bogoraz, "Sternberg's work is finally being completed now and I am going to take it along and send it to Mrs. Sternberg in parts" [AAN f. 250, o. 4, d. 25, l. 67].

AUGUST 25. Boas writes to Bogoraz, inquiring whether Ratner-Shternberg received the materials he sent. Boas explains that Sarra Ratner-Shternberg wanted to make her own additions from notes she had found [AAN f. 250, o. 4, d. 25, l. 69].

1933

Ratner-Shternberg publishes the Russian equivalent of the *Social Organization* manuscript in two editions, one in Khabarovsk, the other in Leningrad (Shternberg, *Giliaki* and *Sem'ia*).

FEBRUARY 10. Ratner-Shternberg writes to Boas, "Since over three months have already gone by since you sent off the manuscript 'The Social Organization of the Gilyak' and it has not arrived (except 4 chapters), I have resolved not to wait any longer . . . and to send the English manuscript back to you.

The manuscript has been completed in accordance with the copy here in a few places, which seemed especially important to me, especially the Introduction.

As far as the chapter on the Gens is concerned, which Mrs. Averkijewa translated [ch. 14 of this edition—B. G.], the Russian copy of this part is an exact copy of the one she translated. Unfortunately I have had a great deal to do with it, as Mrs. Averkijewa's translation was not sufficiently attentive and conscientious. She has left out much that was difficult for her to translate, and has misunderstood some things, e.g. she has translated 'Endosmos' and 'Exosmus' without further explanation as 'Endogamy' and 'Exogamy'!!!, etc. Unfortunately she has refused to correct the translations herself, as she seems to be 'very busy.'

I will send you the manuscript in the next few days. I would be greatly thankful and obliged to you if you would inform me of the manuscript's arrival by return mail.

In the hope that the work will finally be published, for which I express my most heartfelt thanks in advance, I remain with great respect . . ." [APS].

FEBRUARY 21. Boas writes to Ratner-Shternberg, "I am very much troubled to learn that you did not receive all the material. You will remember that we sent part of the English translation by mail a year ago, and another part was delivered by von den Steinem last summer. Then you asked for the Russian ms. I sent this by mail November 5, 1932 . . . . The English translation contained 332 typewritten pages; in all 17 chs. I only hope the whole material may turn up so we can go ahead with it" [AAN f. 282, o. 5, d. 68, l. 23].

MARCH 17. Boas writes to Ratner-Shternberg, "I was glad to receive the manuscript which you returned to me and I will try to get the printing started as soon as possible" [AAN f. 282, o. 5, d. 68, l. 22].

1935

MARCH 27. Ratner-Shternberg convenes a meeting in Leningrad of the committee overseeing Shternberg's posthumous works. Members are I. I. Meschannikov, Bogoraz, A. A. Busygin, Isaak N. Vinnikov, E. G. Kagorov, I. G. Karger, Sarra Ratner-Shternberg, and Ian P. Koshkin. On the reverse side of the memo, Sarra Ratner-Shternberg penned, "August 1936: V. G. Bogoraz—to be excluded by reason of his death; Busygin, Karger and Koshkin, by their political motives; and Vinnikov, one of Shternberg's most loyal students, by his refusal to participate in the editorial collective for personal reasons" [AAN f. 282, o. 1, d. 117, l. 2]. There is no mention of Erukhim Kreinovich, although he is listed as having edited the Gilyak language inserts of both Shternberg *Giliaki* and *Sem'ia*. Beginning in 1937, he spent 18 years in Siberian exile for unspecified anti-Soviet activities [Kreinovich Archive, SOKM]. Koshkin, who was the most active of Ratner-Shternberg's deputies, writing the prefaces for Shternberg, *Giliaki*, *Semi'a*, and 1936, disappeared after his arrest in 1937. Karger, who also studied the Gilyak language, may have assisted in editing. Vinnikov's contribution can be asserted more directly: portions of the Shternberg, *Sem'ia* draft typescript in the AAN include a note from Sarra Ratner-Shternberg stating, "Corrections in the male handwriting are the corrections of I. Vinnikov" [f. 282, o. 1, d. 2, l. 40].

1936

Ratner-Shternberg's editorial collective publishes its final posthumous volume, *Pervobytnaia religiia v svete etnografii* [Primitive Religion in Light of Ethnography], in Leningrad (Shternberg, 1936). She later dies during the siege of Leningrad in 1942.

1950

OCTOBER 13. AMNH loans its library copy of the manuscript to Alfred Kroeber for his opinion on its publication [AMNH].

1951

APRIL 6. Harry Shapiro writes to Demitri Shimkin, proposing that Shimkin consider editing the manuscript. Shapiro observes that while "there are sections of the ms. that deal with rather outmoded points of theory, the essential observations are worthwhile . . ." [AMNH].

APRIL 20. Demitri Shimkin writes to Harry Shapiro, recommending a modified version of the Shternberg manuscript that would "synthesize [von] Schrenck and Shternberg, . . . Soviet and Japanese ethnographers . . . [to give a fuller portrait of] Gilyak and their neighbors." He proposes to complete it in a year's time during his time at the Harvard Russian Research Center, together with Clyde Kluckhohn [AMNH].

APRIL 26. Harry Shapiro writes to Demitri Shimkin, acknowledging Shimkin's idea of a new monograph on Gilyaks co-written with Clyde Kluckhohn, but encourages Shimkin not to give up publishing the Shternberg manuscript wholly [AMNH].

MAY 1. Harry Shapiro writes to Demitri Shimkin, asking that two new chapters be added to the Shternberg manuscript, the first on "Shternberg as an anthropologist, particularly in regard to the development of the discipline in Russia; and also with the Gilyak problem [raised] in his work, Boas' and others, both in regard to the putative connections with American Indians and to the peculiarities of social organization which have made the Gilyak such a favorite topic for students of social structure . . . . The second chapter, which would be considerably more lengthy, possibly seventy or eighty pages long, would be a succinct treatment of those aspects of Gilyak culture, such as the use of the environment and relations with neighboring peoples, including the Chinese, that have been neglected by Sternberg" [AMNH].

OCTOBER 11. Demitri Shimkin writes to Harry Shapiro that he was working on comparing Gilyak to Tungus, Yakut, and Oirot-Turkic kin systems [AMNH].

OCTOBER 12. Demitri Shimkin writes to Harry Shapiro proposing, "First, a rather long introduction outlining the geographical position of the Gilyak, their economy and certain other cultural areas with which Shternberg did not deal. Then would come the main body of the text which would be essentially a reordering of Shternberg's materials both in the ms. you sent me and in some of his other publications in a form somewhat more usable than exists at present. To these basic materials I would propose to add clearly separate paragraphs of discussion in terms of later additions to the problem. All the work would then revolve around the problem of social organization and religion with which Sternberg concerned himself largely, but it would be a somewhat more rounded presentation than could be gained by simply compiling his data" [AMNH].

1952

MARCH 3. Demitri Shimkin writes to Harry Shapiro, noting that he is working on the manuscript together with his assistant, Lawrence Krader, and that they plan to focus on the question of Altaic languages.

1954

JANUARY 4. Demitri Shimkin writes to Harry Shapiro, regretting that because he wanted to spend more time incorporating Russian and Japanese literature to the project, and felt it would be too much work, he is declining further work on the project. He returns the manuscript, noting that "little more than basic spade work was accomplished" [AMNH].

1956

APRIL 7. Thomas Hazard writes to Harry Shapiro to say that he has compared the manuscript to Shternberg, *Giliaki*, and finds it substantively different. He is concerned that it will be difficult to get copies of the relevant Soviet publications for editing work [AMNH].

1958

JANUARY 28. Rodney Needham writes to Harry Shapiro, saying that he learned of the manuscript when he was working in the AMNH in 1957 and would be interested in working on it given its importance in Lévi-Strauss, 1969 (1949) [AMNH].

FEBRUARY 10. Rodney Needham writes to Harry Shapiro that he could oversee the editing if it was done by Mrs. Mary Holdworth, of Russian origin, working at the Institute for Commonwealth Studies in Oxford [AMNH].

1959

NOVEMBER 12. Rodney Needham writes to Harry Shapiro that he would like to write a theoretical introduction for the project, and that Lévi-Strauss might be willing to write a preface [AMNH].

DECEMBER 1. Thomas Hazard writes to Harry Shapiro, regretting that his "personal life has upended work on the ms." He notes that he has received three parts, "One complete Russian text, one incomplete Russian text, and third, the translation into English by Roman Jakobson" [AMNH].[3]

DECEMBER 29. Harry Shapiro writes to Thomas Hazard, asking for the manuscript back so that he can send it to Rodney Needham [AMNH].

DECEMBER 29. Harry Shapiro writes to Rodney Needham, venturing that the translation was made by Roman Jakobson at the request of Boas, asks him to make sure it is verified [AMNH].

1960

MAY 8. Rodney Needham writes to Colin Turnbull, noting that he had agreed to edit the Shternberg manuscript, but that he had his own book to work on, plus a Borneo project. "*Now,* if ever Shapiro starts biting his finger-nails, tapping his foot, and wondering what the hell is happening to that Gilyak job, would you please give him some inkling of [how busy I was]? I don't want to write to him myself because I don't want to begin making excuses . . . . Assure him that Needham is the sort of man (anal complex, etc.) who when he says he will do a thing does it" [AMNH].

1962

JULY 5. Rodney Needham writes to Harry Shapiro, apologizing for delays, but observes, "I think the book is important, and that it is outstandingly valuable in the comparative study of prescriptive alliance in particular" [AMNH].

JULY 11. Harry Shapiro writes to Rodney Needham that the manuscript has been "bumped off repeatedly . . . ," adding, "Please hang on to it."

1969

MARCH 18. Memo in AMNH files reads, "Sternberg ms. received from Needham."

---

[3] An October 1, 1941 letter from Clark Wissler to Boas regretted that there was no money to support Jakobson to work on the Jesup materials. AMNH memos indicate only that Jakobson reviewed the manuscript's contents [AMNH].

APPENDIX B:
AN INTERVIEW WITH ZAKHARII EFIMOVICH CHERNIAKOV
Moscow, June 1996

BY *Bruce Grant*

WORKING ON THE *Social Organization* manuscript in Moscow, in St. Petersburg, and on Sakhalin, it often seemed that answers to the more mysterious parts of the manuscript could be found only in archives. Great was my surprise in Moscow in June of 1996 when I found one of Shternberg's former students, then 96, and heard him talk of the first time he saw Lenin, of Shternberg's chain-smoking lectures, of Bogoraz' bad handwriting, and of the early years of Soviet ethnography. Like many of his academic contemporaries, Zakharii Cherniakov mixed war, revolution, and scholarship in his student life, founding the worker's faculty at the Herzen Institute in Petrograd and later moving over to Leningrad University to take classes with Shternberg, a professor who emerges here as someone who mastered the Machiavellian axiom that it is best to be loved and feared at the same time. Cherniakov brings to life the kind of academic/activist/administrator life that many Soviet ethnographers of the 1920s and 1930s led, not quite following Shternberg's "stationary field method," but living in regional centers such as Murmansk and making periodic visits to indigenous communities. He remained a loyal Communist in the post-Soviet era, lamenting the excesses of Stalinism, but, as he does here, explaining them with a careful logic that belied the fatal roulette game to which so many of his university friends fell victim. He died in November 1997.

FIRST SESSION, JUNE 10, 1996

GRANT: Can you tell me a bit about yourself?

CHERNIAKOV: I was born in May of 1900, in Belarus, in Slavgorod. Before it was called Propoisk. In fact, during the 1950s, I went back there. I can show you a photograph from the local newspaper, a Belarus newspaper.

I lived there with my grandmother, grandfather, and mother until I was 4. Then after my grandparents died, my mother and I went to Warsaw, and Lodz. It was 1905, and we lived there for a year. Then my father arrived. He became a representative for a Polish factory in St. Petersburg and that's where we stayed. In the summer I was always in Finland at my uncle's, that is, the husband of my mother's older sister.

[It was] probably around 10 summers, and it was enough to learn Finnish. So that was up to the First World War. Eventually my uncle sold his property and went abroad. I was finishing school at that time, in May of 1917. I immediately went to the Polytechnical Institute. But the Civil War started. I finished the first year and started in the second, but then changed my mind and became a volunteer in the Red Army to participate in the Civil War. I was on the front in Ukraine, on the Crimean Peninsula. After that, I was a correspondent for a while. I joined the office of the magazine *Krasnyi Kommandir* [*Red Commander*]. When I was discharged, I took part in the formation of the very first Pedogogical *Rabfak* [Worker's Faculty]. I founded the one at the Herzen Institute in Petrograd, and I was its head. But I myself hadn't finished my own university education, so I joined the ethnogeography department under Bogoraz, and eventually even worked as his personal secretary for a year and a half. From 1928 to 1937 I worked on the Kola Peninsula. I was the Secretary for the Committee for the New Alphabet there, and like Kreinovich, who worked on the Nivkh language, I created an alphabet for the Saami language and wrote their first literacy primer. [Sergei N.] Stebnitskii was working on a primer for the Koriaks; his wife was working on a primer for the Chukchi language, together with Bogoraz. Eventually I became director for the Institute of Northern Schools in Moscow. What else can I tell you?

Later, I arrived from Murmansk on a leave, to Moscow. And on the day I arrived, they announced the Second World War. Hitler had attacked us. Being a member of the reserve, I rejoined the army that same day, and I was assigned to work in the General Headquarters [*Genshtab*] in Moscow. I spent the whole war in Moscow. There was nothing going on at the university, since it had been evacuated. However, I oversaw a map-making unit connected with the university. We worked on Eastern Prussia, which was part of Kaliningradskaia Oblast', by the request of the government. A year later, they switched me over to India and I produced some more materials for them on the peoples of India.

After that, I went back frequently to the Kola Peninsula and returned to Saami studies. Even today, despite my age, I still plan on going back. What a sight I should be to them.

GRANT: Can you tell me why you became an ethnographer?

CHERNIAKOV: When I was studying in high school, my father wanted me to become an engineer, and my mother wanted me to become a doctor. I liked history, and always thought ethnography was interesting. I joined the Polytechnical Institute to study engineering, but when the Civil War started, I realized that you couldn't waste time doing things that weren't important, so when I went back to study, I joined Bogoraz' department. When I had been in the Crimea, I met a lot of Crimean Tatars, and that's more or less how my ethnographic education began. Later I saw an announcement in the newspaper that a Geography Institute was being formed, with a Department of Ethnography that Shternberg was heading. I wrote the Polytechnical Institute from the Crimea and asked that they forward my documents there. When I arrived back to Petrograd, all of my documents were already there. At first, because I was still in the army, I was a "military auditor" [*voenno-slushatel'*]; later I became a full-time student. That's more or less how I got into it.

Later, the Institute became part of the University, and became its own Division within the Geographic Faculty, under Fertsman, Aleksandr Ivanovich, a geologist. Bogoraz first suggested that I study the Chukchi. I assented, but we were such a large group. There were 10 or 12 of us, including [Tikhon Z.] Semushkin, and others. I asked Bogoraz whether it was really worth it when I already knew Finnish and I could study Finno-Ugric languages. Everyone wanted to go to the Far East, and no one wanted to study the Saami. Bogoraz thought about it, and said, "Yes, that would be prudent." But then I thought, who would my advisor be? Bogoraz realized I had no one, so he said that he would help me.

GRANT: So you started to study with Bogoraz and Shternberg in 1923 or 1924?

CHERNIAKOV: Right, in 1924, and then by 1927, I had finished. Later I became a researcher at the Academy of Sciences at the Institute for the Study of Peoples where [Nikolai Ia. Marr][1] was the head.

GRANT: Did you attend any of Shternberg's lectures?

CHERNIAKOV: Do you know his book, *Primitive Religion*?[2] It's a compendium of all his lectures, and I was at them.

GRANT: What was Shternberg like as a person?

CHERNIAKOV: Shternberg was a very complicated person, very. He was very serious. [pauses]

Shternberg was a very serious person. His pronouncements were never hurried, always grave. Bogoraz was quite different. He was such a jolly, animated character, with a huge range of interests, always asking after new ideas and new subjects. [Both men] were remarkably erudite, but with completely different styles. Shternberg was a very closed kind of person, while Bogoraz was very open. Bogoraz also used to write fiction, remember. And he was an active journalist. He was a master of paradoxes. He suffered for that in life, because he wrote critical essays in the newspapers all the time, and people got back at him for it. Being a Jew, he even had trouble visiting certain cities. So one day he announced himself a Lutheran, and that problem disappeared instantaneously. The authorities couldn't bear him.

GRANT: So you attended all of Shternberg's lectures on primitive religion?

CHERNIAKOV: I should say that as a lecturer he was very difficult. His lectures were always substantive and very deep, but he read very, very slowly. He would bring entire card catalogues with him to the lecture hall and read out long passages from various cards that he would take from his files. Bogoraz was different. He would just start talking, he would go off on tangents, get distracted, laugh, answer our questions.

---

[1]   Nikolai Ia. Marr was a Georgian linguist who rose to prominence in the 1930s with an economically determined theory of the origin of languages. For more on Marr's influence on ethnography, see Roi Medvedev, "Stalin i iazykoznanie," *Nezavisimaia Gazeta* (April 4, 1997), 14; Yuri Slezkine, "N. Ia. Marr and the National Origins of Soviet Ethnogenetics," *Slavic Review* 55, no. 4 (1996), 826–862; N. Ia. Marr, "Avtobiografiia" (1927) in Nikolai Ia. Marr, *Izbrannye raboty,* 5 vols. (Leningrad, 1933); and Thomas Lawrence, *The Linguistic Works of N. Ja. Marr* (Berkeley: Univ. of California Press, 1957).

[2]   L. Ia. Shternberg, *Pervobytnaia religiia v svete etnografii* (Leningrad: Institut Narodov Severa, 1936).

It was a completely different atmosphere. I remember traveling in a car once with Bogoraz and Stebnitskii when we were going to the offices of Pravda. The whole way in the car he urged us to become part-time writers, and told us all about how to write news articles, you know, the satirical kind [fel'etony]. I remember him saying so enthusiastically, "If you want to do it, then it's always simple." He was a very ebullient personality.

GRANT: Did Shternberg ever talk about Boas?

CHERNIAKOV: Shternberg did, and Bogoraz especially. They both considered themselves to be students of Boas.

GRANT: Did you know Shternberg's wife?

CHERNIAKOV: Sarra Arkadievna? Yes, of course. She was also a complicated person. She was very well educated, very erudite. And she was extremely active in publishing [Shternberg's] archive. Koshkin was her deputy in this matter. He helped her a great deal. Everything that was later published is due to the two of them. As a person—what can I say?—she was very attentive to her husband's students. With Shternberg himself I often talked.

GRANT: Is there a way to explain Shternberg's slow pace for submitting the *Social Organization* manuscript? I wondered if he was occupied with other political matters.

CHERNIAKOV: His slowness was just on the surface, because he always thought everything through very thoroughly. Every word he uttered—how should I describe it—was genuinely weighty [vesomo]. Bogoraz felt this and he submitted to Shternberg in almost all matters. I would say he was even a little afraid of him. We were all afraid of Shternberg in different ways. We loved him but feared him. He was occasionally quite severe with Bogoraz and [Shternberg] never forgot a criticism.

GRANT: Would you say that they were friends?

CHERNIAKOV: Yes, they were very close friends. But it was an unusual friendship since, as I said, Shternberg was a rather sharp personality and Bogoraz had to accommodate this. Bogoraz was a far easier person to get along with.

You have to remember that I oversaw Bogoraz' correspondence when I worked as his personal secretary. He needed one because he had such atrocious handwriting. I got used to it, although with difficulty. He dictated letters to me all the time and in many languages. He knew a number of languages fluently. He had a wide correspondence, with Boas, Langevin, W. E. DuBois, Langston Hughes. With many different people. With his brothers as well—he had one in Rostov-on-the-Don, and another in Paris, a doctor.

GRANT: Which of Shternberg's works did you like the most?

CHERNIAKOV: It's hard to say. I heard all his public lectures, on general ethnography, on the cause of Russian Jewry. They were all interesting.

GRANT: I was asking because I find I have different reactions to different works by him. Some I find brilliant; others, like parts of his work on kinship, I find sometimes difficult to work through.

CHERNIAKOV: I understand you because, truly, kinship is very complicated. I think the word boring is even appropriate. But you know, I remember Shternberg's lectures on kinship. They were difficult to follow. Maybe they were boring, but it's as if they were boring and interesting at the same time.

GRANT: You told me that you were friends with Iurii Abramovich Kreinovich, when you both studied under Shternberg together. Do you know why he chose to study Nivkhi?

CHERNIAKOV: I do. Each of us had a task before them, which was to get to know at least one people in depth. This was something Shternberg insisted on in our program. A profound knowledge of one people, and their language, with no less than a year and a half or 2 years of fieldwork. That was [Shternberg's] school, the "stationary school." He put this task before us. You had to know at least one group before you could go on to other work. Kreinovich was very close to Shternberg. He became one of his main students and chose Nivkhi out of loyalty to him. So he did what most of us did, which was to set out to Sakhalin and collect myths and the like.

GRANT: Did you have a sense of how Shternberg and Bogoraz felt about the Soviet government?

CHERNIAKOV: Quite loyally, really. Very positively, I would say. The most difficult time was after the death of Lenin when Stalin's tsarism began. It was very difficult. But in the early years we were all, in short, enthusiasts. Once I went to hear Lenin speak, at the Congress of the Communist International in 1920. I went with my commander, Vasilii Ivanovich [—]. When we got to the auditorium he said, "Wait, soon you'll feel the full artillery of Marxism." And he was right. That day changed my life.

GRANT: When you read [Shternberg and Bogoraz'] memoirs, you get the impression that the enthusiasm was very genuine.

CHERNIAKOV: On top of that, it was the heyday of the Committee of the North.[3] Bogoraz and Shternberg were members of the Committee, and Bogoraz even ran the Petrograd branch.

GRANT: Did Shternberg take much part in the Committee of the North? I always thought his membership was just a formality.

CHERNIAKOV: What are you saying? He was a very active participant.

GRANT: I think it's because I saw Shternberg's name far more rarely in the Committee archives.

CHERNIAKOV: You just need to take a look at the journal *Sovetskii Sever* [*Soviet North*].

GRANT: When I've read through articles by Bogoraz, I was always confused by his pseudonym "Tan." Do you know where it came from?

CHERNIAKOV: He used Tan from his original name, Natan, so his pseudonym originally was N. A. Tan. He signed all his popular writings that way. His scientific work was just "Bogoraz." Then with time, he started using both, Bogoraz-Tan.

---

[3] The *Komitet sodeistviia narodnostiam severnykh Okrain pri Prezidiume VTsIK* (1924–1935) [Committee for the Assistance to Peoples of the Northern Borderlands] commonly known as the *Komitet Severa* or Committee of the North.

GRANT: Shternberg died in 1927. What kind of atmosphere was there at the time in the world of Petersburg ethnography?

CHERNIAKOV: It was an open battle with supporters of Marr, since Marr's position was diametrically opposed to our position as ethnographers. It was a very sharp opposition. I can even tell you about the map I worked on for my dissertation. I was using the 1926 census to put together a map of languages of the USSR. When the Marrists found out, they wanted me to do it entirely along Marrist lines, I refused to continue and gave up my dissertation right then and there. On principle. The Marrists thought that Indo-Europeanism was an anachronism, and built up their own theory about the origin of all world languages. The Japhetic language family is a reality, one has to look into it, but when Marr got into ancient languages using the same theory, it was a fantasy. By the way, Stalin took part in this fantasy as well, if you see his *Marxism and Linguistics*.[4] But that's what happens when you have people who aren't specialists.

GRANT: So Kreinovich went into the field in 1926. Did you also go off at the same time?

CHERNIAKOV: I went off in 1928, and stayed until 1937. From 1928 to 1937, it was almost 10 years. The advantage was that I grew up knowing Finnish, so it was easy for me to learn the Saami language. I still understand it today.

GRANT: So did you ever see Kreinovich after Shternberg died?

CHERNIAKOV: I saw him not long before he was sent away in 1937. The problem was that he got involved in local politics when he was on Sakhalin. I always stayed out of things like that when I was in Murmansk.[5]

GRANT: So what was Kreinovich's mistake?

CHERNIAKOV: I wouldn't call it a mistake. I couldn't even call it a lack of caution because he was a very cautious person. He just got caught up in the local politics when he was supporting Nivkh interests. You know, on Sakhalin, they were drilling for oil and developing the fish industry. It was hardly as if the local oil barons were interested in ethnography, and Kreinovich protested that they were harming Nivkh communities. So they informed on him to the police.

Many people were surprised that I never got taken away, but the difference is that I never hid anything. I wrote about my grandfather and grandmother, who lived abroad. I wrote about my father who had left in 1922 to live in Palestine. I always told everyone and wrote it down on all my job applications so that I could say it was never a secret. People informed on me too, saying that I had an uncle in Paris and a father in Palestine, that they were anti-Soviet elements. But I could always say, "Well, of course, I've always been open about it." If I had hidden it there wouldn't have even been a conversation. They would have just taken me away.

---

[4]   Iosif Stalin, *Marksizm i voprosy iazykoznaniia* (Berlin: Volk und Wissen Volkseigener Verlag, 1952); published in English as *Marxism and Linguistics* (New York: International, 1951).

[5]   Kreinovich was involved in many conflicts with local fishermen on Sakhalin, enforcing the jurisdiction of the new Soviet fishing collectives Gilyaks had joined. Grant, *In the Soviet House of Culture*, 72–80. By contrast, however, he was much less a figure of formal political life than Cherniakov, who worked in the Murmansk regional administration from 1928 to 1937.

GRANT: In a letter he wrote late in his life, Kreinovich once said that he considered himself too naive, that "innocence is worse than thievery" [*prostota khuzhe vorovstva*]. Did you ever have that feeling about him?

CHERNIAKOV: Oh, looking back, we were all that way. I was an exception only in that I began studying Marxism before the revolution. When I was still in high school, my parents rented out one of their rooms to boarders. Two brothers came to live in our house . . . . They represented themselves as aristocrats, and perhaps they were, but more importantly they were Marxist revolutionaries. They had all the literature—Lenin, Plekhanov, Bogdanov. It was 1915 or 1916. Then suddenly they disappeared. Either they went abroad or went into hiding. But they left all their books behind. So when they left I started to read it all. We were lucky that the police didn't find out since it was a crime to have those kinds of books around. But I kept them right until the revolution.

SECOND SESSION, JUNE 24, 1996

GRANT: So, you started studying in 1925. Can you tell me about the other graduate students you studied with?

CHERNIAKOV: Well, we all had the Ethnographic Division in common. Before the Geographic Institute with the university, and the formation of the Geographic Faculty within the university, I was still in the Geography Institute, in the Ethnography Faculty under Shternberg. He brought together a relatively small group, we were all working in different parts of the country, we would go off and collect data.

As a rule, when we were in the field we didn't think of ourselves as researchers but as civil servants. So when people were stationed in Siberia or the Far East for their research, most of the time they were working in kolkhozes, or an artel, or an elementary school. Shternberg approved of this since this gave us cause to share the problems of the people we were studying. We had common interests with the people we were studying and could see their life as they did. It wasn't like the later Soviet school, when you would go somewhere for 2 weeks and then come back and write it all up. We stayed in the field for a few years, and shared in people's successes and failures. It was just assumed that you would experience at least a few annual cycles—a few winters, a few springs, a few summers. You know, you arrive in the summer, that was the usual tradition. The summer would be spent in language training. You trip your way through the fall, by winter you can more or less speak, and by the following summer you are a real member of the community. That's when you really start your work. It wasn't like someone who just showed up for weddings and funerals.

So, who else was there? Semushkin went to the Chukchi. He eventually became a writer. Stebnitskii went to the Koriaks, and learned the language; he wrote their first primer and translated textbooks. He wrote a grammar for the language. He became a leading specialist in Koriak studies. Kreinovich went to the Gilyaks.

GRANT: Can you tell me about the people here? [We look at the 1926 photograph of him and his colleagues reprinted in the Foreword.]

CHERNIAKOV: Those are my comrades. I could tell you as much as you like about any of them. [N. G.] Shprintzin was a museum worker. She was very close to Bogoraz and worked very closely with him on museum affairs. [Ian P.] Koshkin went to work with Evenks, the same thing. Then there's [Saul M.] Abramzon, he went to work with the Kyrgyz. That was a very different direction than most of us. He got in trouble with the local obkom there. The first secretary of Kyrgyziia wanted to destroy him, but he held out. [Stepan A.] Makar'ev, he studied Vepsy, but he was a fieldworker, and put out a textbook called *Field Ethnography* under Bogoraz' supervision.[6] I see [Pavel Iu.] Moll. He studied the Chukchi. You know who's not here? [Valentin A.] Avrorin—he went to work with Nanaitsy, knew all the dialects. [Elena V.] Talonova was also a museum specialist. She was more of a generalist.

GRANT: Can you tell me which courses of Shternberg's you attended?

CHERNIAKOV: Of course. Material Culture, Social Culture, and Religion. Those were three separate courses. But he began with a general course called Introduction to Ethnography.

GRANT: Which one did you like most of all?

CHERNIAKOV: That's hard to say. Simultaneously we listened to Shternberg's lectures in ethnography and Bogoraz' lectures in ethnogeography. They were two completely different people. Bogoraz had an infectious enthusiasm and won us over with his erudition and wide-ranging curiosity. Shternberg was the absolute opposite. He spoke very unclearly. He muttered, took long pauses between sentences, and smoked constantly, coughing. He stuck very closely to the information he brought with him on index cards that he brought to every lecture. He would often bring whole drawers of these cards with him so that he could respond to students' questions with entire citations that he had transcribed from various books. He was even, to a certain extent, hard to make out at times. And yet his lectures were so substantive. They gave you such a vivid picture of other worlds.

Shternberg lived not far from the university. After the lectures we would often walk in the same direction back to our homes. These were unforgettable conversations for me. He would always talk philosophy and history as we walked. Sometimes I tried to argue with him and he would very patiently explain his positions. For me it was a school of its own, no less than the formal lectures at the university.

GRANT: People say that Shternberg liked to start speaking in Nivkh every now and then during lectures?

CHERNIAKOV: Well, he cited things occasionally, but it was nothing unusual.

GRANT: Do you remember who you read in those courses? For example, in his course on Social Culture?

CHERNIAKOV: We read Tylor's book, *Primitive Culture*. Mostly we read foreign works—Boas, Rivers.

GRANT: Did Shternberg and Bogoraz make references to political topics when they lectured?

---

6   Stepan Andreevich Makar'ev, *Polevaia Etnografiia* (Leningrad: Izdanie etnograficheskoi ekskursionnoi kommissii etnootdeleniia geofaka LGU, 1928).

CHERNIAKOV: Yes, of course, you should consult Bogoraz' publications on the topic. He frequently wrote about the revolution.

GRANT: What about drawing northern peoples toward socialism? Were there those kinds of lectures?

CHERNIAKOV: You know, that wasn't really necessary. All of our lectures in one way or another were about the importance of drawing northern peoples into the Soviet fold, bypassing feudalism and capitalism and entering directly into socialism. That was our mission. It was of course a great achievement and a big mistake. What happened of course is that people left their old lives behind, but had no training to speak of for the new lives they were to participate in. Instead of eliminating traditional cultures, we should have tried to advance them, to elevate them. Instead of eliminating traditional reindeer herding, we should have tried to create an "advanced reindeer herding" [*razvitoe olenevodstvo*].[7] Technically advanced. If we had taught them how to drive motorized sleds, instead of making them leave the taiga, and how to iron their own clothes, that would have been an accomplishment.

GRANT: Was it palpable that a new nationalities policy was in place in the 1930s under Stalin?

CHERNIAKOV: Of course we felt it. It was evident at every step of our work. I mean, we all started out our work learning native languages, writing literacy primers, promoting native intellectuals. And suddenly, we are told that we are supposed to discourage native language use, to attract people instead to the Russian language. Basically, to Russify them.

GRANT: How did the Saami you knew react when that policy came into effect?

CHERNIAKOV: What do you mean "react"? No one ever asked. You have to remember that this was the same time when Stalin ordered that all native children be placed in boarding schools so as to forget the way of life their parents had. People resisted but the resistance was quelled, that's all there was to it. Then there was the whole transfer of nomadic peoples to sedentary life. Whole Saami families were just moved into small towns. It was all looked upon as prudent and even generous.

GRANT: Going back to Shternberg, did he ever talk about his work for Russian Jewry? Was it a large part of his work?

CHERNIAKOV: His study of Jews is a special field unto itself. He was a leader of the Jewish Ethnographic Circle. He read lectures there. I went once. He had a particularly interesting article on this too. It wasn't his specialty, but it occupied much of his time.

GRANT: Did Shternberg ever say anything about his visits to New York?

CHERNIAKOV: He mentioned it in his lectures a number of times, about how both he and Bogoraz had been in America. It's difficult for me to remember the details. They talked about their opinions about international events with some frequency.

---

7   Cherniakov's reference to "advanced herding" seemed a play on the expression used frequently in the Brezhnev period, "advanced socialism" [*razvityi sotsializm*]. His position resonates with the 1920s Soviet policies toward Siberian indigenous peoples, promoting native culture within a strict framework of government supervision.

GRANT: A few days ago, I went to see Shternberg's grave, where the aphorism "All humanity is one" [*Vse chelovechestvo edino*] is written at the head of the gravestone.[8] Was that an idea that often came up in his lectures?

CHERNIAKOV: Of course. But mostly what I remember is the methodology: The stationary method, the practical mastery of the language, and the use of language not only for the receipt of information, but for scientific analysis itself. So language always had a double role: for information, and for analysis in and of itself.

GRANT: After Shternberg and Bogoraz, who were the successful ethnographers?

CHERNIAKOV: [pauses] Of course, there aren't many. There were interesting people, and intelligent people here and there. The Slavists, for example. For example, there is one fellow who is being translated from German now. What is his name? Then we had that specialist in Turkish languages . . . . I forget the name. [Boris Ia.] Vladimirtsov was a specialist in Mongolian languages.

GRANT: In the 1930s, one talks about how much fieldwork diminished after the arrival of Stalin.

CHERNIAKOV: Well, I spent 10 years in the field from 1928 to 1937, so I can't say there was any obstacle. But I also can't say that it was all fieldwork pure and simple, because I worked mainly in Murmansk as the First Secretary there of the Committee for the New Alphabet. In the Murmansk regional offices, I took part in the redrawing of boundaries for the Murmansk okrug. Then again in 1959 I took part in the census for the Kola Peninsula, so I was doing different things. Most of us did that. Vdovin, for example, taught for a few years. I usually went a few times a year for a month. It wasn't a leave of absence, just part of my work, and I always felt comfortable there. People always invited me to stay in their homes, but I didn't want to offend them so I always stayed in the same room in the same hotel.

GRANT: Can you tell me about Shternberg's funeral?

CHERNIAKOV: First I should tell you about his illness. He was living in a dacha just outside of Petersburg. It was in the summer of 1927. He was a friend of Professor Kagarin and his wife. I went to the Kagarins once and he told me that Shternberg was very sick. Sarra Arkadievna met us and told us that he was very sick and couldn't see anyone. He was already on his deathbed at that point.

When he died, Bogoraz was very active in organizing the funeral, and I was his secretary, so Bogoraz and I did much of the work. Preparing documents, ordering the coffin . . . . There was a meeting at the university where his coffin was. After that we went to the cemetery. I remember that I was taking care of various tasks for others, so I went back on forth on my bicycle around the city. The whole group moved rather slowly along Nevskii Prospekt and then over to the Party Committee building on the Moika, where various party officials also made speeches about him. I had to dash about on my bicycle to prepare the meetings, and then finally, I went ahead with the coffin to the cemetery, with Sarra Arkadievna, Koshkin, quite a number of well-known cultural figures. There were a lot of people at the funeral.

---

8   Shternberg is buried in Preobrazhenskoe Evreiskoe Kladbishche in the southern end of St. Petersburg.

At the cemetery, they had asked me to choose a spot, and I had chosen a location beside the famous artist, Antakol'skii, but for some reason, it didn't suit Sarra Arkadievna, and she required that it be moved to another spot. I can't remember why, perhaps it was too shady there. Then they asked me to speak at the graveside in the name of his students. The speech was published somewhere . . . . I can't remember . . . *Vestnik* . . . ? There were only two issues, but the first one included my speech. It was a journal of student works. The first issue was dedicated to Shternberg. The first article is mine, though it didn't carry my name. You should absolutely find it. It would be very useful.

GRANT: Do you know whether Sarra Arkadievna got along with Bogoraz? One gathers from their letters that they were not fond of each other.[9]

CHERNIAKOV: That is also difficult for me to say. I know that their relations were somewhat strained. But I couldn't say they were antagonistic. Now as far as relations between Bogoraz and Shternberg were concerned, I can say. Shternberg often went to Bogoraz for help on his English. Bogoraz had been in the United States longer than he, and he had a much better command of the language. And Bogoraz always helped him. He was always helpful, but rather official with Shternberg.

GRANT: Did you knew Iulia Averkieva? She also did some work on the *Social Organization* manuscript with Sarra Arkadievna.

CHERNIAKOV: I knew her, of course. It was so sad how much time she spent in labor camps. Then there was Koshkin. They shot him, if I recall. It was a horrible, horrible time. The Red Terror.

GRANT: This is why you have to write your autobiography.

CHERNIAKOV: Yes, but you know, I can only write about myself.

---

[9] AAN f. 282, o. 5, d. 70.

Bibliography[1]

Al'kor. *See* Koshkin

Anderson, Barbara, and Brian Silver

1984. Equality, Efficiency and Politics in Soviet Bilingual Education Policy 1934–1980. American Political Science Review 78, no. 4 (October): 1019–1039.

[Anonymous]

1930. Lev Iakovlevich Shternberg: Vazhneishie biograficheskie daty. Ocherki po istorii znanii VII: 7–19.

Austerlitz, Robert

1956. Gilyak Nursery Words. Word 12: 260–279.

1957. A Linguistic Approach of the Ethnobotany of South Sakhalin. Ninth Pacific Science Congress of the Pacific Science Association. Bangkok.

1959. Gilyak Religious Terminology in the Light of Linguistic Analysis. The Transactions of the Asiatic Society of Japan 7: 207–223.

1961. The Identification of Folkloristic Genres (Based on Gilyak Materials). *In* D. Davie et al., eds., Poetics—Poetyka—Poetika. Warsaw: Panstwowe Wydawnictwo Naukow; The Hague: Mouton.

1967. Two Gilyak Song Texts. *In* To Honor Roman Jakobson—Essays on the Occasion of His Seventieth Birthday, 11 October 1966. Vol. 1: 99–113. The Hague: Mouton.

1968. Native Seal Nomenclatures in South Sakhalin. *In* Joseph K. Yamagiwa, ed., Papers of the C.I.C. Far Eastern Language Institute. Ann Arbor.

1974. Paleosiberian Languages. *In* Encyclopaedia Britannica, 15th ed.: 914–916.

1977. The Study of Paleosiberian Languages. *In* Roman Jakobson: Echoes of His Scholarship. Lisse: Peter de Ridder Press.

1978. Folklore, Nationality, and the Twentieth Century in Siberia and the Soviet Far East. *In* Felix Oinas, ed., Folklore, Nationalism and Politics. Columbus, OH: Slavica.

1981. Gilyak Internal Reconstruction, 1: Seven Etyma. Folia Slavica 5(1–3).

1983a. Studies of Paleosiberian Languages. *In* Morris Halle, ed., Roman Jakobson: What He Taught Us. Columbus, OH: Slavica.

1984a. Ten Nivkh Erotic Poems. Acta Ethnographica of the Academy of Sciences of Hungary 33(1–4): 33–44.

1984b. Gilyak Internal Reconstruction, 2: Iron and Questions Related to Metallurgy. Folia Slavica 7(1–2): 38–48.

1984c. On the Vocabulary of Nivkh Shamanism: The Etymon of Qas ("Drum") and Related Questions. *In* Mihaly Hoppal, ed., Shamanism in Eurasia: 231–241. Gottingen: Herodot.

1985a. Etymological Frustration (Gilyak). International Journal of American Linguistics 51: 336–338.

1985b. Gilyak Verse and Music. Proceedings of The International Symposium on B. Pilsudskii's Phonographic Records and the Ainu Culture. Hokkaido Univ. Ural-Altaic Yearbook 58: 143–144.

1986. Gilyak Internal Reconstruction, 3: Ligneous Matter. Folia Slavica.

1988. Lexicography of the Paleosiberian Languages. *In* Dictionaries, an International Encylopaedia. Berlin: Walter de Gruyter.

Averkieva, Julia [Iuliia], and Mark A. Sherman

1992. Kwakiutl String Figures. New York: American Museum of Natural History.

Avgustinovich, F. M.

1872. Zhizn' russkikh i inorodtsev na Ostrove Sakhalin—Vsemirnyi puteshestvennik. Tom 2. St. Petersburg.

1880. Zametki ob Ostrove Sakhaline. St. Petersburg.

Balzer, Marjorie Mandelstam

1978. Strategies of Ethnic Survival: Interaction of Russians and Khanty in 20th Century Siberia. Ph.D. diss., Department of Anthropology, Bryn Mawr College.

1980. The Route to Eternity: Cultural Persistence and Change in Khanty Burial Ritual. Arctic Anthropology 17(1): 77–89.

---

[1] [**Editor's note:** While recognizing that many older Russian encyclopaedic entries and early Soviet publications are incompletely catalogued here, it seemed most useful to include all reference information available, however partial the form.]

1981. Rituals of Gender Identity: Markers of Siberian Khanty Ethnicity, Status and Belief. American Anthropologist 83(4): 850–867.

1982. Peoples of Siberia. *In* Stephen M. Horak, ed., Guide to the Study of Soviet Nationalities: The Non-Russian Peoples of the USSR: 239–252. Littleton, CO: Libraries Unlimited.

1983. Ethnicity without Power. Slavic Review 42(4): 633–648.

1983b. Doctors or Deceivers? The Siberian Khanty Shaman and Soviet Medicine. *In* Lola Romanucci-Ross, ed., The Anthropology of Medicine: 54–76. New York: Praeger.

1987. Behind Shamanism: Changing Voices of Siberian Khanty Shamanism and Cosmology and Politics. Social Science and Medicine 24: 1085–1093.

1992. Dilemmas of the Spirit: Religious Atheism in the Yakut-Sakha Republic. *In* Sabrina Ramet, ed., Religious Policy in the Soviet Union: 231–251. New York: Cambridge Univ. Press.

1993. Two Urban Shamans: Unmasking Leadership in Fin-de-Soviet Siberia. *In* George Marcus, ed. Late Editions: Amid Transitions at the End of the Century: 131–164. Chicago: Univ. Chicago Press.

1995. Homelands, Leadership, and Self-Rule: Observations on Interethnic Relations in the Sakha Republic. Polar Geography 19(4): 284–305.

1996a. Flights of the Sacred: Symbolism and Theory in Siberian Shamanism. American Anthropologist 98(2): 40–53.

1996b. Changing Images of the Shaman: Folklore and Politics in the Sakha Republic (Yakutia). Shaman 4(1–2): 5–16.

1997. Sacred Genders in Siberia: Shamans, Bear Festivals, and Androgyny. *In* Sabrina Petra Ramet, ed., Gender Reversals and Gender Cultures: 164–182. London: Routledge.

BALZER, MARJORIE MANDELSTAM, ed.
1990. Shamanism: Soviet Studies of Traditional Religion in Siberia and Central Asia. Armonk, NY: M. E. Sharpe.

BARKAN, ELAZAR, AND RONALD BUSH, eds.
1995. Prehistories of the Future: The Primitivist Project and the Culture of Modernism. Stanford: Stanford Univ. Press.

BARNES, R. H.
1974. Kédang: A Study in the Collective Thought of an Eastern Indonesian People. Oxford: Clarendon.

BARSUKOV, IVAN PLATONOVICH
1893. O zhizni i podvigakh Innokentiia.
1897. The life and work of Innocent, the archbishop of Kamchatka, the Kuriles and the Aleutian Islands, and later the metropolitan of Moscow. San Francisco: Cubery.

BARTELS, DENNIS A., AND ALICE L. BARTELS
1995. When the North was Red: Aboriginal Education in Soviet Siberia. Montreal: McGill-Queen's Univ. Press.

BATAILLE, GEORGES
1993. The Accursed Share: An Essay on General Economy. Vol. 2–3. New York: Zone. [translated by Robert Hurley]

BEFU, HARUMI, AND JOSEF KREINER, eds.
1992. Othernesses of Japan: Historical and Cultural Influences on Japanese Studies in Ten Countries. Munich: Iudicium.

BILINSKY, YAROSLAV
1980. The Concept of the Soviet People and its Implications for Soviet Nationality Policy. Annals of the Ukrainian Academy of Arts and Science in the United States 37–38: 86–133.

BLACK, LYDIA
1972. Relative Status of Wife Givers and Wife Takers in Gilyak Society. American Anthropologist 74(5): 1244–1248.

1973a. The Nivkh (Gilyak) of Sakhalin and the Lower Amur. Arctic Anthropology 10(1): 1–110.

1973b. Dogs, Bears and Killer Whales: An Analysis of the Nivkh Symbolic System. Ph.D. diss., Department of Anthropology, Univ. Massachusetts, Amherst.

BLOCH, MAURICE
1983. Marxism and Anthropology. New York: Oxford Univ. Press.

BOAS, FRANZ
1909. The Kwakiutl of Vancouver Island. New York: Stechert.

1927 [1911]. The Mind of Primitive Man. New York: Macmillan.

1928. Anthropology and Modern Life. New York: Norton.

1948. Race, Language and Culture. New York: Macmillan.

1973 [1896]. The Limitations of the Comparative Method in Anthropology. *In* Paul Bohannan and Mark Glazer, eds.

High Points in Anthropology: 84–92. New York: Knopf.

BOAS, FRANZ, ed.
1938. General Anthropology. New York: D. C. Heath.

BOGORAS. *See* BOGORAZ

BOGORAZ (BOGORAZ-TAN, BOGORAS), VLADIMIR (NATAN, WALDEMAR) GERMANOVICH (MENDELEVICH)
1909. The Chukchee. Franz Boas, ed. [Memoirs of the American Museum of Natural History Vol. II, pts. 1–3]. Leiden: E.J. Brill, and New York: Stechert.
1922. O pervobytnykh plemenakh. Zhizn' Natsional'nostei 1: 130.
1923. Ob izuchenii i okhrane okrainnykh narodov. Zhizn' Natsional'nostei 3–4: 168–80
1927a. Severnyi rabfak. Sovetskaia Aziia 2: 52–63.
1927b. L. Ia. Shternberg, kak chelovek i uchenyi. Etnografiia 2: 269–282.
1928. L. Ia. Shternberg, kak etnograf. *In* S. Ol'denburg, ed., Pamiati L'va Iakovlevicha Shternberga: 4–30. Leningrad: Akademiia Nauk.
1932. Religiia kak tormoz sotsstroitel'stva sredi malykh narodnostei Severa. Sovetskii Sever 1–2: 142–157.
1935. Voskresshee plemia. Moscow: Khudozhestvennaia Literatura.
1936. Osnovnye tipy fol'klora severnoi Evrazii i Severnoi Ameriki. Sovetskii Fol'klor 4–5: 29–50.
1997 [1928]. Lev. Ia. Shternberg as an Ethnographer. Anthropology and Archaeology of Eurasia 35(3): 17–42. [translation of Bogoraz, 1928, by Stephen Lang]

BOGORAZ, VLADIMIR GERMANOVICH, AND N. J. LEONOV
1928. Cultural Work among the Lesser Nationalities of the North in the USSR. *In* Proceedings of the 23rd International Congress of Americanists.

BOIKO, VLADIMIR IVANOVICH, ed.
1986. Kul'tura narodnostei Severa: traditsii i sovremennost'. Novosibirsk: Nauka.
1988. Nivkhi Sakhalina. Sovremmenoe sotsialno-ekonomicheskoe razvitie. Novosibirsk: Nauka.
1989. Kul'tura narodov Severa: filosofsko-sotsiologicheskii analiz. Novosibirsk: Nauka.

BRASLAVETS, KONSTANTIN MAKAROVICH
1983. Istoriia v nazvaniiakh na karte sakhalinskoi oblasti. Iuzhno-Sakhalinsk: Dal'nevostochnoe knizhnoe izdatel'stvo.

BRETTELL, CAROLINE B., ed.
1993. When They Read What We Write: The Politics of Ethnography. Westport: Bergin and Garvey.

BROWER, DANIEL
1975. Training the Nihilists: Education and Radicalism in Tsarist Russia. Ithaca, NY: Cornell Univ. Press.

BUCKLEY, THOMAS, AND ALMA GOTTLIEB, eds.
1988. Blood Magic: The Anthropology of Menstruation. Berkeley: Univ. California Press.

BUSCHMAN
1852. Ueber die Naturlaute. Abhandlungen der Academie der Wissenschaften zu Berlin.

BUTKOVSKII, IA.
1874. Sakhalin i ego znachenie. Morskoi Sbornik 2 (April): 131–139.
1882. Ostrov Sakhalin. Istoricheskii Vestnik 10: 175–186.

CHARD, CHESTER
1961. Sternberg's Materials on the Sexual Life of the Gilyak. Anthropological Papers of the Univ. Alaska 10(1): 13–23.

CHEKHOV, ANTON
1967. The Island: A Journey to Sakhalin. New York: Washington Square Press. [translated by Luba and Michael Terpak]
1978. Ostrov Sakhalin: Polnoe sobranie sochinenii i pisem. Vols. 14–15. Moscow: Nauka.
1993. A Journey to Sakhalin. Cambridge: Ian Faulkner. [translated by Brian Reeve]

COLLIER, JANE, AND SYLVIA YANAGISAKO, eds.
1987. Gender and Kinship: Essays toward a Unified Analysis. Stanford: Stanford Univ. Press.

COMRIE, BERNARD
1981. The Languages of the Soviet Union. New York: Cambridge Univ. Press.

CRAWLEY, A. E.
1907. Exogamy and the Mating of Cousins. *In* R. R. Marett, W. H. R. Rivers, and Northcote W. Thomas, eds. Anthropological Essays Presented to Edward Burnett Tylor in Honour of his 75th Birthday, October 2, 1907: 51–63. Oxford: Clarendon.

CUNOW, HEINRICH
1894. Die Verwandtschafts-Organisationen der Australneger; ein Beitrag zur

Entwicklungsgeschichte der Familie. Stuttgart: Deik.

CZAPLICKA, MARIE ANTOINETTE
1914.   Aboriginal Siberia: A Study in Social Anthropology. Oxford: Clarendon.

DAVYDOV, GAVRIIL IVANOVICH
1810–1812.   Dvukratnoe puteshestvie v Ameriku ofitserov Davydova i Khvostova. 2 vols.
1977.   Two voyages to Russian America, 1802–1807. Kingston, Canada: Limestone Press.

DEFOE, DANIEL
1789.   The Wonderful Life, and Surprising Adventures of the Renowned Hero Robinson Crusoe. Philadelphia: Charles Cist.
1925 [1790].   The Farther Adventures of Robinson Crusoe. London: Constable.

DEGRAAF, TJEERD
1992.   The Small Languages of Sakhalin. International Journal of the Sociology of Language 94: 185–200.

DELORIA, ELLA CARA
1988.   Waterlily. Lincoln: Univ. Nebraska Press.

DEREVIANKO, ANATOLII PANTELEEVICH, AND VLADIMIR IVANOVICH BOIKO
1986.   Puti kul'turnogo razvitiia Sibiri. In V. I. Boiko, ed., Kul'tura narodnostei Severa: traditsii i sovremennost': 5–13. Novosibirsk: Nauka.

DEWINDT, HARRY
1896.   The New Siberia: Being an Account of a Visit to the Penal Island of Sakhalin, and Political Prison and Mines of the Trans–Baikal District, Eastern Siberia. London: Chapman and Hall.

DOROSHEVICH, VLAS MIKHAILOVICH
1903.   Sakhalin: Katorga. Moscow: I. D. Shchukin.

DUNN, STEPHEN
1979.   The Position of the Primitive-Communal Social Order in the Soviet-Marxist Theory of History. In Stanley Diamond, ed., Towards a Marxist Anthropology: Problems and Perspectives: 173–184. The Hague: Mouton.

ENGELS, FREDERICK
1972.   The Origin of the Family, Private Property and the State: in Light of the Researches of Lewis Henry Morgan. Edited with an Introduction by Eleanor Burke Leacock. New York: International Publishers.

ERMAN, ADOLPH
1833–48.   Reise um die Erde durch Nord-Asien und die beiden Oceane in den Jahren 1828, 1829 und 1830 ausgefuhrt von Adolph Erman. Berlin: G. Reimer.
1871.   Etnographische Wahrnehmungen. Zeitschrift für Ethnologie 3: 162–163.
1970.   Travels in Siberia. New York: Arno Press. [translated from the German by William D. Colley]

FAUBION, JAMES
1996.   Kinship Is Dead. Long Live Kinship. Comparative Studies in Society and History 38: 67–91.

FEIT, HARVEY
1991.   The Construction of Algonquian Hunting Territories: Private Property as Moral Lesson, Policy Advocacy, and Ethnographic Error. In George W. Stocking, ed., Colonial Situations: Essays in the Contextualization of Ethnographic Knowledge: 109–134. Madison: Univ. Wisconsin Press.

FELD, STEVEN
1987.   Dialogic Editing: Interpreting How the Kaluli Read Sound and Sentiment. Cultural Anthropology 2(2): 190–210.

FISON, LORIMER, AND A. W. HOWITT
1880.   Kamilaroi and Kurnai. Melbourne: George Robertson.
1991 [1880].   Kamilaroi and Kurnai; Group-Marriage and Relationship, and Marriage by Elopement/Drawn Chiefly from the Usage of the Australian Aborigines. Introduction by Lewis H. Morgan. Canberra: Australian Institute of Aboriginal and Torres Strait Islander Studies.

FOUCAULT, MICHEL
1990.   The History of Sexuality: An Introduction. Vol. 1. New York: Vintage.

FRAZER, JAMES
1898.   Le Totemisme. Paris: Schleicher. [translated to the French by A. Dirr and J. Van Gennep]
1910.   Totemism and Exogamy. A Treatise on Certain Early Forms of Superstition and Society. London: Macmillan.

FREED, STANLEY A., RUTH S. FREED, AND LAILA WILLIAMSON
1988.   Capitalist Philanthropy and Russian Revolutionaries: The Jesup North Pacific Expedition (1897–1902). American Anthropologist 90: 7–24.

GAGEN-TORN, NINA IVANOVNA
1971.   The Leningrad School of the 1920s.

Soviet Anthropology and Archaeology 10: 146–167.

1975.   Lev Iakovlevich Shternberg. Moscow: Nauka.

GALTSEV-BIZUK, SVIATOZAR DEMIDOVICH
1992.   Toponomicheskii Slovar'. Iuzhno-Sakhalinsk: Sakhalinskoe knizhnoe izdatel'stvo.

GASSENSCHMIDT, CHRISTOPH
1995.   Jewish Liberal Politics in Tsarist Russia, 1900–1914: The Modernization of Russian Jewry. New York: New York Univ. Press.

GELLNER, ERNEST
1976.   The Soviet and the Savage. Current Anthropology 16(4): 595–616.

1988.   State and Society in Soviet Thought. London: Basil Blackwell.

GELLNER, ERNEST, ed.
1980.   Soviet and Western Anthropology. New York: Cambridge Univ. Press.

GESSEN, IOSIF VLADIMIROVICH, M. B. RATNER, AND LEV IAKOVLEVICH SHTERNBERG, eds.
1906.   Nakanune probuzhdeniia: Sbornik statei po evreiskomu voprosu. St. Petersburg: A. G. Rozen.

GLADYSHEV, A. I., ed.
1986.   Administrativno-territorial'noe delenie Sakhalinskoi oblasti. Iuzhno-Sakhalinsk: Dal'nevostochnoe knizhnoe izdatel'stvo.

GLEASON, ABBOTT
1980.   Young Russia: The Genesis of Russian Radicalism in the 1860s. New York: Viking.

GONTMAKHER, PETR IAKOVLEVICH
1973.   O natsional'nom svoeobrazii narodnogo iskusstva nivkhov. In A. I. Krushanova, ed., Istoriia i kul'tura narodov Dal'nego Vostoka: 281–289. Iuzhno-Sakhalinsk: Akademiia Nauk.

1974a. Istoriia kul'tury nivkhov. Diss., Vladivostok State Univ.

1974b. Istoriografiia narodnogo dekorativno-prikladnogo iskusstva nivkhov. In A. I. Krushanova, ed., Voprosy istorii i kul'tury narodov Dal'nego Vostoka. Vypusk 2: 139–152. Vladivostok: Akademiia Nauk.

1974c. Narodnye istoki zhivopisi nivkhskogo khudozhnika S. Gurka. In Iu. A. Sem, ed., Materialy po istorii Dal'nego Vostoka: 288–294. Vladivostok: Akademiia Nauk.

1978.   Khudozhestvennaia obrabotka metalla u nivkhov. In L. I. Sem, ed., Kul'tura narodov Dal'nego Vostoka SSSR [XIX–XX vv.]: 71–74. Vladivostok: Akademiia Nauk.

1981.   K probleme khudozhestvennogo stilia v dekorativnom iskusstve nivkhov. In N. K. Starkova, ed., Etnografiia i fol'klor narodov Dal'nego Vostoka: 93–96. Vladivostok: Akademiia Nauk.

1988.   Zolotye niti na rybei kozhe (Nivkhi). Khabarovsk.

GOODY, JACK
1990.   The Oriental, the Ancient and the Primitive: Systems of Marriage and the Family in the Pre-Industrial Societies of Asia. New York: Cambridge Univ. Press.

GRANT, BRUCE
1995.   In the Soviet House of Culture: A Century of Perestroikas. Princeton, NJ: Princeton Univ. Press.

GRUBE, VLADIMIR
        Linguistische Ergebnisse I. Giljakisches Worterverzeichniss nebst gramm. Bermerkungen. Anhang zum III Bande.

HABERER, ERICH E.
1995.   Jews and Revolution in Nineteenth Century Russia. Cambridge: Cambridge Univ. Press.

HAMAYON, ROBERTE
1990.   La Chasse à l'âme: Esquisse d'une théorie du chamanisme siberien. Nanterre: Société d'ethnologie.

HARRIS, MARVIN
1968.   The Rise of Anthropological Theory. New York: Crowell.

HAWES, CHARLES HENRY
1904.   In the Uttermost East. London: Harper.

HEGEL, G. W. F.
1988 [1840].   Theses on the Philosophy of History. Indianapolis: Hackett. [translated by Leo Rauch]

HENRY, MICHAEL, ed.
1963.   Studies in Siberian Shamanism. Toronto: Univ. Toronto Press.

HIATT, LESTER RICHARD
1996.   Arguments about Aborigines: Australia and the Evolution of Social Anthropology. Cambridge: Cambridge Univ. Press.

HOOGENBOOM, HILDE
1996.   Vera Figner and Revolutionary Autobiographies: The Influence of Gender on Genre. In Rosalind Marsh, ed., Women in Russia and Ukraine: 78–92. Cambridge: Cambridge Univ. Press.

HOWITT, K. W.
1885. Australian Group Relations [paper presented to the Smithsonian Institute].

HUMPHREY, CAROLINE
1991. "Icebergs," barter and the mafia in provincial Russia. Anthropology Today 7(2): 8–14.

IADRINTSEV, NIKOLAI MIKHAILOVICH
1891. Sibirskie inorodtsy, ikh byt i sovremennoe polozhenie. St. Petersburg: N. M. Sibiriakov.
1892. Sibir' kak koliniia v geograficheskom, etnograficheskom, i istoricheskom otnosheniiakh. St. Petersburg: M. M. Stasiulevich.

INNOKENTII. See VENIAMINOV

IOKHELSON (JOCHELSON), VLADIMIR (WALDEMAR) IL'ICH
1900. Materialy po izucheniiu iukagirskago iazyka i fol'klora. St. Petersburg: Imperatorskaia Akademiia Nauk.
1907a. Etnologicheskie problemy na severnykh beregakh Tikhogo okeana. Izvestiia IRGO 43: 1–30.
1907b. Etnologicheskie problemy na severnykh beregakh Tikhogo okeana. Izvestiia IRGO 43: 1–30.
1908. The Koryak. Jesup North Pacific Expedition, Vol. 10. Leiden : E. J. Brill.
1922. Pervye dni narodnoi voli. St. Petersburg: Tipografiia No. 15.
1926. The Yukaghir and the Yukaghirized Tungus. Jesup North Pacific Expedition, Vol. 13. Leiden : E. J. Brill.
1928. The Gilyak. In Peoples of Asiatic Russia: 57–60. New York: American Museum of Natural History.
1933. The Yakut. New York: American Museum of Natural History.

JAKOBSON, ROMAN
1957a. Notes on Gilyak. Studies Presented to Yuen Rin Choo. Academia Sinica. Bulletin of the Institute of History and Philosophy 29(pt. 1): 255–281.
1957b. Paleosiberian Peoples and Languages: Bibliographical Guide. New Haven, CT: Human Relations Area Files Press.

JOCHELSON, WALDEMAR See IOKHELSON, VLADIMIR IL'ICH

KAN, SERGEI
1978. Lev Shternberg: From Revolutionary Populism to Evolutionary Anthropology. [unpublished manuscript]
n.d. The Mystery of the Missing Monograph or Why Boas Did Not Include

Shternberg's "The Social Organization of the Gilyak" in the Jesup Expedition Publications. [unpublished manuscript]

KENNAN, GEORGE
1871. Tent life in Siberia, and adventures among the Koryaks and other tribes in Kamchatka and Northern Asia. London: S. Low and Marston.
1981. Siberia and the Exile System. New York: Century.

KOHLER, JOSEF
1897. Zur Urgeschichte der Ehe: Totemismus, Gruppenehe, Mutterrecht. Zeitschrift für vergleichende Rechtswissenschaft 12: 187–353.
1901. Das Recht der Hottentots. Zeitschrift für vergleichende Rechtswissenschaft 15: 341–342.
1975 [1897]. On the Prehistory of Marriage: Totemism, Group Marriage, Mother Right. Chicago: Univ. Chicago Press. [translated from the German by R. H. Barnes and Ruth Barnes. Edited with an Introduction by R. H. Barnes]

KORANASHVILI, GURAM
1980. Morgan's Influence on Marx: The Question of Asiatic Society. Dialectical Anthropology 5: 249–253.

KOSHKIN (AL'KOR), IAN PETROVICH
1933a. L. Ia. Shternberg kak issledovatel' narodov Dal'nego Vostoka. In Lev Ia. Shternberg, Giliaki, orochi, gol'dy, negidal'tsy, ainy: xi–xl. Khababovsk: Dal'giz. [written by Shternberg, edited by Koshkin]
1933b. Predislovie redaktora. In Lev Ia. Shternberg, Sem'ia i rod u narodov Severo-Vostochnoi Azii: iii–xvi. Leningrad: Institut Narodov Scvcra. [written by Shternberg, edited by Koshkin]
1936. Predislovie redaktora. In Lev Ia. Shternberg, Pervobytnaia religiia v svete etnografii: iii–xv. Leningrad: Institut Narodov Severa. [written by Shternberg, edited by Koshkin]

KOSHKIN (AL'KOR), IAN PETROVICH, ed.
1934. Iazyki i pismennost' narodov severa. Moscow: Gosudarstvennoe uchebno-pedagogichcskoe izdatel'stvo.

KOZYNIUK, V.
1996. Ostrova teriaiut, materik nakhodit. Sovetskii Sakhalin (April 12): 2.

KRADER, LAWRENCE
1974. The Ethnological Notebooks of Karl Marx. Assen, The Netherlands: Van Gorcum.

1979.   The Ethnological Notebooks of Karl Marx: a Commentary. *In* Stanley Diamond, ed., Toward a Marxist Anthropology: 153–171. The Hague: Mouton.

KRASHENINNIKOV, STEPAN PETROVICH
1755.   Opisanie zemli Kamchatki. St. Petersburg: Imperatorskaia Akademiia Nauk.
1972.   Explorations of Kamchatka. Portland, Oregon Historical Society. [translated with an introduction and notes by E. A. P. Crownhart-Vaughan]

KRASNOV, A.
1894.   Na Sakhaline [iz vospominanii puteshestvennika po vostoku Azii]. Istoricheskii Sbornik 55: 383–410, 713–737.

KREINOVICH, ERUKHIM ABRAMOVICH (IURII)
1928.   Rasselenie tuzemnogo naseleniia v sovetskoi chasti strany. Dal'nevostochnoe statisticheskoe obozrenie 12(51): 1–9.
1929.   Ocherk kosmogenicheskikh predstavlenii giliakov. Etnografiia 7(1): 78–102.
1930a. Rozhdenie i smert' cheloveka po vozzreniam giliakov. Ibid. 9(1–2): 89–113.
1930b. Sobakovodstvo u nivkhov i ego otrazhenie v religioznoi ideologii. Ibid. 12(4): 29–54.
1932a. Giliatskie chislitel'nye. Trudy Instituta Narodov Severa 1(3): 1–26.
1932b. Cuz Dif [Novoe Slovo] Nachal'naia uchebnaia kniga. Leningrad: Gosudarstvennyi uchebno-pedagogicheskoe izdatel'stvo.
1934a. Morskoi promysel giliakov derevni Kul'. Sovetskaia Etnografiia 5: 78–96.
1934b. Nivkhskii iazyk. Trudy po lingvistike Instituta Narodov Severa 3(3): 81–122.
1934c. Kolkhoznye zametki. Sovetskii Sever 3–4: 184–188.
1935a. Okhota na belugu giliakov derevni Puir. Sovetskaia Etnografiia 2: 108–115.
1935b. Kniga dlia chtenia. Moscow-Leningrad.
1936.   Perezhitki rodovoi sobstvennosti i gruppovogo braka u giliakov. Trudy Instituta Antropologii, Arkheologii i Etnografii 4: 711–754.
1937.   Fonetika nivkhskogo (giliakskogo) iazyka. Trudy po lingvistike Instituta Narodov Severa 5.
1955.   Giliaksko-tunguso-manchurskie iazykovye paralleli. AN SSSR, Institut Iazykoznaniia, Doklady i Soobshchenia 8: 135–167.
1973a. Nivkhgu. Zagadochnye obitateli Sakhalina i Amura. Moscow: Nauka.
1973b. O perezhitkakh gruppovogo braka u nivkhov. *In* Iu. V. Maretin, ed., Strany i narody Vostoka 15. Moscow: Nauka.
1974.   Medvezhii prazdnik u nivkhov. *In* Drevniaia Sibir': 339–348. Novosibirsk.
1977a. La fête de l'ours chez les Nivkh. Ethnographie 74–75: 195–208.
1977b. L. Ia. Shternberg kak issledovatel' nivkhskogo iazyka. *In* E. G. Bekker, ed., Iazyki i toponimiia. Tomsk: Tomskii Pedogogicheskii Institut.
1980.   O Shmidtovskom dialekte nivkhskogo iazyka. *In* N. V. Andreev, ed., Diakhroniia i tipologiia iazykov: 133–144. Moscow: Akademiia Nauk.
1982.   O kul'te medvedia u nivkhov. *In* V. V. Petrov, ed., Strany i narody vostoka 24: 244–283. Moscow: Nauka.
1987.   Etnograficheskie nabliudeniia u nivkhov 1927–1928gg. Ibid. 25: 107–123. Moscow.
ms.   Istoriia moego otnosheniia k arkhivu L. Ia. Shternberga. [unpublished manuscript archived at SOKM]

KROL', MOISEI
1929.   Vospominaniia o L. Ia. Shternberge. Katorga i Ssylka 8–9 [57–58].

KRUPNIK, IGOR
1996.   The Bogoras Enigma: Bounds of Culture and Formats of Anthropologists. *In* Vaclav Hubinger, ed., Grasping the Changing World: Anthropological Concepts in the Postmodern Era: 35–52. London: Routledge.

KRUPNIK, IGOR AND SMOLIAK, ANNA VASIL'EVNA
1982.   Sovremennoe polozhenie korennogo naseleniia Severa Sakhalinskoi Oblasti. Moscow: Institute of Ethnography. [Dokladnaia zapiska, po materialam poezdki s sentiabria 1982 g.]

KWON, HEONIK
1993.   Maps and Actions: Nomadic and Sedentary Space in a Siberian Reindeer Farm. Ph.D diss., Dept. of Social Anthropology, Cambridge Univ.

LABBÉ, PAUL
1903.   Ostrov Sakhalin: putevye vpechatleniia. Moscow: M. V. Kliukin. [translated from the French]

LANTZEFF, GEORGE
1943.   Siberia in the Seventeenth Century:

A Study of the Colonial Administration. Berkeley: Univ. California Press.

LAPIDUS, GAIL WARSHOFSKY
1984. Ethnonationalism and Political Stability: The Soviet Case. World Politics 36, no. 4 (July): 355–380.

LATYSHEV, VLADISLAV M.
1996. Dorogoi Lev Iakovlevich. Iuzhno-Sakhalinsk: SOKM.

LAUFER, BERTHOLD
1902. The Decorative Art of the Amur Tribes. New York: Memoirs of the American Museum of Natural History.

LAWRENCE, THOMAS
1957. The Linguistic Works of N. Ja. Marr. Berkeley: Univ. California Press.

LEBEDEV, G.
1920. Vymiraiushchie brat'ia. Zhizn' Natsional'nostei 19: 76.

LEACH, EDMUND RONALD
1961. The Structural Implications of Matrilateral Cross-Cousin Marriage. In Edmund Leach, ed., Rethinking Anthropology: 54–104. London: Athlone Press.

LÉVI-STRAUSS, CLAUDE
1949. The Elementary Structures of Kinship. Boston: Beacon.
1963. Structural Anthropology. Vol. 1. New York: Basic Books.

MAJEWICZ, ALFRED E., ed.
1992a. Collected Works of Bronislaw Pilsudski. Vol. One: The Aborigines of Sakhalin. Steszew, Poland: International Institute of Ethnolinguistic and Oriental Studies.
1992b. Collected Works of Bronislaw Pilsudski. Vol. Two: The Aborigines of Sakhalin. Materials for the Study of the Ainu Language and Folklore. Steszew, Poland: International Institute of Ethnolinguistic and Oriental Studies.

MAKAR'EV, STEPAN ANDREEVICH
1928. Polevaia etnografiia. Leningrad: Izdanie etnograficheskoi ekskursionnoi kommissii etnootdeleniia geofaka LGU.

MALININ, V. A.
1972. Filosofiia revoliutsionnogo narodnichestva. Moscow: Nauka.

MALINOWSKI, BRONISLAW
1913. The Family among the Australian Aborigines. London: Univ. London Press.

MANCHEN-HELFEN, OTTO
1992. Journey to Tuva. Los Angeles: Ethnographic Press, Univ. Southern California. [translated and annotated by Alan Leighton]

MARR, NIKOLAI IA.
1933. Izbrannye raboty. 5 vols. Leningrad.

MARSHALL, WILLIAM E.
1873. A Phrenologist among the Todas. London.

MARX, KARL
1964. The Economic and Philosophical Manuscripts of 1844. New York: International Publishers.
1965. Pre-Capitalist Economic Formations. Edited with an Introduction by Eric Hobsbawm. New York: International Publishers.

MARX, KARL, AND FRIEDRICH ENGELS
1983. The Manifesto of the Communist Party. New York: International Publishers.

MARZHETTO, IGOR
1995. Neftegorsk krichal troe sutok. Argumenty i Fakty 25, no. 766 (June): 5.

MAUSS, MARCEL
1898. Review of J. G. Frazer. Le Totemisme. L'Anneé Sociologique (2nd Year): 202.

MCCONKEY, JAMES
1971. A Journey to Sakhalin. New York: Coward, McCann and Geohagen.
1986. To a Distant Island. New York: Dutton.

MCLENNAN, JOHN FERGUSON
1865. Primitive Marriage. Edinburgh: A. and C. Black.
1886. Studies in Ancient History; Comprising an Inquiry into the Origin of Exogamy. London: MacMillan.

MEDVEDEV, ROI
1997. Stalin i iazykoznanie. Nezavisimaia Gazeta (4 April): 14.

MEDVEDEVA, L. M.
1992. Iz istorii sakhalinskikh lagerei. Kraevedcheskii Biulleten' 2: 12–24.

MORGAN, LEWIS HENRY
1851. League of the Ho-de-no-sau-nee, Iroquois. Rochester, NY: Sage.
1868. A Conjectural Solution of the Classificatory System of Relationship. Proceedings of the American Academy of Arts and Sciences 7: 436–477.
1871. Systems of Consanguinity and Affinity of the Human Family. Washington, D.C.: Smithsonian Institution.
1877. Ancient Society. New York: Henry Holt.
1900. Pervobytnoe Obshchestvo. [translation of Morgan 1877]
1963. Ancient Society. Cleveland: World Publishing.

MURDOCK, GEORGE PETER
1949.   Social Structure. New York: Macmillan.

NANJUNDAYYA, HEBBALALU VELPANURU
1906–1915.   The Ethnographical Survey of Mysore. 15 vols. Bangalore: Government Press.

NEEDHAM, RODNEY, ed.
1971.   Rethinking Kinship and Marriage. London: Tavistock.

NORDENSKIÖLD, ADOLF ERIK
1880.   Vegas fard kring Asien och Europa. Stockholm: F. & G. Beijers.
1881.   The Voyage of the Vega Round Asia and Europe: With a Historical Review of Previous Journeys Along the North Coast of the Old World. London: Macmillan. [translated from the Swedish by Alexander Leslie]

NOVEMBERGSKII, NIKOLAI IAKOVLEVICH
1903.   Ostrov Sakhalin. St. Petersburg: Dom prizreniia maloletnykh bednykh.

OL'DENBURG, S., ED.
1928.   Pamiati L'va Iakovlevicha Shternberga. Leningrad: Akademiia Nauk.

OSOKIN, B.
1996.   Programma predpologaet, chinovnik raspologaet. Sovetskii Sakhalin (27 July 1995).

OSSENDOWSKI, FERDINAND
1924.   Man and Mystery in Asia. New York: Dutton.

OTAINA, GALINA ALEKSANDROVNA
1971.   O nazvaniiakh tsveta v nivkhskom iazyke. Trudy Instituta Istorii, Arkheologii i Etnografii Dal'nego Vostoka 8: 106–109. Vladivostok.
1977a.   Nivkhskie toponimy; Lichnye imena nivkhov. In Iu. A. Sem, ed., Filologiia narodov Dal'nego Vostoka [Onomastika]: 67–75, 86–93. Vladivostok: Dal'nevostochnyi Nauchnyi Tsentr AN SSSR.
1979.   Sovremennost' i izmeneniia v soznanii nivkhov. XIV Tikhookeanskii Nauchnyi Kongress—Sotsial'nye i Gumanitarnye Nauki 2: 29–31. Khabarovsk.
1981.   Nivkhskie narodnye pesni. In N. K. Starkova, ed., Etnografiia i fol'klor narodov Dal'nego Vostoka: 110–123. Vladivostok: Dal'nevostochnyi Nauchnyi Tsentr AN SSSR.
1978.   Kachestvennye glagoly v nivkhskom iazyke. Moscow: Nauka.
1983a.   Otrazhenie etnokul'turnykh protsessov v nivkhskom iazyke. In N. K.

Starkova, ed., Traditsii i sovremennost' v kul'ture narodov Dal'nego Vostoka: 53–56. Vladivostok: Akademiia Nauk.
1983b.   Fol'klornye motivy v romane V. Sangi "Zhenit'ba Kevongov." In G. I. Lomidze, ed., Vzaimodeistvie literatur narodov Sibiri i Dal'nego Vostoka: 252–256. Novosibirsk: Nauka.
1984.   Otrazhenie mifologicheskikh i religioznykh predstavlenii v nivkhskom iazyke. In N. K. Starkova, ed., Kul'tura narodov Dal'nego Vostoka: traditsii i sovremennost': 157–164. Vladivostok: Akademiia Nauk.
1985.   Istoriia sobraniia i izucheniia nivkhskogo fol'klora. In L. Ia. Ivashchenko, ed., Voprosy izucheniia narodov Dal'nego Vostoka SSSR v otechestvennoi i zarubezhnoi literature: 110–119. Khabarovsk: Akademiia Nauk.

PANFILOV, VLADIMIR ZINEVEVICH
1973.   Nivkhsko-altaiskie iazykovye sviazi. Voprosy Iazykoznaniia 5: 3–12.
1976.   Kategorii myshleniia i iazyka, stanovlenie i razvitie kategorii kachestva. Voprosy Iazykoznaniia 6: 3–18.

PANOV, A. A.
1905.   Sakhalin kak koloniia. St. Petersburg: I. D. Sykin.

PASTERNAK, BURTON
1976.   Introduction to Kinship and Social Organization. Englewood Cliffs, NJ: Prentice-Hall.

PIKA, ALEKSANDR IVANOVICH
1989.   Malye narody Severa: iz pervobytnogo kommunizma v real'nyi sotsializm. In Perestroika, glasnost', demokratiia, sotsializm: V chelovecheskom izmerenii. Moscow: Progress.
1994.   Neotraditsionalizm na Rossiiskom Severe. Moscow: Akademiia Nauk.

PIKA, ALEKSANDR IVANOVICH, AND BORIS BORISOVICH PROKHOROV
1988.   Bol'shie problemy malykh narodov. Kommunist 16: 76–83.

PILSUDSKII, BRONISLAW
1905.   Pis'mo komandirovannogo na O. Sakhalin B. O. Pil'sudskogo (na imia sekretaria Komiteta) IRKISVA 5: 24–30.
1907 [1898].   Nuzhdi i potrebnosti sakhalinskikh giliakov. Zapiski izucheniia amurskogo kraiia 4(4): 1–38. Vladivostok. [first published in ZPOIRGO (April 20th, 1898) 4(4): 1–38]

1909a. Aborigeny Ostrova Sakhalina. Zhivaia Starina 2–3: 3–16.

1909b. L'accouchement, la grossesse et l'avortement chez les indigènes de l'île Sakhaline. Bulletins et Mémoires de la Société d'Anthropologie de Paris 10: 692–699.

1910.   Rody, beremennost', vykidyshi, bliznetsy, urody, bezplodie i plodovitost' u tuzemtsev ostrova Sakhalina. Zhivaia Starina 73–74.

1913.   The Gilyaks and Their Songs. Folklore 34: 477–490.

1964.   The Aborigines of Sakhalin. Human Relations Area Files 10: 1–16. [translated by A. Holborn]

1989 [1904]. Iz poezdki k orokam ostrova Sakhalina v 1904g. Iuzhno-Sakhalinsk: Akademiia Nauk.

1990 [1911]. Poeziia giliakov. Kraevedcheskii Biulleten' 1: 76–111. [translated from the Polish by V. M. Drakunov]

1996a. Dorogoi Lev Iakovlevich. Pis'ma L. Ia. Shternbergu. Edited with an Introduction by Vladislav M. Latyshev. Iuzhno-Sakhalinsk: SOKM.

1996b. Materials for the Study of the Nivhgu (Gilyak) Language and Folklore. Steszew, Poland: International Institute of Ethnolinguistic and Oriental Studies.

POLEVOI, BORIS
1995.   Sakhalinskaia kollektsia P. I. Suprunenko. Vestnik Sakhalinskogo Muzeia 2: 144–155.

POPKIN, CATHY
1992.   Chekhov as Ethnographer: Epistemological Crisis on Sakhalin Island. Slavic Review 51(1): 36–51.

RADCLIFFE-BROWN, ALFRED R.
1913.   Three Tribes of Western Australia. Journal of the Royal Anthropological Institute 43: 143–194.

1952.   Structure and Function in Primitive Society. London: Cohen and West.

RADLOV [RADLOFF], VASILII VASIL'EVICH
1884.   Aus Sibirien. Leipzig: T. O. Weigel.

1894.   Die altturkischen inschriften der Mongolei. St. Petersburg: Eggers.

RAEFF, MARC
1956.   Siberia and the Reforms of 1822. Seattle: Univ. Washington Press.

RAKOWSKA-HARMSTONE, TERESA
1974.   The Dialectics of Nationalism in the USSR. Problems of Communism 23 (May–June): 1–22.

RATNER-SHTERNBERG, SARRA ARKADIEVNA
1928.   Lev Iakovlevich Shternberg i Muzei Antropologii i Etnografii Akademii Nauk In S. Ol'denburg, ed., Pamiati L'va Iakovlevicha Shternberga: 31–70. Leningrad: Akademiia Nauk.

1931.   L. Ia. Shternberg, kak polevoi etnograf. Priroda i Liudi 17–18, 19.

1935.   L. Ia. Shternberg i Leningradskaia etnograficheskaia shkola 1904–1927 gg. Sovetskaia Etnografiia 2: 134–154.

REICHARD, GLADYS A.
1938.   Social Life. In Franz Boas, ed., General Anthropology: 409–486. New York: D. C. Heath.

RESHETOV, A. M.
1994.   Repressirovannaia etnografiia: liudi i sud'by. Kunstkamera 4: 185–221; 5–6: 342–369.

RICHARDSON, SAMUEL
1795.   Clarissa. Boston: Samuel Hall.

RIVERS, W. H. R.
1906.   The Todas. London: Macmillan.

1907a. Marriage of Cousins in India. Journal of the Royal Asiatic Society (July): 611–640.

1907b. On the Origin of the Classificatory System of Relationships. In W. H. R. Rivers et al., eds. Anthropological Essays presented to Edward Burnett Tylor: 309–324. Oxford: Clarendon.

RUBIN, GAYLE
1975.   The Traffic in Women: Notes on the "Political Economy" of Sex. In R. Rieter, ed., Towards an Anthropology of Women: 157–210. New York: Monthly Review.

SAHLINS, MARSHALL
1976.   Culture and Practical Reason. Chicago: Univ. Chicago Press.

SANGI, VLADIMIR MIKHAILOVICH
1961.   Nivkhskie legendy (Perevody).

1965a. Pervyi vystrel: Rasskaz i Povest'.

1965b. Lozhnyi gon, i Izgin. Moscow: Molodaiia Gvardiia.

1967a. Semiperaia ptitsa. Vladivostok.

1967b. Legendy Ykh-Mifa. Moscow: Sovetskaia Rossiia.

1971.   "Mudraia" nerpa. Moscow: Sovetskaia Rossiia.

1975.   Zhenit'ba Kevongov. Moscow: Sovetskii pisatel'.

1981.   U istoka: romany, povesti, rasskazy. Moscow: Sovremennik.

1982.   Devochka-Lebed'. Iuzhno-Sakhalinsk.

1983.   Izbrannoe. Leningrad: Khudozhestvennaia literatura.

1985a. Legendy i mify Severa. Moscow: Sovremmennik.

1985b. Puteshchestvie v stoibishche Lunvo. Moscow: Sovremennik.

1985c. Mesiats runnogo khoda: romany, povesti, rasskazy, skazki. Moscow: Sovetskii Pisatel'.

1986. A Stride across a Thousand Years, Works by Writers of the Soviet North and Far East. Moscow: Progress.

1988a. Otchuzhdenie. Sovetskaia Rossiia (11 September).

1988b. Bez umileniia. Literaturnaia Gazeta (1 April).

1989a. Pesn' o nivkhakh. Moscow: Sovremennik.

1989b. Shtoby krona ne ogolilas'. Literaturnaia Gazeta (15 February): 1,7.

1989c. Polozhenie o gosudarstvenno-kooperativnoi agrofirme 'Aborigen Sakhalina'. [unpublished bulletin]

1989d. Protokol konferentsii 'Aborigen Sakhalina' Nogliki (4 Oct. 89). [unpublished bulletin]

SANGI, VLADIMIR MIKHAILOVICH AND GALINA ALEKSANDROVNA OTAINA

1981. Nivkhskii iazyk. Uchebnik i kniga dlia chteniia dlia pervogo klassa (sakhalinskii dialekt). Leningrad: Prosveshchenie.

1993. Bukvar'. 3rd ed. St. Petersburg: Prosveshchenie. [Nivkh language reader]

SAPIR, B., ed.

1974. Lavrov-gody emigratsii. 2 vols. Dordrecht, Holland: D. Reidel.

SCHNEIDER, DAVID

1984. A Critique of the Study of Kinship. Ann Arbor: Univ. Michigan Press.

SCHRENCK, LEOPOLD VON. See VON SCHRENCK, LEOPOLD

SCHUSKY, ERNEST. L.

1972. Manual for Kinship Analysis. 2nd ed. New York: Holt, Rinehart and Winston.

SCHWEITZER, PETER

1989. Spouse-Exchange in North-Eastern Siberia: On Kinship and Sexual Relations and their Transformations. Vienna Contributions to Ethnology and Anthropology 5: 17–38.

SHRENK, LEOPOLD VON. See VON SCHRENCK, LEOPOLD

SHORT, JOHN

1869. An account of the hill tribes of the Nilgiris. Transactions of the Ethnological Society of London. n. ser., vol. 7. London: J. Murray.

SHTERNBERG, LEV (KHAIM) IAKOVLEVICH

1892. Moskva, 14 oktiabria. Russkie Vedomosti 284 (October 14): 1. [report on the presentation of Shternberg's research to the Obshchestvo Liubitelei Estestvovania, Moscow, October 10, by N. A. Ianchuk]

1893a. Sakhalinskie Giliaki. Etnograficheskoe Obozrenie 17(2): 1–46.

1893b. Besedy o Sakhaline. Vladivostok 42, 43, 44.

1894. Besedy o Sakhaline. Vladivostok 11, 18, 22, 24.

1895a. Besedy o Sakhaline. Vladivostok 9, 20, 26).

1895b. Ot Vladivostoka na Amur. Vladivostok 44, 46, 48, 51.

1896a. Puteshestvie na krainyi sever o. Sakhalina. In Sakhalinskii kalendar': 16–53.

1896b. Pis'ma s Sakhalina. Vladivostok 11, 18, 20, 26.

1896c. V Blagoveshchenske. Iz vospominanii turista. Vladivostok 6, 10, 16, 18.

1896d. Orochi Tatarskogo proliva. Vladivostok 47, 48, 50, 51.

1897. Ostrov Sakhalin. In Sibirskii torgovo-promyshlennyi i spravochnyi kalendar': 442–469. Irkutsk.

1899a. Beregovye seleniia o. Sakhalina. Priamurskie Vedomosti 264, 266, 267.

1899b. K voprosu o belokuroi rase v Srednei Asii. Vostochnyi Vestnik 7, 8.

1900a. Obraztsy materialov po izucheniiu giliatskogo iazyka i fol'klora. Imperatorskaia Akademiia Nauk, Izvestiia 13(4): 387–434.

1900b. Udskaia okruga Primorskoi oblasti. In Sibirskii torgovo-promyshlennyi i spravochnyi kalendar'. Irkutsk.

1900c. Sravnitel'noe izuchenie religii. In ESBE.

1901a. Giliaki. Bol'shaia Entsyklopediia.

1901b. Novye izdaniia Akademii Nauk v oblasti fol'klora i lingvistiki, po izucheniiu chukotskogo i koriatskogo iazykov i fol'klora, sobrannye V. G. Bogorazom i V. I. Iokhel'sonom. Zhurnal ministerstva narodnago prosveshcheniia. June: 189–202.

1901c. Strela; Tabu; Tylor; Tatuirovanie; Teoriia rodovogo byta; Teroteizm; Topor; Totemizm; Traur; Tretichnyi chelovek; Trizna; Trofei; Trudovoe nachalo. In ESBE.

1902. Tungusskoe plemia; Tungusy; Turki;

Turkmeny; Tiurki I tiurko-tatary; Ubezhishcha i ubezhishchnye goroda; Ubiistvo starikov i detei; Ubor golovnoi; Udiny; Uzbeki; Ukrasheniia; Umykanie; Usynovlenie; Fallicheskii kul't; Fetish i fetishizm. *In* ESBE.

1903a. Khoziain v pervobytnoi religii; Tsvet cheloveka; Tsygane; Charodeistvo; Cherkesy; Chelovechestvo; Chort; Chukchi. *In* ESBE.

1903b. Chto takoe doistoricheskaia arkheologiia. Vestnik i biblioteka samoobrazovaniia 2: 127–132.

1903c. [Review of Gabriel de Mortillet. Doistoricheskii Mir (Russian Edition). Originally published as Le prehistorique: entierement refondue et mise au courant des dernieres decouvertes. Paris: C. Reinwald, 1900.]

1903d. Shabash ved'm. *In* ESBE.

1903e. [Review of L. Krzhivitskii. Psikhicheskie rasy]. Russkoe Bogatstvo 2: 37–41.

1903f. [Review of Nikolai Nikolaevich Kharuzin. Etnografiia. St. Petersburg, 1901]. Ibid. 8: 64–68.

1904a. Putevoditel' po MAE Akademii Nauk. St. Petersburg: Akademiia Nauk.

1904b. Bemerkungen über die Beziehungen zwischen der Morphologie der gilyakischen und amerikanischen Sprachen. XIV Internationaler Amerikanisten-Kongress: 137–140. Stuttgart.

1904c. Endogamiia i eksogamiia; Eskimosy; Etnografiia. *In* ESBE.

1904d. [Review of Lavrentii Sokolovskii. Chelovekovedenie. Translation from German. St. Petersburg.]

1904e. Translation from the German (of parts concerning Central Asia) of Hans Ferdinand Helmolt, Der Treppenwitz der Weltgeschichte. Geschichtliche Irrtumer, Entstellungen und Erfindungen. St. Petersburg.

1904f. Giliaki (I). Etnograficheskoe Obozrenie 28(60): 1–42.

1904g. Giliaki (II). Ibid. 28(61): 19–55.

1904h. Giliaki (III). Ibid. 28(63): 66–119.

1905a. Kul't inau u plemeni ainu. *In* Ezhegodnik Russkogo antropologicheskogo obshchestva pri S. Peterburgskom Universitete: 289–308.

1905b. [Review of Henry George, The Writings of Henry George. New York: Doubleday and McClure]. Russkoe Bogatstvo 3: 97–99.

1905c. [Review of Sergei Kotliarevskii. Sovremennyi katolitsizm. St. Petersburg]. Ibid. 1: 156–161.

1905d. [Review of Bogdanovich. Ocherk proshlogo i nastoiashego Iaponii]. Ibid. 4: 66–68.

1905e. [Review of V. G. Bogoraz, The Chuckchee, Vol. 1]. American Anthropologist 7 (2): 320–324.

1905f. Die Religion der Giliyaken. Archiv fur Religionswissenschaft 8: 244–247.

1906a. The Inau Cult of the Ainu. *In* Berthold Laufer, ed., Boas Anniversary Volume: Anthropological Papers Written in Honor of Franz Boas: 425–437. New York: G. E. Stechert.

1906b. Tragediia shestimillionogo naroda. *In* I. V. Gessen et al. eds., Nakanunie probuzhdeniia: Sbornik statei po evreiskomu voprosu: 163–187. St. Petersburg: A. G. Rozen.

1907. Natsional'nye techeniia v russkom evreistve. Svoboda i ravenstvo 5(25 January): 2–6.

1908. Materialy po izucheniiu giliatskago iazyka i fol'klora. Tom 1: Obraztsy narodnoi slovesnosti. Chast' Pervaia: Epos. St. Petersburg: Imperatorskaia Akademiia Nauk.

1909. Iz zhizni i deiatel'nosti V. V. Radlova. Zhivaia Starina 2–3: 3–25.

1910a. Inorodtsy. *In* Formy Natsional'nogo dvizheniia v sovremennykh gosudarstvakh. Pp. 531–574. St. Petersburg: Obshchestvennaia Pol'za.

1910b. Buriaty. Ibid.: 625–653.

1911a. Aleuty. NESBE.

1911b. Animizm. NESBE.

1911c. Russkii etnograficheskii muzei. Zhivaia Starina 2–4: 453–472.

1912a. The Turano-Ganowanian System and the Nations of Northeast Asia. Proceedings of the XVIII Congress of the Americanists: 319–333. London.

1912b. Noveishie raboty po antropologii evreev. Evreiskaia Starina 3: 3–30.

1913a. Gruppovoi brak. Russkaia entsiklopediia.

1913b. Eniseiskie ostiaki. Ibid.

1913c. V. F. Miller kak etnograf. Zhivaia Starina 22: 417–425.

1914a. Kratkaia programma dlia sobiraniia etnograficheskikh svedenii priminitel'no k narodam Sibiri. *In* Sbornik instruktsii programm dlia uchastnikov ekskursii v Sibir'. 2nd ed.:

212–251. St. Petersburg: Obshchestva izucheniia Sibiri i ulushcheniia ee byta.

1914b. Klassifikatorskaia sistema rodstva. Russkaia entsyklopediia.

1914c. Kuzennyi brak. Ibid.

1916a. Antichnyi kul't bliznetsov pri svete etnografii. *In* Sbornik MAE, Vol. 3: 133–189. St. Petersburg: Akademiia Nauk.

1916b. Instruktsiia dlia registrirovaniia etnograficheskikh kollektsii. St. Petersburg: Akademiia Nauk.

1918. V. V. Bartol'd. Biograficheskie svedeniia. *In* Biograficheskii slovar'. p. 6. St. Petersburg: Istoricheskoe obshchestvo.

1924a. Problema evreiskoi natsional'noi psikhologii. Evereiskaia Starina 1: 5–44.

1924b. [Review of Fritz Kohn. Die Juden als Rasse und Kulturvolk.] Ibid.: 378–380.

1924c. Rol' sokhraneniia imeni v evreiskom levirate. Ibid.: 177–179.

1925a. Dukhovnoi iubelei russkoi etnografii i etnograficheskikh muzeev. Priroda 7–9: 46–66.

1925b. Muzei antropologii i etnografii Akademii Nauk. Chelovek i Priroda 9: 47–54.

1925c. Kul'tura u sibirskikh narodov. *In* Sbornik Muzeiia Antropologii i Etnografii 5: 717–740.

1925d. Divine elections in primitive religions. Proceedings of the XXI International Congress of Americanists.

1926a. D. N. Anuchin kak etnograf. Etnografiia 1–2: 7–13.

1926b. Iafeticheskaia teoriia pri svete etnografii. Postanovleniia i rezoliutsii 2-ogo kraevedcheskogo s''ezda v Batume.

1926c. Kraeved i kraevedenie. Ibid.

1926d. Sovremennaia etnologiia. Noveishie uspekhi, nauchnye techeniia i metody. Etnografiia 1–2: 15–43.

1926e. Etnografiia. Tikhii okean. *In* Russkie nauchnye issledovaniia: 147–172. St. Petersburg: Akademiia Nauk.

1927a. Kastren—atlasist i etnograf. *In* Pamiati Kastrena: 35–56. St. Petersburg: Akademiia Nauk.

1927b. Kul't bliznetsov v Kitae i indiiskie vliianiia. *In* Sbornik MAE 6: 1–18.

1927c. Izbrannichestvo v religii. Etnografiia 1: 3–56.

1928a. Problema evreiskoi etnografii. Evreiskaia Starina 12: 11–16.

1929a. Ainskaia problema. *In* Sbornik MAE, vol. 8: 334–374.

1929b. The Ainu problem. Anthropos 24: 755–799.

1929c. Der Zwillingskultus in China und die indischen Einflusse. Baeseler Archiv 13: 31–46.

1930. Der antike Zwillingskult im Lichte der Ethnographie. Zeitschrift fur Ethnologie 1–3: 152–200.

1933a. Giliaki, orochi, gol'dy, negidal'tsy, ainy. Khabarovsk: Dal'nevostochnoe knizhnoe izdatel'stvo. [edited with a preface by Ian P. Koshkin (Al'kor)]

1933b. Sem'ia i rod u narodov Severo–Vostochnoi Azii. Leningrad: Institut Narodov Severa. [edited with a preface by Ian P. Koshkin (Al'kor)]

1936. Pervobytnaia religiia v svete etnografii. Leningrad: Institut narodov Severa. [edited with a preface by Ian P. Koshkin (Al'kor)]

1974a. Shamanism in Religious Election. *In* Stephen and Ethel Dunn, eds., Introduction to Soviet Ethnography: 61–85. Berkeley: Highgate Road Social Science Research Station. [translation of Shternberg, 1936, pages 347–360]

1974b [1884]. Politicheskii terror v Rossii 1884. *In* B. Sapir, ed. Lavrov-gody emigratsii. Vol. 2: 572–94. Dordrecht, Holland: D. Reidel.

n.d. The Social Organization of the Gilyak. Archives of the Dept. of Anthropology, AMNH. [unpublished Russian typescript]

n.d. Sotsial'naia organizatsiia giliakov. Archives of the Dept. of Anthropology, AMNH. [unpublished English typescript]

n.d. Sem'ia i Rod: Sotsial'naia zhizn' giliakov. AAN, f. 282, o. 1, d. 2.

n.d. Obshchestvennoe i bytovoe ustroistvo u giliakov. Ibid., d. 41.

SHTERNBERG, LEV IAKOVLEVICH, ED.

1900–1909. ESBE, Vols. 61–82. [all ethnographic materials]

1903–1914. Izvestiia Russkogo komiteta po izucheniiu Vostochnoi i Srednei Azii. Vols. 1–10 of the First Series and 1–3 of the Second Series.

1906. Ko dniu semidesiatilietiia Vasiliia Vasil'evicha Radlova. St. Petersburg.

1910–1911. NESBE. Vols. 1 and 2. [all ethnographic materials]

SIEBOLD, PHILLIP FRANZ VON. *See* VON SIE-
BOLD
SIIKALA, ANNA-LEENA AND MIHÀLY HOPPÀL
1992.   Studies on Shamanism. Helsinki:
        Finnish Anthropological Society.
SLEZKINE, YURI
1989.   Russia's Small Peoples: The Policies
        and Attitudes toward the Native
        Northerners 17th c.–1938. Ph.D. diss.,
        Univ. Texas at Austin.
1991.   The Fall of Soviet Ethnography, 1928–38.
        Current Anthropology 32(4): 476–484.
1992.   The Soviet Far North: 1928–1938.
        Slavic Review 51(1): 52–76.
1993.   Savage Christians or Unorthodox Rus-
        sians? The Missionary Dilemma in
        Siberia. *In* Galya Diment and Yuri Slez-
        kine, eds., Between Heaven and Hell:
        The Myth of Siberia in Russian Culture:
        15–32. New York: St. Martin's Press.
1994.   Arctic Mirrors: Russia and the Small
        Peoples of the North. Ithaca, NY: Cor-
        nell Univ. Press.
1996.   N. Ia. Marr and the National Origins
        of Soviet Ethnogenetics. Slavic Review
        55(4): 826–862.
SMITH, GRAHAM, ed.
1990.   The Nationalities Question in the
        Soviet Union. New York: Longman.
SMOLIAK, ANNA VASIL'EVNA
1953.   Ekspeditsiia G. I. Nevel'skogo i pervye
        russkie etnograficheskie issledovaniia
        v Priamur'e, Primor'e i na Sakhaline.
        Sovetskaia Etnografiia 3.
1960.   Zametki po etnografii nivkhov Amur-
        skogo Limana. Trudy Instituta Etno-
        grafii 56: 92–147.
1963.   O nekotorykh etnicheskikh protses-
        sakh u narodov nizhnego i srednego
        Amura. Sovetskaia Etnografiia 3: 21–30.
1967.   O sovremennom etnicheskom razvitii
        narodov Nizhnego Amura i Sakhalina.
        Ibid. 3: 95–103.
1970.   Sotsial'naia organizatsiia narodov
        nizhnego Amura i Sakhalina (novye
        materialy o nivkhakh). *In* I. S. Gur-
        vich, ed., Obshchestvennyi stroi u nar-
        odov Severnoi Sibiri: 264–299. Mos-
        cow: Nauka.
1971.   Osnovnye puti razvitiia ekonomiki,
        kul'tury i byta za gody Sovetskoi vlasti
        u narodov basseina nizhnego Amura i
        Sakhalina. *In* I. S. Gurvich, ed., Osu-
        shchestvlenie leninskoi natsional'noi
        politiki u narodov Krainego Severa:
        314–341. Moscow: Akademiia Nauk.

1974.   Rodovoi sostav nivkhov v XIX—
        nachale XX v. *In* Sotsial'naia organi-
        zatsiia i kul'tura narodov Severa:
        176–217. Moscow: Akademiia Nauk.
1975a. [Review of Kreinovich, 1973a] Sovet-
        skaia Etnografiia 2: 171–173.
1975b. Etnicheskie protsessy u narodov Nizh-
        nego Amura i Sakhalina. Moscow:
        Nauka.
1977.   [Review of Taksami, 1975]. Sovetskaia
        Etnografiia 6: 130–134.
1978.   O starinnykh promyslakh materi-
        novikh nivkhov. *In* Polevye issledo-
        vaniia Instituta Etnografii za 1976 g.:
        86–93. Moscow.
1979.   O vzaimnykh kul'turnykh vliianiiakh
        narodov Sakhalina. *In* I. S. Gurvich, ed.,
        Etnogenez i etnicheskaia istoriia naro-
        dov Severa: 43–77. Moscow: Akademiia
        Nauk.
1982.   Narody nizhnego Amura i Sakhalina.
        In I. S. Gurvich, ed., Etnicheskaia
        istoriia narodov Severa: 223–257. Mos-
        cow: Akademiia Nauk.
1991.   Shaman: Lichnost' i funktsii. Moscow:
        Nauka.
1992.   Spisok osnovnykh trudov. Etnogra-
        ficheskoe Obozrenie 3: 140–143.
SOKOLOVA, ZOIA PETROVNA
1990.   Narody Severa SSSR: Proshloe, nas-
        toiashchee i budushchee. Sovetskaia
        Etnografiia 6: 17–32.
SPENCER, BALDWIN, AND FRANK GILLEN
1899.   The Native Tribes of Central Aus-
        tralia. London: Macmillan.
SSORIN-CHAIKOV, NIKOLAI
1998.   Stateless Society, State Collective, and
        the State of Nature in Sub-Arctic Sibe-
        ria: Evenki Hunters and Herders in the
        20th Century. Ph.D. diss., Stanford
        Univ.
STALIN, IOSIF
1951.   Marxism and Linguistics. New York:
        International.
1952.   Marksizm i voprosy iazykoznaniia.
        Berlin: Vok und Wissen Volkseigener
        Verlag.
STANIUKOVICH, T. V.
1964.   Muzei antropologii i ctnografii imeni
        Petra Velikogo. Leningrad: Akademiia
        Nauk.
1970 [1964].   The Museum of Anthropology
        and Ethnography named after Peter
        the Great. Leningrad: Nauka.
STEPHAN, JOHN J.
1971.   Sakhalin: A History. Oxford: Clarendon.

1992.   "Cleansing" the Soviet Far East, 1937–1938. Acta Slavica Iaponica 10: 43–64.

SUNY, RONALD GRIGOR

1993.   The Revenge of the Past: Nationalism, Revolution and the Collapse of the Soviet Union. Stanford: Stanford Univ. Press.

SWANTON, JOHN REED

1905.   Contributions to the Ethnology of the Haida. Leiden: E. J. Brill.

TAKSAMI, CHUNER MIKHAILOVICH

1959a. Vozrozhdenie nivkhskoi narodnosti. Iuzhno-Sakhalinsk: Sakhalinskoe knizhnoe izdatel'stvo.

1959b. Zhilye i khoziaistvennye postroiki nivkhov Amura i Amurskogo limana. Avtoreferat. Leningrad.

1960a. Sovremennaia kul'tura i byt narodov severa. In Doklady i soobshcheniia nauchnoi konferentsii po istorii Sibiri i Dal'nego Vostoka: Sektsii istorii i etnografii sovetskogo perioda: 104–105. Tomsk.

1960b. Sovremennye nivkhskie seleniia i zhilishcha. Sovetskaia Etnografiia 1: 23–37.

1961a. Seleniia, zhil'e i khoziaistvennye postroiki nivkhov Amura i zapadnogo poberezh'ia Ostrova Sakhalina. In Trudy Instituta Etnografii 64: 98–166.

1961b. Issledovatel', drug i uchitel' nivkhov. In Ivan A. Senchenko, ed., Issledovateli Sakhalina i Kuril: 108–131. Iuzhno-Sakhalinsk: Sakhalinskoe knizhnoe izdatel'stvo.

1964.   Dar nivkhov Muzeiu antropologii i etnografii. In Sbornik Muzeiia antropologii i etnografii. 22: 191–199. Moscow: Institut etnografii.

1967a. Nivkhi (Sovremmenoe khoziaistvo, kul'tura i byt). Leningrad: Nauka.

1967b. Ustanovlenie sovetskoi vlasti i organizatsii sovetov sredi nivkhov. In Velikii oktiabr' i malye narody severa. Leningrad: Institut im. Gertsena.

1969a. Geograficheskie predstavleniia nivkhov i ikh ispol'zovanie russkimi issledovateliami Sakhalina i nizov'ev Amura. Izvestiia Vladisvostokskogo Geograficheskogo Obshchestva 101(1): 41–48.

1969b. Nekotorye voprosy fol'klora i iskusstva nivkhov [Iz istorii sobrianiia i izucheniia fol'klora] In Uchenye Zapiski 383: 138–151. Leningrad: Institut im. Gertsena.

1969c. Pervobytnye otnosheniia i religioznye verovaniia u nivkhov. Strany i Narody Vostoka 8: 53–69.

1970.   Odezhda nivkhov. In S. V. Ivanov, Odezhda narodov Sibiri: 166–195. Leningrad: Nauka.

1971.   K voprosu o kul'te predkov i kul'te prirody u nivkhov. In Trudy Muzeia Antropologii i Etnografii 21: 201–210.

1972.   Nivkhi. Voprosy Istorii 10: 212–217.

1974.   Problemy istorii nivkhskogo etnosa i ego kul'tury. In Kratkoe soderzhanie dokladov godichnoi nauchnoi sessii Instituta Etnografii AN SSSR 23–26 (July 1974): 85–88. Leningrad: Akademiia Nauk.

1975.   Osnovnye problemy etnografii i istorii Nivkhov. Leningrad: Nauka.

1976.   Predstavleniia o prirode i cheloveke u nivkhov. In I. S. Vdovin, ed., Priroda i chelovek v religioznykh predstavleniiakh narodov Sibiri i Severa: 203–216. Leningrad: Nauka.

1977a. Nivkhi. Problemy khoziaistva, obshchestvennogo stroiia i etnicheskoi istorii. Doktorskoi avtoreferat. Moscow: Institut Etnografii im. Miklukho-Maklaia.

1977b. Sistema kul'tov u nivkhov. Sbornik Muzeiia Antropologii i Etnografii 33: 90–116.

1978a. Problèmes de l'ethnogenèse des Nivkhes. Inter-Nord 15: 65–78.

1978b. Dve sud'by narodov ostrovnoi zemli [O nivkhakh i ainakh Sakhalina i nizhnego Amura]. In Dva Mira—Dve Sud'by: 65–72. Magadan.

1979.   Vliianie khristianstva na traditsionnye verovaniia nivkhov. In I. S. Vdovin, ed., Khristianstvo i lamaizm u korennogo naselenii Sibiri: 115–126. Leningrad: Nauka.

1980.   Problemy etnogeneza nivkhov. In I. S. Gurvich, ed., Etnogenez narodov severa: 196–211. Moscow: Nauka.

1981a. Shamanstvo u nivkhov. In Problemy istorii (po materialam vtoroi poloviny XIX–nachala XXv): 165–177. Leningrad: Nauka.

1981b. Nivkhi. In Rasy i Narody 2. Moscow: Institut Etnografii.

1982.   K vershinam znanii [o razvitii kul'tury i prosveshchenii u nivkhov za gody Sovetskoi vlasti]. In Porodilis' na Amure: Ocherki: 145–159. Khabarovsk.

1984a. Obshchie cherty v dukhovnoi kul'ture narodov Priamuria i Sakhalina. *In* Chuner M. Taksami, ed., Etnokul'turnye kontakty narodov Sibiri: 74–83. Leningrad: Nauka.

1984b. Nivkhskoe pis'mo. *In* Sakhalinskii Literaturno-Khudozhestvennyi Sbornik: 178–187. Iuzhno-Sakhalinsk: Dal'nevostochnoe Knizhnoe Izdatel'stvo.

1987. Sootnosheniia traditsionnogo i novogo v kul'ture narodnostei Severa. *In* V. I. Boiko, ed., Problemy sovremennogo sotsial'nogo razvitiia narodnostei Severa. Novosibirsk: Nauka.

1988. Peoples of Siberia: Ethnic Traditions and Education of Children. [paper given at the 12th ICAES, Zagreb; held in Lenin (now the Russian State) Library, Moscow]

1989. Liudi u kromki zemli. Pravda (3 March): 3.

TAN, N. A. *See* BOGORAZ

TOKAREV, SERGEI A.
1966. Istoriia russkoi etnografii. Moscow: Nauka.

TROITSKII, NIKOLAI
1996. Druz'ia naroda ili besy? Kak i kogo zashchishchali narodniki. Rodina 2: 67–72.

TVARDOVSKAIA, V. A.
1973. People's Will. Great Soviet Encyclopaedia 17: 617–618. New York: Macmillan.

TYLOR, EDWARD BURNETT
1976. Primitive Culture. New York: Gordon Press.

URBAN, GREG
1996. Metaphysical Community: The Interplay of the Senses and the Intellect. Austin: Univ. Texas Press.

VAINSHTEIN, SEVYAN
1980. Nomads of South Siberia. Edited with an Introduction by Caroline Humphrey. New York: Cambridge Univ. Press.

VAKHTIN, NIKOLAI B.
n.d. Franz Boas and the Shaping of the Jesup North Pacific Expedition, 1895–1900: A Russian Perspective. [unpublished manuscript]

VENIAMINOV, IVAN (IOAM) [*later*, INNOKENTII, SAINT, METROPOLITAN OF MOSCOW AND KOLOMNA]
1840. Zapiski ob ostrovakh Unalashkinskago otdela.

1984. Notes on the islands of the Unalashka District. Translation of Zapiski ob ostrovakh Unalashkinskago otdela. Kingston, Canada: Limestone Press. [translated by Lydia T. Black and R.H. Geoghegan; edited with an introduction by Richard A. Pierce]

1993. Journals of the Priest Ioann Veniaminov in Alaska, 1823 to 1836. Fairbanks: Univ. Alaska Press. [translated by Jerome Kisslinger; introduction and commentary by S. A. Mousalimas]

VENTURI, FRANCO
1960. Roots of Revolution: A History of the Populist and Socialist Movements in Nineteenth Century Russia. New York: Knopf.

VINNIKOV, ISAAK NATANOVICH
1928. Leo Sternberg. Anthropos 23: 135–140.

VLADIMIROV, ANDREI
1992. Rodovye khoziaistva: vozvrashchenie k istokam. Svobodnyi Sakhalin (9 July): 7.

VON SCHRENCK [SHRENK], LEOPOLD
1855. Voyages [Lettres de M. Léopold Schrenk a l'Académicien Middendorf (Lu le 13 avril 1855)] *In* Bulletin de la Classe Physico-Mathematique de l'Academie Imperiale des Sciences de St.-Petersbourg. Vol. 14: 40–46, 184–192, 217–222 [in German]. Leipzig: L. Voss.

1860–1900. Reisen und Forschungen im Amur-Lande in den Jahren 1854–1856 im Auftrage der Kaiserl. Akademie der Wissenschaften zu St. Petersburg. St. Petersburg: Eggers.

1883. Ob inorodtsakh Amurskago kraiia, Tom 1. St. Petersburg: Izdanie Imperatorskoi Akademii Nauk.

1899. Ibid., Tom 2.

1903. Ibid., Tom 3.

VON SIEBOLD, PHILLIP FRANZ
1897. Nippon. Archiv zur Beschreibung von Japan und dessen neben- und schutzländern Jezo mit den südlichen Kurilen, Sachalin, Korea und den Iukiu-Inseln. 2 Vols. Wurzburg: L. Woerl.

VUCINICH, ALEXANDER,
1988. Darwin in Russian Thought. Berkeley: Univ. California Press.

WEINBERG, ROBERT
1993. Blood on the Steps: The Revolution of 1905 in Odessa. Bloomington: Indiana Univ. Press.

WEINER, ANNETTE
1976.   Women of Value, Men of Renown. Austin: Univ. Texas Press.

WESTERMARCK, EDVARD ALEXANDER
1891.   The History of Human Marriage. London: Macmillan.
1893.   Geschichte der menschlichen Ehe. Jena: H. Costenoble.

WILKEN, GEORGE ALEXANDER
1893.   Handleiding voor de vergelijkende Volkenkunde van Nederlandsch-Indie. Leiden : E. J. Brill.
1921.   The Sociology of Malayan Peoples. Kuala Lumpur: Commercial Press. [translated by G. Hunt]

1962 [1893].   Manual for the Comparative Ethnology of the Netherlands East Indies. New Haven: Human Relations Area Files. [translated by S. Dumas Kaan]

WIXMAN, RONALD
1984.   The Peoples of the USSR: An Ethnographic Handbook. Armonk, NY: M. E. Sharpe.

ZOLATAREV, A. M.
1933a.   K voprosu o genezise klassoobrazovaniia u giliakov. Za Industrializatsiiu Sovetskogo Vostoka 3.
1933b.   O perezhitkakh rodovogo stroia u giliakov raiona Chome. Sovetskii Sever 2: 52–66.

Index

NOTE: Italicized page references are to illustrations.

A

abbreviations, list of, ix
adoption, 155–156
affection among married couples, 13
affinity
  agnatic kinship and; see agnatic kinship,
    generally
  cognatic kinship and; see cognatic kinship,
    generally
  defined, v
age, role in kinship terminology, 99
agnates, defined, v, 12
agnatic kinship, generally, 14–20
  ascending line within the clan, 15, 17–18
  brothers and sisters, class of, 16–17
  cousins, 17
  defined, 14–15
  descending line within the clan, 16, 18–20
  fathers and paternal uncles, 17–18
  grandfathers and grandmothers, 17
  husbands within the clan, 18
  list of terms; table 1, 24
  man's own generation, 16–17
  mothers within the clan, 18
  sisters and brothers, class of, 16–17
  uncles, paternal, 17–18
  wives within the clan, 18
Agniun, Konstantin, *206*
Ainu settlement, 13, 37–38, 46, 85–86, 112
  matriliny principles, 37
akhmalk (father-in-law), v, 15, 20, 21, 22,
  27, 30, 58
  near and remote, 22–23
Aleut, 113, 118–121
algebraic kinship formulae, 103–107
Al'kor, Ian Petrovich; see Koshkin, Ian Petrovich
alliance, clan; see clan alliance
ancestor deities, 158–159
Ancient Society (Morgan), xxxix, xxxvii,
  102, 108
Andrews, Lorin, xxxviii
ang'rei; see *pu* (marriageable husband) and
  ang'rei (marriageable wife)
animals
  bear; see bear
  dog, religious ceremony for killing of, 42
  symbolic relationship with, xxxvi–xxxvii
archival and field research for English edition, xx–xxi

ascending line within the clan
  agnatic kinship, 15, 17–18
  sexual intercourse and marriage prohibited
    between generations in direct and most
    remote collateral, 40–42
Australia
  cousin marriage, 91, 95–107
  Dieri people, xliii, 64–65
  evolution of marriage, 93, 95–107
  genetic link between Gilyak system and
    natives of, 95–107
  group marriage studies, xli–xliii, 47, 51,
    57, 64–65

B

bear
  festival, *135, 139*, 157, 160–161, 176,
    181–182
  ritual kin, regarded as, xxxvi–xxxvii
  vengeance, ritual, 162–163
benevolent deity, 161
bestiality, 129–130
bctrothal ceremony, 51, 136–137, 140–141,
  202–203
  kettles used in, 145–147, 180, 210
birds of prey as souls of murdered kinsmen,
  164
"black Gilyak," 6–7
Bloch, Maurice, xl
Bloody Sunday massacre in St. Petersburg, xlv
Boas, Franz, xliii, xliv–xlix, xvii, xxiv, 248
  commissioning *Social Organization* man-
    uscript, excerpts, 233–241
Bogoraz, Vladimir, liii, xlv–xlvi, xlvii–xlviii,
  xxiii, xxviii, xxxiv, 247–249, 252–255
  correspondence on *Social Organization*
    manuscript, excerpts, 238–239
  graduate students, photograph with (1926),
    xlviii
bride-price or bride-wealth, v, 48, 49, 52–54,
  137–138, 141–147, 181, 210
  articles of, 143, 181
  dowry and, 144–147
  installment payments, 145
  return of, 148
brotherhood, custom of fictive, 181
brothers and sisters, generally
  agnatic kinship, 16–17
  cousins distinguished, 17
  marriage prohibited between, 40–42
  sexual intercourse prohibited between,
    40–42
  terminology used for addressing, 5
  tuvng (brothers and sisters, real and classi-
    ficatory), vi, 15–18, 20, 22–25, 35
Buschman, 31–34
business conversation, restrictions on, 71–72

273

Bygar tribes of Sathpuras, India, marriage
between cousins, 51

C

census of Gilyak settlements, 5–9, 13, 53–54
Chekhov, Anton, xxx, xxxii
Cherniakov, Zakharii Efimovich, li, lii,
245–255
Chernyshevskii, Nikolai, xxvii
chess, playing, *101*
Chukchi, 113, 116–117
circumstantial terms, 23, 28–30
clan, defined, v
clan alliance, 153–183
adoption, 155–156
akhmalk-imgi clan, 154–156
bear festival, celebration of, 157, 160–161,
176, 181–182
communal property principles, 159–160
daily activities of Gilyak boy, 173–174
deities, clan; see deities, clan
disputes, resolution of, 177
economic system, 174–175
fishing, 174–175
hunting, 174–175
murder within clan, 39, 50, 128, 162–169
name of clan, 172
out-of-wedlock children, 154
ransom received or paid in cases of
vengeance, 161–169
relations between clans, 178–183
sins, avoidance of, 169–170
taboos, avoidance of violation of, 169–170
vengeance, ransom received or paid in
cases of, 161–169
classificatory kinship system, 5, 13
age, role of, 99
agnatic kinship; see agnatic kinship, generally
algebraic kinship formulae, 103–107
cognatic kinship; see cognatic kinship,
generally
comparison of terms of relationship with
those of Ural-Altaians and Paleo-
Asiatics, 31–38
defined, v, 5
descriptive or circumstantial terms, 23,
28–30
lovers, terms used by, 30
matrilineal organization, 149–152
neighboring tribes, relationship of Gilyak
nomenclature to, 37–38
Paleo-Asiatics and Ural-Altaians, comparison of terms of relationship with those
of, 31–38
parents, terms for; comparison with those of
Paleo-Asiatics and Ural Altaians, 31–38
pilang (great, grand), 28–29

plural of terms or relationship, 29–30
secondary substitutive terms, 23
sexual intercourse and marriage; **see** sexual intercourse and marriage
Turanian system among Dravidian natives
of India, 93–94, 97–107, 113–114
Ural-Altaians and Paleo-Asiatics, comparison of terms of relationship with those
of, 31–38
classificatory terms, defined, v
clothing, traditional, xxxv, 8, 19, 147
cognates, defined, v
cognatic kinship, generally, 15, 20–23
agnatic relationship outside the clan, 23
akhmalk (father-in-law), near and remote,
22–23
clanswomen, position of, 20
cousins, 20, 21
defined, 15
list of terms; table 1, 24
collateral kin, defined, v
Committee of the New Alphabet, lii
Committee of the North, li, xiv
communal property principles, 159–160
consanguinity, defined, v
conversation, restrictions on, 70–72, 212, 221
correspondence on *Social Organization*
manuscript, excerpts, 233–244
cousin marriage; **see also** *pu* (marriageable
husband) and *ang'rei* (marriageable wife)
Ainu settlement, 112
Aleut, 113, 118–121
algebraic kinship formulae, 103–107
Australian natives, genetic link between
Gilyak system and, 91, 95–107
brothers and sisters distinguished from
cousins, 17
Chukchi, 113, 116–117
cognatic kinship, 20
cross-cousins, defined, v
evolution of marital institutions and, 90–94
Ganowanian system among Indian tribes
of North America, 99–107, 113
India, Dravidian natives of, 93–94, 97–107
Kamchadal, 113, 116, 118
Koriak, 113, 116–118
Morgan's theories on, 98–121
North Asian peoples, 110–121
parallel-cousins, defined, vi
Punaluan system in Hawaii, xli, xxxviii,
99–101
rites, 132–148
sexual intercourse, prohibitions, 41–42
Tungus tribes, 110–112
Turanian system among Dravidian natives
of India, 93–94, 97–107, 113–114
Yukaghir, 113–116
cross-cousins, defined, v
Cunow, Heinrich, 99